THE SHOTGUN BOOK

Jack O'Connor

THE

SHOTGUN

BOOK

SECOND EDITION, REVISED

New York: Alfred·A·Knopf   *1978*

SECOND EDITION, REVISED

The following chapters originally appeared in Outdoor Life *Magazine and are used by permission of* Outdoor Life: *7, 10, 11, 13, 15, 16, 17, 18, 19, 21, 23, 24, 25, 26.*

Library of Congress Cataloging in Publication Data

O'Connor, Jack, 1902–1978.
  The shotgun book.

  Includes index.
  1. Shot-guns. 2. Shooting. 3. Hunting.
I. Title.
GV1179.023   1978   799.2'0283   77–92795
ISBN 0–394–50138–1
ISBN 0–394–73562–5 pbk.

To BILL RAE
My editor for many years and
my good friend

ACKNOWLEDGMENTS

I should like to express my gratitude to Eugene Duffield, president of the Popular Science Publishing Company, and to Bill Rae, editor of Outdoor Life, *for permission to use material which has previously appeared as articles and parts of articles in* Outdoor Life; *to Angus Cameron, my editor at Knopf, for keeping me working; to my secretary, Fran Nelson, for preparing the typescript; to Paul Nolt of the Lolo Sporting Goods Company, Lewiston, Idaho, for his helpful advice on handloading; and to my wife, Eleanor, for putting up with me while I hole up to write a book.*

—Jack O'Connor

Contents

1. *A Brief History of the Shotgun*   *3*
2. *The Classification of the Modern Shotgun*   *16*
3. *Types of Double-Barrel Shotguns*   *28*
4. *The European Double-Barrel Shotgun*   *40*
5. *The Double Gun in the United States*   *53*
6. *Pump and Automatic Shotguns*   *69*
7. *The Shotgun Barrel*   *84*
8. *The Choke in the Shotgun Barrel*   *93*
9. *The Variable Choke Devices*   *115*
10. *Patterning Your Shotgun*   *123*
11. *Sights on the Shotgun*   *134*
12. *The Shotgun Stock*   *142*
13. *Shotgun Fit*   *154*
14. *Shotguns for Various Purposes*   *162*
15. *The Shotgun Gauges*   *176*
16. *Guns and Loads for Pheasants*   *186*
17. *Quail Guns and Loads*   *193*
18. *Combination Guns*   *202*
19. *The Shot Shell and Its Components*   *208*

CONTENTS

20. *Ballistics of the Shot Shell* 222

21. *The Shot Pellet* 240

22. *The Elements of Shotgun Shooting* 250

23. *To Lead or Not to Lead* 263

24. *It's the Angles* 276

25. *Hitting Birds Afield* 284

26. *Big Game with a Shotgun* 295

27. *Learning on Clay Targets* 305

28. *Handloading Shot Shells* 313

29. *Shotgun Miscellany* 323

INDEX 333

Note about the Illustrations

The illustrations for this book—except for the diagrammatic drawings that are printed with the text—are all grouped together for convenience of study. They will be found following page 150.

THE SHOTGUN BOOK

CHAPTER 1

A Brief History

of the Shotgun

THE use of the shotgun as a sporting weapon goes back to about the beginning of the eighteenth century when the first shotguns that could be handled and pointed effectively at flying game were produced in England. Before that time, the sporting shotgun and the military musket differed mostly in ornamentation and intent. Both were smooth bores. Both were generally long of barrel, heavy, and slow to handle. Like the musket, the early sporting shotgun was a flintlock and was to remain a flintlock for at least another century.

These early sporting guns used cast "swan shot" running 200–250 to the pound or smaller shot made by chopping up sheets of lead. Since this "shot" was roughly in the form of cubes, its action was erratic and its ballistic properties were pretty sad. The combination of excessive weight, long barrel, slow ignition time, and poor ballistic performance made these early sporting guns unsuited for anything but short-range pot shooting of sitting game.

In the eighteenth century, British gunmakers shortened the barrels of these ponderous guns, did away with the stock to the muzzle, improved locks and pan covers, and began experimenting with turning out double-barrel flintlock muzzle loaders. Joseph Manton in the late flintlock era made beautiful and graceful double flint-lock guns that can be shot and handled with pleasure today. Fine London-made sporting guns were put in handsome felt-lined fitted cases with compartments for the various accessories—powder horn, shot pouch, vent pick, cleaning rod, etc. I can remember seeing such a fitted case of a somewhat later era—one for a London double caplock gun brought to this country by my Irish grand-father before the Civil War.

Not only were the guns improved in the late eighteenth century but also the powder and the shot. French and British chemists learned to manufacture stronger and more reliable black powder, blended and standardized as to grain size. A Britisher named William Watts developed the process of pouring molten lead through shower pans with holes of various sizes to produce round shot easily and cheaply—the same process that is used in shot towers today.

The first quarter of the nineteenth century saw the development of the caplock shotgun, in which a pellet of fulminate of mercury was substituted for the flint and steel of the flintlock. The use of the fulminate was the discovery of Alexander Forsyth, a British clergyman, but the perfection of the cap itself was the work of another Britisher named Joshua Shaw, who migrated to the United States. He invented the caplock system as we know it. After about 1825, all newly manufactured arms used this system and many flintlocks were adapted to it. The caplock, unlike the flintlock, could be used in wet weather. In addition, it provided a much faster ignition time and hence made wing shooting easier.

Better guns, better powder, better shot, and faster ignition re-sulted in wing shooting's becoming a popular sport for the rich and leisured. Col. Peter Hawker's famous book on wing shooting, *In-structions to Young Sportsmen*, appeared in 1814 and was reprinted many times until the last edition in 1922. The British were the first keen wingshots, and hunting over dogs as well as shooting driven grouse and pheasants was fashionable. In the United States there was much interest in the sporting shooting of grouse, ducks, geese, pigeons, woodcock, and snipe.

The first successful breech-loading shotguns were made possible by the development of the Lefaucheaux pinfire cartridge. Lefaucheaux made guns to fire the cartridge, and this revolutionized shotgun manufacture. Lancaster and Daw, London gunsmiths, brought out their versions of centerfire shot shells and breech-loading shotguns to fire them. After the American Civil War, double-barrel breech-loading shotguns, at first with outside hammers but later hammerless, were manufactured not only in Great Britain but also in Germany, Austria, Spain, Belgium, France, and Italy. In the United States doubles were made by Ithaca, the Hunter Arms Company (L. C. Smith), Colt, Parker, Remington, the Syracuse Arms Company, the old (Uncle Dan) Lefever Company, and by others.

Choke boring came into common use in the late 1870s and early 1880s and by about 1890, the double gun had so nearly reached perfection that any changes after that time were matters of refinement. Wildfowl guns shot patterns about as tight as guns do today. Many of these old guns were superbly finished, checkered, and engraved. The automatic selective ejector had been perfected. Factory-loaded cartridges were reliable and relatively cheap.

The period from about 1875 until 1914 was the golden age of the shotgunner in America. Upland game birds and waterfowl were incredibly plentiful. Hunters were relatively few, as the cheap transportation of the automobile hadn't sent hordes of hunters scurrying through the country to invade every likely looking covert. Clean farming and the use of pesticides had not killed off the upland game, and the draining of marshes had not decimated the waterfowl. Seasons were long, bag limits were generous, and law enforcement sketchy. There was much interest in live-pigeon shooting and trapshooting at clay targets. This was also the day of the market hunter, and game was served in all fine restaurants.

In those days shotguns and shotgunning had a prestige they do not enjoy today. Whereas upland game had increased because of the introduction of farming into new areas, the big game had been heavily overshot and was not nearly as plentiful in the United States then as it was to be fifty and sixty years later. Back in the 1880s and 1890s sportsmen made long trips simply for shotgun shooting, something that seldom happens today. Rich Easterners would send out their dogs in the baggage car, take staterooms in the Pullman, and go to the Dakotas for prairie chicken and sharptail, down south for quail, to the Canadian provinces for ducks, geese, and prairie chickens, to the Mississippi flyway for ducks. Sometimes they would establish elaborate camps out on the prairie, but at other times they would board at some sod buster's farm or at some small-town hotel. Then they would rent livery-stable buggies and drive out to hunt. The poor man would take a trolley to the end of the line and then walk or catch a local train that went into the country.

I can remember those horse-and-buggy days myself. I grew up in the Salt River Valley of Arizona. My maternal grandfather was a solid and well-to-do citizen who was a keen bird shot. When I was seven or eight he bought me a single-barrel 20 gauge, and we used to ride out in a rubber-tired buggy for quail, whitewing, or mourning doves behind Pet, my grandfather's fine trotting mare.

Before the First World War, much wheat was raised in the valley. There was still mesquite forest along the rivers for nesting ground, and whitewings were present by the hundreds of thousands. In the shortsighted manner of the time, the hunters started gunning for the birds as soon as they invaded the valley from Mexico to nest and to feed on the wheat. Rich men from California and even from as far away as New York came into the low hot valley, established luxurious camps along some canal bank, and shot up case after case of shells. None of us had any idea that shooting the birds during the nesting season would soon cause them to diminish. On many occasions my grandfather and I brought home one hundred or more whitewings from an afternoon's shoot—a whole washtub full of birds.

In those days the ordinary small town had only a handful of hunters. The Salt River had not been drained of its last drop of water for irrigation at that time and was a clear, year-round stream. Thousands of ducks came through the valley every fall, and when I was in my teens I used to hunt them with an old Model 97 Winchester 12-gauge pump gun I had bought secondhand. Rarely did I see another hunter, either on the river for ducks or in the nearby brush for the beautiful Gambel's quail. Today the river where I used to hunt is a dry and dusty bed of sand littered with tin cans, empty beer bottles, and old automobile tires. The brush patches where I used to hunt quail have become real-estate developments full of jerry-built houses sprouting television antennas and all exactly alike. A mountain where my grandfather killed a desert bighorn ram is now surrounded by voluptuous winter homes.

Not only were the years between 1875 and 1914 the golden days of shotgun shooting, they were also the golden days of the double-barrel shotgun. Today a rich Texas sportsman or a Californian who has made a fortune in real estate or by manufacturing some electronic gadget for a ballistic missile has along with his Cadillac a gold-plated Weatherby big-game rifle as a prestige item. This costs him from $500 to $2,000. If he hunts birds or shoots clay targets, he probably owns a machine-made, mass-produced pump or automatic shotgun.

Before the First World War, it was the shotgun that was the prestige item. The solid, well-heeled, respectable citizen who took any interest in sport was expected to have at least one good shotgun, along with a set of fine British straight razors, one for each day of the week. He was also expected to keep up at least one good well-cared-for horse and a buggy. In large cities the man of substance was expected to maintain a carriage and a matched team.

My own grandfather was a bit of a gun nut. I can remember several of his shotguns. All were doubles. He looked upon pump-guns as inventions of the devil, and he regarded those who used automatics as unsound and contemptible fellows who were probably secret socialists and not above robbing widows and orphans. Among others he had an Ithaca, a high-grade Parker, and a Purdey, which spent most of its time in an oak-and-leather case lined with dark red billiard cloth. Grandfather had imported it from England and when my grandmother found out that it had cost him $600 she was so mad she liked to died. But when he went deer hunting he used a Winchester Model 94 .30/30 carbine that cost him $15.

So let's take a look at one of these old doubles from the classic days of the shotgun. In spite of the fact that "fluid" homogenous steel barrels were developed in the 1880s, chances are that a double manufactured between 1885 and 1910 had some sort of twist barrels made of a combination of iron and steel. Such barrels were stronger than the older barrels made of a sheet of iron or mild steel wrapped around a mandrel and welded. They were not nearly as strong as tubes turned, drilled, and reamed from solid-alloy steel-bar stock, but old notions die slowly, and for many years figure on the barrels of a shotgun was considered a mark of quality. Until the outbreak of the First World War, twist and Damascus barrels were optional for all double guns with any pretenses to class.

Although smokeless powder was used almost universally by the early 1900s, shotgun users still demanded long barrels, and most of these classic doubles had barrels 30, 32, 34, and even 36 inches long. Black powder burns at the same rate confined or unconfined, and if a lot of powder was used, a long barrel was needed to burn it. Hence, it was the universal belief (and one held even today) that the longer the barrel, the "harder" the gun shot. In 1910 a 30-inch barrel was on the short side, and a 28-inch barrel was considered quite short and handy. A 26-inch barrel was almost unheard of. Actually, as we shall see in the chapter on shotgun ballistics, what amounts to practically full velocity is developed by modern shotgun powders in barrels 24 inches long.

In the early 1900s, doubles with outside hammers were on their way out, but many guns were still made with them. The Anson & Deeley hammerless box-lock action had been invented in England in 1875, and it had been modified and copied wherever shotguns were made. The American L. C. Smith and Syracuse guns were sidelocks, but the Fox, the Parker, and the Ithaca were box locks.

In the 1870s and 1880s, the 10 gauge was the most popular gauge, but in the 1890s, the 12 gauge took its place for all-round use. The 8 gauge was well liked for wildfowl shooting, and even some 4 and 6-gauge guns were made. Anyone who used a 20 or a 16-gauge gun was considered a bit on the eccentric side. Some 24-gauge doubles were made in the United States and many were made in Belgium. The 28 gauge did not come along until about 1903, when it was pioneered by the Parker Gun Company. The .410 gauge did not even exist then, except in embryonic form in the shape of such little pest cartridges as the .44XL.

Most shotgun stocks before the First World War were much more crooked than they are today. Whereas the standard American mass-produced shotgun stock in the 1960s has a length of pull of 14 inches, a drop at comb of 1⅝ inches and at heel of 2½ inches, the old timers had comb drops of from 1¾ to 2 inches and drops at heel of from 3 to as much as 4 inches. As we shall see in the chapter on stocks, dimensions like these caused unpleasant recoil, and to the modern shooter they seem slow to mount and awkward to point.

By 1910 a few trapshooters were experimenting with Monte Carlo combs and beavertail fore-ends, but most shotguns had splinter fore-ends and conventional buttstocks. The usual shotgun had a horn or composition buttplate, but the higher grades had butts of plain checkered wood, skeleton buttplates, or heel and toe plates to prevent the wood from denting or splitting.

Automatic ejectors were almost universal on the better grades of guns and selective single triggers were available at an extra charge.

In the better grades, the wood used in the stocks was much handsomer than is commonly seen today. Fine, well-figured French walnut was used in British and Continental guns and for the better grades of American-made doubles. The checkering done in those days has never been surpassed, and the higher the grade of the gun the finer, sharper, and more elaborate the checkering.

Except for the cheapest grades, all doubles had some engraving. The more expensive grades had a great deal, and like fine and precise checkering, engraving was considered one of the marks of a good gun. A good double required much handwork, but that was not of great moment back in the 1890s and early 1900s, as wages were low. An old-timer who had been with a company that had been making double guns for a half century told me that in 1895 he was paid 10 cents an hour and finally when he was making 25 cents an hour he felt that he was in the chips and got married.

In those days the second most expensive A. H. Fox gun retailed with automatic ejectors for $215, and the most expensive, a veritable dream gun, for $500. The beautifully checkered stock was of fine Circassian walnut. The piece was beautifully engraved on breech and frame. The guns were made to order and the buyer had his choice of barrel length, boring, stock style, and dimensions. A gun of the same quality today would cost $5,000, and the "second best" could not be purchased for $2,000.

Comparatively few of the pre-World War I double guns were luxury items with Circassian walnut stocks and fine checkering and engraving. Most sold at modest prices. In 1915, the first year the Parker Trojan was on the market, it sold for $27.50. Before 1914 it was possible to buy a double-barrel shotgun with automatic ejectors from the big mail-order houses for $20 to $35.

In the heyday of the double, tens of thousands of these inexpensive guns were sold in the United States, and in my more than twenty years as a shooting editor, I have received thousands of letters about them. Correspondents want to know when they were made, who made them, where they were made, what they cost new, where they can get parts, and how much they are worth.

Most of these requests are enough to send a conscientious gun editor to the bottle. For one thing, many of these guns bear private brand names. A big hardware jobber or a mail-order house would, let us say, order one thousand 12-gauge double guns and have a private brand name stamped on them. Sears, Roebuck and Montgomery Ward have used dozens of private brand names. The Simmons Hardware Company and the Shapleigh Hardware Company, both St. Louis jobbers, used many different private brand names. So did Hibbard, Spencer & Bartlett of Chicago and the Marshall, Wells Company of Duluth, Minnesota. Makers of cheap guns, such as Harrington & Richardson, Stevens Arms Corporation, and Hopkins & Allen, made guns under various of their own private brand names. One long used by Stevens, for example, is "Springfield," something which causes the uninitiated to think guns of that name were made at the Springfield arsenal in Springfield, Massachusetts, where the 1903 "New" Springfield and the M-1 Garand came into being.

Sears, Roebuck not only bought and sold guns stamped with their private brand names from various manufacturers but also made guns themselves in a manufacturing subsidiary at Meriden, Connecticut, called the Meriden Arms Company. In addition, tens of thousands of cheap Belgian guns were imported, generally marked with private brand names, and sold. The picture is made all the more confusing because the jobbers often did not bother to trademark the names of their fanciful gun companies and in some cases the same name was used by more than one concern.

Here are some of the many private brand names used at one time or another by Sears: Aubrey, Black Beauty, Challenge Ejector, Chicago, Colton Firearms Company, Eastern Arms Company, Empire Arms Company, Featherlight, Fryberg & Company, Gibralter, Long Range Wonder, Long Tom, Meriden, Ranger, Super Ranger.

Many of these old doubles had twist or Damascus barrels. Most of them were soft and shoddily made and have long since shot loose. Parts are impossible to obtain. No one that I have ever heard of collects old private-brand-name shotguns with Damascus barrels, and consequently they are worth nothing. Even those with some type of fluid-steel barrels often are chambered for 2½ or 2⅝-inch shells and the wisdom of using them with modern 2¾-inch shells is doubtful. Even if they have serial numbers it is impossible to trace them, and the harried chaps who work for the big mail-order houses won't go through the records to find out when and where they were made and what they cost. Nevertheless, for the next fifty and maybe one hundred years, people will dig great-grandpa's old fowling piece out of the attic and write to gun editors about them. This poor starveling can only send them Form Letter No. 21 saying that identification would be beyond the powers of a swami with nine crystal balls and then reach for the jug.

The single-barrel repeating shotgun has many advantages over the double. One is the somewhat doubtful one of the single sighting plane over one barrel. Another is that such a gun of necessity has a single trigger. Yet another is that the shells are ejected automatically in the case of the self-loading shotgun or with a short forward-and-back motion of the slide handle in the case of the pump. Perhaps the most important advantage of all is the fact that tolerances are not nearly as important with the repeater as they are with the double, and repeaters lend themselves more easily to mass production.

Initially, the fact that repeaters carried more than two shells was deemed a great advantage, particularly for wildfowl shooting. Today, federal law limits all repeating shotguns to three shots if they are to be used on migratory birds, and some states limit such guns to three shots for all game. Consequently, the extra shots are of less importance. Repeaters began to catch on during the late 1890s and early 1900s when there were many ducks and geese and much market hunting was done.

However, in many ways the repeater is inferior to the double. For one thing, the repeater always looks like a machine, whereas a well-made and well-finished double is a work of art. For another, the double does not have the long receiver of the repeater and consequently is shorter and handier with the same length of barrel. The double is generally better balanced, since the weight is more nearly between the hands. The double is also safer, since one can open the gun and tell at a glance if it is loaded or not.

Actually, the first repeating shotgun with a single barrel made in the United States came before the days of breech loading. It was a Colt with a revolving cylinder like the Colt cap-and-ball revolvers. This came out in 1839 and an improved model appeared in 1855.

Another primitive repeater that came along during the transition period between muzzle loading and breech loading with fixed ammunition was the Roper, which appeared in 1867. The charges were contained in reloadable steel containers with a nipple for a percussion cap. They were placed in a rotating cylinder. The gun featured a choke tube screwed to the muzzle, a gadget on the order of the variable choke devices popular today.

Two abortive pump guns appeared during the 1880s—the Spencer and the Burgess—but neither was successful as both designs were full of bugs. The first really successful repeating shotgun was the Winchester Model 1887, a lever action invented by that firearms genius John Browning. In fact, John Browning, more than anyone else, is the father of the repeating shotgun.

The Model 1887 was initially made only in 10 gauge but later came out in 12 gauge. Barrels were 30 and 32 inches in length and were furnished in Damascus and laminated steel as well as in fluid steel. Capacity of the guns was four shots in the tubular magazine under the barrel and one shot in the chamber. Manufacture of the gun continued until 1901, when some changes were made in the gun and it was continued in 10 gauge only under the designation Model 1901. These old guns were as ugly as sin, slow to operate, but strong, rugged, and reliable. An uncle of mine had one and I did some duck hunting with it when I was a kid. I still remember how it kicked.

The first successful pump gun was also an invention of John Browning and manufactured by Winchester—the Model 1893. It had a visible hammer, side ejection, solid breech, and tubular magazine. It was made in 12 gauge only, as the 12 was by that time taking the play away from the 10 gauge and with its smaller shells a 12 was easier to manufacture than a 10. Safety was the hammer at half cock, as was the case with lever-action big-game rifles.

Barrels for the 1893 were chambered for 2⅝-inch shells and were 30 and 32 inches in length. They were regularly furnished in fluid steel but could be had in laminated or Damascus on special order. The magazine held five shots. Guns were solid frame—which means they could not be taken down.

After a few years the Model 1893 was improved and brought out as the famous Model 1897, which was made in both 12 and 16 gauge and which was manufactured continuously until the middle 1950s. Many thousands of these old Model 1897s are still in use. I had one at one time and shot many doves, whitewings, quail, and ducks with it. The 1893 is much rarer. The only one I have ever seen outside of the Winchester museum at New Haven was one that was standing in the corner of an abandoned cabin in the Yukon.

The first successful self-loading shotgun was also a John Browning invention. It was the Remington Model 11 and it was made from 1905 until 1948. It was then superseded by another recoil-operated gun known as the Model 11–48.

The long-recoil system with the recoiling barrel is one of the most reliable of all systems. The Browning autoloaders (with the exception of the double automatic employing the short-recoil system), made in Belgium and sold in the United States by Browning

Arms Company, are substantially the same gun as the original Model 1911 Remington, and the Savage self-loader is based on the same design.

Remington's original pump gun was the Model 1910. It was based on Pedersen patents. It was a hammerless job. Winchester's famous Model 1912 came out in January 1913 in 20 gauge with a 2½-inch chamber and with a 25-inch barrel. The Model 1912 was designed by Thomas C. Johnson of the Winchester staff and is the most famous and best liked of all the 12-gauge hammerless repeaters.

Winchester had less luck with its first self-loading shotgun, the Model 1911. It likewise was designed by Johnson, but he had helped Browning make out his application for patent on what had become the Remington Model 11 and had done such a good job of it that he had made it difficult for anyone to design a self-loading shotgun without infringing on Browning patents. Manufacture of the Model 1911 was discontinued in 1925. It was revived as the Model 40 in 1940, but it was never a satisfactory or popular gun and was dropped.

Repeating shotguns have been made by many American firms— Marlin, High Standard, Savage, Ithaca, Mossberg—and the repeater is the typical American scatter gun. Europe, with its lower wages, has remained the home of the double, but the repeater is making inroads even there. As we have seen, the Browning automatic is made in Belgium and distributed over the world. At least one pump gun is made in France and two or three makes of automatics are turned out in Italy.

Turn of the Century Gun Prices

A Sears, Roebuck catalog issued in 1902, shortly after the turn of the century and the year I was born, lists a DH grade Parker double with Damascus barrels, imported walnut stock, and fine checkering for $73.60; an Ithaca double, also with Damascus barrels, European walnut stock, engraving, and good checkering for $37.60—about the price of a VH grade Parker.

A double ejector with Damascus barrels, built by the long

defunct Union Arms Company of Toledo, Ohio, is listed at $18.75, and a double-barrel "Sam Holt" hammer gun for $8.95.

An early pump gun, also by Union Arms, sold for $14.92, and a Winchester Model 97 pump gun for $17.82, but you could get a single-barrel Long Range Wonder for $3.98. By comparison a Model 94 Winchester in the then rather new .30/30 caliber cost $14.75; a Model 95 Winchester lever-action rifle in .30/40 cost $21.35. If you were content with the same rifle for the black powder cartridge, you could buy it in .38/72 caliber for $17.82.

But back in those days men raised families on a dollar a day. My father was a newspaperman who kept a horse and buggy, drank sour-mash bourbon, and smoked good cigars. At the time I was born his salary was $125 a month.

CHAPTER 2

The Classification

of the Modern Shotgun

SHOTGUNS are used all over the world today and in many different forms. The African native hunts with a smoothbore muzzle loader, which costs $4 or $5 but which nevertheless represents a great investment to him. He loads it with whatever he can get his hands on—shot if he can afford it and find it, stones, pieces of scrap iron—almost anything. He wounds a lot of game but he also kills a lot, far more than is ever taken by the American or Continental sportsman on safari. He almost never shoots at birds and never takes a wing shot. Instead he bangs away at big game.

Particularly in Tanganyika, there are tens of thousands of these muzzle loaders in the hands of native hunters, and in 1953, when I made a long safari there, a high percentage of all the game shot by my companions and me had been previously wounded by muzzle loaders. The finest sable antelope I have ever taken had a rusty iron slug buried in the muscles of his rump.

The shotgun is so enormously popular because the man armed with one and equipped with proper ammunition can take almost any game from birds and small deer to lions and tigers. In central Asia tribesmen armed with muzzle-loading flintlocks build blinds and lie in wait for the wonderful *Ovis poli*, the wild sheep that is generally considered to be the world's finest and rarest trophy. In Iran, village shikaris kill ibex, red sheep, and the larger sheep called urial with muzzle loaders, but they have to stalk very close to do so. India is full of muzzle loaders and also cheap Spanish breech-loading shotguns. Using buckshot or round "pumpkin balls," the natives shoot deer and even take a pop at an occasional leopard or tiger with them.

The American farm boy has his single-barrel or bolt-action shotgun and with it he takes pheasants, rabbits, and quail. In many densely populated sections of the United States it is illegal to hunt deer with anything other than a shotgun with buckshot or slugs.

Shotguns vary enormously in cost. The Iranian shikari or the American farm boy pays from $10 to $30 for his gun. The wealthy European may put out $10,000 for a matched pair of guns built by Holland & Holland, Boss, or Purdey. An American Winchester Model 21 can cost over $4,000. Just as the willow pole in the hands of a barefoot, freckle-faced farm boy may catch more trout than the sportsman's fancy and expensive handmade rod of split bamboo, so a machine-made bolt-action shotgun may throw just as dense a pattern and kill just as far as a Winchester Model 21 or a Boss. It won't handle as fast, point as surely, look as handsome, or be as much of a joy to own—but that is something else again.

The difference in cost between a machine-made pump gun and a high-class double comes largely from the handwork involved, just as the cost or the handwork is responsible for much of the difference between the cost of a Chevrolet and a Cadillac. The cost of the steel that goes into the pump or the double is inconsequential in any case.

The Single-Barrel Shotgun

The cheapest and some of the most expensive shotguns are single-barrel, single-shot guns. The expensive guns are the single-barrel trap models. The cheapest are the farm-boy pot guns, the kind of gun that most of us begin our shooting with. These have been made by the hundreds of thousands and competition is ferocious.

Profit, if any, is literally figured in cents. Every effort is made to turn them out as cheaply as possible, because if one retails for $30, let us say, and another for $29.50 the cheaper gun will get the sales. Frames are generally cast to save money. Chokes are swaged, also to save money. Stocks are of the cheapest possible wood. They are turned on a machine and finished by a sprayed-on coat of lacquer. Little if any handwork can be put in on adjustment for smooth operation, as handwork is expensive. The stocks are not checkered, as checkering, too, costs money.

Some of these guns are hammerless, but some like that classic, the old Iver Johnson Champion, are made with hammers. Since automatic ejectors for single barrels can be non-selective, many are so equipped. At times these single shots have sold for less than $10. Now they generally cost $30 and more.

The amount of choke in the barrels of most of them is indefinite, since swaging in the choke is not the most exact of processes. Patterns of those I have shot run from 55 to 65 percent, or within the range of modified and improved-modified. This is about right. Since these guns are not bought by sophisticates, most of them are made with 28 and 30-inch barrels. Because many believe that the longer the barrel is the harder the gun shoots some single shots are made with 36-inch barrels even today and in the past some were made with 40-inch barrels. I often get letters from some old-timer who writes of the Long Range Wonder of his youth. It was, he says, the hardest shooting gun he ever saw and would kill single ducks regularly at 125 yards.

These cheap single shots are useful guns. They may be rough. They aren't beautiful, but most of them pattern well enough, and they introduce most of us to the wonderful sport of scattergunning. They are good farm guns and good guns to take along on a rough pack trip to pick up some ducks and grouse.

The Lever-Action Shotgun

There isn't much use for a lever-action shotgun, as most of us cannot operate the lever fast enough to drive in a quick second shot. However, as we have seen, the first successful Winchester repeating shotgun was the Browning lever-action Model 1887 made in 10 and 12 gauge; the revised Model 1901 in 10 gauge only was manufactured until 1920. Marlin at one time made a lever-action .410, and after World War II, a lever-action shotgun known as the Kessler was manufactured for a while. These guns were all repeaters. Some of the single shots were operated by levers. Shotguns were built on the Winchester Model 89 falling block action operated by a lever, and shotguns were also built on the famous Remington-Rider rolling block action.

The Bolt-Action Shotgun

The bolt action is too slow for shotgun use, as it is even slower than the lever action—so slow that it is almost impossible even for a skilled operator to get in a second shot on a covey rise. However, tens of thousands of bolt-action repeating shotguns have been made because they are cheap to manufacture, and the fact that they are repeaters gives them more sales appeal than the single shots.

The first such shotguns I remember were made in Germany during the inflation period in the early 1920s and employed old Model 98 Mauser actions. All I saw were in 12 gauge, and the locking lugs at the head of the bolt were inoperative as the receiver ring had to be opened up to let the 12-gauge barrel in. Only the auxiliary locking lug at the root of the bolt held the bolt in the receiver. Sometimes this crystallized and sheared off and then there was hell to pay. These guns were sold all over North America. They bore such names as "Geco" and cost but a few dollars. I still hear of one now and then.

For many years several concerns have made inexpensive bolt-action shotguns which compete in the beginner's market with the single shots. These generally hold one shell in the chamber, two in a clip magazine. They are satisfactory farm and pot guns, and when fitted with receiver sights or scopes they do well for shooting deer with rifled slugs. These bolt-action guns have been made by Harrington & Richardson, by Mossberg, by Stevens, and by Marlin.

The Pump Gun

The pump gun is the most popular type of repeating shotgun in the world today. For many years the pump was an American phenomenon, but pump-action shotguns are now being manufactured and sold in Europe. Even in Britain, the citadel of shotgun conservatism, pumps are being used more and more—particularly by men of moderate means who cannot afford the expense of a flossy London-made double, just as they cannot afford a grouse moor or a shoot for driven pheasants.

A pump gun is simple, rugged, and relatively cheap to make as it requires a minimum of handwork, and it can be shot about as fast as an automatic. The pump has its faults. For one thing, it is never as handsome a piece of ordnance as a good double. For another, the pump tends to be overlong, for the barrel is hitched to a long receiver. The pump does not have the advantage of two degrees of choke for the first and second shots, and as the shells are fired and ejected the balance changes slightly. What the pump does have, however, is a single sighting plane, great ruggedness and reliability, three or more shots, a built-in single trigger, rapid ejection.

For years the standard pump gun was fearfully heavy and clumsy, as the great demand was for 12-gauge guns with 30 or 32-inch full-choke barrels. Now pumps are made with receivers of lighter alloy steel or Duralumin. Barrels tend to be shorter and more open. Stocks have improved and, as a consequence of all this, pumps are handier weapons than they used to be.

John M. Browning had his hand in most gun developments around the turn of the century, including the development of the pump gun. As we have seen, he was the inventor of the Model 1897 lever-action shotgun and the Model 1893 Winchester pump with the visible hammer. It is not generally known but he was also the father of the Model 520 Stevens pump gun, the first pump with a solid breech. He also invented the Remington Model 1917 pump, on which the present Ithaca Model 37 was based.

Remington at one time made very fine double guns, as well as top-break single shots, but the company turned out its last double in 1910. The Remington pump, the Model 10, was made between 1907 and 1929. It was a solid-frame hammerless that ejected at the bottom. It was made in 12 gauge only, but the Model 1917 was made in 20 gauge only. The Model 1910 was followed by the Model 1929, which in turn was superseded by the Model 31. This popular gun came out in 1931 and was made until 1949.

The longest lived, best loved, and most successful pump gun ever built is the Winchester Model 12, which first appeared in 1913 as a handsome little 20 gauge with a 25-inch barrel. The 12 and 16-gauge Model 12s came out in 1914, the now discontinued 28 gauge in 1934. Hundreds of thousands of Model 12s have been used all over the world and the gun has been made in field, trap, skeet, riot, and various special models. It is common to see a Model 12 that has been used so much that all the blue has worn off and its metal shines like a new silver dollar. In most cases, however, these old guns still function smoothly, shoot well, and their insides are bright and clean. Many of these have fired a half million shells with no service except the replacement of an occasional minor part.

The Model 12 was dropped in 1964 and replaced by the Model 1200, a cheaper gun to manufacture. However, it has been revived in 12 gauge only.

Today, expired patents and much experience in manufacture have made all pump guns more or less alike. All are hammerless, solid breech guns. Most eject at the side but some eject at the bottom of the receiver. All have tubular magazines under the barrel. They are made by Savage-Stevens, by Remington, Winchester, High Standard, Marlin, Mossberg, and Ithaca. Some have checkered stocks, some do not; some have factory-installed variable choke devices, but most do not. They are all pretty much the same breed of cat.

The Automatic

Properly speaking, the shotguns generally called "automatics" should be called "semi-automatics" or "self-loaders." By definition an automatic fires as long as the trigger is held down, whereas the trigger of the semi-automatic or self-loader must be pulled for each shot. A gun capable of doing all the work of ejecting the empty cartridge case, inserting a new shell into the chamber, and cocking the piece is an old dream. Two forces can be used to accomplish this. One is that of the expanding gases. The other is recoil.

The first successful automatic shotgun was the invention of John Browning. Browning used the long-recoil system, in which the whole barrel and breech block locked together recoil for several inches. Then the breech block is held back while the barrel goes forward. His gun was first offered to Winchester, but Browning wanted a royalty for each gun made, whereas the brass at Winchester wanted to pay a flat fee. He then offered the gun to Remington, but while he was waiting to see the head of that company, Marcellus Hartley, that famous man died of a heart attack. Browning then went to Belgium, where he made arrangements for the manufacture of the gun by Fabrique Nationale. Later it was brought out as the Model 11 by Remington. F. N. still makes and sells the Browning automatic in Europe and the rest of the world. F. N. also makes the many Browning guns sold by the Browning company in the United States. Remington made the Model 11 from 1905 until 1948, when it was replaced by a streamlined version of the same gun called the Model 11-48.

Just as the Model 12 Winchester pump gun was the standard by which all other pump guns were judged, so the Remington Model 11 was the standard automatic. Until recently, I am told, the Browning automatic imported from Belgium and marketed by the Browning company was still a best seller among the automatics. With its square receiver it is somewhat homely in this streamlined age. It is heavy, but it is rugged, reliable—and it works. It is made in 12, 16, and 20 gauge. As the Remington Model 11, it was made only in 12 gauge. Patents for the gun have long since expired, and the Savage automatic is pretty much a copy of the original Browning—square receiver and all.

Since the war, the long-recoil system used by the Browning and the Remington Model 11 has been less popular than it was among American manufacturers. Remington has brought out a series of gas-operated semi-automatics. The High Standard automatic is also gas operated. The obsolete Winchester Model 59 automatic used the short-recoil system by means of the slip-chamber invented by "Carbine" Williams. The Model 1400 is gas operated.

The majority of shooters are not bothered by the "double shuffle" of the long-recoil type of automatic, but some object to it. Actually, the recoil with an automatic of that type is increased as the slamming back of barrel and breech block adds to recoil. If the recoil mechanism is not properly adjusted, the recoil becomes unpleasant. There is no doubt but that the kick of the gas-operated and short-recoil guns is somewhat softer.

The long-recoil operated guns are no longer as popular as they were in skeet shooting, and they have never been very popular for traps because the ejected cases annoy other shooters on the line. The pump gun is popular for skeet, and the most widely used type for trapshooting.

In the 1970s, there is no doubt but that the automatic shotgun is increasing its share of the market. The new automatics are lighter than the old, have better lines, and are more pleasant to shoot. The Remington 1100 has been a great success at trap and on waterfowl.

The Double-Barrel Shotgun

World War II just about killed off the American-made double-barrel shotgun in both the side-by-side and over-and-under forms. For one thing, the tastes of the American shooter had been swinging over to the single-barrel repeater for a few generations. For another, the old gun craftsmen who turned out the better American doubles were dying off or retiring in the 1940s and no young men were coming along to replace them. Another reason is that the costs of hand labor skyrocketed during and after the war.

In 1941, the great Parker side-by-side double was still being made by Remington at Ilion, New York. After peace broke out, a few Parkers were assembled from parts but manufacture was never resumed. The Ithaca Gun Company, which for generations was famous for its doubles, saw the handwriting on the wall and went into the manufacture of pump guns before the war. The company made some doubles after the war but found their manufacture unprofitable and discontinued all doubles. Ithaca now makes pump shotguns, .22 rifles, and a very expensive single-barrel trap shotgun.

The Hunter Arms Company, makers of the L. C. Smith side-by-side doubles, went broke. After the war, the business was bought by Marlin and moved to New Haven, Connecticut, but Marlin had labor troubles, couldn't make the guns at a profit, and so folded up the operation.

Winchester never made any money through the manufacture of the famous Model 21 side-by-side double, even though after the war the price was raised annually. Now the Model 21 is strictly a custom proposition, with the cheapest Model 21 retailing for $3,000 and the most expensive for over $5,000. Only a trickle of Model 21s are coming through.

The only other maker of side-by-side doubles in the United States in the 1970s is the Savage-Stevens combine. They turn out Fox and Stevens guns, but although they are strong, serviceable guns they are by no means fine guns. They are made with nonselective single triggers and are available with automatic ejectors. They are turned out with a minimum of handwork.

The side-by-side double has hardly changed since the turn of the century, and what changes have taken place are in the nature of refinements. Automatic ejectors were perfected in the late 1880s and early 1890s. Single triggers were worked out in the early 1900s. A smooth-working, nicely balanced double does not lend itself to mass production, and the world's fine doubles are either very expensive or are made in countries with low wage scales.

There is still a considerable market for good double guns in the United States, for a secondhand Parker or Winchester Model 21 of good grade and in good condition will sell for from two to five times its original cost. A few fine doubles are imported from England, some from Belgium, Italy, Austria, and Spain.

The Over-and-Under

Shotguns with barrels one above the other, instead of side by side, are relatively popular in the United States. The leader is the famous Browning Superposed gun designed by John Browning, made in Belgium, and imported and sold in the United States by the Browning Arms Company. It is a premium-quality gun with selective single trigger, selective automatic ejectors. It is made with watch-like precision.

The only American-made over-and-under in the same class with the Browning was the Remington Model 32, which was made from 1932 until 1942. Whereas the Browning is available in all gauges, the Remington was made only in 12 gauge. It was a particular favorite with skeet shooters.

Savage made an inexpensive over-and-under double before the war, but did not resume its manufacture after the conflict was over. Marlin made an over-and-under known as the Model 90 and continued it after the war. It has now been dropped.

If an over-and-under shotgun with selective single trigger, selective automatic ejectors, good balance, good wood, and good finish could be produced in the United States to sell at from $200 to $250 it would no doubt have an excellent sale. However, the production of any smooth-working, well-finished double requires so much handwork that I doubt whether it is possible to produce one and pay American wages. Winchester's new Model 101 over-and-under is made in Japan. It is rugged, well made and finished, reliable, but in 12 gauge on the heavy side. The production of fine doubles requires painstaking fitting of small, intricate, and delicate parts, many hours of skilled work with files and polishing stones. In Spain and Italy such labor can be obtained for $2.50 to $3.50 a day. In the United States such labor demands and gets that much an hour.

Guns Classified According to Use

Shotguns are classified not only as to the type of action but also as to use. *The upland gun* is used for hunting such game as quail, pheasants, and grouse. Such guns are generally light, usually have short barrels, and have open boring. In the past the classic upland gun has been a double with barrels about 26 inches long and bored improved cylinder and modified. Often such guns were in 16, 20, or even 28 gauge, rather than 12 gauge. Nowadays the upland gun is apt to be one of the new light automatics with a short open barrel.

The wildfowl gun is generally heavier than the upland gun; it has a longer barrel and a tighter choke. The classic wildfowl gun is a 12-gauge double with 30 or 32-inch barrel bored modified and full or full and full. Often it has 3-inch chambers so that the 12-gauge magnum loads can be used. Whereas the upland gun is light because it has to be carried long distances between shots, the wildfowl gun is ideally heavier so its recoil will be less unpleasant for the heavy shells used on ducks and geese. Today the special wildfowl gun is one of the heavier automatics such as the Browning or one of the heavier pump guns chambered for the 3-inch magnum shells. Some wildfowl enthusiasts have imported heavy side-by-side double guns from Spain and Italy for the 10-gauge, 3½-inch magnum shell. However, more 12-gauge guns are used in wildfowl shooting than all other gauges put together.

The all-around gun is a compromise and it does fairly well on everything. A good bet is a 12 or 16-gauge pump or automatic with 26 or 28-inch barrels bored modified. Even better perhaps would be such a gun fitted with one of the variable choke devices.

Shotguns for deer hunting have been brought out under various names such as "Slugster," "Deer Slayer," or "Slug Special" since the war. These are pumps or automatics with short (22 or 24-inch) straight cylinder barrels fitted with iron sights. Such guns are handy in woods shooting, and up to 75–100 yards they are about as accurate as iron-sighted rifles in ordinary hands.

Trap guns almost always have 30 or 32-inch barrels with ventilated ribs. Generally, they are pump guns but some are special single shots. They are generally bored improved-modified or full and have longer and straighter stocks than do game guns, since the clay targets are always rising.

Skeet guns have short (generally 26-inch) barrels bored to throw as wide a pattern at 20–25 yards as is possible, since skeet is a fast, short-range game. Generally, skeet guns are pumps or automatics with ventilated ribs. Stocks have more drop at heel and comb than do trap guns, as skeet targets are generally falling instead of rising. At one time most skeet guns were fitted with variable choke devices but now most simply have plain skeet-bored barrels, usually with ventilated ribs. Over-and-under shotguns with open borings are used by many at skeet but the side-by-side double is now seldom seen in serious skeet shooting, as most contestants feel they do better with the single sighting plane.

Riot guns are special cylinder bored guns with very short barrels, the descendants of the "sawed off" shotguns used by express messengers and sometimes by gangsters. The riot gun is designed to throw a lot of buckshot fast. It is used by law enforcement officers and bank guards; it was also used for close-range fighting by the American army during both world wars.

CHAPTER 3

Types of Double-Barrel
Shotguns

THE side-by-side double-barrel shotgun as it is known today was largely developed in nineteenth-century England. When break-open breech-loading double-barrel shotguns first came into being with the invention of the shot shell, all manner of systems were tried. Guns were made with under levers, with side levers, and with various odd systems. Locks were equally strange. By the 1880s, however, the double-barrel shotgun began to look very much as it does today. The use of the top lever became just about universal by the 1890s, but under-lever double rifles were built as late as the early 1930s.

The first successful break-open breech-loaders all had outside hammers, but in the 1870s hammerless doubles were being built. The Anson & Deeley hammerless box-lock action, the action which most box locks copy today, was, for example, patented in 1875. The old hammer gun died hard, because, I presume, of the natural conservatism of the human race. A 1902 Sears, Roebuck catalog I have at hand shows about a third of the doubles offered for sale with hammers. Hammer guns were made in the United States as late as 1920, and some are still made today in Spain, Belgium, and

Austria. For more information on the subject the interested reader should refer to W. W. Greener's *The Gun and Its Development*.

In some of the early attempts to make breech-loading shotguns, the breech was opened to load or to remove the cartridge by sliding the barrels back and forth, by turning the barrels over, or by sliding them to the side. But very quickly almost all gun barrels were made to rotate in a vertical direction. An exception still being made today is the French Darne, an unconventional creation with a sliding and locking breech but stationary barrels.

The use of the top-break system meant that some means had to be developed to control rotation and to lock barrels and frame strongly together at the time of firing. To accomplish this, projections called "lumps" or "lugs" are fitted to the barrel group. A hinge pin is fitted into the forward portion of the frame or action body. Then a hook is machined into the front of the forward lump to fit it. Barrels are held to the frame by one or two under bolts activated by the top lever. Many double guns have some type of top bolting. A common one is the doll's head, a round extension of the top rib with a V bite which bolts together and strengthens the union of barrel group and action body. The Greener crossbolt is a tapered pin worked by the top lever. When the gun is ready to fire, the bolt locks action body and barrel group together as it passes through a hole in the extension rib. The Greener crossbolt is commonly seen on guns of Continental manufacture, both side-by-side and over-and-under, and even on double rifles. Many American doubles used a bolt through the extension rib, although they did not use the Greener crossbolt. The American-invented rotary bolt was used in the L. C. Smith and the Ithaca. The Winchester 21 has no extension rib and no top bolt at all. According to an old brochure on the Winchester Model 21: "With the strong Winchester frame of improved design and under bolt of ample size and strength, a top bolt is not needed. . . . This simplifies construction and leaves the breech free from the usual projection that interferes with the loading and removal of shells. The Winchester bolt works lengthwise with wedge action and is housed immediately below the breech face of the frame. It wedges into its step on the rear of the barrel lug and forces the breech of the barrels down firmly on the water plate of the frame under the stress of a durable coiled bolt spring. Its design is such that it neither sticks nor can it in any degree permit breech looseness to develop from recoil."

Winchester says that the "shooting loose" so common with double guns starts at the hinge because of wear between the hinge pin and the main barrel lug, which results from soft metal and rough handling as well as from shooting. The way to cure it, Winchester says, is by good design, good metal, and proper metallurgy. Top bolts can only hold the barrels down and not up against the standing breech. I think Winchester has something. I have never seen a Model 21 that has shot loose, but I have seen plenty of doubles with top bolting that were so loose they rattled like castanets. Whatever type of bolting is used, it is necessary that all fitting be close and exact if the gun is to remain strong, tight, and smooth.

There are three types of shotgun actions in general use—the box lock, the sidelock, and the Blitz, on which the firing mechanism is carried on the trigger plate. There are theoretical advantages and disadvantages to all of these, but all of them, if well made and fitted from good materials, are adequately strong and satisfactory.

All of the box locks are modifications of the Anson & Deeley system, the first successful hammerless action, patented in 1875. With it, tumbler assemblies, sears, springs, safety, cocking levers are mounted in the frame, or "action body." With the sidelocks these are all carried on the sideplates, which are separate from but fitted to the frame. There are two types of sidelocks, the back action and the bar action. Of the two, the back action is considered to be the stronger and is the one generally used in England for magnum waterfowl guns and for sidelock double rifles. Sidelocks can be easily removed by the use of a screw driver or, in the case of the hand-detachable sidelocks seen on many expensive British and Continental guns, with no tools at all. Another advantage of the sidelock is that the sideplates give a greater area for engraving and in general make up into a somewhat handsomer gun. Some boxlock guns are made with false sideplates for the sake of appearance and of the engraving area.

The Blitz or trigger plate-lock system has so far as I know never been used in the United States, and in Britain only with the Dickson round action, but it is used a good deal by European makers. The Winchester Model 21 uses a box lock, and so did the Parker, the Remington, the Ithaca, the Fox, and the Iver Johnson. The

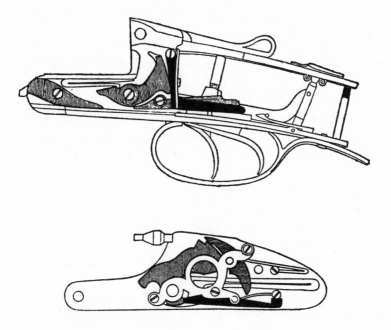

TOP: Anson and Deeley system box lock. This uses flat springs. Most American box locks used coil springs. BOTTOM: Back action side lock.

doubles made by the long-defunct Union Arms Company of Toledo, Ohio, were sidelocks, and so were the guns put out by the Baker Gun Company of Batavia, New York, an outfit which went out of business about 1910. The last surviving American sidelock was the L. C. Smith, made by the Hunter Arms Company, a concern which was finally folded not long after the end of World War II.

Most high-class double guns have selective automatic ejectors, which throw the empty shell or shells from the chambers clear of the gun. If one barrel has been fired, but the other has not, the ejector "selects" the fired case and ejects it clear of the gun. Both shells are "extracted" or pulled out of the chambers, then the ejector kicks out the fired one. Some snappy ejectors throw the fired cases ten or fifteen feet and with considerable velocity. The tried and true Southgate ejector was perfected in the 1890s and is still widely used.

Most double-gun manufacture in the United States was semi-custom in that within limits it was possible to obtain special stock dimensions and chokes to order. It was the practice to list guns without automatic ejectors and then charge extra for them. Most cheap doubles have "extractors," which means that the fired shells are extracted part way from the chamber to facilitate easy removal, but they must be taken out by hand. The mechanisms for automatic ejectors are housed in the fore-end. They are tricky mechanisms, which have to be "timed," or properly adjusted. If not timed, they sometimes do not eject or they eject unfired as well as fired shells. If there is any choice in the matter, the man ordering a double should always specify automatic selective ejection. It is a great convenience in a hot corner, when the hands are cold or when the shooter is wearing gloves.

Most double guns have two triggers, one for the right barrel, and one for the left. Such triggers have their advantages. For one thing the double-barrel shotgun with two triggers is in effect two guns with two triggers and two locks hitched together on one stock. If one set of locks goes haywire, the other will still function. For another thing, the two triggers enable the shooter to make instant selection of the barrel and choke he wants to use. Incidentally, the almost universal use of double triggers in Britain is responsible for the British addiction to stocks with straight grips, as the right hand can then be moved back and forth slightly as each trigger is pulled.

Yet, the two triggers have their disadvantages. A length of pull that is right for one trigger is not right for the other, and the pull dimension is therefore a compromise. Also, yanking two triggers has always been annoying to me and after using single triggers I would no more go back to double triggers than I would go back to a straight razor. And for another thing, unless the front trigger is hinged (as it often is on high-class European doubles), it has a tendency to bruise the trigger finger.

For my money a single trigger on a double gun is well worth the extra cost—IF IT IS GOOD. Many of the foreign single triggers are lousy. They double (fire both barrels at once) or balk (do not fire the second barrel). The first trigger of a Franchi over-and-under gun I have doubled about half the time with duck loads (3¾ drams and 1¼ ounces of shot) and about every fifth time when I was using trap or skeet loads. However, the Franchi people seem to have licked the single-trigger problem and the replacement trigger has given me no trouble. Some of the classiest British makers are pretty coy about accepting orders for guns with single triggers, and many of the British single triggers are not very satisfactory.

American single triggers, on the other hand, have been very satisfactory. In my family we have four Winchester Model 21s, all with single triggers—a 12, two 16s, and a 20. The oldest gun is my wife's 16 gauge, which I purchased in 1939 or 1940. It doubled once when I was shooting skeet with it. The fault was my own, I believe. I held the gun too loosely, and it recoiled against my finger. The other guns have been fired many thousands of rounds at skeet and on game without a single malfunction.

The only American single trigger which ever gave me consistent trouble was one on a 12-gauge Ithaca. I returned it to the factory for adjustment and from then on it was all right. As far as I know, the single triggers on the old Fox guns, the Parkers, and the L. C. Smiths were beyond reproach. The Miller single trigger, made in both selective and non-selective styles, is built like a watch and I have never heard of any trouble with one. I have a non-selective Miller on a beautiful little Arizaga 20 gauge. Miller has come to the rescue of many a man who has had a good foreign gun with a poor trigger and he has fitted hundreds to American doubles that originally did not have the feature. (The company's address is Miller Trigger Company, Millersburg, Pennsylvania.)

Non-selective single triggers are easier and cheaper to make than selective triggers. They have been put on relatively cheap guns upon occasion—the Marlin Model 90 over-and-under, for example, the Ithaca-made Lefever, and the Fox Model B, which is still manufactured. Ninety percent of the time a single trigger which fires the open barrel first is all a man needs, but now and then the selective feature comes in handy. When shooting skeet some like to shift the selector to fire the closer patterning barrel first for the outgoing target and to retain the open barrel for the incomer. With a double-barrel trap gun with one barrel modified and the other full, it is handy to have a selective trigger so that the modified barrel can be used for 16-yard rise and the full-choke barrel for handicap shooting. In Scotch grouse shooting the best practice is to fire the choked barrel first, taking the first bird out of a covey at 35 or 40 yards and using the open barrel for the second bird.

With the exception of the Greener safety, which is on the left side of the stock just above the triggers, all safeties for double-barrel shotguns are on the tang. The tang is a much more convenient location for a safety than the side of the stock or the forward portion of the trigger guard, where the crossbolt safety of many pump guns is.

Some double guns have "automatic" safeties that go on safe when the top lever is operated to open the gun. I loathe such safeties with a purple passion and think they should be prohibited by constitutional amendment. Fortunately these safeties can generally be rendered non-automatic quite easily by a gunsmith. Automatic safeties are particularly bad on a double rifle to be used on dangerous game. An acquaintance of mine rented a double in Africa and was out after buffalo with an unarmed native game scout. He shot a buffalo but the wounded animal ran into the bush. The hunter opened his double, ejected the fired case, and reloaded. He was used to a non-automatic safety on his shotgun. When the buffalo came at him his rifle was on safe and he almost pulled the triggers off trying to get it to fire. He was so badly pounded by the buffalo that he was in a hospital for months, and he would have been killed if the buffalo hadn't already been dying when it attacked him.

Actually, the safeties on double guns only lock the triggers—not the tumblers (hammers)—and it is possible for a hard blow to jar a gun off when on safe. I was hunting with a young dog once and was chasing a wounded pheasant with the gun on safe when for some reason or other that damned dog ran between my legs and tripped me. I hit the ground with a resounding crash. The gun was on safe but it went off—fortunately not at me or the dog. Now when I am in the presence of birds I almost never carry a gun on safe—but I always know where it is pointed. There is really no such thing as a safe gun, only a safe hunter.

Some British and Continental makers turn out what they call "self-opening" guns. They could with equal honesty be called "hard-closing" guns. The self-opening feature consists of two little spring-activated studs that project through the water table of the frame and bear against the flats of the barrel near the breech. When one turns the top lever to the right to unlock the gun, the spring-loaded studs push the barrel up sharply. But the gun has to be closed against the spring pressure. I can do without this feature.

An American was once talking over the specifications of a double he intended to order from a British maker. The subject of the self-opening feature came up, and the gunmaker handed him a self-opening gun to demonstrate the feature.

"It sure does open nicely," the American said, "but it is hard as hell to close."

"My dear Mr. Jones," the gunmaker said coldly, "my customers do not close their own guns."

And this is true when the "gun" has a matched pair of doubles. He takes two birds as the covey or flock—or whatever they call a bunch of grouse in Britain—comes in toward the butts (blinds). He opens his gun, hands it to his loader, takes the second gun from him, turns, and (theoretically) takes two going away. I understand now, however, that loaders are seldom employed in Britain. With the peasants getting uppity, it is hard enough to secure beaters, let alone loaders. In 1939 I spent several pleasant days shooting grouse, Hungarian partridges, and pheasants in Scotland and never a loader did I lay eyes on.

The Over-and-Under

The classic shotgun of Europe is the side-by-side double, and far more side-by-side game guns are sold there than over-and-unders even though many good over-and-unders are manufactured in England and on the Continent.

In the United States the demand for a quality double leans to the over-and-under, and more Browning over-and-unders, called by that firm the Superposed, are sold than any other gun that costs over $500. The only other quality over-and-under ever built in the United States was the Remington Model 32, which during the depression cost more than the Browning. It did not survive the war.

The over-and-under has its advantages. The most obvious is the single sighting plane, a virtue also enjoyed by the single-barrel trap gun and the various repeaters. Many who like the single sighting plane claim they cannot shoot double-barrel guns with their wide muzzles.

I am rather inclined to think that they are talking through their hats and that their notion is based on prejudice rather than reason. When one actually shoots a shotgun by seeing the muzzle or muzzles in relation to his target, as one should do, he is not aiming, he is "pointing." I don't think it makes any difference in the accuracy with which the shot charge flies to the target whether the muzzle is narrow or broad. Like many other things in shooting it is all in the mind. I shoot side-by-side doubles, over-and-unders, and repeaters. If the stocks fit and the guns balance properly, I shoot them pretty well. If they don't fit and balance, I don't do so well. I notice that I do a bit better on upland game with a double and a bit better on skeet with the single sighting plane of an automatic. However, I think the difference lies in balance rather than sighting plane. The double, with its weight more between the hands, is a livelier gun, faster to get on with on the straightaways and gentle angles of upland hunting. The automatic, with its balance forward to give a slight muzzle heaviness, swings steadier for the crossing shots at skeet and makes it more difficult for me to practice my pet sin of slowing my swing.

However, a man shoots a gun well if he is convinced he is going to shoot it well, and if a man thinks he is going to shoot better with an over-and-under, he should by all means get one.

Another advantage of the over-and-under is that the recoil of the more open barrel, which is always the bottom barrel, comes back on a straight line against the shoulder and is felt less than the recoil of a side-by-side double or a repeater, for in these the barrel is carried higher and there is a greater angle to accentuate recoil. The recoil of the side-by-side double is always at an angle and creates torque. Yet another advantage of the over-and-under is that the hands are carried in line and theoretically anyway it is easier to point a gun if the left hand is parallel to the right. With the side-by-side double the left hand is carried a bit higher than the right and presumably this tends to cause high shooting.

But the over-and-under also has its faults. Some such guns are rather bulky, the fine Browning among them. I for one do not consider any over-and-under as handsome and sleek as a fine side-by-side. A minor criticism is that the over-and-under presents more surface and is hence harder to hold and control in the wind. Another is that the over-and-under has to be opened wider to eject the fired cases and to reload.

Over-and-unders are made in both sidelock and box-lock styles. Some use under bolts, and this type of construction means a thick frame from top to bottom. The British makers, such as Boss, Woodward, and Holland & Holland, and also the Italian firm of Beretta do not use under bolts. Instead they lock up by the use of lugs machined into the rear face of the barrels. Such a design makes for sleek, handsome lines, and particularly in 20 gauge, such guns are the handsomest of their tribe. The now obsolete but mourned Remington Model 32 was another over-and-under without under bolts.

The over-and-under most often seen in the United States is the excellent Browning. In all grades it is a good gun. In the higher grades it is a superb gun with fine wood and tasteful engraving.

Of the Continental over-and-under guns, the Merkel is one of the best and most famous. It uses underlugs and locks up on top with a Greener crossbolt, which on the Continent is called the Kersten fastener. All the Merkels are good and the better ones are really superb pieces of craftsmanship, beautifully checkered and lushly engraved. They are made in East Germany, but a firm in Switzerland makes a specialty of handling Merkels and many Americans import them from there. (Abercrombie & Fitch, the great sporting-goods store in New York that recently closed, also used to carry them.)

I have had no experience with the higher-grade Franchis, an Italian over-and-under imported by Stoeger. However, I have one in field grade, which at one time sold for about $300. It is a box lock with under bolts and no top fastener. It is a sound and good-looking gun, plain but with hard, straight-grained wood and nicely checkered.

The Italian Beretta over-and-under is often seen in this country in the form of the Silver Hawk, a nice-handling gun with a single trigger but extractors rather than ejectors. For a man who wanted an over-and-under but who was also feeling economical, this struck me as a good buy. The higher-grade Berettas, which sell in Italy at from $1,000 to $5,000, are real masterpieces of the gunmaker's art, superbly finished, elaborately engraved, and sweetly balanced. The top-grade Beretta over-and-under 20 gauge is about as pretty a little trick as you'll ever see.

For some time I played with an over-and-under Spanish AYA (Aguirre & Aranzabal) Model 37 in 16 gauge. This is the most expensive gun made by that large Spanish firm. The hand-detachable sidelocks were superbly made, polished, engine turned, and gold plated. The gun balanced superbly, and the wood was sensational. AYA doesn't give the gun away even in Spain, but for a gun of this class, the checkering should be better and the selective single trigger ought to select.

Excellent Belgian-made over-and-under guns are imported by the Continental Arms Company of New York, a Fifth Avenue firm which every gun nut should visit. I have never seen a Belgian Francotte over-and-under, but I hear they are fine guns, and the better Francotte side-by-side doubles are among the world's best.

No finer over-and-under guns are made anywhere than the Holland & Holland, Boss, and Woodward guns turned out by the famous London makers. All are similar. They are shallow-frame, side-bolted, sidelock guns, nicely checkered and fitted, and superbly engraved. They also are very, very expensive.

The Winchester Model 101 is a good-looking gun that superficially resembles the Browning but is actually quite different. The one I played with struck me as being reliable and very strong. The automatic ejectors work, the single trigger selects, does not double or balk. The stock dimensions are standard American and almost anyone can shoot it well. The wood is better than average, and the engraving and checkering, although not distinguished, are better than average. It is made in field, skeet, and trap styles, and all guns have ventilated ribs. It is offered in 12 and 20 gauge, and the expensive Winchester Model "skeet set" has interchangeable .410, 28, and 20-gauge barrels and forends. The Model 101 is made under Winchester supervision in Japan.

CHAPTER 4

The European

Double-Barrel Shotgun

THE double-barrel shotgun is manufactured today in all industrial countries with a tradition of making firearms—the United States, Great Britain, France, Belgium, Spain, Germany, Czechoslovakia, Finland, Austria, Italy, Russia, and Japan. Some very good doubles have been made in Sweden by Husquvarna and possibly in other Nordic countries, and some in Hungary. However, some guns made in countries not noted for the manufacture of sporting firearms seem actually to have been assembled rather than made. Tubes, frames, and locks have come from Belgium and Germany. Many times one comes across double guns bearing the name of a French or Hungarian maker that had German or Belgium proof marks.

In Europe the tradition of firearms manufacture is very ancient and guns tend to be produced in areas where for generations there have been many skilled gun craftsmen. Suhl and Zella-Mehlis, both now in the Russian zone of Germany, were famed gunsmithing centers. The Basque country of Spain, particularly around Eibar, has for hundreds of years been a center of gun manufacture. The owners of the largest Spanish shotgun factory bear the typical Basque names of Aguirre and Aranzabal. The Austrian village of Ferlach is a famous gunmaking center that turns out not only shotguns but combination guns, double rifles, and magazine rifles. The area around Liége, Belgium, has not only the great Fabrique Nationale plant that makes the F. N. and Browning guns but many smaller gunsmithing concerns that make some very fine over-and-under and side-by-side doubles. The good Franchi and Beretta over-and-under and side-by-side guns are made in northern Italy.

In Great Britain the guns with the most prestige are made in London, the home of Purdey, Holland & Holland, and Boss. Excellent guns are also made in Birmingham, where the Westley Richards factory is located. John Dickson & Son, a very fine maker, is in Edinburgh.

The United States is the home of mass production, and indeed the making of interchangeable parts tested with "Go" and "No Go" gauges originated in American gunmaking when Eli Whitney went into the production of army muskets. It is natural then that the United States should specialize in the making of guns that lend themselves to mass production.

In many parts of Europe the tradition of skilled hand labor is strong and in many countries the apprentice system is still in full flower. The American who makes cut No. 16 on a shotgun frame, then puts the partially machined part into a pile, which then goes to the next machine, is interested in his dreary occupation only for his wages and the fringe benefits. The European craftsman is not so highly paid but he tends to take more pride in his work. This is also true today of the relative handful of fine American stockers, engravers, and gunsmiths who do the best custom work. It was also true of the fine workmen who built the high-grade Parkers, the L. C. Smiths, and the Winchester Model 21s in the United States before the war.

Once in the late 1930s, on a visit to a factory noted for the production of fine American shotguns, I was struck by the fact that most of the craftsmen were in their fifties and sixties. Not long after that the war came along. By the time it was over many of these men were dead or had retired. They have never been re-placed, as few young men these days have the patience to want to learn a skilled trade that requires a long apprenticeship.

The production of a first-rate double gun requires skillful hand-work and lots of it. Parts have to be fitted by hand filing—and some of the parts are almost as small and delicate as those of a watch. Wood should be carefully and painstakingly fitted to metal. Engraving requires the most skilled and precise of handwork and so does good checkering. To see how workmanship has slipped, one has only to compare a prewar Winchester Model 21 of good grade with one turned out after the war. The Model 21 is an excellent gun. It is exceedingly strong, well designed, and made of fine materials. However, the careful and painstaking handwork one found in the prewar guns simply isn't there today. My son Brad-ford has a 16-gauge Model 21, as does my wife. I have a 20 and a 12. I am a booster for the gun but I am aware of the problems the Winchester management has in securing skilled labor for their pro-duction.

The same problem is present in England, and the difficulty of finding good workmen is one of the troubles that now assail the British gun trade. We were in the war for four years. The British were in it for six. Old workmen died off. New ones didn't come along by the apprentice route to replace them, for after the war the young Englishmen wanted to get married and buy television sets and motor bikes. They could get better wages working on a machine in a factory than they could as apprentices at some dank and musty gunmaker's shop.

The falling off in the quality of British firearms is most apparent in the magazine rifles turned out by the better British makers. The best are far below the standards set by such individual American craftsmen as Leonard Mews, Al Biesen, or Lenard Brownell. The worst are about the quality of the stuff turned out by Joe Doaks, who runs Ye Olde Gun Shoppe, sells fishing tackle, and repairs lawnmowers. The very best British shotguns are still among the finest in the world, and of course a British double rifle by Holland & Holland or Purdey is in a class by itself. But, alas, some of the shotguns, as well as the magazine rifles, now being turned out by once famous and respected makers would make the founders of those august concerns turn over in their graves.

The war is one reason for the British decline. Another is the wave of egalitarianism that has hit Britain. With income taxes and death duties being what they are, the British gentry no longer have the money to spend on fine guns. Today a high percentage of the customers of the flossy British gunmaking concerns are Americans and Continentals.

A British sportsman today is more apt to look around and try to pick up a gun secondhand than he is to order a new one. Old guns of famous make are in great demand and in most cases they bring much more now in Britain than they did when new, from thirty to fifty years ago.

A famous British name on a shotgun adds a good 50 percent to its value. Holland & Holland, Purdey, Woodward (absorbed by Purdey since the last war), Boss, Westley Richards, Churchill, Dickson—all are to shotguns what Tiffany is to jewelry, Rolls-Royce is to automobiles, and Messrs. Patek and Philippe are to watches.

Things have not gone well in the British gun trade since the war. Some ancient and respected firms have folded and some have consolidated. As I noted above, Purdey has absorbed Woodward. The firm of Stephen Grant & Joseph Lang is an amalgamation of a whole covey of gunmakers—Charles Lancaster, Fredrick Beesley, Harrison & Hussey, and Watson Brothers. The last time I was in London the famous firm of John Rigby was not building any shotguns or double rifles—only rather indifferent magazine rifles on Mauser actions. It appeared to be living off the sales of the popular .416 Rigby cartridge, a "proprietary" job manufactured by Imperial Chemical Industries but sold at that time only by Rigby.

The ancient and ritzy firm of Holland & Holland has been moved from 98 New Bond Street, where its sales rooms have been located since the Norman Conquest, to 13 Bruton Street, and amalgamated with the Westley Richards sales agency and W. J. Jeffery.

All the London gun and rifle-building firms are small, high-cost operations. How many shotguns they make in a year I haven't the faintest idea, but it cannot be very many. I doubt if all of them combined build more than twenty double rifles a year—and making such weapons may soon become a lost art. Demand is so small and the British gun trade is in such a parlous state that Imperial Chemical Industries, the British loading trust, is just about out of the business of loading centerfire rifle cartridges. This means, of course, that most of the famous double rifles are now orphans.

Of the famous old British firms, it strikes me that the only ones showing much vitality are Holland & Holland, Boss, and Purdey. These three produce fine side-by-side and over-and-under shotguns, double rifles, and reasonably good magazine rifles. All firms are loaded with tradition and prestige. They have built guns for British and Continental royalty and nobility, Indian maharajas, Middle Eastern potentates, and American millionaires who as youngsters were herded around by English nannies, who went to Groton or St. Marks and then on to Yale or Princeton, who are apt to buy Peel shoes, have their clothes tailored in Savile Row and their shirts made on Bond Street.

To the conservative old rich, a fine British double (or, better, a matched pair) in a fitted oak-and-leather case was a status symbol comparable to an old but perfectly kept chauffeur-driven Rolls-Royce, a string of polo ponies, a 185-foot steam yacht, a love affair with a French countess, or, in the days before the airplane, a six-month safari in East Africa. Alas, like many of the other customers of the London gunsmiths, men of this type are dying off. The Indian maharajas have had their lands seized and have been put on such skimpy government allowances that many of them are down to their last elephant. The Middle Eastern potentates have been shot and the Egyptian millionaires have taken it on the lam to the French Riviera. The big money in England today is not in the hands of the huntin'-and-shootin' set, but in the hands of real-estate speculators. Oddly enough, I am told that many of the orders the London makers receive for expensive double rifles and shotguns come from the other side of the Iron Curtain—gifts apparently to big-shot communists.

A fine British gun is a handsome thing as well as a prestige item. Almost all have double triggers, straight grips (or hands, as the

British call them), good checkering in diamond patterns, conventional splinter forends, stocks of very good French walnut with long, sweeping, dark lines. With a few exceptions, most of their single triggers aren't too hot, and only their American customers ever order beavertail forends or buttstocks with pistol grips. Most of these utilize flat instead of coil springs.

The 12 gauge is just about universal in Britain, but the British 12-gauge shot shell (cartridge to them) is in a 2½-inch case and uses 1 1⁄16 ounces of shot. As a consequence, the British "game gun" is lighter than its American counterpart and weighs from 6½ to 7 pounds. Their wildfowl guns are heavier and chambered for 2¾ and 3-inch shells. The London makers, of course, chamber the guns they build for Americans for the 2¾-inch American standard shells.

When I was shooting grouse in Scotland, my British friends thought my 12-gauge Model 21 Winchester, which weighs 7½ pounds, quite heavy. They were also surprised that it cost as much as it did and yet had no engraving. Churchill had plugged 25-inch barrels in England for many years, but the guns my British pals shot all had 28 and 30-inch barrels. They thought my 26-inch barrels a bit odd.

In England the best-grade guns more often than not have sidelocks. These are presumed to give better trigger pulls, have more area for ornamentation, and enable a stronger gun to be built as less wood has to be cut away to inlet the action into the buttstock. However, some first-grade box-lock guns are built.

The most prestigious gun built in England is the Purdey. The sales office is at 57 South Audley Street in London's West End, hard by the lush Dorchester Hotel, where I have stayed to recuperate from several safaris. Purdey makes a fine side-by-side double in 20, 16, and 12 gauge with any barrel length or boring. Standard chambers are 2¾ inches but one can order 2½-inch chambers in the 20 or 12 and 2 9⁄16 inches in the 16. These Purdeys use the bar-action sidelock and Purdey side clips. They are of a refined and conservative elegance seldom equaled and rarely surpassed. The Purdey action has been widely copied. The Woodward over-and-under is a very handsome shallow-frame sidelock gun, as elegant as the Purdey. Either the Woodward or the Purdey sells for about the price of a fine automobile.

Holland & Holland is famous for its double-barrel and magazine rifles and also for its development of such rifle cartridges as the .300 and .375 Magnum, but the firm also produces fine shotguns. Its best doubles have hand-detachable back-action sidelocks. The firm also sold a box-lock gun, which is not completely made in the London factory. Holland also made a fine and handsome over-and-under (which the British call an "under and over") in design much like the Boss and the Woodward. The H & H sidelocks can be taken off by turning a little lever on the left-hand plate. It removes the screw which holds the plates to the frame. This feature has been widely copied, particularly in the better Spanish guns.

Boss, 41 Albemarle Street, London, is strictly a custom outfit and turns out side-by-side and over-and-under guns which many aficionados of British smoothbores consider finer even than the Purdeys. They are not, however, quite so expensive.

The Westley Richards guns are made in Birmingham, but their sales office in London has been amalgamated with Holland & Holland. The Westley Richards guns are for the most part box locks and, indeed, the firm is the developer of the Anson & Deeley box lock, the action from which most modern box locks are descended. Guns could be obtained with detachable locks that were removed by a hinged floor plate, and they can be ordered with extra sets of locks. The firm also makes sidelock guns and has turned out magazine and double rifles.

John Dickson & Son, 21 Frederick Street, Edinburgh, builds three types of shotguns—sidelock, Anson & Deeley box lock, and the Dickson "round" action, which had a lock attached to the trigger plate like the European Blitz action. The Dickson round-action and sidelock guns cost about $1200. The box-lock gun is cheaper. Locks of Dickson guns, except for their cheapest box lock, are gold plated to prevent rust. The firm makes a single trigger.

British guns bearing famous names and even British guns bearing not-so-famous names have great prestige and are in great demand over the world. They often bring astounding prices. I heard not long before I wrote this in the fall of 1976 that a pair of Purdeys had recently changed hands for about $30,000. A friend of mine in the fall of 1976 paid $11,000 for a Holland & Holland double rifle for the obsolete .465 Nitro Express cartridge. With the billowing inflation in Britain the price of a new British gun of famous make is fantastic. At present prices I would not consider England a particularly good place to buy a firearm of any sort.

A best-grade British gun made prior to World War II was a very fine gun and the workmanship was of the best, but the British "game gun" (read "upland gun") was too light for the average American shot shell and often has chambers that are too short. Today a great many British guns leave much to be desired. I have seen poor fitting and sloppy checkering on postwar British guns by famous firms. Some of the wood in the stocks of guns costing thousands of dollars has been only fair. The British gun trade, alas, has seen better days!

The Belgian city of Liège is the home of the great Fabrique Nationale plant, where tens of thousands of Browning over-and-under shotguns, automatic shotguns, big game rifles, and .22s have been turned out for the American market and distributed by the Browning Arms Company. In Europe the sales are handled by Fabrique Nationale and the guns are called FNs.

The best of the Belgian guns are very fine indeed, with lines and conservative scroll engraving much like the best British guns. Guns made by Francotte and La Beau Corelay are generally very good. I am not acquainted with French shotguns but there are supposed to be about three small firms building fine shotguns in Paris. One outfit is strictly a one-man proposition. The proprietor does all the metalwork, makes all parts from scratch, stocks, and engraves.

The ancient cities of Brescia and Gardone in northern Italy are home to a great variety of gun-making firms. Pietro Beretta produces everything from moderately priced boxlock side-by-sides and over-and-unders to some of the finest shotguns made anywhere. My favorite pheasant gun as of 1976 is a Beretta Model 450 EL, a lovely 12-gauge sidelock with fancy wood, superb fitting and checkering, and lovely engraving. Around 1965 it cost me with two sets of barrels (26-inch improved cylinder and modified, and 28-inch modified and full), all in an oak and leather trunk case with brass fittings, something over $1,000 in Rome. I suspect it would cost at least $5,000 today.

The SO series of sidelock over-and-unders by Beretta are fine guns. They have trim lines since they lock up with lugs on the sides of the breech. Anyone who has ever seen a Japanese-made Ithaca SKB over-and-under can tell instantly that the SKB designers also have seen Berettas. Probably the handsomest 20-gauge over-and-under ever turned out was the Beretta ASEELL, a box lock with dummy sideplates. One I had weighed 5¾ pounds with 26-inch barrels. Wood and checkering were lovely. Engraving was the stuff dreams are made of. But I never shot it very well. It was just too light and whippy. I sold it when I realized that at my age I had more guns than I could use.

Bernardelli is another good Italian firm that, like Beretta, turns out a variety of guns. Some are very good, some are knockabout grade. A relatively new North Italian firm is Perazzi. It specializes in slickly designed, beautifully pointing trap and skeet guns. These have caught on well in the United States. Perazzi also makes lovely field guns. I visited the Perazzi factory on the way to Iran for a sheep hunt in 1970. There I saw the most beautiful sidelock 12-gauge side-by-side I have ever laid eyes on. It was mechanical and artistic perfection. The price was $2,500. I didn't buy it. I would guess that today it would sell for at least $7,000. Another new firm, Fabri, likewise turns out exquisite guns and has a fine reputation. Some Italian guns, as we have seen, are among the world's finest. Some are run-of-the-mine, and among them are guns that are downright trashy. On the whole, though, Italy has been since the war one of the best places in the world to buy a shotgun.

The Spanish picture is even more mixed than the Italian. One of my pet 20-gauge pheasant guns is a Spanish creation of little-known make—an Arizaga. I have had it twenty years and have shot many dozens of pheasants, sharptail grouse, quail, and Hungarian partridges. Like many Spanish single triggers made in those days, the one on the little Arizaga didn't work, but otherwise it has been a fine little gun. The wood is very good but not exhibition grade. The checkering is good. The engraving is a competent job of medium grade. The lines of the stock and forend are handsome indeed. The gun has two sets of 26-inch barrels—improved cylinder and modified, modified and full. This all cost me, plus duty and air transportation, $210. But this, mind you, was the price in 1956. Today the Spanish price of the gun would be at least $1,000. Arizaga is located in Palancia de las Armas, a town near Éibar. I have never visited the place. When I was in Éibar I was told that Arizaga had taken a contract for a large number of cheap guns for an American concern and at the time was not making any fine guns.

Like Liège in Belgium, Suhl in Germany, Ferlach in Austria, and Brescia in Italy, Éibar is a city of gunmakers. Handguns are made there, and so are a few not very good double rifles, but mostly the gunsmiths of Éibar turn out shotguns. These range all the way from the cheapest and roughest of single-shots designed and priced to be sold to Indian poachers and African tribesmen to very flossy pieces with excellent wood, superb engraving, and fine mechanical tuning. I have been told that there are about 100 firms in Éibar that put their names on guns. Some have their own plants from start to finish. Others do part of the work, and farm out the rest. One small outfit may do only engraving, another only stocking, yet another the fitting of barrels. Some entrepreneur may get an order for 500 12-gauge sidelock guns with automatic ejectors, single trigger, and some engraving. He may then farm out all the work and pay someone to assemble the parts. Many such guns have been hastily made, sloppily assembled. Sometimes the ejectors eject and sometimes they do not.

But many very fine guns are turned out in Éibar. The largest of the Éibar manufacturers is AYA, Ai-Yah, or Aguirre & Aranzabal. Like most Spanish manufacturers AYA makes guns of all grades. I was quite impressed by the plant and the workmen. AYA has all the latest technical gadgets. It can make scientific hardness tests, inspect by microscope, and so on. But AYA has a room full of good engravers. Barrels are also "struck"—filed lengthwise to remove the waves. The stocks are finished by being dunked in linseed oil that is allowed to dry. When a coat gums, it is rubbed down to the bare wood with water and pumice by a little old man who looks 101 years old.

The better AYA guns (and indeed most good Spanish guns) are copies of fine British guns. I understand that the sidelocks on AYA guns are copies of the Holland hand-detachable locks. I ordered and received a beautiful little AYA No. 1 in 20 gauge. I likewise ordered a pair of 12-gauge guns known as the XXVSL Model. In the main, these last are copies of the British Churchills with 25-inch barrels and narrow ribs, which, according to Master Salesman Churchill, gave the shooter the same effect with 25-inch barrels as did 30-inch barrels with the regular rib. These two guns balance and point exactly the same. Even the stock wood is well matched. These lovely guns weigh 7 pounds. I generally use the light field load of 3¼ drams of powder and 1 ounce of No. 6 shot on pheasants. If I revealed what I paid for the two guns, someone would probably have me arrested, but remember I bought them in the days when the dollar was up and the Spanish peseta was down. Those were the good old days!

Ugartechea is another fine Spanish maker, the firm that used to turn out presentation guns which the late General Franco gave to heads of state. Years ago a friend of mine received from Spain an Ugartechea he had ordered at the same time he received a British gun of famous make. He looked the two guns over. To his layman's eye there seemed to be little difference. Both were sidelocks with nicely engraved sideplates and good but not spectacular wood. He paid a gunsmith to take them apart and look them over. The gunsmith said both were fine guns and he could not see $10 difference in their value. Any American gun lover who goes to Éibar should visit Ugartechea.

An exceedingly interesting Éibar gun company is Garbi. If anyone wants to know how the British built guns in the 1870s, Garbi is the place to go. There is *no* power machinery. Parts are filed out by hand, fitted, polished, and hardened. Frames are filed out of rough forgings or bar stock by hand. Holes that could be put in with a drill press in seconds are made with a file. I asked a workman when he knew if a part was properly hardened. "I take a file to it!" he told me. Garbi guns are highly thought of by Spanish shooters and are widely used on clay targets and live pigeons.

Ugartechea will not make a gun with a single trigger, but many Spanish concerns will. For a while the Spanish had a hell of a time with single triggers. Many of them doubled, probably because of the recoil of the hot loads the Americans used. Sometimes they "balked"—didn't fire the second barrel. The nonselective single trigger on my fine little 20-gauge Arizaga *always* doubled. I sent the gun to the Miller Trigger Company, Millersburg, Pa., for a nonselective trigger. It has served me faithfully for many thousands of shots for twenty years. A running mate to the 20, a sleek little 28-gauge with 25-inch barrels, had a nonselective single trigger that worked nicely for ten years. When it gave up the ghost I had it replaced with a trigger by Griffin & Howe. The selective triggers on my matched pair of 12-gauge AYAs had pulls of about 9 pounds when I received them—apparently assurance by AYA that they would not double. I had them adjusted by a very remarkable gunsmith named George Hoenig, 6521 Morton Drive, Boise, Idaho. Since then they have worked like charms.

If the American visiting Spain cannot go to Éibar, a good place to see a variety of Spanish shotguns is Diana, Serrano, 70, Madrid. In Italy I know of no better place than Armería E. Casciano, 115, Piazza Benedetto Cairoli, Rome.

In comparing Spanish and American prices, I noticed that American retail prices were about three times those of the lowest prices to dealers at the Spanish factories and about twice what Madrid retail prices were. As an example, a gun that sold for $100 at the factory in Éibar brought almost twice that in Madrid and around $300 in the United States. This, incidentally, was a good gun except for a single trigger that doubled about half the time with heavy loads. The Spanish also make beautiful leather goods for the gun nut—trunk-type gun cases, leg-o'-mutton cases, cartridge belts, shell and game bags, handsome leather cases for a pair of guns to be used when the secretario carried the guns from one firing point to another.

I imagine that in 1977 it is still possible to get a good, medium-grade but handsome shotgun for $300 to $400 at the Spanish factory price. Such a gun would probably sell for $1,000 to $1,200 at retail in the United States. Like shotgun prices everywhere, Spanish prices have gone up. A medium-grade AYA that seven or eight years ago sold at the Éibar factory for $200 now costs $800 at retail in Madrid and about $1,500 in this country. Guns are not going to get cheaper.

For whatever the reason, shotgun manufacture has languished in France. The only French-made shotgun I have ever had any experience with was a 16-gauge double I rented in Fort Archambault in what is now Chad. I wanted it to knock off guinea fowl when I was on a hunt for Sahara and sub-Sahara game in 1958. That was really some shotgun. The trigger pulls were about 15 or 20 pounds. The razor-sharp comb has a drop of about 1¼ inches but the heel drop was about 3½ inches. That bloody gun punished me worse than any gun I have ever shot.

I have seen a few doubles marked with the names of Paris makers, but I suspect that they were imported from Belgium, as they had Belgian proof marks. Rich Frenchmen generally buy fine Belgian or British guns. I have met some of them in Paris and in what used to be called French Equatorial Africa and I have yet to see one with a French rifle or shotgun.

The Japanese are fine and painstaking workmen, as shown by the excellent optical goods and electronic equipment turned out in Japan. The Winchester over-and-under shotgun introduced in 1962 is made by a Winchester subsidiary in Japan. Winchester simply bought into a Japanese company and moved in supervisory personnel for quality control. It is a good sound gun of medium grade. Other Japanese over-and-unders are imported into the United States, but I have not seen all of them. The Valmet from Finland is an inexpensive over-and-under with a single trigger but with extractors, not automatic ejectors. The Swedish rifle-manufacturing firm of Husquvarna makes box-lock and sidelock shotguns in various grades. I had a chance to acquire one of their box-lock doubles and it is an excellent weapon. So far as I know, the guns are not imported into the United States.

CHAPTER 5

The Double Gun

in the United States

AT present, in the 1970s, the manufacture of high-quality double-barrel shotguns in the United States is just about a thing of the past. One of the reasons for this sad state of affairs is changing public taste. There has been a drift away from the double to the pump and automatic ever since the introduction of the old Winchester Model 97 hammer pump gun over eighty years ago. But basically it is high labor costs which have shot down the makers of double guns one by one. Fine shotguns are largely made by patient and skillful human hands. Remington quit making doubles in 1910, the Baker Gun Company of Batavia, New York, about 1912. The original Lefever Company gave up and sold what assets it had to Ithaca just after World War I. Parker was a victim of the depression and sold out to Remington in 1934. After World War II, Remington assembled a few Parkers from parts made prior to the war, but never resumed manufacture of Parker guns.

Like Parker, the Ansley H. Fox Company of Philadelphia was killed off by rising costs and dropping demand. The company went broke and sold out to the Savage Arms Corporation of Utica, New York, which continued the manufacture of Fox guns on a reduced scale, but World War II ended the true Fox gun. Savage still makes an inexpensive double under the Fox name but actually it is a gun of Stevens design. The war also finished the Hunter Arms Company, makers of the L. C. Smith guns. The firm went broke during the war, and just afterwards the machinery, tools, and assets were purchased by Marlin and moved to New Haven, Connecticut. Then Marlin had labor troubles, found that the L. C. Smith guns could not be made profitably, and, after an unsuccessful attempt at revival, folded the operation.

During the depression, Iver Johnson made some rather good doubles at a very reasonable price but never resumed manufacture after World War II. Savage and Marlin turned out inexpensive over-and-under shotguns during the depression. Savage made no more of them when peace broke out, but Marlin continued the over-and-under Model 90 for some years before they gave up. Few people know that three-barrel guns or "drillings" were at one time produced in the United States. During my years as a shooting editor, I have had letters from several dozen people who owned these American-made drillings and wanted information about them. The concern that made them was founded in 1898 at Wheeling, West Virginia, as the Wheeling Gun Company, but the name was soon changed to the Hollenbeck Gun Company. In 1904 the firm again changed its name, this time to the Three-Barrel Gun Company and moved to Moundsville, West Virginia. In 1907 the firm was reorganized and called the Royal Gun Company. It was apparently in financial hot water during most of its existence and finally went broke in 1911. The guns I have heard of were all, if I remember correctly, made with two 12-gauge barrels over a .32/40 barrel, and the shotgun tubes of the one gun I have seen were of twist. The guns sold for from $75 to $500.

Cheap shotguns were made by the tens of thousands by the Crescent Firearms Company of Norwich, Connecticut, a manufacturing subsidiary of The Folsom Arms Company, a big New York jobber. This outfit stamped literally dozens of private brand names on guns that were to be sold by various jobbers. One model it made might be sold under two dozen private names—all of non-existent "arms companies"—the Elgin Arms Company, the Central Arms Company, etc. Even today I constantly get letters from readers who want to know if such firms are still in business. Not only did most jobbers have private brand names but some had several of them. Sometimes such names were calculated to make the buyer think he was getting a gun of famous make—Barker for Parker, for example, W. Richards for Westley Richards of England, even J. Manton & Company. I have had many letters from those who have "W. Richards" and "J. Manton" guns. They think their pot-metal wonders are genuine Westley Richards and Joseph Mantons and are sure that they are immensely valuable. The depression brought the activities of Crescent to a close.

Sears, Roebuck owned a manufacturing subsidiary called the Meriden Arms Company at Meriden, Connecticut, and made guns under many private brand names. Hopkins and Allen of Norwich, Connecticut, made doubles under private brand names as well as its own. The firm stopped manufacturing sporting firearms after 1914 when it got a big contract to make Model 1891 7.65 mm. Mausers for the Belgian government. At the end of World War I, it went out of business. The Union Arms Company of Toledo, Ohio, made guns under its own name and stamped with private brands—a pump model as well as doubles—but I can find very little about it.

It is not generally known that Colt made double-barrel shotguns as well as pistols, revolvers, slide-action rifles, and, believe it or not, a few double-barrel rifles in .45/70 caliber and on shotgun actions. Colt's first double-barrel shotgun, a hammer job, came out in 1878 in 10 and 12 gauge. A hammerless model appeared in 1883 and was made in 10 and 12 gauge until 1900.

The Parker

The most famous and probably the most highly regarded of all American-made side-by-side double guns is the Parker. It was manufactured at Meriden, Connecticut, from 1868 until 1937, when Remington, who had bought Parker in 1934, decided to close the Meriden plant and move the machinery to Ilion, New York. The last Parkers, probably assembled from parts on hand, came out of Remington's Ilion factory in 1947.

Like most American doubles, the Parker was a box lock on the Anson & Deeley pattern. The cheaper grades, the VH and the Trojan were very plain, though sound and well-made guns. Peter H. Johnson, in *The Parker: America's Finest Shotgun*, estimates that approximately 58,000 VH grade guns and about 50,000 Trojans were sold. A catalog issued early in the depression listed the Trojan with two triggers at $60.50 and with a single trigger at $89.10. The VH, a sound but plain gun, was $79.50 with double triggers and extractors, $129 with automatic ejectors and single trigger. The DHE with single trigger and automatic ejectors was listed for $217.30. It had better wood, better checkering, and a modest amount of engraving. By the time the purchaser got to the CHE ($251.50 with double triggers and $282.30 with single trigger), he had a very handsome gun indeed. The stock was French walnut, the checkering about 22 lines to the inch. There was more engraving and a silver crest plate on the stock. The customer was given the choice of a skeleton buttplate or a rubber recoil pad and the choice of a straight or a pistol grip. The stock had a very cute little arrowhead carved in the wood above the rear of the trigger guard, and the little gadget broke up the plain lines. I wanted a CHE so bad I could taste it in those days but I could never dig up the $282.30! Only about 5,000 CHE Parkers were ever turned out.

The higher-grade Parkers were all beautifully engraved, had handsomely checkered stocks of fine French walnut, and were in every respect just about as good box-lock guns as money could buy—both in Europe and in the United States. The BHE sold for $385.99, the AHE for $528.30 with single trigger, the AAHE for $763.20 with single trigger, and the A–1 Special for $915.60 with single trigger. Only 13,000 guns in BHE grade were made, 5,600 in AHE, and 320 each in AAHE and A–1 Special. Like most manufacturers of high-class double guns, Parker also made single and double-barrel trap guns and guns bored especially for skeet—Skeet In and Skeet Out, roughly improved cylinder and quarter choke.

A great many old Trojan and VH Parker shotguns are for sale these days, most of them with extractors and double triggers and most of them in rather poor condition. Since I wouldn't be caught dead with a shotgun without a beavertail forend, automatic ejectors, and a single trigger, I consider none of these rare bargains. It seems to be a law of human nature that the man who buys the cheapest gun of any make seldom takes care of it but that the chap who buys a deluxe gun almost always takes care of it. Generally those who own old Trojans and VH guns have an exaggerated idea as to their value. The high-grade Parkers one comes across are almost always well taken care of and usually they are worth four or five times what they cost new. A mint-condition CHE or BHE Parker will bring from $1,000 up, and if the Parker collector runs into a good AHE or AAHE, the sky's the limit. The Parker was the Pierce-Arrow and the Cadillac of American-made shotguns and it was the gun bought by the well-to-do sportsmen of the interior United States. A rich New Yorker who had gone to Groton and Yale might shoot a Purdey, but the Iowa banker or the Arizona wholesale merchant who graduated from the school of hard knocks or at best went to the state university used a CHE Parker. All of the high-grade Parkers are today rare and in great demand. So are Parkers in such odd gauges as the magnum 10, the .410, and the 28—a gauge introduced by Parker, incidentally.

The Ithaca

The Ithaca Gun Company began business in 1880, as a partnership between W. H. Baker (a gun designer who was the designer not only of the first Ithaca but also of the Baker, later made at Batavia, New York, and of the L. C. Smith), L. H. Smith, brother of the L. C. Smith who made double guns and typewriters, J. E. Van Natta, and Dwight McIntire. Very shortly Van Natta's interest was purchased by George Livermore. I knew Uncle George, who was Ithaca's president and chairman of the board when I was a fledgling gun editor in the late 1930s. He died at a great age, a few years after World War II. The firm has been purchased from the Smith family by General Recreation, a conglomerate.

Ithaca built double guns from 1880 until 1948, but just before World War II the management saw the handwriting on the wall and tooled up to make a pump gun based on the same Browning design used for the 20-gauge Model 17 Remington. Right after the war, the firm was making about one thousand pump guns a month and decided to drop the double.

Ithaca turned out several models of box-lock shotguns, the last being the NID model, which came out in 1925, a gun with an extension rib and a rotary bolt. Ithaca was the first concern to produce guns for the monstrous 3½-inch 10-gauge magnum shell developed by Western Cartridge Company. It also produced a 20-gauge double-barrel pistol which it called the auto and burglar gun. The firm still builds a single-barrel trap gun, the only one now made in the United States.

At different times Ithaca purchased the assets of four bankrupt makers of shotguns—the Union Arms Company, the Wilkes-Barre Gun Company, the Syracuse Gun Company, and the Lefever Arms Company. Ithaca cashed in on the Lefever name, as the Lefever Company under Uncle Dan Lefever made a good-quality sidelock double. Between 1921 and 1947 the firm made about 250,000 Lefever Nitro Special doubles, inexpensive guns with extractors and either double triggers or non-selective single triggers. They also made an even cheaper double called the Western Arms Long Range gun.

The Ithaca doubles were a lot of gun for the money, but in the higher grades they were neither as elegant nor as expensive as the Parkers, the Foxes, and the L. C. Smiths. In early depression days the Field Grade Ithaca with extractors and double triggers retailed for $39.75. Ejectors were $12.95 extra and the selective single trigger was $21.60 extra. Back in 1927, when I got married, I bought my wife a No. 2 grade 20-gauge bored improved cylinder and modified and with 26-inch barrels. It had automatic ejectors and single trigger and cost less than $100.

The No. 4 grade Ithaca was a pretty showy gun with considerable checkering, a stock of American burl walnut, some engraving. It sold in those days for $151.60 with single trigger and ejectors—a real bargain. The No. 5 cost $189.60 with ejectors but double triggers, the No. 7, $379.20. It was a real fancy job with fine checkering in an elaborate pattern and a good deal of showy but rather shallow engraving.

The Ithaca double guns were well designed and reliable, but they were never quite in the class of the Parker, the Fox, and the L. C. Smith. The locks were not quite as carefully fitted and polished. Even in their higher grades they were never stocked with French walnut, and the engraving, though showy, was not as well executed as was that on the other good-grade guns. The checkering was not as carefully and flawlessly done. However, the Ithaca sold for about half what the other companies got for a corresponding grade. Ithaca doubles were made in all gauges from .410 to Magnum 10.

The L. C. Smith

Manufacture of the L. C. Smith gun began in 1880 at Syracuse, New York, but the tools and manufacturing rights were bought from the L. C. Smith Company by the Hunter Arms Company of Fulton, New York, in 1888. At the time that Hunter purchased the L. C. Smith, it was manufacturing a three-barrel gun.

The L. C. Smith was one of the few sidelock guns ever made in the United States. When Hunter started making the guns, many of them had exposed hammers, as the hammerless gun was then just becoming popular. And for many years hammer guns were kept in the line. The firm introduced its excellent Hunter single trigger in 1904. Its first guns were in 10 and 12 gauge. The 16 came out in the 1890s and the 20 gauge in 1907. The guns were never made in .410 or 28 gauges. Like most other manufacturers of double guns Hunter made double-barrel trap models, skeet models, and a single-barrel trap gun.

Apparently the firm imported most of its barrels in rough forged condition from Europe. British Sir Joseph Whitworth fluid-steel barrels were used in the better grades, and until World War I, Belgian Damascus or fluid-steel barrels were optional on the cheaper grades.

A pre-World War I Smith catalog I have shows the cheapest hammerless double, the No. oo selling for $37 with extractors, $47 with automatic ejectors. It is a plain gun without engraving, with a stock of English walnut, and with a minimum of checkering. The No. o at $65 with ejectors, $50 without, or $90 with ejectors and single trigger and the No. 1 at $105 with single trigger and ejectors are plain guns with a little better wood and a very small amount of engraving.

The Pigeon ($172 with single trigger and ejectors) and the No. 4 ($200 with the same equipment) were stocked in good French walnut, had some neatly executed engraving, and the barrels were either of Nitro steel or chainette Damascus.

The top-grade guns (the A–3 at $725 with ejectors and single trigger, the A–2 at $425, and the Monogram at $400) all had barrels of Sir Joseph Whitworth fluid steel, superbly executed engraving, fine and precise checkering in elaborate patterns. I remember one of these high-grade Smiths. It belonged to a banker friend of my grandfather. He didn't think any more of that gun than he did his right arm. I can still remember how he, my grandfather, and I used to ride out in two light buggies behind handsome trotting mares to where we would shoot whitewings. While I clutched my single-barrel Iver Johnson 20 gauge, I used to watch the banker take his Smith 16 out of its leg-of-mutton case and assemble it carefully and gently. I thought it a handsomer gun than my grandfather's Parker or even his Purdey. Knowing of my admiration, the banker promised that when I was a little older he'd let me shoot it. But, somehow, I never got to.

In the early years of the depression, the cheapest L. C. Smith was the Field Grade, which sold for $59 with automatic ejectors, $45 without. This is the L. C. Smith most often seen. It was not a fancy gun. It had no engraving, the stock was of straight-grained American walnut, and the checkering was plain and rather coarse. However, I can testify that the Smith Field Grade was a sound and rugged gun. I shot one for several years. It was a 20 gauge with automatic ejectors and 30-inch barrels, and it was the only shotgun I had for a time. I bought it secondhand in 1932 for $17.50 with a leather leg-of-mutton case. I shot quail, ducks, and doves with it, and in Mexico I sometimes had a guide carry it for me in a saddle scabbard when I was hunting whitetails, so if we ran across a covey of fool quail I could jump off and pot a few.

In those days the Ideal Grade with a bit of engraving, better wood and checkering, sold for $99.25 with single trigger and automatic ejectors, the more elaborate Specialty Grade, a good gun indeed for $149.20, was similarly equipped. The Crown Grade Smith was a truly fine gun at $292.50. The top-grade Smiths, the Monogram at $525, the Premier at $917, and the De Luxe at $1,290 were all superb guns, with French walnut stocks handsomely and precisely checkered, superbly engraved, perfectly fitted and finished. I don't imagine that many of these great Smiths were built—in the depression years anyway.

I visited the plant where those fine guns were turned out a year or two before we got into World War II. I was struck by the fact that almost all the workmen were old men and I wondered what would happen to the company when they died or retired. The Hunter Arms Company went into bankruptcy during the war. It was purchased by Marlin and moved to New Haven right after the war. There labor trouble closed it the second and last time. And so perished the last sidelock gun to be made in the United States, a gun that has never had the reputation its sterling qualities deserved.

The Winchester

Right now the American-made double-barrel shotgun that probably enjoys the most prestige is the Winchester Model 21, which has now been made for over forty-five years. The reputation of the 21 is such that guns in good condition that sold for a little over $100 twenty-five years ago now bring from $300 to $500 in the second-hand market.

The Model 21 has had an exceedingly curious career. Originally brought out in 1931, right in the worst part of the depression, it retailed in its cheapest form with splinter fore-end, double triggers, and extractors rather than ejectors for $59.50. The skeet grade, a real honey of a gun, with selective single trigger, automatic ejection, beavertail fore-end and choice of straight or pistol grip, retailed for $127.95. Wood in the stocks of the prewar Model 21 skeet and trap guns was good American walnut, often with some nice figure. Checkering was extensive and quite well done by hand. Buttstocks and fore-ends were very well designed. There was no engraving except on special order.

Winchester would also undertake to make custom-grade Model 21s with stocks of figured French or American walnut, dimensions and engraving to order. Some of these custom Model 21s were very elegant guns indeed. I have seen some at Abercrombie & Fitch in New York and at the Winchester factory in New Haven for which I would gladly rob a bank. My son Bradford has a custom Model 21, a 16 gauge with two sets of barrels, one bored Skeet No. 1 and No. 2, the other bored modified and full. It has a straight-grip stock of well-figured American black walnut and a skeleton buttplate, the only one I have ever seen on a 21. I got the gun on a trade. What it originally cost I haven't any idea.

I believe the Model 21 Winchester double is probably the strongest, most rugged, and most trouble-free double ever made. My wife's 16 gauge is now over thirty-five years old. It has had good care but a lot of use. I even took it on a two-month safari to East Africa with me in 1953 and shot no end of sand grouse, guinea fowl, and francolin with it. It has been used for skeet, pheasants, quail, even ducks. Its only malfunction was doubling once when I was shooting skeet with it, but I think it was my fault because I held the gun too loosely. I have a 21 in 12 gauge with two sets of barrels, one bored Skeet No. 1 and No. 2 (about cylinder and modified) and the other bored modified and improved-modified, and also a 20 gauge for the 3-inch shell. The barrels of the 20 gauge are 26 inches long and bored modified and full. It has been restocked with a superb piece of Circassian walnut I picked up in Iran. At present prices these four Model 21s in the family add up to quite a piece of scratch.

Like most American-made doubles, the 21 is of box-lock construction. It has no extension rib and no top bolt. I have yet to see a 21 that has shot loose, whereas I have seen doubles with more bolts than a Mississippi jail house that have shot so loose they rattled like lumber wagons. The selective single trigger on the 21 is one of the world's best. The four Model 21s in my family have been used a total of sixty-six years and have been fired thousands of times. The only one that has ever doubled is my wife's 16 and, as I said, that happened just once.

Winchester Model 21 frames are made of heat-treated alloy steel. No better or more wear-proof material has ever been put in a shotgun. The barrels are mechanically interlocked with dovetails, instead of being brazed together near the breech as is the case with many doubles. This way there is no risk of warping the barrels or destroying the temper. Barrels are forged of chrome-molybdenum steel and are enormously strong. They are assembled by fitting the interlocking dovetails together and sweating and pinning them into position. Small barrel parts are completely finished before they are assembled. An old Winchester catalog published about forty-five years ago says that one Model 21 was fired 2,000 times with proof loads, each of which gave 7½ long tons pressure. This means about 16,500 pounds per square inch, or 50 percent more than the pressure developed by the most potent shot shell. Firing pins are integral with the hammers (tumblers) and a Model 21 can be snapped indefinitely without hurting anything.

In its more than forty-five years of life, the Model 21 has been made in many styles and many gauges. A .410 Model 21 is a rarity but a few have been made on 20-gauge frames. The 28 gauge on the 20-gauge frame was always made on special order only. The guns have been made in 12 gauge with both 2¾ and 3-inch chambers, in 16 gauge with 2¾-inch chambers, and in 20 gauge with both 2¾ and 3-inch chambers. Actually, Model 21s with 3-inch 20-gauge chambers were in use by Winchester officials long before they were available to the general public. Such special 21s were used to develop the present 20-gauge 3-inch magnum shell, which is now loaded to handle 1¼ ounces of shot. No Model 21s were ever made in 10 gauge, but two or three double rifles in .405 Winchester caliber were built in the early 1930s. One of them, I believe, is now in the Winchester museum at New Haven, and another was used on a brown-bear shoot in southeast Alaska. Barrels were furnished in all lengths from 26 to 32 inches, with both raised-matted and ventilated ribs.

Winchester added a Model 21 in Tournament Grade in 1932 and made it until 1936. Other grades followed: Trap Grade, 1932–40; Standard Grade trap gun, 1940; Standard Grade skeet gun, 1933; Trap Grade skeet gun, 1933–40; Custom Grade, 1933–41; Duck Gun, 1940; De Luxe, 1943.

Sometime in the late 1930s, Winchester decided not to make any more guns with extractors and double triggers. Just when this old standard-grade gun was dropped I cannot say. Even the Winchester bible, *Winchester Rifles & Shotguns* by George R. Watrous, an official Winchester publication, does not tell this. A Stoeger catalog published just after the war shows a standard gun with single trigger and automatic ejectors but splinter fore-end. Beavertail fore-ends are listed as extras on field guns. Incidentally, all Model 21 field guns had automatic safeties, which I consider an abomination in the sight of the Lord. Trap and skeet guns have always had non-automatic safeties, something which has caused the Godly to rejoice.

One of my most bitter regrets is that I didn't buy U. S. Steel at 40 right after the war and another is that I didn't lay in a better supply of Model 21s at the same time. In 1946 a Winchester Model 21 skeet gun sold for $203.75, the standard grade for $185. From then on the price went up—and UP. I bought a 12 gauge with two sets of barrels about 1950 and a 20 gauge for the 3-inch shell in 1955. In 1958 the field gun retailed for $425 and the skeet gun for $440. By that time Winchester had changed the checkering pattern on the Model 21 stocks. The patterns were skimpier and the checkering less well done. At the same time the price was going up, the quality of the gun, at least in appearance, was going down.

The trouble was that Winchester executives had been taking a hard look at the Model 21 operation, had done some cost analysis, and had discovered that a Model 21 was yet to be sold at a profit—if the Model 21 was assigned its share of the overhead. Let us suppose that the checkering on a gunstock costs $25 in wages. If the concern is to break even, about $75 must be added for overhead. Since the manufacture of a good double requires a lot of handwork, it can be seen that it is very difficult to make one at a price the average sportsman will pay and still turn a modest profit—if the model is charged with little things like taxes, advertising, and executives' salaries.

Finally, Winchester gave up on standard Model 21s and announced that the gun would be custom made to special order only. It is now offered in three grades, all with some engraving and fairly fancy checkering patterns—the custom grade at $4,000, the Pigeon grade at $5,500, and the Grand American with two sets of barrels and a British trunk-type case at $7,500. This last is an elaborately engraved and checkered gun, incidentally. The prices make the Model 21 a real luxury item now. Production, I understand, is only about one hundred guns a year. Actually prices are on application.

Besides the Model 21, Winchester has made two other experiments in producing double guns. One was the Model 24, an inexpensive mass-produced and rather homely job. It had double triggers, extractors, no checkering, and was a rather amorphous-looking creation. It did, however, have a well-shaped stock and it handled and shot well. Right after the war, it sold for $53.50. It was discontinued about 1956.

Winchester's other experiment with the double gun is the Model 101. It is made in Japan in a factory controlled by Winchester. An over-and-under, it looks superficially like the Browning but has many important points of difference. It is a good gun, but by no means a deluxe gun. It has a little engraving, fairly good checkering. Most important, the selective single trigger selects, does not balk or double, and the automatic ejectors eject. It is made in 12, 20, 28, and .410 gauge in field and skeet models and 12 gauge for trap. It is a bit heavy, to my way of thinking. I have a Model 101 "skeet set" with barrels and forends in 20, 28, and .410 gauge.

The Remington

The ancient firm of Remington got into the manufacture of side-by-side doubles very early with the Remington Whitmore, a break-open hammer gun, in 1874. An improved hammer gun followed in 1882 and was made until 1910. A hammerless gun made its appearance in 1894 and was made in various styles and grades until 1910, when Remington got out of the double-gun business. Guns had automatic ejectors, barrels of Damascus, ordnance, or Sir Joseph Whitworth steel. The highest-grade Remingtons were beautifully engraved, handsomely checkered, and stocked in fine European walnut. My only experience with a Remington double was with a trap gun belonging to my father. It threw the most consistently dense patterns I have ever had any experience with—between 75 and 80 percent. At 30 yards it would put so much shot into the rear end of a quail that his little bottom looked like the business end of a salt shaker. The Remington doubles of highest grade sold for $750, a lot of money at the turn of the century!

Remington's last experiment in making a double gun, other than the Remington-made Parker, was the over-and-under Model 32. It was born of the depression in 1932 and was a victim of World War II, since manufacture ceased in 1942 and was never resumed. The Model 32 was made in field, skeet, and trap versions, all with automatic ejectors. Early in its history the Model 32 sold for $99.50 in field grade with two triggers, $116 with single trigger. The skeet model was $119 and the trap model with ventilated rib, $144.90. Skeet and trap models had selective single triggers as standard equipment. Higher grades with some engraving and fancy wood were sold for from $250 to $385.

A novel feature of the Model 32 was that the barrels were not joined. The guns were all nicely stocked and had superb balance. The only time I ever shot a Model 32, I broke my first 24 at skeet.

These Model 32s are still in great demand, particularly for skeet shooting, and one in good condition will bring several times its new cost. The West German firm of Heinrich Krieghoff makes a copy of the Model 32. It is imported into the United States and sells fairly well. Somehow the German copy has never seemed to me to have quite the balance of the original.

The Remington over-and-under Model 3200 is supposed to be a modern version of the Model 32, but it has a blobby stock, and at 8¼ pounds in the skeet version it is too heavy.

The Fox

The A. H. Fox Company of Philadelphia made box-lock double guns for many years, many of them very high-class guns superbly finished and decorated and stocked in fine imported walnut. Before World War I the firm used a high proportion of barrels imported from England and from Germany.

The most common Fox was the Sterlingworth, which in the early 1930s sold for $39.50 with extractors, $52.50 with automatic ejectors. The A grade Fox had a little line engraving and sold for $57. With automatic ejectors it was called the AE and sold for $70.

The higher-grade Utica-made Fox guns were the XE at $185, the DE at $275, and the FE at $500. All had stocks of European walnut, automatic ejectors. The Fox-Kautsky single trigger was available at an extra charge. Fox specialized in 12-gauge magnums for the 3-inch shell overbored to give shorter shot columns and better patterns. Like the rest of the double-gun makers, Fox turned out a single-barrel trap gun. Fox guns were made in 12, 16, and 20 gauge, never as far as I am able to find out in .410 or 28.

After the war all of the Savage operation was moved to Chicopee Falls, Massachusetts, and the manufacture of the true Fox gun was never resumed. The Fox gun of today is actually a Stevens, a stout enough but rather roughly made gun.

The Browning

The best-selling quality shotgun in the United States since the end of World War II has been the over-and-under, or "Superposed," Browning. It is an American brand, but it is manufactured in Belgium for the Browning Arms Company of Ogden, Utah, by Fabrique Nationale. The Browning gun was designed by that firearms genius, John Browning, at a time when he felt that repeaters designed to hold more than three shells might be legislated out of existence.

The Browning Superposed is one of the world's most successful over-and-under designs, along with the Merkel, the Boss, and the Italian Beretta. It is painstakingly made and fitted. It is a special favorite with skeet and trap shooters, and many Brownings are in use that have been fired thousands upon thousands of times with never a malfunction. The selective single trigger is one of the most successful of such designs. The shifting mechanism of the trigger completely disconnects between the first and second shots, thereby preventing doubling. All Browning Superposed guns are made with automatic ejectors.

Early in the depression the gun sold for $79.80 in the standard model, but now, sad to say, it is several times that. It is made in field, skeet, and trap models, with various barrel lengths, and in several grades. Even the standard Grade I has some engraving and good checkering. The Diana, Pigeon, Pointer, and Midas grade guns have progressively more engraving, selected European walnut stocks, and fine, precise checkering seldom seen on a factory-produced gun these days. As this is written, in late 1976, the story is that the field-grade Browning Superposed has been discontinued and only the higher grades will be marketed.

The Superposed is made in 12, 20, 28, and .410 gauges, and it is possible for the skeet shooter to have one gun with extra sets of barrels and fore-ends in all gauges. Guns in 12 gauge bored for the 3-inch shell are available for long-range wildfowl shooting. All 20-gauge Brownings are chambered for the 3-inch shell. Precision made and finished as they are, the Browning is an investment for a lifetime, and it will probably be worth more at the end of the shooter's life than it was when he bought it.

CHAPTER **6**

Pump and Automatic

Shotguns

THE pump or slide-action shotgun is the dominant type of shotgun in the United States today. More money is spent for pumps than for shotguns of any other type, and possibly more pumps are sold than the cheaper single shots and bolt actions. Just about every American manufacturer of shotguns makes a pump.

In 1976 pump guns were being made in the popular gauges— .410, 20, 16, 12. No pump gun has ever been made in 10 gauge and only one in 28 gauge.

The first pump gun was the Spencer. It was designed by Christopher C. Spencer, who brought out the Spencer carbine of Civil War fame, and it was manufactured at Windsor, Connecticut. I find one listed in a catalog put out by a St. Louis jobber in 1884. Then the gun retailed for $60, a lot of money in those days; but it had some engraving on the receiver and a checkered pistol grip and slide handle. The Spencer looked unlike the pumps available today. The magazine was a tube under the barrel and held five shots. It was hammerless. The Spencer company fell on evil times and the parts and assets were bought by Bannerman of New York, a concern that dealt in surplus military equipment. Bannerman, I understand, assembled the parts and sold Spencers for many years. I can remember Bannerman advertising Spencer pump guns when I was a gun-struck urchin reading my grandfather's copies of the old *Outdoor Recreation*. Another forgotten pump gun was made by the Union Arms Company of Toledo, Ohio. I have never laid eyes on one. Yet another odd repeater was the Burgess which was made in Buffalo and was operated by a sliding pistol grip.

The first Winchester repeating shotgun was not a pump, but a lever action, the Model 1887. It was designed by John Browning and the manufacturing rights were purchased for a flat fee by Winchester. It was made in both 12 and 10 gauge with 30 and 32-inch barrels. The magazine was a tube under the barrel and held four shells. The barrels were regularly made of fluid steel, but Damascus barrels were available on special order. The Model 1887 was manufactured until 1901. At that time it was revamped a bit and called the Model 1901, but after that it was made in 10 gauge only.

The Model 1887 and the Model 1901 were among the homeliest shotguns ever made. Their appearance is enough to put anyone with an eye for beauty and line into a state of shock. An uncle of mine had a Model 1901 in 10 gauge, and I used to borrow it to shoot ducks. I still remember that evil musket with horror. The lever made it slow to operate. Drop at comb and heel were excessive and the gun kicked like three mules. Nevertheless, I was convinced that with this monster in my hands I could nail ducks at 100 yards. I seldom hit a duck with it at any distance since I was quite small and the gun was awfully big, but now and then I did scratch one down at long range.

Actually, the lever is a poor means of operating a repeating shotgun. It is not nearly as fast as the slide handle of the pump. A few other lever-action shotguns have been made, but none have been wildly successful. Marlin made one for a time in .410 gauge, and after World War II, a lever-action shotgun called the Kessler was manufactured for a time.

Winchester's first pump gun was the Model 1893. Like the Model 1887 it was a Browning design. It was a solid-frame gun with visible hammer and a tubular magazine under the barrel.

The first Winchester catalog announcement describes the operation of the gun as follows:

This gun is operated by a sliding forearm below the barrel. It is locked by the closing motion and can be unlocked only by pushing forward the firing pin, which may be done by the hammer or by the finger. When the hammer is down, the backward and forward motion of the sliding forearms unlocks and opens the breech block, ejects the cartridge or fired shell and replaces it with a fresh cartridge.

The construction of the arm is such that the hammer cannot fall or the firing pin strike the cartridge until the breech block is in place and locked fast. The trigger touches the sear only when the gun is closed—that is, the hammer cannot be let down except when the gun is locked. Having closed the gun and set the hammer at half cock, it is locked both against opening and pulling the trigger. While the hammer stands at the full chock notch, the gun is locked against opening.

To open the gun lift the hammer to full cock and push forward the firing pin, pulling back the action slide.

The Model 1893 was made in 12 gauge only with 30 and 32-inch barrels of Damascus on special order but otherwise of fluid steel. Trouble developed with the pressures of smokeless powder loads. The Model 93 was discontinued, redesigned, and reissued as the Model 97, one of the most widely used and deeply loved of all repeating shotguns. Few of the old Model 93s are left outside of the Winchester museum at New Haven, Connecticut, and the collections of Winchester fans. The only one I can remember seeing was standing rusted and forlorn in the corner of an abandoned Indian cabin by a lake in the Yukon, along with a decaying Model 1879 Winchester single-shot rifle for some forgotten black-powder cartridge.

The Model 1897 had a visible hammer and a strengthened frame made slightly longer in order to handle 2¾-inch 12-gauge shells as well as those with 2⅝-inch cases. The frame was covered so the ejection was entirely from the side. The gun could not be opened until a slight forward movement of the slide handle released the action slide lock. In firing, the recoil did this, but in the absence of recoil the slide handle had to be pushed forward manually in order to release the action slide lock.

Originally brought out in 12 gauge and in solid frame only, the Model 97 was made in take-down form in 1898 and in 16-gauge take-down in 1900. The Model 97 was not discontinued until 1957. During the sixty years of its manufacturing life, it was made in many different forms—as a field gun, a trap gun, a trench gun with a 20-inch barrel, a riot gun, and even as a skeet gun. It was made with fluid-steel barrels regularly, but it could also be had with Damascus barrels. It was the first Winchester shotgun made for the 2¾-inch 12-gauge shell and the first Winchester chambered for the 16-gauge shell. Over one million of the guns were sold. Tens of thousands of these strong, reliable old guns are still in use. In the fall of 1963, I ran across a farmer hunting pheasants with one. The stock looked pretty grim and every vestige of bluing had long since been worn off the barrel and receiver. Nevertheless, the action operated smoothly and there were no pits in the barrel. The farmer, no spring chicken himself, said his father had bought it in the early years of this century.

My first repeating shotgun was a Model 97, a 12 gauge with a 30-inch full-choke barrel. I never loved it. It had too much drop at comb, was too long, too muzzle heavy, had too much choke. I didn't do too badly on ducks and doves with it when I had plenty of time, but when I tried quail in the brush they baffled me. Such faults as I have in handling a shotgun I trace to that damned old Model 97.

Marlin made a pump gun, the Model 1898. Like Winchester's Model 1897 it had a visible hammer and indeed looked very much like the Model 97. It was made in 12 gauge only with a 30-inch full-choke barrel. It was a take-down. The Union Arms Company pump, which was also being sold in the early years of this century, was hammerless.

Remington's first pump gun was the Model 10, a 12 gauge which came out in 1907 and was made until 1929. It was made in various degrees of chokes and with barrels from 26 to 32 inches in length. Fired cases were ejected at the bottom. The Model 10 was a good-looking gun with a streamlined receiver. Some are still in use.

Winchester's first hammerless pump gun was the Model 12, the most popular pump gun ever made in the United States. A side-ejecting gun, the Model 12 was first made in a handsome little 20 gauge with a 25-inch barrel. Chambers were for 2½-inch shells. Later the Model 12 appeared in 12, 16, and 28 gauge. The Model 42 in .410 only is no longer manufactured but it is a revised Model 12. The Model 12 has been made in many different barrel lengths, from 25 to 32 inches, and in field, trap, skeet, and riot models and in various grades. It is a fairly expensive gun to manufacture, and in 1964 the field model was discontinued in favor of a new pump called the Model 1200, which uses a Duralumin receiver and multiple locking lugs on the forward portion of the breech bolt. It is a much cheaper gun to manufacture than the Model 12, which now is being made only in trap and skeet models. The Model 12 has been revived with cast parts at a higher price.

The Remington Model 17, which was made between 1921 and 1933, was similar to the Model 10. It was a bottom ejector and was made in 20 gauge only. The Model 29 Remington pump was made in 12 gauge only and was a sort of an enlarged Model 17.

The Model 31 Remington, which is still widely used, replaced the Model 17 and the Model 29. It was famous as a fast-handling, smooth-working gun and thousands are still in use. It was made in 12, 16, and 20 gauge and was a side ejector. It was made in all grades.

After the war, Remington decided once more to redesign its line of pump shotguns for easier and cheaper manufacture. The result was the Remington Model 870. It took the place of the Model 31 and was made in 12, 16, and 20 gauges, in various grades, and in field, trap, and skeet models. These guns are smooth working, nicely stocked, and fast handling. They have sold very well indeed.

Before World War II, the Ithaca Gun Company saw that the market for doubles was falling off and the guns themselves were getting more expensive to manufacture. As a consequence, the company tooled up to make a pump shotgun—the Model 37. This gun has been made ever since and has sold well. It is a bottom ejector and bears more than a passing resemblance to the Remington Models 10 and 17, patents on which have expired. It is made in 12, 16, and 20 gauges in various grades and barrel lengths and is available in a special model for deer hunting.

Because a huge market exists for the pump gun in the United States, just about every arms manufacturer has got into the act. Marlin long made two types of pumps, one with a visible hammer—the Model 42–A—and two hammerless, the Model 43–A and the Model 53–A. All were turned out with various barrel lengths and degrees of choke. They were killed off by the depression and the war. The present Marlin pump gun is partially produced in France.

Savage has also been in the pump-gun business for many years. The Model 21 was produced in 12 gauge only with 26, 28, 30, and 32-inch barrels and with borings from cylinder to full choke. A novel feature was a tang safety like those on double-barrel guns instead of the usual crossbolt safety in the trigger guard of most pump guns. In 1964 Savage was producing its Model 30 in .410, 20, 16, and 12 gauge, with plain barrels and ventilated ribs, with and without the Savage variable choke device, in various barrel lengths. One model is made for southpaws with the ejection on the left side of the receiver.

The Mossberg company entered the field late with the slide-action Model 500 shotgun. It is made in 20, 16, and 12 gauges, in various barrel lengths, degrees of choke, both 2¾ and 3-inch chambers in 20 and 12 gauge, and with the Mossberg C-Lect Choke if ordered. Like the old Savage Model 21, the Mossberg has a top tang safety. Mossberg also furnishes special "Slugster" barrels for hunting deer with rifled slugs.

High Standard, which started as a manufacturer of automatic pistols, got into the shotgun business after World War II by making shotguns for Sears, Roebuck, and now sells a complete line of pumps in .410, 20, 16, and 12 gauges in all grades, varieties, barrel lengths, degrees of choke, with plain barrels, ventilated rib barrels, and a Mossberg variable choke device. High Standard pumps are also furnished with special slug barrels equipped with rifle sights. The guns are made in models for trap and skeet. They are good-looking, sound, and reliable guns.

Harrington & Richardson is another entrant in the pump-gun field with a conventional line. The Model 400 is made in 12 and 16 gauges and the Model 402 in .410 gauge. Only 28-inch full-choke barrels are furnished.

Another postwar maker of pump guns is the Noble Manufacturing Company of Haydensville, Massachusetts, a company which makes pump guns in .410, 20, 16, and 12 gauge.

In spite of the fact that the pump gun is the dominant shotgun type since before World War II, I am not a mad aficionado of pump guns. Most of them made today are essentially alike. Most are hammerless, side-ejecting guns and all have tubular magazines under the barrel. Some have tang safeties. Others have crossbolt safeties in the forward part of the trigger guard. To me at any rate, none of them have the charm and beauty of a good double. All are pieces of machinery rather than works of art. Those with barrels longer than 26 inches are muzzle heavy for many uses because the barrels are tacked onto long receivers. Some operate more smoothly than others. Some have better lines than others. In my experience the smoothest operating of the lot are those made by Remington and by High Standard, and the best looking of the lot are the high-grade Remington Model 870s and the Winchester Model 12 trap and skeet guns.

Some bold manufacturer of pump guns should bring out a gun for upland shooting with a 24-inch barrel and then one would get that balance and fast handling of a double. Pumps with the popular 28-inch barrel length are to me somewhat muzzle heavy and slow for upland shooting, although all right for waterfowl and for traps, and pumps with 30-inch barrels are too clumsy and sluggish for any purpose. The crossbolt safeties with which most pumps are equipped are slow and awkward, and the actions of many pump guns are stiff and rough to operate.

On the other hand, pump guns are adapted to cheap mass production and the fact that some can be sold for a little over $100 shows that some profound thought has gone into the manufacturing. I think that in time the self-loading or automatic shotgun will to a great extent replace the pump. It is about as cheap to manufacture, and it will do everything the pump will do and in most hands it will do it a little faster.

The "Automatics"

There are two forces that can be used to operate a shotgun to make it eject the fired case, cock itself, and chamber a fresh live shell. One is the force of recoil, and the other is the force of the expanding powder gases. Each of these forces can be utilized in different ways. Shotguns which eject the fired shell, recock themselves, and chamber a new cartridge are properly called "self-loaders" or "semi-automatics," but "automatic" is the popular term and will be used here.

John Browning's successful automatic shotgun was recoil operated. He first offered it to Winchester, and Thomas C. Johnson, the head Winchester designer, helped him work out the patent application. Browning had always sold the rights to his previous inventions for lump sums, but this time he wanted a royalty deal. As this was against Winchester policy, Browning was refused. As mentioned before, he took his invention to Remington, but while John Browning and his brother Matthew were waiting to see the Remington president, the president dropped dead of a heart attack. John Browning then took his invention to Europe where he made a deal with Fabrique Nationale at Liége. Browning automatics made by Fabrique Nationale are sold in the United States by the Browning Arms Company of Ogden, Utah, and throughout the rest of the world by the Belgian firm itself. Later Browning came to an agreement with Remington to produce the gun at Ilion, New York, and to sell it in the United States on a royalty basis. It came out as the Model 11 in 1905 and was made until 1948.

Those Browning-Remington guns used the long-recoil type of automatic mechanism. In this system the barrel and the breech bolt locked together recoiled for several inches. The breech bolt is then held back while the barrel goes forward.

A gun of this sort has two separate return springs, one to return the barrel and another to return the breech block. The breech block is locked to the barrel when the piece is fired and the pressure drives it about four inches to the rear. It is then arrested by striking a stop. Locked to the breech block, the barrel goes to the rear. The return springs for both breech block and barrel are compressed. When the breech block has reached the limit of its rearward motion, it is caught and held in that position by a latch. Then as the barrel return spring pushes the barrel forward, the breech bolt unlocks itself and allows the barrel to go forward. The empty cartridge case held to the breech block by the extractor is ejected as the barrel goes forward. When the barrel reaches its forward position, it strikes a lever which drops a latch and allows the breech block to come forward. As it does so, it feeds a new cartridge.[1]

The present Browning automatic and the old Remington Model 11 were made under the same patents and appear almost identical. Tens of thousands of these rugged, homely old guns are still in use. The defunct Winchester Model 1911 and Model 1940 were both long-recoil automatics. The Savage Model 750, which has been manufactured for many years, is also a long-recoil automatic; it is now somewhat streamlined but once it looked much like the Remington and the Browning. The Franchi and Breda automatics made in Italy also use the long-recoil system.

Many shooters never did like the square receiver of the Browning, Remington, and Savage automatics. Some owners of these weapons were so shaken up by their appearance that in the late 1930s they had the New York gunsmithing firm of Griffin & Howe "streamline" them by extending the buttstock up to the square end of the receiver.

After the war, Remington discontinued the classic Model 11 and brought out the streamlined version called the 11–48. In 1964 this model is still being manufactured in all gauges—.410, 28, 20, 16, and 12. It is the only American shotgun that is available in the complete series of gauges.

Winchester discontinued the Model 12 pump gun in 28 gauge along in the late 1950s and later the Model 42 pump in .410. As a consequence, Remington just about has a monopoly of small-bore

[1] Summarized from Julian S. Hatcher's *Hatcher's Notebook*, p. 53.

and sub-small-bore skeet guns. Some Model 12 pumps in 28 gauge are seen on the skeet field as well as some Model 42s in .410. A few skeet shooters have Browning over-and-under guns with extra barrels in 20, 28, and .410 gauges, but most of the small-bore and sub-small-bore shooters I have seen in recent years are shooting the Remington Model 11–48.

The long-recoil system is a good reliable system that has worked for over two generations, but many shooters have never liked it. For one thing, the slam of the barrel as it comes back adds to the recoil. For another, many shooters have been annoyed by the "double shuffle" of the gun going off and then the smack of the barrel as it reaches the end of its travel. Automatics operated on the long-recoil system have friction rings that cut down on the recoil. They are set at various positions for light and heavy loads and if they are not properly adjusted the recoil is pretty annoying.

These old recoil-operated Brownings and Remingtons have taken a lot of game in their day. They were particularly deadly duck and goose guns. At one time, extension magazines were sold for them and with these they could really pour out the lead. Once many years ago I was hunting turkeys with a chap armed with one of these stuffed full of shells loaded with No. 2 shot. We sneaked up on a big bunch of turkeys. I got one with a rifle but my pal emptied his automatic. There were dead and dying turkeys all over the place!

An interesting shotgun operated by the short-recoil system is the Browning Double Automatic, a two-shot weapon invented by Val Browning. It appeared on the American market after the last war. This was a handsome gun made with both steel and Duralumin receivers. The barrel recoils only about one-half inch against two sets of springs. One powerful spring is in the fore-end. Behind the breech block, one within the other, are two more springs. As the barrel moves, it is cushioned by spring action. The double automatic is a very pleasant gun to shoot. The loading port is on the left side of the receiver and it snatches the shell like a hungry dog grabbing a piece of meat.

What with this and that, Winchester has had difficulties with its automatic shotguns. Winchester's first autoloader was the Model

1911. It was the gun developed to compete with the Browning-designed Remington Model 11, which came out in 1905. As we have seen, the Winchester designer, T. C. Johnson, was faced with the tough problem of designing a long-recoil automatic that would not infringe on the Browning patents he himself had helped to draw up.

He finally succeeded after a fashion and the Winchester Model 1911 was the result. It developed weaknesses in use, but these faults of design were corrected. The recoil of this gun was divided, its main force being absorbed by a buffer at the lower front end of the receiver and the rest by a similar device forming a cushion between the bolt and the rear end of the receiver. The Model 1911 was never considered a particularly satisfactory gun. It was discontinued in 1925, and for fifteen years Winchester was without a self-loading shotgun. Then a revised edition of the Model 1911 was introduced. It was the Model 1940, a rather good-looking gun of streamlined appearance. However, some pretty bad bugs appeared and it was discontinued in 1941. As I understand it, Winchester replaced unsatisfactory Model 40 guns with New Model 12 pumps.

After World War II, the shift in repeating shotguns tended to be toward self-loaders, so Winchester brought out their Model 50, a gun which operated on a novel short-recoil system. In the Model 50, unlike the long-recoil self-loaders such as the Remington Model 11 and the short-recoil Browning double automatic, the barrel does not move. Instead, Winchester in designing the Model 50 used the principle of the recoiling chamber or "slip chamber," which was developed by "Carbine" Williams. It has been used in the Colt "Ace" pistol and the Remington Model 550 automatic .22, which handled .22 short, long, or long rifle ammunition. The chamber, bolt, and inertia rod are locked together and move one-tenth of an inch when the gun is fired. This starts the inertia rod on its cycle of unlocking the bolt, extracting and ejecting the empty shell, reloading, and locking the bolt.

It is my understanding that the Model 50 never sold particularly well. In its original form it was a rather heavy gun, weighing well over eight pounds. Since the design called for a lot of machinery in the buttstock, the gun was butt heavy. Winchester brought out a "featherweight" model in 12 gauge only with a Duralumin receiver. Later this model was given a barrel made of fiber glass wound around a steel liner. It is now made in 12 gauge only, whereas the Model 50 was made in both 12 and 20 gauge. The Model 59 is a light gun, weighing only 6½ pounds. It was available with barrels threaded for the "Win-Lite" Choke—ventilated tubes with various degrees of constriction that screwed onto the barrel.

The Model 59 is butt heavy (and also muzzle light) but it is well stocked and I have always shot very well on upland game with it. Many others have too. Shooting at Nilo Farms near Alton, Illinois, the year it was introduced, fellow gun editors Larry Koller, Warren Page, and I killed twenty-eight bobwhite quail with twenty-nine shots and I don't think any of us missed a pheasant put up by dogs during the two-day shoot.

I strongly suspect, however, that as soon as the present supply of parts on hand is used up, the Model 59 will be dropped. The tendency these days is toward gas-operated automatics and Winchester has one in the new Model 1400.

Gas-Operated Self-Loaders

Expanding powder gas is pretty violent stuff, and early efforts to produce gas-operated automatic rifles and shotguns were not wildly successful. They were not nearly as reliable as those operated by recoil, as they were given to broken parts and functional failures.

The M–1 "Garand" military rifle was gas operated. It was a fine and reliable combat arm with which we fought World War II and the Korean War. As soon as the war was over, designers began to work on the problems presented in designing gas-operated sporting arms. The result has been that the gas-operated self-loaders are out in front. Remington and Winchester have both dropped their recoil-operated big-game rifles. Remington now makes the Model 742 in various calibers including the .280 and the .30/06 and Winchester chambers its own gas-operated rifle, the Model 100, for the .243, the .284, and the .308.

The first American gas-operated shotgun was turned out by the High Standard Company for Sears, Roebuck. It had a gas system somewhat like that on the German Gewehr 41 autoloading rifle.

All the operating parts are confined in the rather large fore-end of the High Standard J. C. Higgins. The gas piston is a collar fitted over the tubular magazine. The gas is fed into a cylinder through three ports about one foot ahead of the chamber. It then goes into a piston which transmits the movement of the operating rod to the bolt slide, which has about one-half-inch free travel before it unlocks the bolt. This is to give the shot time to get out of the barrel and the pressures time to drop. When the breech block has reached the limit of its travel and the case has been ejected, the operating spring around the tube feeds in a fresh cartridge and locks up the breech.

The original J. C. Higgins autoloader made for Sears, Roebuck proved to be a good, rugged, reliable gun. It was on the heavy side, as it weighed around 8½ pounds, but it handled well and functioned without a whimper. For some years High Standard was in the long-gun business with a full line of pump guns and gas-operated automatics in 12 and 20 gauge.

After World War II wound up, the Remington company took a long look at the business of manufacturing rifles and shotguns and decided to see if there was not some way to make it reasonably profitable. Ruthlessly, they dropped the guns they had been manufacturing by traditional methods—and losing money on. They got smart designers, some from the automobile business. They junked obsolescent machinery, got new, efficient machines, used more stamped and cast parts. One of their successful innovations was to use the same basic receiver for a whole family of shotguns and rifles. Another was the perfection of the process of pressing checkering patterns in by a combination of heat and pressure.

As we have seen, the Remington Model 11–48 was a long-recoil self-loader, the old Model 11 streamlined and turned out by manufacturing short cuts. The Model 58, Remington's first gas-operated shotgun, employed the same basic receiver as the 11–48 and looked just about like it.

The gas-operated Model 58, however, had no recoiling barrel, and consequently recoil is much less noticeable. A barrel ring with two gas vents passes around the magazine tube. The gas goes through these vents into a gas cylinder in the forward portion of the magazine tube which contains a double-bar operating rod hinged to the breech block. When the powder of the shell begins to burn, causing the gas to form and expand and the shot and wads to move up the bore, gas is fed out of the vents to strike the piston and start it to move rearward. The shot is out of the muzzle before the breech is unlocked. The fired shell is ejected, and as the breech block returns to battery it picks up and chambers a loaded cartridge. On the end of the magazine tube of the Model 58 is a rotating cap marked H and L. Turned to H, the three gas vents are open for use with maximum loads. Turning to L closes two of the vents off for use with light field and skeet loads.

The Model 878, which followed the Model 58, used the same standard receiver as the Model 11–48 and the 58. It also employed many of the same parts and felt and handled the same. However, the Model 878 had a self-adjusting gas piston, which operated the breech mechanism with the correct force when any loads, heavy or light, were used. The Model 58 and the Model 878 were both successful guns, good-looking, and with nicely shaped stocks of good dimensions. They became favorites on the skeet field and were widely used in the duck marshes and in the uplands.

Now both models are obsolete, as they have been superseded by the latest Remington gas-operated job, the Model 1100. This fine autoloader was introduced in 12 gauge and 12-gauge magnum in 1963, but it is now made in 16 and 20 gauges as well.

In general appearance the Model 1100 is much like the Model 11–48, the 58, and the 878. A good many changes from the Model 878 were made in the operating parts. The longer barrel extension is forged in one piece with the barrel. The piston, which was inside the magazine tube on previous models, now surrounds the magazine tube and slides on it. The gas cylinder is part of the magazine-tube bracket on the barrel. The action spring, which moves the breech block back to battery, is in the stock. Like the Model 878, the Model 1100 handles all loads without adjustment. Barrels for the Model 1100 are interchangeable without special fitting.

I was introduced to the Model 1100 Remington one miserable wintry day at Lordship, a gun club on Long Island Sound near Bridgeport. After being suitably brainwashed, we gun writers were allowed to shoot the gun. I was bundled up in all the clothes I could put on and even at that I was half frozen. We had been told, though, that the recoil was quite soft, less than that of the Model 58 or 878, and much less than that of the rugged Model 11–48. I found this was indeed true. Later I shot a Model 1100 on geese in Maryland. I used the fearsome 2¾-inch magnum loads with 1½ ounces of shot, and the recoil was not at all bothersome—certainly no more than a double with the ordinary field load with 1⅛ ounces of shot. Another excellent characteristic of the Model 1100 is that it doesn't throw the ejected cases into the next county. Instead, they tumble out gently and land a few feet away.

The Model 1100 weighs 8 pounds in 12 gauge with 28-inch barrel, somewhat heavy for an upland gun, but fine for skeet or waterfowl. In comparison, my Model 58 12-gauge skeet gun with 26-inch barrel with ventilated rib weighs 7½ pounds, also a bit heavy for the uplands. The Model 1100 is also made in 28 and .410 gauges with plain and ventilated rib barrels.

The use of impressed "checkering" on the latest Model 1100 guns has enabled Remington to decorate them with a very ornate and elaborate checkering pattern—one that if hand done would probably cost $150. However, no impressed checkering gives the hands a no-slip hold like real checkering filed painstakingly into the wood.

Late in the summer of 1964, Winchester brought out that company's first gas-operated self-loading shotgun. It was light, good-looking, and had a soft recoil. It was the Model 1400. This has been replaced by a rugged 12-gauge autoloader of new design. This is the Super-X.

CHAPTER 7

The Shotgun Barrel

THE shotgun barrel is simply a long cylinder generally made of steel. At one end is the chamber, which is enlarged to accept the shell (cartridge). The other end is usually closed up a bit to control the pattern. This is the choke portion of the barrel. The barrel of a repeating shotgun is screwed into the receiver. The twin barrels of a double gun are held against the action face or standing breech by under bolts, side bolts, and generally some sort of a top bolt.

The earliest shotgun barrels were made by wrapping a sheet of iron around a mandrel, heating it red hot, and hammering it until it was lap welded. This method was all right with black powders and low pressures. W. W. Greener, the British gunmaker and author of books on guns and gunsmithing, says in *Modern Shotguns* (1888) that these barrels were no good. Be that as it may, many thousands of cheap shotguns had barrels made by this process. Greener also says that many of the barrels turned out in the 1880s and 1890s marked "decarbonized steel" were simply made from pieces of lap-welded iron, and actually steel without carbon *is* iron. As a long-time practicing gun editor who has received tens of thousands of letters from readers, I must have answered many hundreds from people who had cheap and ancient doubles marked "decarbonized steel." Barrels were also made by the same method but with a piece of mild sheet steel. Because of the weld, such barrels are not strong.

Later it became fashionable to make barrels out of various combinations of steel and iron. They were variously called "twist," "skelp," "laminated," and "Damascus." These were made by taking long strips of steel and iron and twisting and welding them together. These twists were then pounded flat, wound around a mandrel in a spiral, and welded. The ribbons were composed of two, three, and four spiral twists. The more the twists, it was thought, the finer the barrel. The resulting tube was reamed out to bore diameter, choked, and chambered.

It is easy to detect a twist or Damascus barrel because one sees some sort of a spiral, whorly, or speckled pattern. The reason for this is that the iron and steel take the blue (in this case "browning") differently, with resulting contrast in color and value. In my more than a score of years as a gun editor I have had thousands of letters from owners of guns with these old twist barrels. Often they say they do not think the barrels are twist because the figure cannot be seen when they polish them bright with emery cloth or steel wool. The reason for this is that the browning is polished off and both kinds of metal are left bright. Even at that, though, a careful examination will show a pattern.

Sometimes barrels are marked "Damascus Finish" and have the pattern etched or painted on. These barrels are generally weaker than twist and are simply lap-welded pieces of mild steel or even iron.

These barrels are not very strong. They were made for black-powder loads which gave a breech pressure of about 5,000 pounds per square inch. Even modern low-brass trap loads give pressure twice as high and in effect every modern shell is a tough proof load for an old twist barrel. Barrels made of a combination of iron and steel lack the tensile strength of modern steel, and even the best of them have "grays" caused by impurities in the material and minute cracks in the welds where rust can begin.

Yet for many years, some sort of a figure on a barrel was considered by the layman to be a guarantee of quality. The use of figured barrels was almost universal in the 1890s and widespread until about the time of World War I. It was possible to order a high-grade Parker with Damascus barrels as late as 1920. Most twist barrels were made in Belgium and even many British-made guns used Belgian tubes. Later, the British learned to make satisfactory tubes out of the various types of twist, and characteristically claimed them superior to the Belgian product. As far as I know, no Damascus barrels were ever made in the United States. Instead, makers of American double guns imported their tubes, sometimes from England but generally from Belgium. Before World War I, high-grade Parkers, Lefevers, L. C. Smiths, and other double guns were either regularly made with imported twist tubes or such tubes were offered as a choice. The popularity of such material for barrels is shown by the fact that the purchasers of even some early repeaters had the option of twist barrels. Among them were the Model 1893 and 1897 Winchester pumps and the Model 1887 Winchester lever action in 12 and 10 gauge.

Many old guns with twist barrels are still in use, often with the very hottest of modern loads including the 12-gauge 2¾-inch magnums. Many get away with this dangerous practice. I recall one old chap with a cheap and rickety old double that rattled like a castanet every time it was touched. Some of the iron was so badly rusted that it was eaten away and the barrel actually had holes in it. Yet he was shooting South Idaho pheasants with progressive-powder loads with 1¼ ounces of shot and 3¾ drams of powder. Incidentally, these old twist barrels were generally pretty soft and often the choke portion at the muzzle would be so worn that what had once been a full-choke barrel would deliver cylinder patterns.

Along in the later 1930s I warned a chap with a good-grade Parker that twist barrels were not safe with modern smokeless powder. He told me I was full of prunes and went ahead shooting high-brass maximum loads. Not long after, he blew out one barrel when he was shooting some shells that had been sitting out in the 140-degree heat of southern Arizona's direct September sunlight. These old guns usually blow forward of the chamber. Sometimes they injure the left hand. Sometimes they don't, but always they scare the hell out of the shooter when they let go.

I get many letters from chaps with these old guns, many of

which are beauties with fine wood, good engraving, and beautiful checkering. What to do with them? If they want to shoot them as they are, it will be necessary for them to handload shells with black powder, as manufacture of all black-powder shot shells was discontinued during World War II. If the owner of such a gun is allergic to black powder, he will either have to hang Old Betsy on the wall or have it rebarreled.

A new set of barrels can be made for a gun in Belgium, Austria, or possibly in Spain. The last time I inquired, replacement barrels cost from $125 to $175 if for a non-ejector and from $25 to $50 more for an ejector. To justify these prices, the gun equipped with new barrels would have to be of very high quality. Another way of skinning the cat is to fit new steel tubes into the breeches of old barrels. Some years ago Frank Lefever & Sons, 114 East Main Street, Frankfort, New York, was doing this job for $125. The firm also fitted new barrels for $175 and up. This same job of fitting new tubes into the breech is done by Westley Richards at their Birmingham plant in England.

Since the end of World War I, the use of shotgun barrels made of solid-steel blanks or billets has been universal. The popular name for such steel is "fluid" steel because the first barrels of the type used by English-speaking people were those which the inventor, Sir Joseph Whitworth, gave to solid-steel tubes of his manufacture. In the 1890s and early 1900s, tubes of Whitworth Fluid Steel were widely used in quality guns in the United States as well as in England. Fluid-steel tubes were also imported into both the United States and England from Germany, where they were made by Krupp and by Siemens. A London-made Jeffery double rifle in .400 Nitro Express caliber that I own has all the proper British proof marks, but the barrels are made with Krupp steel. I have had hundreds of letters from G.I.'s who liberated shotguns and combination guns in Germany during the last war. They want to know more about their guns and they write me that they were made by "Krupp" or by "Krupp Flusshahl." Krupp tubes were also imported by American double-gun makers, but I believe that the use of American tubes was pretty general after the end of World War I.

I suspect that in Europe there is more to gun building than meets the eye. I know I have come across guns marked with the names of Paris custom gunmakers that were apparently entirely made in Belgium, Austrian guns with German tubes, and German guns with Belgian tubes. In England today I understand that practially all shotgun tubes are made by one firm, Vickers. Once just before the last war I was in the factory of a fine builder of double guns. Depending on the grade, the barrels were variously marked with fanciful names "Chromax Steel," "Acme Steel," etc. All were made from exactly the same tubes.

Today, most American concerns make their own barrels by drilling a hole in a blank, then reaming it, chambering it, turning it to the correct outside contour, and choking it. However, I have been told that some concerns buy their barrels in a semi-finished state, already drilled and reamed, from a deep-hole drilling company. One concern performs most of the operations of barrel-forming by forging in an intricate and costly machine.

In Europe the choke is reamed into the barrels, and since the barrels are made up, they are usually left full choke until the individual gun is ready to be assembled. Then the degree of choke that has been ordered is put in by reaming out a bit of metal, shooting, reaming some more, polishing, shooting, reaming. In the old days of the double companies in the United States, the gun buyer could order the exact pattern he wanted with any size shot and any brand of shell and he could be reasonably sure of getting about what he ordered. My last custom-made American double was a fine Winchester Model 21 ordered to give 55 percent in the right barrel with 1¼ ounces of No. 6 shot and 65 percent in the left. When I received it, I patterned it with 10 shots for each barrel with Western Super X. It came out 57 and 68 percent. By fiddling around, reaming, and patterning, skilled gun borers could often turn out barrels that would give a more open pattern with light, low-brass loads and small shot than with larger shot and heavier loads, in effect giving the man who ordered the gun two guns instead of one. I know this defies all the laws of physics and mechanics but that is what the old-time gun builders tell me.

Today choke is not reamed into the muzzles of repeating shotguns made in the United States. Instead the choke is left on the outside in reverse near the muzzle when the barrel is contoured. Then the end of the barrel is put into a machine that swages or pounds it outside in. Only an occasional gun is shot for pattern. One outfit which I visited patterned one pump gun in ten but shot all of them for functioning.

Some cheap single-barrel guns simply have an indefinite amount of choke swaged in by pushing the end of the barrel inward. The steel liners used in the barrels of the Winchester glass-barrel Model 59s have swaged choke. Miles of fiber glass is then wrapped around the barrel. These are light, strong, and satisfactory. Experimental barrels have been made of high-tensile aluminum alloy, but have not been used in production models. Attempts have been made to make barrels of seamless steel tubing, but I understand that there is no saving over conventional methods. Eventually, barrels for repeating shotguns will probably be entirely forged around mandrels having choke, bore, and chamber in reverse, a method by which some rifle barrels are now made.

It takes no genius to discover that the center distance between holes in the barrels of a double gun is much greater at the breech than at the muzzle. As the barrels are assembled, they are bent or "beveled" toward the muzzle so the barrels will shoot to the same place at 40 yards and not crossfire. The barrels are properly bent by a process known as "Englishing," which consists of bending the barrels by hammering tapered nails inserted under wires. The two barrels of high-grade doubles made largely by hand generally shoot right together. Often the barrels do not, as "Englishing" is a painstaking task which takes a lot of patience and know-how. A wide cylinder or improved cylinder pattern will cover a good many sins, but it is common to find a pair of full-choke barrels that throw cockeyed patterns.

When choke devices are fitted to single-barrel guns, the gadget on the end of the barrel is in effect a higher front sight, and unless the barrel is bent upward to compensate, the barrel equipped with a choke device will almost always shoot low. I have seen guns with carelessly fitted choke devices that shot from 1½ to 2 feet low at 40 yards. Cockeyed barrels are more common than most people think. Some barrels throw patterns not only high or low but also right and left.

The chamber in the breech end of the shotgun barrel is simply an enlarged hole to contain the shell or cartridge. The point where it is contracted to bore diameter is known as the "cone." Chambers are made in various lengths from 2 inches for some short British 12-gauge shells to 3½ inches for the 10-gauge magnum. Today the most-used chamber in the United States is 2¾ inches long. It is standard for 28, 20, 16, and 12-gauge guns. However, 3 inches is the standard chamber length for the .410 and for 20 and 12-gauge guns chambered for the 3-inch magnum shell. Formerly, .410 and 20-gauge guns were made with 2½-inch chambers, 16-gauge guns with 2%6-inch chambers, 28-gauge guns with 2½, then later 2⅞-inch chambers, and 12s with 2⅝-inch chambers.

Chambers in American 12-gauge barrels were standardized at 2¾ inches right after World War I. The 16-gauge chamber was standardized at 2¾ inches in 1929, the 20-gauge chamber at 2¾ inches in 1926. A 3-inch chamber became standard for the .410 in the early 1930s when Western and Winchester brought out the 3-inch .410 shell and a gun to shoot it. The 28 gauge was standardized at 2¾ inches before the last war.

In England the standard game (upland) gun is made with 2½-inch chambers, but wildfowl guns are made with 2¾ and 3-inch chambers. On the Continent, 12, 16, and 20-gauge guns are made with 65-mm. (2½-inch). Some, particularly those for the American market, are turned out with 70-mm. (2¾-inch) chambers. Some Continental guns are also made with 3-inch chambers. European guns are commonly stamped with gauge and chamber length on the flats under the breech of the barrels. A "12–70" is, of course, a 12 gauge with 2¾-inch chambers and a "20–65" would be a 20 with 2½-inch chambers. If a European gun is not stamped for chamber length, the chamber is generally 65 mm. Shooting long shells in short chambers raises pressures a bit, as the end of the case crowds into the cone and the wads have to force their way past it. Many believe that shooting short shells in long chambers opens up patterns, but this is questionable. The considerable experimenting I have done shows little if any difference between patterns with 2¾-inch shells in a 2¾-inch and in a 3-inch chamber.

We have inherited many notions from the days of black powder, and one of them is that the longer the barrel is the harder it shoots. This notion had some basis in fact. Before the days of choke boring, long barrels did throw somewhat denser patterns since the long barrel gave the shot charge time to outrun the wads and the wads did not smash into the rear of the shot at the muzzle and disrupt the pattern. For another, it took a long barrel to burn large quantities of black powder. Today the length of the barrel has little to do with velocity delivered and almost nothing to do with the pattern. Most modern shotgun powders are pretty well consumed in 24 inches of barrel length, and a 26-inch barrel gives almost as much velocity as a 32-inch barrel. Actually, if full velocity is developed in a short barrel, the long barrel will give a little less velocity because as the push of the powder gases falls off, friction begins to slow the shot charge down.

Barrel length should be decided on, then, on some other basis than delivered velocity. A short barrel handles faster, is quicker to get on with, and is preferred for upland shooting and for skeet. Nowadays the standard length for the barrels of a double gun to be used in the uplands is 26 inches. Skeet shooters who use side-by-side and over-and-under doubles like 26 and 28-inch barrels. The double-barrel gun used for trap and for wildfowl shooting generally has a 30-inch barrel but sometimes one 32 inches long. It is a custom with manufacturers of repeating shotguns to make barrels bored "skeet" or improved cylinder 26 inches in length. Guns bored modified are generally 28 inches long, although 26-inch modified barrels can be obtained on repeating guns made by Ithaca and Browning. Full-choke barrels are available in 28 and 30-inch lengths and in some cases in 32 inch.

The long barrel puts the muzzle farther away from the face, and hence the shooter is less aware of report and muzzle blast. It swings steadier and gives a longer sighting radius for trapshooting and birds taken against the sky, such as doves and ducks.

For the pump or automatic used in the uplands, I think even a 26-

inch barrel is a bit long, as a repeating shotgun with a 26-inch barrel is about as long overall as a double with a 30-inch barrel. To me a repeater used on upland game balances better with a barrel from 22 to 24 inches in length. However, no factory guns are made with barrels that short, and the only way to obtain one is to have a variable choke device fitted for the preferred length. For me, even a 26-inch barrel on a repeater is adequately long for wildfowl and a gun so equipped generally has about the same balance as a double with a 30-inch barrel.

At one time, shotguns with 36 and even 40-inch barrels were common, and those who owned them were convinced that they were universally "hard shooters" that would knock off ducks at 110 yards. A cheap single shotgun with a 40-inch barrel was sold by Sears, Roebuck around the time of World War I. These guns were called "Long Toms" and those who owned them were convinced that they "shot like rifles" and would take ducks at fantastic distances. Sad to say, it was all in their minds, but the notion lingers on. And when Savage brought out a single with a 36-inch barrel about 1960, it enjoyed a good sale to the unsophisticated.

For the past fifty years there has been a slow, almost glacial, shift toward shorter barrels, smaller gauges, lighter guns, and more open boring. Before the last war, the best seller among repeating shotguns was the 30-inch, 12-gauge, full-choke barrel and many 32-inchers were sold. In the early 1960s, the best seller was still the 12 gauge, but the barrel most in demand, from some manufacturers anyway, was the 28-inch modified. Few 32-inch barrels are seen today, and the popularity of repeaters with 26-inch barrels is increasing. At one time, barrels bored improved cylinder were almost unknown except among the quail shooters of the South and worldly characters like the woodcock and ruffed grouse hunters of the East. Now, even in the unsophisticated West, many gunners order repeaters bored improved cylinder and doubles bored improved cylinder and modified, both with 26-inch barrels.

CHAPTER 8

The Choke

in the Shotgun Barrel

BEFORE the invention of choke boring, all shotgun barrels were made as straight cylinders throughout. Patterns were wide, and the sure killing range even of a heavily loaded 12 gauge was not much over 30 yards. At 25 yards these guns in cylinder bore delivered 70 percent patterns—70 percent of the charge in a 30-inch circle. Kills were made, of course, at much greater distances, but such kills were a matter of luck. Either the bird ran into a cluster of shot or he was hit by one pellet in a vital place.

The discovery of choke boring did more to increase the killing range of the shotgun than any other development. Instead of being a 30-yard weapon, the shotgun became with choke boring a 50-yard weapon. Shot is harder and more uniform today than it was fifty years ago. Shot shells are loaded more uniformly. New gas-seal wads and the pie crimp have improved patterns, so has the use of protective plastic collars around the shot charges. But compared with choke boring, all of these improvements have been relatively minor.

The late Capt. Charles Askins, former arms and ammunition editor of *Outdoor Life*, gave an Illinois duck hunter named Fred

CHOKE SPECIFICATION.

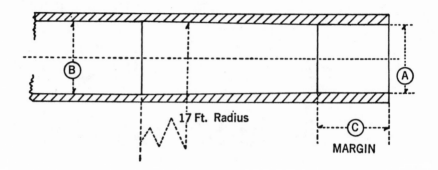

17 Ft. Radius

MARGIN

Full Choke

MODEL	GAUGE	A		B		C	
		MIN.	MAX.	MIN.	MAX.	MIN.	MAX.
	12	.694	.699	.730	.735	⅝	⅞
	16	.640	.645	.670	.675	⅝	⅞
ALL	20	.590	.595	.615	.620	⅝	⅞
	28	.528	.532	.550	.555	½	¾
	32						
	.410 BORE		.393	.410	.415*	½	11/16

Salvage .415

Modified Choke

MODEL	GAUGE	A		B		C	
		MIN.	MAX.	MIN.	MAX.	MIN.	MAX.
	12	.715	.720	.730	.735	⅜	⅝
	16	.655	.660	.670	.675	⅜	⅝
ALL	20	.603	.608	.615	.620	⅜	⅝
	28	.541	.544	.550	.555	⅜	⅝
	.410 BORE	.400	.403	.410	.415*	⅜	⅝

Salvage .415

Kemble the credit for the invention of the choke boring. According to him, Kemble tried constricting the muzzle of a 10-gauge barrel he bored, but he had too much constriction and the barrel was overchoked. It shot worse than a straight cylinder. Discouraged, he tried to bore out the "choke" but left a little in. To his surprise and delight, the gun then shot beautiful dense patterns. He discovered what he had done and thereby found the secret of choke. Whether he was the first man or not to choke a gun barrel successfully, he did do much to publicize choke boring. He never patented his idea.

Kemble probably discovered choke boring independently about 1870, but his experiments were preceded by those of an English gunmaker named W. R. Pape, who patented a method of choke boring in 1866. In his patent claim he said that his method was to bore the barrel one size smaller than the gauge wanted. Then he rebored to within one inch or so of the muzzle for the gauge wanted, and finished the choke by tapering from the end of the larger bore to the end of the muzzle. His method produced the type of choke known as "conical," "taper," or "American" choke.

Taper choke is widely used today. One American gun manufacturer has until recently cut all degrees of choke with the same reamer, running it into the muzzle farther for improved cylinder boring, for example, than for modified or full choke. Most of these taper chokes are cut with a slight radius. Whether the radius does the patterns any good or not I cannot say. One engineer with long experience in the shotgun field is doubtful.

Most high-class guns employ another method of choking—a cone followed by a cylindrical portion or "parallel" at the muzzle. This system has been called "standard choke," "English choke," "conical-parallel choke." With fine handmade guns it is the practice to leave the parallel portion of the choke a bit undersize. It gets its final reaming and polishing by cut and try. The barrel borer shoots the gun, looks over the pattern, reams out a bit of choke, shoots it again, reams it until he is satisfied.

In the old days high-class American double guns were individually regulated and to some extent handmade. The customer order-

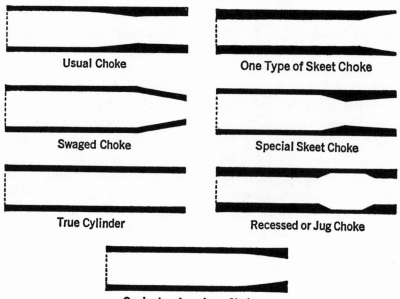

Usual Choke

One Type of Skeet Choke

Swaged Choke

Special Skeet Choke

True Cylinder

Recessed or Jug Choke

Conical or American Choke

These drawings are greatly exaggerated to illustrate the point. Almost all the European guns are choked by the "English" or "conical-parallel" method, but many American guns have been choked by the use of a simple cone cut with a slight radius. Recess choke or "jug choke" is simply a makeshift method of putting a little choke in a gun that for some reason has a cylinder barrel with no choke at all. The purpose of choke is to control pattern—to make it smaller and denser than it would be if thrown from a straight cylinder barrel in most cases, but larger and thinner in the case of some skeet chokes.

ing a high-grade Ithaca, Parker, L. C. Smith, or Winchester Model 21 could specify what pattern he wanted with what load. Then the gun company would do its best to follow directions. One of my pet possessions is a fine custom-made Winchester Model 21 12-gauge gun with two sets of barrels—one set bored Skeet No. 1 and No. 2 and the other marked modified and improved-modified. I picked out the Skeet No. 1 and No. 2 barrels at the factory. I patterned several guns and chose the barrels that gave the widest and evenest patterns. The choke barrels were then made to order and I specified that the right barrel throw a 52 percent pattern with the pheasant load of 3¾ drams of powder and 1¼ ounces of No. 6 shot, and the right barrel 62 percent with the same load. When the gun arrived I took it out and patterned it. The shots from each barrel averaged 54 and 64 percent with No. 6, 56 and 67 percent with No. 4.

With mass-produced guns such meticulous handwork and patterning is of course economically impossible. Most pump and automatic shotguns are not patterned before they leave the factory. One outfit I know of patterns every tenth gun that comes off the assembly line.

Another type of choke is the recess choke. As far as I know, no factory uses it, but it is a makeshift used to put some choke back in barrels that have had all the choke cut off. For this type of choke a recess is cut in the barrel starting about one-half inch back of the muzzle and extending 1½ to 2 inches back toward the breech. This enables the shot column to expand a bit and then compress, and if the job is skillfully done, a straight cylinder barrel patterning from 35 to 40 percent can be turned into an improved cylinder or modified barrel patterning from 45 to as much as 55 percent.

Some skeet chokes are of yet another type. Instead of the conical portion being followed by a parallel, it is followed by a bell. This is supposed to spread the pattern a bit more than would a true cylinder, and actually, as far as I can tell, such patterns are not much different from the straight cylinder ones. A bell reamed in at the muzzle of a straight cylinder barrel is also supposed to spread the pattern a bit.

The variable choke devices employing a cage allow the shot column to expand as in the recess choke and it is then squeezed down by a tube. Variable choke devices of the collet type employ the conical type of choke. Those that use tubes employ the conical-parallel type.

High-grade double guns made in Europe have the choke reamed by the method described by Pape almost a hundred years ago, and the barrels of many repeaters are so reamed. However, within the past few years some of the repeating-shotgun manufacturers have employed another method. The bore of the barrel is left throughout as a straight cylinder, but when the exterior of the barrel is finally turned to contour, the "choke" is left in reverse on the outside at the muzzle. Then the muzzle is put into a die and swedged outside in. A roll-swedging machine is also used for the same thing. These methods are quicker and cheaper than reaming but apparently just as satisfactory. Yet another method long employed for cheap shotguns is simple swedging—reducing the muzzle by forcing it into a conical die. This has long been used for the single-barrel shotguns sold for a few dollars, and it is also the method used to choke the steel liners used in the glass barrels of the Winchester Model 59 automatic.

The choked portion of the shotgun barrel is from 1 to 3 inches in length. Generally the choke portion cut to deliver a full-choke pattern is longer than chokes for improved cylinder and modified patterns. One skilled barrel borer at a major factory told me that the cylindrical portion of the conical-parallel type of choke should be long enough to contain the entire shot charge. For that reason, barrels of magnum 12-gauge shotguns made to handle the 1⅞-ounce charge of the 3-inch magnum shell generally have longer choke portions than barrels choked for standard loads.

According to *The Mysteries of Shotgun Patterns*, by George G. Oberfell and Charles E. Thompson, the shorter the choke portion of the barrel at the muzzle is the less the constriction needed to deliver full-choke or 70 percent patterns. The following table is from their book.

Length of Choked Section Required for 12 Gauge Gun with .729 Bore Diameter	Diameter of Muzzle End of Conical Type Choke for 70 Percent Pattern Efficiency
1.0 inches	.710 inches
1.5 inches	.705 inches
2.0 inches	.700 inches
2.5 inches	.695 inches
3.0 inches	.690 inches
3.5 inches	.685 inches

Their experiments showed that there was nothing to be gained by using a choke section longer than 2½ inches in a conical or taper choke and that with the conical-parallel choke nothing was to be gained with a parallel portion over ½ inch long. This finding is in direct opposition to the testimony of my old barrel borer. Experimenting with chokes varying in length from 4 to 1⅝ inches, they got the densest patterns with a tube with a choke portion 2 inches in length. This tube gave 77 percent patterns.

As a practicing shooting editor, I get many letters requesting an easy way to decide how a shotgun is choked. My correspondents feel that if they but knew it they could apply some magic formula, some measurement that would tell them how their guns would pattern without the tiresome business of shooting the darned thing.

Alas, this is not so.

There is but one way to tell how a gun is bored and that is by what sort of patterns it throws. If it will deliver 70 percent or more of its shot charge in a 30-inch circle at 40 yards, it is a full-choke gun, no matter what the diameter of the muzzle is. A gun that will deliver 60 percent is classified as modified, and one that delivers 45 percent is improved cylinder. One also can order a barrel bored improved-modified (a favorite first barrel for a double to be used at traps) and such a barrel is supposed to give about 65 percent patterns. A quarter choke gives about 50 percent patterns. Skeet No. 1 or "Skeet In" barrels are approximately cylinder choked, and the Skeet No. 2 or "Skeet Out" barrels I have measured and patterned are indistinguishable from modified barrels of the same make.

Long experience with the consuming public has shown gun manufacturers that no one ever protests if his gun patterns more densely than advertised, but that if patterns are less dense than factory specifications, all hell breaks loose. Actually, the average gun buyer does a pretty slipshod job of patterning. A method often used is to put a tin can on a fence post and shoot at it. If by some chance a cluster of shot hits the can and makes it look like the top end of a salt shaker, the gun owner is sure he has a "hard-shooting" gun and he is filled with euphoria. If, on the other hand, his smoothbore puts only two or three shots in the can, he knows why he has been missing those birds and comes bellowing back to the retailer and the retailer sends the gun to the factory. The lads at the factory check the patterning of the gun, find that it delivers around 70 percent, then return it to the retailer. The consumer accepts it with skepticism and from that time on is convinced that his gun is not a "hard shooter" and has barely enough power to knock off a bull butterfly at 50 feet.

It is for this reason that most factories are exceedingly coy about committing themselves as to the patterns their guns will deliver. In the 1950 edition of the *Winchester Ammunition Handbook*, the following specifications for the various types of choke are given:

Full Choke	65–75%
Improved Modified (¾ *choke*)	55–65%
Modified, Skeet No. 2	45–55%
Improved Cylinder (¼ *choke*)	35–45%
Cylinder, Skeet No. 1	25–35%

These claims are modest to the extreme, particularly for the more open borings. It is not uncommon to find barrels marked modified that will pattern around 70 percent, and very often improved-modified barrels will throw dense full-choke patterns. Improved cylinder barrels that throw 50–55 percent patterns are a dime a dozen, and now and then a barrel marked "improved cylinder" will pattern more than 60 percent. Cylinder and skeet barrels often pattern 40 percent or a bit above. Right after the war I ordered a No. 4 grade Ithaca double with two sets of barrels, one bored modified and full and the other (presumably) improved cylinder in both barrels. At skeet I didn't do so well with the improved cylinder barrels. I noticed that if I hit a target it disappeared in a cloud of blue smoke, but when I missed, I missed clean. Finally, I got around to patterning the gun at 20 yards, something I should have done as soon as I got it. Both barrels shot small patterns that averaged about what one would expect from an improved-modified barrel. At 40 yards the barrels averaged almost 70 percent. I returned the gun to the factory, where some of the choke was reamed out. It then threw 50 percent patterns with 1⅛ ounces of No. 9 shot with the left barrel, about 55 percent with the right. These were actually quarter choke and weak modified patterns, excellent for general upland shooting but still too small and dense for short-range skeet shooting.

The British have standarized on a constriction of .040 inch (40 points of choke) for a 12-gauge barrel bored full choke, on 30 points of choke for improved-modified or ¾ choke, 20 points for modified or half choke, and 10 points for improved cylinder or ¼ choke.

American gun manufacturers usually use less constriction. One reason for this is that American factory-loaded shot shells are the world's best and will give denser patterns with less constriction than will foreign shot shells. The old rule of 40 points of choke for a 12-gauge gun bored full choke no longer holds.

After measuring the bore diameter and the muzzle diameter of thousands of guns, Williams Gun Sight Company, which does much shotgun work and installs many thousands of variable choke devices annually, published average figures for three prominent makes of shotguns, as shown in the chart on p. 102.

As the figures in the chart will show, the amounts of constriction put in the barrels by the various manufacturers vary considerably. Browning's modified choke has only 7 points less constriction than Winchester's full choke, which by English standards is about an improved-modified. Any 12-gauge gun with 40 points of constriction is probably overchoked for American ammunition and patterns are generally better if the choke is "relieved" or reamed out. A friend of mine bought an expensive German Merkel, found the full-choke barrel had 40 points of constriction but patterned only 62 percent. He had an intelligent gunsmith work it over by the cut-and-try method. He wound up by reaming 8 points out of the parallel and getting patterns of over 70 percent. Another chap I know bought a beautiful and expensive Belgian double with 26-inch barrels bored improved cylinder. At skeet he shot so poorly with it that he was about to give up the game. Then he patterned the gun and found he was getting patterns that ran over 60 percent. He had some judicious reaming done until he was getting 32-

Below is a chart that has been compiled after checking many thousands of guns. Your barrel might vary from the chart because of the wide variance of bore diameters, and that is just another reason why, if you really want to find just how much choke there is in your gun, you must check the constriction with an inside barrel micrometer. Don't use a dime in the muzzle to get the measurements.

	BROWNING BD–.725	REMINGTON BD–.730	WINCHESTER BD–.725
12 GAUGE			
Full Choke	.687 AC–.038	.694 AC–.036	.669 AC–.031
Modified	.701 AC–.024	.712 AC–.018	.714 AC–.016
Improved Cylinder	.712 AC–.013	.721 AC–.009	.623 AC–.007
Cylinder	.725 AC–.000	.730 AC–.000	.730 AC–.000
16 GAUGE	BD–.665	BD–.673	BD–.664
Full Choke	.628 AC–.037	.640 AC–.003	.633 AC–.031
Modified	.640 AC–.025	.656 AC–.017	.648 AC–.016
Improved Cylinder	.649 AC–.016	.665 AC–.008	.657 AC–.007
Cylinder	.665 AC–.000	.673 AC–.000	.664 AC–.000
20 GAUGE	BD–.611	BD–.619	BD–.614
Full Choke	.578 AC–.033	.590 AC–.029	.587 AC–.027
Modified	.593 AC–.018	.604 AC–.015	.600 AC–.014
Improved Cylinder	.603 AC–.008	.613 AC–.006	.609 AC–.005
Cylinder	.611 AC–.000	.619 AC–.000	.614 AC–.000

BD–Inner Bore Diameter   AC–Amount of Choke

inch patterns at 22 yards. Now he is happy but also wiser. And he makes better scores at skeet.

In its catalog the Williams company writes:

When the hunter or shooter asks the question, "What choke would you suggest that I get in a gun?", the answer cannot be given directly until you find out just to what use the shooter wishes to put the gun. There really is no all-around choke in a standard gun, anymore than there is one club that can be used to play a round of golf. In a 12 gauge gun for skeet we prefer to use a gun that has anywhere from .003 to .004 of choke. For 16 yard trap targets around .020 to .022 in choke. For handicap trap targets usually a gun with about .031 to .037 seems to work out about best. On pats or quail the more open type of gun is preferred, while on pass shooting of ducks or geese a higher degree of choke is desired. In this latter case, however, it is better to have one of the Magnum guns. For pheasants and other upland game the shooter should select the choke that fits his particular case.

Generally speaking, the foreign guns are tighter in choke than our domestic models. We no longer pay much attention to the amount of choke marked on the barrel, whether it is improved cylinder, modified, improved modified, or full, because a choke in any one of the settings is a matter of degree, and very few companies have the same set rule of what constitutes each of the above mentioned chokes. Their own tolerances are considerable, and there is quite a variance even in the same make and model of gun in the various choke markings.

This whole business of constriction is complicated by the fact that the surface of the choke itself has an important bearing on the density of patterns. It would seem reasonable to assume that the choke with a very smooth surface would pattern better than one with a rough surface. Actually, just the opposite is true.

I first learned of this phenomenon from the late E. Field White, the inventor of the Poly Choke. His theory was that when the choke is glass-smooth the wads are not retarded, smash into the rear of the shot column, and scatter the shot. On the other hand, if the surface of the choke is roughed up, the lighter wads are retarded, lag behind the shot charge, do not smash into the shot column, and do not disperse the patterns.

He also told me that it is possible to get full-choke patterns from a cylinder barrel if the barrel is long enough and a bit rough. The greater friction of the wads in the long barrel causes them, he told me, to lag behind the shot. Such a barrel will throw dense patterns, he said, and this is the basis for the widely held belief that the longer the barrel is, the tighter the patterns, and the greater the killing range.

It is common for pattern efficiency to fall off in trap guns that have been shot thousands of times until the choke portion of the barrel has been polished glass-smooth by the passage of the shot. Patterns are then brought back to full choke by roughening up the choke portion with emery cloth or by some other means. An engineer who was formerly the head of the department of research and development of one of the major manufacturers tells me that he found the condition of the surface of the choke to be almost as important in getting tight patterns as the amount of constriction. Experiments by Oberfell and Thompson verify the necessity for a slight roughness of the choke for the best patterns.

It is generally believed by shotgun users that if they shop around and try various makes of shot shells in their guns, they will find one brand that will perform better than the others. Oberfell and Thompson found that this was not true, that a barrel that threw good patterns with one make of American ammunition did about as well as with another. However, shot shells which use the protective plastic collars around the shot charges usually give denser patterns.

Yet, it is true that most barrels seem to prefer one size of shot to others. A 12-gauge pump bored full choke that I had would pattern a bit over 70 percent with 1¼ ounces of No. 4, slightly under with No. 6, but only about 65 percent with a 1¼ ounces of No. 7½. A 16-gauge double, bored improved cylinder and modified, would pattern less than 40 percent with the open barrel if the maximum load of 1⅛ ounces of No. 6 was used. But with the trap load of No. 8, patterns went about 50 percent.

Generally speaking, almost any barrel will pattern very well with the light trap loads. Guns will throw denser patterns with copper-plated shot than they will with ordinary shot because the plated shot is harder and fewer pellets are deformed. With heavy loads, most barrels pattern better with large shot than with small, probably for the same reason.

In spite of many claims to the contrary, any barrel that will *consistently* deliver 70 percent patterns is a very good full-choke barrel. Barrels which consistently pattern 75 percent are rare and barrels that pattern 80 percent and above are just about non-existent and in a class with the featherweight sporting rifle that will always shoot ¾-inch groups. When the proud rifle owner says that he has a light sporter that shoots ¾-inch groups, he means that he once shot a ¾-inch group with it, and when the shotgunner says he has a gun that patterns 80 percent, he means that he once shot an 80 percent pattern.

Most American gun manufacturers are now using less constriction to obtain wanted patterns than they did formerly. As we have seen, a 12-gauge gun with 40 points of constriction is probably overchoked for modern ammunition and would shoot better if the choke were "relieved" or reamed out. This phenomenon is often seen with variable choke devices of the collet type. Set at full choke these gadgets often deliver considerably less dense patterns than when they are set at modified. I had a 16-gauge pump at one time. It was equipped with a Poly Choke. Set at full, it patterned about 60 to 65 percent, but set at modified it patterned around 70 percent.

Individual patterns may vary 10 or 15 percent from shot to shot, so an average of at least ten shots should be taken. The old dime test which is part of American folklore is utterly without value. The bore diameters of 12-gauge shotguns can vary from .719 to .740. The same amount of constriction in the two barrels would allow a dime to drop through one muzzle but not the other, yet both would shoot 70 percent patterns.

Two barrels with the same bore diameter and the same amount of constriction at the muzzle may produce very different patterns because of the different length and angle of the choke and because of the condition of its surface.

Barrels marked improved cylinder often give modified patterns and it is routine for barrels marked modified to pattern between 65 and 70 percent. Modern fast-burning powders have improved patterns. So have the new types of wads which seal off the powder gases and keep them out of the shot column, and so do frangible top wads and wadless (pie) crimps. Plated shot improves patterns, as do the protective collars used in Winchester Mark 5 and Remington ammunition with the "Power Piston." In the summer of 1964, Federal Cartridge Company also introduced a plastic shot protector.

Selecting the Choke

One fall I hunted pheasants for a few days in California's Sacramento Valley. The first day I used barrels bored Skeet No. 1 and No. 2 on a Model 21 Winchester 12 gauge. The year before at the same club I had hunted along sloughs choked with cattails. Hardworking Labs had booted the birds out and shots were at from 15 to 25 yards. I had done fairly well, but I had decided that if I had used barrels that were more open, I'd have done better. The next year we hunted another area. Shots were longer—at from 30 to almost 40 yards. Shooting the Skeet No. 1 barrel first, I didn't kill a single bird stone dead. One bird I would have sworn was knocked cold ran when it hit the ground and the dogs didn't recover it.

From that time on I switched to barrels bored modified and improved-modified. I didn't kill all the birds I shot at, but every bird I hit was stone dead. The last day, shooting in a big rice field at a private club, I killed nine birds with eleven shots. That isn't the best shooting I have ever done, nor yet the worst; but the point is that I either missed those birds or dumped them cold. One miss was at close range and I would probably have nailed it with the skeet barrel. The other bird was the second of an attempted double. Two cocks got up out of the rice stubble together. One went northwest, the other straight south. I dumped the first bird, whirled and missed the second. I was probably tangled up in my own feet, shot behind. The degree of choke I was using had nothing to do with it.

Earlier during the hunting season I was out after pheasants with a 20-gauge double bored modified and full but I blundered into a thicket that was crawling with California valley quail. Shots were as close as 10 feet and few were farther than 15 yards. At this short range, patterns were so small and dense that it was almost like trying to hit the birds with a rifle. I managed to connect with one bird that flashed across an opening in front of me. When I picked him up, his head was gone but there were no shot in the body. I managed to get ten birds, but with pretty heavy expenditure of ammunition, and most of the birds I picked up were pretty badly mangled.

Not long before I wrote this, I shot a couple of rounds of skeet with a young physician friend of mine. He is an experienced and good field shot but he has shot little skeet. He was using an automatic with a full-choke 12-gauge barrel. He broke a 15 and a 16 out of 25. He either missed his targets clean or they vanished in a cloud of black smoke. This was the first skeet I had shot in almost a

PELLETS WITHIN 30 INCH CIRCLE AT 40 YARDS

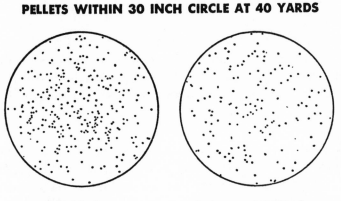

Full Choke　　　　**Improved Cylinder**

The difference between patterns thrown by various degrees of choke is that the open chokes throw wider, thinner patterns.

—*courtesy Browning Arms Co.*

year. I managed to miss the high-house birds at stations 1, 2, and 3 each time. Then I settled down and broke the rest for two 22s. Few of my birds were smoked, but the big pattern definitely broke them. If my friend had been using a bit more pattern he would have scored in the 20s.

Choosing the right degree of choke for the business in hand is an important part of wing shooting. Anyone using a full-choke gun for close range shooting misses a lot of birds he would hit with a wider pattern, and he mangles many birds that would have been good on the table with less shot in them. Anyone using too open a pattern at long range will cripple birds he would have dumped nicely if he had hit them with more shot.

All of this wind in the willows has been included only to show that measuring the hole in the end of the shotgun barrel is not a very good way to determine the pattern percentage one will get out at 40 yards. As we have seen, the stamped designation on the barrel (IMP CYL, MOD, OR FULL) is a better indication but by no means perfect. Different manufacturers have different notions as to how an improved-cylinder or a modified barrel should pattern.

Actually, this business of percentage of shot delivered into a 30-inch circle at 40 yards is only a convenient device for measurement and for practical purposes is relatively meaningless. What should be of primary interest to the gunner is the size of the pattern with which he has to work—and the ranges at which he actually kills his birds.

For the sake of comparison, patterns are taken in a 30-inch circle at 40 yards, but far more game is killed at under 40 yards than over. Most gunners tend to think of a shotgun as a long-range weapon, when it is not. They tend to judge their guns by the patterns thrown at 40 yards and farther instead of by the evenness of shot distribution and the width of the pattern at average range.

The choice of the degree of choke depends on the game on which the gun is to be used and the conditions under which it is shot. The man who hunts bobwhite quail, which usually lie very tight and flush at the feet, needs less constriction and a wider pattern than the chap who hunts the wilder-flushing Gambel's and scaled quail of the West. The man who hunts quail, woodcock, and ruffed grouse in the brush needs a wider pattern than the man who shoots in open stubble fields and grasslands. In addition, the fast shot needs less choke than the slow, deliberate shot.

I once knew a very fine performer on Gambel's quail in Arizona who hunted with a Parker trap gun bored full choke in both barrels. I am not the fastest shot that ever lived but with that *escopeta* I would have chewed those birds to pieces. For him it was just right. He shot as deliberately as if he had been using a rifle and it was seldom that he dropped a bird at under 40 yards. With that gun and with that timing, he would have looked pretty bad on grouse or woodcock in the brush, but on mourning doves and desert quail he and his hard-shooting gun made a wicked combination.

Another acquaintance of mine can nail two birds while I am thinking about shooting one. Taking pheasants over a dog, he kills them almost on the end of the barrel. This chap does his upland gunning with a pump bored Skeet No. 1.

Obviously, the larger the pattern the easier it is to hit with. It is also obvious that the pattern with a wide spread at short range thins out more quickly than does the pattern that is small and dense at short range.

Here is a table taken from Maj. Gerald Burrard's work, *The Modern Shotgun*, giving the spread of the whole shot charge at various ranges:

Degree of Choke	\ Range in Yards						
	10	15	20	25	30	35	40
Cylinder	19	26	32	38	44	51	57
Improved Cylinder	15	20	26	32	38	44	51
Half Choke (Modified)	12	16	20	26	32	38	46
Full Choke	9	12	16	21	26	32	40

While we are at it, at 6 feet the bulk of the shot pellets from a cylinder bore are dispersed in a pattern 2¼ inches wide and from a full choke, 1½ inches. This concentration of shot at very close range makes the shotgun one of the deadliest of all firearms at a few feet. It is said that if a hunter is armed with a shotgun and buckshot, and that if he is cool enough to point his gun right and to hold his fire until the last moment, he is safe even from a charging lion. I once killed a whitetail buck at very short range with a shotgun and No. 7½ shot. The entrance hole was about 3 inches in diameter.

At 45 yards a shot charge from a full-choke gun will spread out to about 48 inches and at 50 yards to about 60 inches. A modified pattern will cover about 54 inches and at 50 yards about

66 inches. At that range the coverage of an improved cylinder is enormous—something that explains why so many birds are hit at long range with an improved cylinder but so few are killed.

Some types of shooting demand the widest possible spread. Shooting quail, woodcock, and grouse in the brush is one of them. Obviously, it is far easier to hit a bird at 20 yards with the 32-inch pattern from a cylinder or skeet bore than with a 16-inch pattern from a full-choke barrel. That most popular of all American shotgun targets, the cottontail rabbit, is also generally shot at very close range and the more pattern thrown at him the better.

The game of skeet is also a close-range business calling for plenty of pattern. Most targets are broken at 20 to 25 yards and some are broken much closer. Many effective skeet guns are simply old pumps or automatics with all the choke removed by sawing off the barrel behind the choke. Some barrels bored Skeet No. 1 or simply marked "Skeet" are weak improved cylinders with a few points (4 to 8) constriction, but some are bored with a bell at the muzzle. Skeet borings differ greatly. Some skeet guns throw patterns that are indistinguishable from those thrown by straight cylinder borings. Others give rather tight improved-cylinder patterns.

For some shooting, even the relatively wide patterns of the skeet or cylinder bore give patterns too small. Somewhat larger patterns can be obtained by several means. One Missouri quail hunter imported a Belgian double with one barrel bored straight cylinder and the other rifled at the muzzle. He reported great success with it. A chap I know owns such a gun. I borrowed it and patterned it. The rifling did definitely spread out the patterns at short range.

Wider patterns can also be obtained in a modified or full-choke barrel by using "brush" or "scatter" loads. In these the shot charge is separated by cardboard partitions. In the early days of skeet, all boxes of skeet loads contained two of these scatter shells. They were to be used on the targets shot at the No. 8 station, which come directly toward the gunner and which are broken at a range of a few feet. I understand that a Belgium loading company puts up shells loaded with cubical shot in order to obtain greater dispersion and wider patterns.

If *all* shooting were to be done within 30 yards and a shot seldom taken at over 25 yards, anyone would be foolish to use any boring but straight cylinder or Skeet No. 1. The wide patterns enable one to get by with fairly sloppy holding and at short ranges turn fair shots into crack shots. The first time I ever used a Skeet No. 1 boring on birds was about twenty-five years ago in southern Arizona. I found a spot in a mesquite forest where the doves were coming over fast and low and I seldom had a shot at over 30 yards. When I used the open bore, I had misgivings and planned to switch if I found myself wounding. But I left the skeet barrels on all afternoon and never shot better in my life. A dove, though, is an easy bird to bring down, and will fall and stay put with a hit that would enable a quail to escape.

For most upland gunning, the improved cylinder with its denser, slightly smaller pattern is a better bet. A good barrel so bored will throw a 26-inch pattern at 20 yards and a 32-inch pattern at 25 yards. It is deadly to about 35 yards, and at that distance it is, with its 44-inch pattern, easy to hit with. Some guns bored improved cylinder actually give weak modified or quarter-choke patterns (50 to 55 percent) and will kill nicely to 40 yards. A gun which will deliver 50 percent patterns at 40 yards is an exceedingly useful instrument and will do for about 90 percent of all shooting. But, alas, such a barrel is difficult to come by.

With its 35-yard range an improved cylinder is to be selected for all-around upland gunning. It will double very nicely at skeet, and it is deadly on ducks and geese coming into decoys within 35 yards. Thicken up the patterns with the 2¾-inch 12-gauge magnum loads with 1½ ounces of shot, and an improved cylinder becomes a 40-yard gun. BUT the improved cylinder is no boring for the slow shot who rides his birds out. However, if reaction time is fairly fast an improved-cylinder boring will turn a fair shot into a good one, a good one into a crackerjack.

The most versatile and useful of all borings is modified or "half choke." Modified is supposed to give a 60 percent pattern, and barrels so bored have from 14 to 18 points of choke in 12 gauge as bored in this country. With some loads an occasional gun so bored will pattern close to 70 percent, but the most useful modified patterns run 55 to 60 percent. Most gunners will do better at 16-yard rise trapshooting with a barrel bored modified than with one bored full.

With an ounce of shot in a 20 gauge, a modified barrel will kill to at least 35 yards and often to 40. In a 16 or a 12 gauge with 1¼ ounces, and modified will kill to 45 with the right size of shot for the particular bird. At 40 yards, all the shot thrown by a good modified barrel will be contained in a 46-inch circle—a bit larger than the 4-inch pattern of the full choke. However, at that distance the modified barrel is much easier to kill with because the shot are pretty evenly distributed, whereas with the full choke the center is dense, the edges thin. Most gunners will kill cleaner with a modified—and probably kill farther.

For the one-gun average man who uses a pump or automatic on everything from quail to geese, modified is the boring to be selected. He'll kill just as far with it as with a full choke, wound less game, make more hits. It is also the proper boring for the second barrel of the upland double and for the first barrel of the double used on ducks. Most trapshooters will do better at 16-yard rise with a barrel bored modified than they will with a full choke. Full choke is for pass-shooting at waterfowl and for use in trapshooting at handicap or for the second barrel at doubles. Full choke has no place in the uplands and little place in shooting over decoys.

Notions as to killing range vary, but one American manufacturer, after extensive experimenting, concluded that it takes five No. 4 shot to make a clean kill on a duck the size of a mallard. With a full-choke gun of whatever gauge patterning 70 percent, they estimate that the sure killing range is 43 yards with 1 ounce of shot, 46 with 1⅛, 49 with 1¼, and 55 with 1½. Even with the 3-inch 12-gauge magnum handling 1⅞ ounces of shot, the *sure* killing range isn't much over 60 yards.

Choosing the proper amount of choke is an important part of good shotgun shooting, be it with an integral choke or one of the various choke devices. Some shooting, as we have seen, demands all the spread the gunner can possibly get—and some the densest pattern possible. In general, it is a good rule to use the widest pattern that will give a clean kill at the average maximum range. The upland gunner who uses an improved cylinder and never shoots at beyond 35 yards will have a far better record than the chap who uses a full choke and shoots at everything he sees. Another good rule is: When in doubt use modified. With its fairly wide patterns, its generally good shot distribution, and its excellent range, a modified, or 55 to 60 percent pattern is the most useful of all chokes.

The following table shows the approximate amount of constriction ordinarily used at the muzzle by one manufacturer to give the several well-known degrees of choke boring:

Gauge	Boring	Bore Diameter	Muzzle Diameter	Constriction	% at 40 yds. in 30-in. circle
10	Full Choke	.775	.740	.035	70
	Modified	.775	.758	.017	60
	Imp. Cyl.	.775	.768	.007	50
	Cylinder	.775	.775	None	40
12	Full Choke	.725	.695	.030	70
	Modified	.725	.710	.015	60
	Imp. Cyl.	.725	.719	.006	50
	Cylinder	.725	.725	None	40
16	Full Choke	.662	.638	.024	70
	Modified	.662	.650	.012	60
	Imp. Cyl.	.662	.657	.005	50
	Cylinder	.662	.662	None	40
20	Full Choke	.615	.594	.021	70
	Modified	.615	.605	.010	60
	Imp. Cyl.	.615	.611	.004	50
	Cylinder	.615	.615	None	40
28	Full Choke	.550	.533	.017	70
	Modified	.550	.542	.008	60
	Imp. Cyl.	.550	.547	.003	50
	Cylinder	.550	.550	None	40
.410 Bore	Full Choke	.410	.396	.014	70[1]
	Modified	.410	.405	.005	60
	Imp. Cyl.	.410	.408	.002	50
	Cylinder	.410	.410	None	40

[1] Percentages for .410 gauge obtained at 25 yds.

Percentage in 30-in. Circle at 40 yds.
from Patterns Actually Fired

Gauge		Marked	Percent	Loads	
12		Imp. Cyl.	66	1¼	#7
12		Modified	71	1¼	#7½
20		Modified	69	⅞ oz.	#8
12 ⎫		Full	78	1¼	#7½
12 ⎪ same		Full	80	1¼	#6
12 ⎪ barrel		Full	80	1¼	#4
12 ⎭		Full	85	1¼	#7
12		Modified	80	1¼	#6
12		Imp. Cyl.	71	1⅛	#8
.410		Modified	92 (at 25 yds.)	¾ oz.	#9
12		Modified	67	1¼	#7½
12		Skeet No. 2	57	1⅛	#7½
20		Imp. Cyl.	46	1	#7½
12		Skeet No. 1	36	1⅛	#8

The above percentages of single patterns actually fired would tend to show that guns do not always pattern the way they are marked, and that with the new kind of ammunition they pattern much closer than they are marked. These are *not* averages. They are simply patterns fired at random.

CHAPTER 9

The Variable Choke Devices

PUTTING a gimmick on the end of a shotgun barrel to vary the degree of choke is a very good idea—and a very old one. The Roper choke, tubes with various degrees of constriction, were used on repeaters at the turn of the century. The ends of the barrels were threaded for the device, and the tubes were screwed on. I have seen pictures of the gadget but I have never laid eyes on one in the flesh. How many tubes were furnished I have no idea.

The modern variable choke device is something over forty years old. There are two main types. One obtains the difference in degrees of choke by interchangeable tubes. This type, basically the same idea as the old Roper choke, was developed by Colonel Cutts of the U. S. Marine Corps. He sold the idea to the Lyman Gun Sight Company, and this firm has been making the Cutts Compensator ever since. The other type of variable choke device is the adjustable collet, which can be squeezed down or opened up to vary the patterns. This type was worked out by the late E. Field White, a mechanical engineer who made a fortune in the automobile industry and who developed and manufactured this device late in life. As far as I know, the term "variable choke device," which is now universally used, is my own invention. I may be wrong about this but I cannot remember seeing the term used prior to my own use of it in *Outdoor Life* in the late 1930s.

Patents on the Cutts Comp and the Poly Choke have now expired, and various manufacturers have turned out similar choke devices. Sometimes tube and collet are combined with a ventilated "cage" which diverts the powder gases and reduces recoil to some extent. The Poly Choke is made in both ventilated and solid form, and the Cutts Comp can be purchased with an adjustable collet which can be screwed into the cage and used instead of a tube. The Weaver Choke, now no longer made, was turned out by W. R. Weaver, the scope manufacturer, and was like the Cutts Comp in

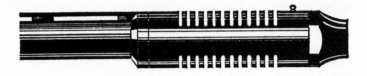

Lyman's Cutts Compensator with skeet tube attached.

that it consisted of a ventilated cage equipped with baffles. The cage was threaded to the end of the barrel, and the various tubes, to give different degrees of choke, were screwed into it. The POWer PAC, made by the Pachmayr Gun Works of Los Angeles, was of the same type, but the tubes extended back into the cage and picked up the shot charge there. This device has been discontinued.

A talking point of the Cutts Comp, the obsolete Weaver Choke, and POWer PAC is that the tubes squeeze down and control the shot charge after some of the pressure has been taken off of it by the diversion of the gases to the side. The Ventilated Poly Choke, on the other hand, diverts the gases *after* the shot charge has passed through the collet. Both schemes seem to work well.

The Simmons Choke, sold for a year or two by Simmons Specialties of Kansas City, Missouri, consists of three tubes which can be screwed into a short adapter-sleeve attached to the barrel. One tube gives a slight degree of choke; another, patterns that are about modified; and the last tube is supposed to give full-choke patterns.

Winchester's "Win-Choke" consists of tubes of various diameters to control patterns screwed into the muzzles of Model 1200 pumps.

In addition to the chokes of the tube-and-collet type, some devices have been made that change the degree of choke automatically. One of the first was the Jarvis Choke, now no longer manufactured. It would change with successive shots from cylinder, to modified, to full. All this sounds like a splendid idea but the device was heavy, complicated, and expensive. It never caught on and is now no longer made. Poly Choke made for a time a device which would change the degree of choke automatically, but this has been discontinued.

An interesting device for the gadget-loving American shooter was the Adjustomatic Choke made by the Hartford Gun Choke Company, the maker of the Cyclone Choke which is similar to the Poly Choke. The Adjustomatic had six choke settings marked on a rotating sleeve. To operate the automatic changing, a button underneath is pressed and a spring pushes the choke to the rear in its most "open" position. When the gun is fired, the device is carried forward, contracting the choke fingers by means of a collar. There are three settings available—the C-I (cylinder and improved cylinder), I-M (improved cylinder-modified), and M-F (modified-full). With the device set for C-I, the second shot will be fired at I-M. In addition, the device could be set to stay at any degree of choke.

The collet-type choke devices have been, on the whole, more popular than those of the tube type. Partly, this is because the degree of choke is more easily changed with this type of choke—a mere "twist of the wrist," as the Poly Choke company used to advertise. Another reason is the long-continued and convincing advertising campaign that the Poly Choke company under E. Field White put on. He advertised nine degrees of choke (something which is open to argument) and he advertised better and more consistent patterns (something which is also open to argument) but the customers were convinced and had Poly Chokes fitted to their guns by the thousands.

The Herter Company of Waseca, Minnesota, makes two collet-type chokes, one with a ventilated sleeve and one without. These are very similar in essentials to the corresponding Poly Chokes. The same can be said of the Cyclone Choke made by the Hartford Gun Choke Company. Mossberg makes a collet-type choke called the C-Lect Choke for shotguns of its manufacture, and the Savage-Stevens combine also turns out a choke of this type for its shotguns. High Standard had its own variable choke device and for a time manufactured its version of the POWer PAC. An Italian auto-

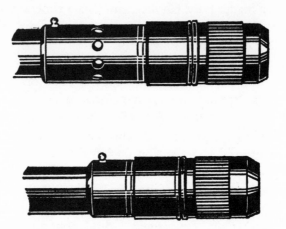

Lyman collet-type chokes ("Lymanchoke").
TOP: with "recoil chamber"; BOTTOM: without.

matic, the Breda, comes equipped with a series of tubes giving various degrees of constriction.

The various choke devices have real advantages. The most obvious, of course, is that they permit changing the degree of choke and consequently the size and density of the pattern delivered. Another is that the owner of a pump or automatic shotgun can have a variable choke device installed to give him any barrel length he wishes. The gadgets also permit choke to be put into barrels which either have lost their choke portion through some accident or have never had any, as is the case with the riot guns widely sold as surplus. With riot guns the length of the choke device is an advantage, too, as the 20-inch barrels of these guns are too short for good balance. A relatively light 12-gauge repeater equipped with a variable choke device is a good and inexpensive approach to the all-around gun. With such a weapon one can shoot skeet, quail, doves, ducks—just about anything. The cost is a fraction of what one would have to pay for a good double with two sets of barrels.

Still, it must be admitted that those who own guns equipped with variable choke devices do not use the adjustable feature nearly as much as they think they are going to. Beginners, particularly, are fascinated by this "nine degrees of choke" business, just as they are fascinated by the adjustable feature of variable power rifle scopes. They fancy themselves casting a judicious eye over the covert and changing the choke settings in the field as the occasion arises. Actually, they seldom do. The upland hunter sets his gadget at improved cylinder or thereabouts and leaves it there. The pheasant hunter probably uses modified. The duck hunter usually uses the full-choke setting and lets it go at that. It would seem both logical and sensible for the hunter to adjust his choke to a more open setting when he is about to enter brush territory where the shots will be short. It would be logical, but he simply doesn't do it.

The variable choke devices have their shortcomings as well as their virtues. One of the main objections is the installation. Some of them have been put on by all manner of gunsmiths. Some of the jobs have been poorly done, and it is not unknown to see one of the gadgets go sailing off into the wild blue yonder. Another fault is that the devices are larger than the plain barrels. As a consequence, anyone who shoots by lining up the front bead on one of the gadgets with the receiver will often find that his gun patterns low.

This low shooting can be corrected by giving the barrel a slight upward bend to bring the pattern to point of aim. Thirty years ago, one choke manufacturer said in his literature that this bending of the barrels was necessary and was done routinely when his chokes were installed. This drove the customers mad. He changed the phrasing to "straightening" the barrel and then everyone was happy. But, alas and alack, many a choke device is put on without bending, straightening, or anything else and often a gun so equipped will shoot low, to the right, to the left, or in some other direction. All of this saddens the handful of customers who are actually smart enough to pattern their guns. If I have had one letter of complaint about this over the years, I have had a thousand.

Another objection to the variable choke devices is that it is doubtful if any of them improve the looks of a gun. This is something that anyone can get used to, and I for one have no objection to the looks of the gadgets. However, some gun lovers loathe all of them.

Yet another objection is that those with ventilated cages, although they reduce recoil to some extent, increase muzzle blast and make it unpleasant for any shooter standing alongside a gun so equipped. Many shooters dislike the sharp crack given by the diverted gases, even when they are behind the gun. For this reason, trapshooters object to shooting on a squad with anyone using a gun with a ventilated cage. Variable choke devices are almost never seen in trapshooting.

Bore diameters of shotguns vary to some extent even in guns of the same make and they vary considerably from make to make. Therefore a collet device or a tube will give different patterns when installed on barrels of various diameters. Some outfits ream barrels to give uniform dimensions before the installation of the devices. Other outfits make the gadgets of various sizes to be fitted to barrels with different diameters.

The W. R. Weaver Company found the sales of the excellent Weaver Choke falling off years ago. Bill Weaver decided to stop advertising his choke and to concentrate his advertising instead on his scopes. Manufacture of the Weaver Choke was finally discontinued in, I believe, 1961. Another variable choke device that has bitten the dust is the Shooting Master, a collet-type choke that was made in Massachusetts. Ken Richards, who manufactured it, died along about 1958 or 1959 and his business was liquidated. As I have written above, the Jarvis Choke did not long survive. When I wrote the first edition of this book, the variable choke devices had pretty well lost their onetime popularity. They are in even worse shape today. Some worked well but, as we have seen, many of them were put on so poorly that they made the gun shoot cockeyed, and none of them patterned any better than a good comparable "solid" choke. Today the Cutts Compensator is still manufactured, as is the Poly Choke. The Emsco·Choke made at Waseca, Minnesota, the home of George Leonard Herter, sounds to me like a spin-off of the Herter Vari-Choke, a device very similar to the Poly Choke. The Win-Choke is factory-installed only on the Winchester Model 1200. The blackest mark against the devices has been poor installation.

For what it is worth, my experience has been that the choke devices employing tubes tend to give better wide-open patterns for skeet and for upland shooting than do the collet-type chokes. The tube chokes also have given me denser full-choke patterns. However, a collet-type choke properly installed is handy, easy to adjust, and gives a useful range of patterns from improved cylinder to generally about improved-modified. Of these I prefer the plain to the ventilated type because of its neater appearance and also because I do not care for the sharp muzzle blast.

Some pretty fruity stuff has been written about the excellence of the patterns delivered by some of the choke devices, but I have not found that they pattern any better than equivalent integral chokes and often not as well. It is true that the devices employing ventilated cages reduce recoil, but recoil reduction is accomplished at the expense of unpleasant muzzle blast.

It is a curious thing that many people who have been shooting shotguns for years and have never patterned them, very often pattern their guns when they get them equipped with variable choke devices. Sometimes they find that no matter how they adjust the choke they get about the same sort of pattern. They also find on occasion that their guns shoot low or off toward the old Finnegan place. Then there is a fearful howl. There are lemons among choke devices, just as there are lemons among automobiles.

The best variable choke device is no better than its installation, and some jobs of putting on these muzzle devices have been very sad indeed. Probably the best way to get one installed is to have the job done by a good, properly equipped, and conscientious local gunsmith. Then if any bugs develop, the customer has his worthy smith close at hand. The poorest way to get one of the gadgets put on is to turn it over to some jackleg gunsmith without the necessary knowledge and equipment. Unfortunately, good, well-equipped, and conscientious gunsmiths, like beautiful women, good cooks, and skillful writers, are not found behind every briery bush. Fortunately, most of the rash of self-nominated gunsmiths who set up business after the last war have gone back to repairing lawn mowers and driving trucks but there are still some lulus at large. If there is any doubt, the customer should send the gun back to the manufacturer of the choke device for installation—but even then some of the jobs are by no means perfect.

Since modern powders develop just about their full velocity in 22 to 24-inch barrels, the man getting a choke device installed can write his own ticket as far as barrel length is concerned. I see no point whatsoever in an overall length on a pump or automatic of over 26 inches, since a repeater with a 26-inch barrel has about the same butt-to-muzzle measurement as a double with a 30-inch barrel. Actually, for upland shooting with a repeater, I like an overall barrel length of 24 inches and some bold souls are having Poly Chokes fitted to give an overall barrel length of only 22 inches. They swear by them.

The man with several guns; the man with a pump or automatic with two barrels, one bored improved cylinder, let us say, and one bored modified or full; the man with a double with two sets of barrels—none of these has much use for a variable choke device. These gadgets, however, are a great boon to the man who wants to use one gun and one barrel for everything. A light 12, a 16, or a 20-gauge magnum equipped with a properly installed and properly functioning variable choke device has the nearest thing to an all-around gun yet invented.

CHAPTER 10

Patterning

Your Shotgun

FOR years writers on firearms have been needling their readers
to sight in their big-game and varmint rifles, to shoot them at targets, and to find out where the bullets are going and make correc-
tions. I don't know how many times I as a practicing gun editor
have pointed out that just because a rifle was presumably sighted in
at the factory, it could not be taken for granted that the factory
expert held it the way the ultimate buyer does, or that he used the
same kind of ammunition and the same bullet weight.

That preaching has gradually sunk in. There are still careless
fellows who never shoot their deer rifles at paper targets, but they
are a much smaller segment of the hunting population than they
were a few years ago. The great majority of shotgun users, on the
other hand, never in their lives pattern a shotgun, and thus have no
real idea of its performance. Now and then some of them will take
a pop at a tomato can or a piece of writing paper tacked to a fence
post. Such shooting teaches them nothing about their guns but
they let it go at that. In a way I do not blame them, since the
proper patterning of a shotgun is a laborious chore. I have done a

lot of it, and I should have done more, because many are the lessons it teaches.

The man who spends a morning with his favorite scatter gun, a variety of loads, wide sheets of paper, and something to pin them to will be well rewarded. He may find that his gun isn't shooting to point of aim at all, or that his presumably full-choke gun throws so thin a pattern at 40 yards with the load he has been using that hitting a bird the size of a mallard would be only an accident.

One good way of preparing a patterning setup is to get a roll of butcher's or wrapping paper 48 inches wide, cut it into 48-inch squares, and tack the squares to a suitable frame as you need them. Lumber for such a frame recently cost me $1.65, a sum which shouldn't break anyone. Most skeet and trap clubs have patterning frames, and anyone who has access to one is in luck. An outfit in California makes 32-inch patterning charts with a 15-inch circle inside a 30-inch circle. One sheet has life-size drawings of a quail and a mallard duck for the guidance of the gunner who is studying killing patterns. Another sheet has the 15-inch inner circle filled with side views of clay targets to assist the skeet or trapshooter in evaluating his pattern at various ranges. These sheets are very handy if the gun shoots where it looks and if one is able to center the pattern in the 30-inch circle. Alas, though, many shotguns shoot low or high or to port or starboard.

Yet another way is to use a sheet of iron 5 feet square. This is painted with a mixture of lard oil and white lead. The patterns are shot, inscribed, then painted out with a brush and another pattern shot. This is a convenient method, since the sheets of iron do not blow down, but it is quite a production for the casual pattern shooter.

The standard way of taking patterns is to shoot at a sufficiently wide sheet of paper at 40 yards, then to inscribe a 30-inch circle that will enclose the most shot holes. Next, one counts the number of holes within the circle and compares the total on a percentage basis with the total number of shot in the charge. It is wise to open a shell and pattern the number of pellets in a charge, as pellet sizes differ slightly from make to make.

Patterns for 20, 16, and 12-gauge guns are taken at 40 yards.

Those for .410s are taken at 30 yards. Loading companies give varying standards, according to degree of choke, but the usually accepted figures are about like this:

Full choke, 70–80 percent; improved-modified, 65 percent; modified or Skeet No. 2, 55–60 percent; quarter choke, 50 percent; improved cylinder, 45 percent; cylinder and Skeet No. 1, 35–40 percent.

These figures are open to considerable debate, and many gunmakers will maintain that it's cutting things too fine to list improved-modified or quarter choke. They hold that shells from the same box, shot through the same barrel, may very well make a full-choke pattern one time, an improved-modified the next, and a modified somewhere in the course of the string. What really counts, if you want to classify your choke, is the *average* pattern of five shots—or still better, of ten shots.

Suppose then, that our first chore is to classify the choke we have with the shells we ordinarily use. We start out by shooting five patterns at five big sheets of paper, listing the pertinent data on each, for example: Remington Model 1100, 12 gauge, 28-inch barrel, marked full choke, 40 yards; Remington Nitro Express, 1¼ ounces of No. 6.

Then, when we have our five sheets, we can inscribe the 30-inch circle to enclose the most shot on each. It is then helpful to quarter the circle and count the shot holes in each quarter, checking off each hole with a pencil. Then the four totals are added to give you the grand total in the circle. (It is also interesting to compare the number of shot in each quarter. If the gun patterns well, each segment should have approximately the same number.)

As an example, take a pattern I recently made. It came out as follows: 54, 41, 52, 52; total, 199.

It was made at 40 yards with Western Super X, 1¼ ounces of No. 6 shot. Since there are 279 shot in that charge, I divide 199 by 279 to obtain the precentage. Result is 71 percent, which is, of course, a full-choke pattern. Curious thing in this instance is that the barrel is marked modified. But of that, more later.

This 30-inch circle at 40 yards is only an arbitrary standard, and a rather unfortunate one, because 90 percent of all game is killed at shorter ranges than the 40 yards at which most guns are patterned. That includes wildfowl too!

What pays off, then, is not the pattern delivered at 40 yards, but the pattern delivered at shorter ranges, where game is actually killed.

Anyone who really wants to know how effective his shotgun is

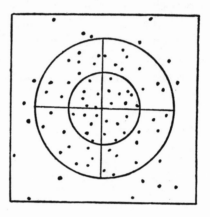

It helps to quarter the 30-inch circle drawn around the greatest number of shot, then to inscribe an inner 15-inch circle. Shot in four quarters should be nearly equal. In full-choke pattern, shot should be concentrated in center.

should not stop with patterning it at 40 yards. He should also shoot at 10, 20, and 30 yards. If he does he will really have his eyes opened.

On countless occasions I have seen good shots miss a quail or even a pheasant at 10 yards and kick themselves for being stupid, maladroit dolts with hardly enough co-ordination of eye and muscle to scratch themselves. (I have done such missing myself!) And I have seen these same men cut down a straightaway pheasant at 40 yards and congratulate themselves as being rather wicked shotgun pointers.

But what about it? Let's say our shooter had a full-choke gun. At 10 yards he probably had a pattern about 8 inches wide, whereas at

40 yards he had a killing pattern perhaps 36 inches wide. The close "easy" shot was far more difficult! Hold dead on a sharply rising bird at that distance with a pattern like that and you'll miss him every time. Center him and you'll chew him to pieces.

One season I killed a California valley quail that went by me like a bullet; when I shot I don't believe he was more than 10 feet from the muzzle of my gun. I swung fast and fired just as the muzzle swung past him. The bird fluttered down with his head gone and not a single shot in his body. I remember missing a big cock pheasant at about the same distance, actually not more than 10 feet from the muzzle. Not a shot hit him from the first barrel, but I waited him out to about 25 yards and nailed him with the second barrel—a far easier shot.

Most of upland game birds are shot at ranges between 20 and 30 yards, as are the majority of ducks shot from a blind. Actually, more birds are probably killed at ranges of less than 25 yards than beyond that distance. A 35-yard shot is a long one at an upland game bird.

So the question is: Just what sort of patterns are we working with at these distances?

At 20 yards the average full-choke gun throws, on the average, a killing pattern about 13 to 16 inches wide. A modified pattern at that distance should run around 16 to 20 inches. That's better, but still not really good for short-range shooting, because such a pattern is powerfully easy to miss with. A tight improved-cylinder (¼ choke) pattern at 20 yards will run 20 to 24 inches, or around 1 inch to 1 yard, and give enormously more hitting area than the 1-foot spread of the full choke. Few people have the skill to do very well with a full-choke gun at 20 yards or so. They simply cannot point well enough, and for that reason a high proportion of the birds they hit are caught on the edge of the small, dense pattern and feathered with a few deformed shot. At short upland ranges, the wider and evener distribution of the improved-cylinder or even of a Skeet No. 1 choke not only makes more kills but cleaner ones.

The skeet shot with proper timing breaks his birds at about 20 yards, and he needs all the pattern he can possibly get. That's one reason why most of the hotshots have guns equipped with a Cutts Compensator with a spreader tube or with skeet-bored barrels. I recently patterned No. 9 shot at 20 yards with a Cutts Compensator with the spreader tube and got target breaking patterns running between 30 and 36 inches. Another similar device patterns slightly smaller, averaging around 30 inches. I also patterned a Winchester Model 21 16-gauge skeet gun bored Skeet No. 2 and Skeet No. 1 (right). Patterns ran between 20 and 22 inches, the No. 2 barrel making the slightly smaller ones. I like double shotguns, and I use them in the field constantly. For skeet, though, some improved cylinder barrels and some bored presumably for skeet do not throw a pattern wide enough to put a gunner on a par with lads using spreader devices.

In this one the joke's on me:

I once got a fine double gun with two sets of barrels—one set presumably bored modified and full, the other improved cylinder in both barrels. I wanted to use the close-bored set for ducks and for pheasants, and Huns at the end of the season, and the open ones for skeet and general upland shooting.

The gun fitted me exactly, handled like a dream. I have never shot better in the field with any other. But I did notice that I missed with the open barrels if my hold was the least bit sloppy, and also that when I centered a bird he had a lot of shot in him. I patterned the close-choked barrels and found that the patterns they shot were terrific—around 75 percent with No. 4 shot in the left barrel, believe it or not, and an average of around 70 percent with the right barrel.

It took me a long time to get around to patterning the set of "open" barrels. Even though the gun fitted me perfectly, balanced and swung beautifully, I couldn't do very well at skeet. I noticed that when I hit a target it was smoked and when I didn't smoke it I missed it clean. Well, I found, when I got around to patterning, that at 20 yards my "open" barrels were giving me patterns that ran 15 or 16 inches. At 40 yards they were patterning an average of 68 to 72 percent respectively. In other words, the factory had shipped me a set of barrels marked improved cylinder that were actually throwing improved-modified and full-choke patterns. And that explained a lot of things to me! The skeet shooter with a gun throwing a 15 or 16-inch pattern at 20 yards is really working under a handicap—and so is the chap who shoots upland game with the same small pattern at the same distance.

I used to hunt quail with an old rancher who for years had shot an ancient blunderbuss with twist barrels. He did very well with it, even though the barrels were worn so thin at the muzzle that a man risked cutting his fingers in handling it. But it got results, and the rancher took pride in having "the hardest-shooting dad-blamed old gun in the country." When I finally talked him into retiring it, he bought a new one bored full choke—and couldn't hit a thing with it.

So we patterned the two guns. The old job with soft twist barrels had no constriction whatsoever—it had long since been shot out. It threw a pattern that pretty well filled a 30-inch circle at 20 yards, and that was why he had been hitting with it. His new gun threw a tight full-choke pattern, with all shot within a 10 to 12-inch circle, and his skill simply wasn't up to it.

When anyone wants to sell a variable choke device or a new shell, the sales talk is always about its wonderful full-choke patterns. Some very nice guys once spent most of a day demonstrating to me a new variable choke that would pattern 80 percent at 40 yards with large shot, and throw a killing pattern on a large duck at 60. All that was of very limited advantage to the ordinary gunner. Actually, at 40 yards, the schnozzle put from 50 to 60 percent of the shot in a 15-inch circle and was therefore almost as specialized an object as a ballistic missile and almost as worthless for all-around use. This same gimmick happened to throw one of the widest, evenest skeet patterns at 20 yards I have ever seen and, with another tube, one of the most useful patterns I have ever seen for all-around hunting—wide, even, round as a silver dollar. The lads, however, were determined to sell it on the basis of its full-choke performance for long-range pass-shooting. Probably they were smart, at that, because most of us are impressed by 40-yard performance, and by that alone.

The precise degree of constriction in a barrel doesn't have very much to do, in many cases, with the pattern delivered. Once at the gun club I was patterning a barrel that was reputedly an improved cylinder. When she threw a 70 percent pattern, I raised my voice to cry out that I had been jobbed with a full-choke barrel. My pals rushed over, thrust dimes into the muzzle, and then triumphantly assured me that my gun was *not* full choke. The heck it wasn't! No matter how it was bored it was throwing full-choke patterns with anything I put into it. What we're concerned with is patterns, and not so many thousandths of an inch of constriction as measured by an inside micrometer.

I am not enough of a technician to know all the answers on this one, but I have a sneaking suspicion that the advent of the star crimp, gas seal wads, plastic wad columns, and protective plastic collars for shot charges, has upset the applecart in this choke business. Shot shells often pattern more densely than they used to. A few years ago a gun that would consistently pattern 70 percent or better was something to brag about, but now it's not too uncommon to find a shell-and-gun combination that will throw patterns running from 75 to 80 percent, particularly with shot like No. 6 and larger. I believe a few sessions at the pattern board will convince many chaps who thought they were using a modified choke that they were actually getting full-choke patterns, and even some improved cylinder barrels will turn up murderously tight patterns.

What we're after is not the densest long-range pattern we can get, but the widest, most even killing pattern at the longest *ordinary* range at which we shoot with a particular gun. On most birds, the pattern that fills 30 inches at this hypothetical range is what we want, *if we can get it.*

The hunter of the bobwhite quail in the jack oaks, where few shots are taken at more than 25 yards, wants every bit of spread he can get, any way he can get it. And so does the man who shoots ruffed and blue grouse in the timber.

Run-of-the-mine upland shooting and decoy shooting on ducks require a pattern that will kill, let us say, to 35 yards so there's no use sacrificing spread at 25 and 30 yards to obtain killing density way out at 40, 45, and even 50 and 60 yards for the shot that turns up once in ten or fifteen times.

For pass-shooting on ducks, geese, or even doves, a man needs all the pattern density he can get at outside ranges. But the choke that shines in this particular field is worthless for quail and grouse, and puts even the pheasant and Hungarian-partridge hunter under a handicap.

So the smart scattergunner should cook himself up a pattern board and some pattern sheets, and dash out to see what his gun actually does under the conditions under which he uses it. He'll learn a lot of interesting things. He may find, for example, that the full-choke 20 gauge he had always thought of as "shooting like a rifle" actually throws a wider pattern than his modified 12 gauge, and that the little .410 throws a wider pattern yet. He may find that those "easy" short-range shots he has been missing are actually very difficult because, at 15 or 20 yards, Old Betsy is throwing a pattern almost as hard to hit with as a rifle bullet. Or he may find that with the No. 4 shot he has been using at mallards on the pass, he could center a bird in his pattern and yet never scratch it in five shots out of ten.

Or he may find that his gun habitually shoots low, right, high, or over toward the Finnegan place. I'll never forget one experience I had with a gun I had not patterned. It was a Winchester glass-barreled Model 59 fitted with a choke device the manufacturer wanted me to try out and write up. The gun came one morning. It fitted and handled nicely, so I put on the modified tube and took it pheasant hunting with me. My dog and I walked up a brushy draw and I heard some pheasants going out ahead of me. In the stubble above the head of the draw, my Brittany was on point. I booted out a big cock, missed it. In a few minutes my dog pinned down another. I also missed that. A third miss convinced me that something was wrong. I let off a shot at a stone in a cutbank and I could see the pattern was striking well below the point of aim. Patterning the gun later, I found that at 20 yards the top portion of the pattern was about at the point of aim—or where the muzzle rested. The center of the pattern was, of course, so low that hitting anything would be an accident.

No one really knows his shotgun until he has given it a workout with the pattern sheets!

Quantity of Pellets in Various Shot Shells

Load	⅞ oz.	1 oz.	1⅛ oz.	1¼ oz.
No. 2	77	88	99	110
No. 4	119	136	153	170
No. 6	195	223	251	279
No. 7	262	299	336	374
No. 7½	302	345	388	431
No. 8	358	409	460	514
No. 9	512	585	658	731

Short-Range Patterning

A pattern that will put 70 percent of the shot in a 30-inch circle at 40 yards (full choke) will measure 7 inches at 10 yards if flyers are disregarded. A 60 percent or modified pattern will cover 10 inches at 10 yards and an improved-cylinder pattern that will do 46 percent at 40 yards will measure 15 inches at 10 yards.

TO DETERMINE PATTERN PERCENTAGE

1. Set up a piece of paper about 20 inches square exactly 10 YARDS from the MUZZLE of the gun.

2. Select the load you want to test, and shoot at center of paper.

3. Now draw a circle around the resulting pattern, BUT DO NOT include those pellet holes which obviously are "Flyers."

4. Measure the diameter of this circle, then compare it with the corresponding figure on the chart. To determine WHAT PER-CENTAGE OF PATTERN you are getting at 40 yards, see Column 2. Column 3 will give you the maximum killing range of that pattern, assuming that your shot size is sufficiently large to kill at that distance.

This method was worked out by the late Ken Richards, manu-facturer of a collet-type choke known as the "Shooting Master." He was a pessimist as to the killing range of shotguns and most will disagree with his conclusions.

Circle diameter in inches on paper 10 yards from gun muzzle	Percentage of pattern in 30-inch circle at 40 yards	Maximum killing range of pattern in yards
5½	77	50
6	75	48
6½	73	46
7	71	44
7½	69	42
8	67	40
9	64	38
10	61	36
11	58	34
12	55	32
13	52	30
14	49	28
15	46	26
16	43	24
17	40	22
18	37	20

Sights on the Shotgun

SEVERAL times a year I hear from citizens who have invented shotgun sights that take all the guesswork out of shotgun shooting and make the rawest beginner an expert overnight. Some of these gadgets are very ingenuous indeed, and the sales pitch that goes along with them sounds convincing. The only thing wrong with them is that almost none of them help the man behind the gun shoot any better than he could without them. The more complicated and elaborate they are, the more generally they are useless. Most of them are designed by people who don't know anything about shooting a shotgun and are sold to those who know less.

One time a hunter with one of these gimmicks showed up at my house and gave me a sales pitch that would have sold an electric heater to a sinner frying in hell. The man using a gun equipped with one of these wonders simply could not miss, he told me. You just looked through the gadget a certain way, under certain conditions, yanked the trigger, and whatever you were shooting at came down.

The more he talked, the more convinced I was that he knew about as much about the art of shooting a shotgun as I know about the fertility rites of the Watusi. I finally told him that I would like a demonstration, that I had a hand trap, some clay targets, and that we could do some shooting on the grounds of the local trap-and-skeet club without having the gendarmes on our neck.

So out we went. I used to be a fairly decent tennis player back during the administration of Chester A. Arthur, and since the technique of hurling a clay pigeon out of a hand trap and that of smacking a forehand drive are similar, I can make the clays sail out right smartly. It saddens me no end to report that my inventor with his foolproof sight hit about one target in ten. Finally, he called a halt and told me that for some reason he never could hit clay targets in spite of the fact that he never missed a bird. If we could only go pheasant shooting together, he said, he'd give me proof that his gadget was a real tiger.

Then he turned to me. "Do you think it will sell if I put it on the market?" he asked.

I told him I thought it would. In the first place, this gadget of his was a cute little creation. In the second, his sales pitch would sound convincing to anyone who didn't know much about hitting with a shotgun. In the third place, the world is full of people who would like to become good shotgun shots without going to the trouble of working at it.

Every human being that ever lived was born with a yen for magic, a deep-seated conviction that he can excel in almost anything if he can only get hold of some gimmick or be told some "secrets." He feels that somehow there is an easy way to excel in almost anything. Women like to believe that if they could only afford some rare and costly perfume to dab behind their ears, handsome and charming men driving Rolls-Royces and wearing suits tailored on Savile Row would batter down doors for the privilege of holding their hands. They like to be told that if they take a couple of magic pills a day they can eat like harvest hands and still have girlish figures, or that they can achieve the same result by trussing themselves up in those astounding suits of armor called foundations. They look sourly indeed on anyone who tells them that to have a fetching figure they have to be born with the right bones and the right proportions and that to keep what nature gave them they have to exercise and to forgo unseemly bouts with the knife and fork.

And we men, in our own way, are just as easily conned as the gals. We like to believe that we can become executive types with iron wills and steel-trap minds if we take ten easy lessons, or that by reading a book we can acquire the terrifying ability to remember everybody's name, date and place of birth, occupation and date of wedding, and names and number of children.

And many of us would like to believe that there is a magic shortcut to learning to shoot a shotgun, and if only we could discover just what it was, we'd be set. There are some aids to pointing a shotgun barrel in the right direction, but none of them make the gun self-pointing, none of them pull the trigger, and none of them keep the gun swinging. Alas, the magic shotgun sight is in the class with the scatter gun with the 100-yard killing range and the big-game cartridge so deadly that a hit just anywhere will bowl an animal over.

But he who hunts deer with a shotgun and rifled slugs is someone else again. He needs sights. He also needs to sight in as if he were using a rifle, and in actuality he is using a substitute for a rifle. The man using a shotgun for wing shooting can do very nicely without any sight at all—even the conventional bead at the end of the barrel.

In fact, any gimmick put on a shotgun that draws the shooter's attention *away* from the target, particularly if it draws toward the breech, probably does more harm than good. It is almost optically impossible for anyone to focus his eyes on any sort of a rear sight, the front sight, and the target at the same time. Young eyes can make a pretty fair stab at it. Old eyes cannot.

I have a Model 21 12-gauge shotgun with two pairs of 26-inch barrels. One set is bored modified and improved-modified and has no middle bead. The other is bored skeet No. 1 and No. 2, and has a middle bead. So far as I know, I have yet to notice the middle bead when I was shooting at anything, be it live bird or target. Actually, most people notice even the front bead only in a subconscious sort of way. I have a little Spanish 28-gauge double that is a lot of fun to play with, and for about three months I had been going out a few times a week to bust clay targets thrown from a hand trap by one of the family. Then someone who was examining the gun happened to notice that the small gold front bead had dropped off, something I had not been conscious of. With my eyes on the target, my point of reference, my "sight" if you wish, had simply been the muzzles. I swung and the gun went off when relationship of bird and muzzles looked right.

In reality, the front sight of the shotgun is the muzzle, the rear sight the human eye. Raise the eye and the gun shoots higher. Lower it and the gun shoots lower, just as is the case with the rear sight on a rifle. The *comb* of the stock, which governs the position of the eye, is in effect the elevation mechanism for the rear sight. Trapshooters, probably the most serious and knowledgeable scattergunners, are well aware of this function of the comb. That is why they use high combs, so that they'll see more barrel. Then the shot charge goes high and catches the rapidly rising target. And that too is why they like the level Monte Carlo comb, as then constant elevation is maintained, no matter where they put the cheek.

Aiming the shotgun as one would aim a rifle by lining up a front and rear sight is fatal to fast, relaxed shooting. Not long ago, an inventor of a shotgun sight told me that those who used the shotgun depended too much on the spread of the shot pattern. I responded that on the contrary, they did not depend on it enough. The shotgunner does not hit with a single bullet, he hits with a cloud of shot pellets with a spread of from 10 to 50 inches, depending on the choke and the range. It is far more important for him to shoot fast and to keep his gun moving than it is for him to be precise, in the sense that the rifleman with his single bullet is precise. Trying to be extra precise, thinking of the shot charge as a bullet, leads the gunner to the most fatal of all errors in shotgun shooting—slowing and stopping the swing.

Shotgun rear sights take various forms. The small, gold plastic or ivory bead halfway down the rib does no harm. On the other hand, I doubt whether it does any good, for I have never noticed one when shooting. A generation or so ago there was a fad for large globe or ring sights that clipped to the rear of the barrel. I tried guns so equipped. I doubt whether they did any harm, but I am convinced they made pointing no more exact, no faster. I simply ignored the ring and shot as I always did. Right after the war, some optical rear sights that were supposed to revolutionize shotgun shooting came out. They were marked by concentric rings. The gunner was supposed to put the center ring on what he wanted to hit and let go. The gimmicks stuck up above the receiver like sore thumbs. They were made of glass and were fragile. They raised the line of sight and took the cheek away from the comb, tended to make the shooter an arm swinger instead of a body swinger, an aimer instead of a pointer. They took his attention away from the muzzle and the target and put it to the rear. They were difficult to line up, easy to knock cockeyed. I thought they were turkeys and said so. They had their brief moment in the sun and were then forgotten. For years after their manufacture ceased, they were advertised for a fraction of their original cost by cut-rate sales companies.

One of the damndest gadgets I have ever seen was a rear sight to be clipped to the breech. It consisted of a bar on which were dots of various colors. If the gunner thought the bird was crossing at, let us say, 30 yards, he matched up the red dot with the front bead and let go. If it was 40 yards away, he used the yellow dot; if 50 yards away, he used the green dot. Whether you did this with the sustained lead (pointing out) or the fast swing, the inventor did not say. Just as screwy was a complicated metal ring sight consisting of converging lines and metal circles. You were supposed to pick out the line on which the bird was flying, swing up and keep the bird on the line for the proper angle, and then cut loose.

Shortly before the last war, the W. R. Weaver Co. brought out a 1X shotgun scope, and even before that some shotgunners used Zeiss 1½X scopes on shotguns. Oddly enough, there is much to be said for such a sight. For one thing, it puts target and aiming point in the same focal plane and for cases of extreme far-sightedness this is a good idea. For another, the sight is adjustable so that the pattern can be centered wherever one wants it. For yet another, it uses the "pointing" principle of aligning two objects, just as one sees the relationship of shotgun muzzle and target. For shotgun use, the scope was and is furnished with a very large and conspicuous dot, for deer hunting, generally with a post.

This is the queen of the sights for the man hunting deer with rifled slugs in heavy brush, and it is also a useful sight for wing shooting. I had, at one time, a 16-gauge pump equipped with a 1X Weaver scope and used it extensively. It worked out very well. It was fast and easily enabled me to call my shots. I believe I killed a higher percentage of straightaway quail with that gun than with any other I have ever used. The reason was that with it I didn't shoot over. It is a very speedy sight, good on skeet as well as on birds. The late Bill Weaver used it, and if there was a better wing shot in this country than Weaver, I have yet to hunt with him. I have seen him kill three Hungarian partridges on a covey rise, and what that guy couldn't do to quail isn't worth doing. The 1X Weaver has been replaced by a 1.5X.

Another useful gimmick that could be classed as a sight (or at least a sighting device) is the ventilated rib. It is dearly beloved by the trap and skeet shooters, and I think rightly. It leads the shooter's eye to the target, makes pointing quick but precise, and, I think, increases the shooter's confidence in hitting. Money spent for a ventilated rib is, I am convinced, well spent.

I have often heard shooters say that they cannot shoot a double as the sight of the twin tubes bothers them. I have also heard some say that they do not like single-barrel guns as they find the less conspicuous muzzle slower to pick up. For my part, I have never been able to detect any difference. If a gun fits me and balances well, I can shoot it, be it double, pump, or automatic. If it doesn't balance and fit, I can't shoot it as well. I can do better on upland game with a double than I can with a repeater (or at least I think I can), but I believe that is because with 26-inch barrels, the double is livelier and faster for quick shooting. At skeet I can do a bit better with a pump or automatic because the balance is farther forward and the gun swings more evenly, and it is more difficult to commit my own pet sin of slowing down my swing. Otherwise, I can do as well with one type as with the other.

But some are annoyed by the slim tubes of the single-barrel small-gauge repeaters—.410, 28, and 20. They claim they are not conspicuous enough. One cure that has been tried is a muzzle bandage, a wad of white adhesive tape wrapped around the muzzle so that relationship of muzzle and target can be quickly ascertained. I tried this on a .410 pump for skeet and I believe it helped. The Cutts

Compensators with aluminum tubes left bright serve the same function.

I also think that there is probably a real advantage in large and conspicuous front beads. I don't think dinky little gold beads are ever noticed, as the gunner by-passes them as reference points and instead uses the muzzle as a whole. But large ivory, red plastic, or fluorescent beads are horses of another shade. These are not only attractive but useful, and I am all for them. These should be *large*. Most of them are too small. To be useful, one should be conspicuous and to be conspicuous, it should be in the neighborhood of one-quarter inch in diameter. Those about the size of a No. 6 shot, as some are, do no good as they simply are not seen.

Sights made for the slug-using shotgun are a must for those who are unfortunate enough to live in an area where they cannot use a rifle for deer. But these are not shotgun sights in actuality, but sights for what amounts to a makeshift rifle. They should always be removed from the dual-purpose shotgun when it is used for wing shooting, as the presence of the rear sight is fatal to quick pointing and fast shooting.

It saddens me to say this, but there is only one way to learn to be reasonably good with a shotgun. That is to do a lot of shotgun shooting. There is no shortcut. Instruction helps, and in fact is very important. Even some reading helps, so that the principles of shotgun shooting are understood. Critical watching of the performance of a good shotgun shot also helps, just as it helps to see a good man do his stuff in any sport, be it golf, broad jumping, pole vaulting, or tennis.

A good-fitting, well-balanced shotgun makes shooting easier, but the beginner with the best shotgun in the world is still a beginner, just as a bum tennis player with the finest racket in the world is still a bum tennis player. In these days, people do not have an opportunity to learn to shoot a shotgun well on game. There is simply not enough game and the seasons are too short.

Anyone who wants to become handy with a smoothbore has little choice but to shoot at clay targets. And of all clay target games, the most useful in making anyone an all-around shot is skeet. Anyone with normal eyes and muscular co-ordination who has good instruction and shoots a hundred rounds of skeet should be a fairly good shotgun shot—far better than the average duck or pheasant hunter. He will have learned how to mount a gun, the necessity of swinging and keeping the gun swinging. He will have formed the habit of focusing on the target instead of on the barrel and receiver, of pointing rather than aiming as with a rifle, of shooting fast instead of dawdling around. At the end of the hundred rounds of skeet he should be able to shoot with about anyone in the field or in the duck blind and at least not look foolish. He probably won't be a crack shot, but at least he won't be lousy.

This hundred rounds of skeet will cost him about $300. It would be wonderful if we could buy $300 worth of skill with a $5 shotgun sight, but like the plump lady's reducing pill, the doggoned things just don't produce!

CHAPTER 12

The Shotgun Stock

BECAUSE rifles and shotguns are shot and handled differently, stocks for the two weapons have many points of difference. The shotgun stock is longer than the rifle stock and generally a bit straighter—at least in the case of the shotgun stock as compared with the stock of a rifle to be used with iron sights. For most shooting, the rifle should be held firmly and steadily, but not hard enough to cause tremor, whereas the shotgun is held less firmly and is generally fired when the weapon is moving. As a consequence the close, full pistol grip, which is just about mandatory on a good rifle stock, is optional on the shotgun stock, and a cheekpiece, which is generally demanded by the serious rifle shooter, is seldom seen on the shotgun stock.

A typical rifle stock to be used with iron sights by a man of average height will have a drop at comb of 1¾ inches, drop at heel of about 2¾ inches, and length of pull (center of trigger to center of buttplate) of about 13½ inches. The pitch down of the rifle stock, which is determined by the angle of the buttplate, is generally from 3 to 4 inches.

A typical American mass-produced shotgun stock has about the following dimensions: drop at comb, 1½ inches; drop at heel, 2½ inches; length of pull, 14 inches; pitch down from the 26-inch barrels of a double gun, 1 to 2 inches. The longer and straighter the stock, the less the recoil effect, and as a consequence experienced scattergunners generally shoot longer and straighter stocks than do beginners. Since there is nothing particularly natural about mounting a shotgun, beginners generally feel more comfortable with shorter stocks and more drop at heel than they later learn to like. Many experienced shooters prefer stocks with only 2 inches drop at the heel, and some like zero pitch. Since trapshooters call for their targets with their guns mounted and always shoot at rising targets, they generally prefer longer stocks than field or skeet shooters. Stocks on trap guns average pulls of about 14½ inches and an occasional one is seen that is 15 inches or so in length.

I am six feet and one-half inch tall in my stocking feet. I feel that I am best fitted with a shotgun stock with a length of pull of 14¼ inches. But I like my rifle stocks 13½ inches long—¾ inch shorter than what seems right for my shotgun stocks. A rifle stock with a pull of 13¾ inches seems a bit long and awkward to me and a 14-inch pull is annoying.

A properly designed shotgun stock of correct dimensions should enable the shooter to mount his gun quickly with his right eye in line with the barrel and target. It should also be designed so he can swing smoothly and steadily. The stocks should also minimize recoil, keep the hands away from the hot barrel, and ideally be a thing of beauty.

Almost all shotguns wear two-piece stocks. The exception is the bolt-action shotgun, which is primarily a rifle-type. It has a one-piece stock like the similar bolt-action rifle. There are three schools of stock design—the American, the British, and the German. American stocks almost always have pistol grips (or "hands" as the British say). They have full, rounded combs, wider and longer buttplates. On an average they are straighter than European stocks but possibly not as straight as some the British are now building. They generally have large, hand-filling fore-ends on pumps and automatics and "beavertail" fore-ends on doubles. American stocks are generally a bit shorter than the British, somewhat longer than the German.

Stocks on fine, handmade British game guns almost always have straight grips, skimpy fore-ends which do little more than cover the metal. British guns are generally conservatively and elegantly

SHOTGUN GRIPS.

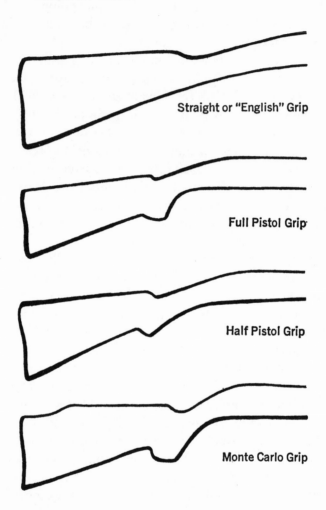

Straight or "English" Grip

Full Pistol Grip

Half Pistol Grip

Monte Carlo Grip

engraved with handsome scroll. The checkering is laid out in diamond patterns, and in the most expensive grades it is quite good. There is nothing showy about a fine British shotgun such as a Boss or a Purdey, but it is quietly elegant. The lines are sleek and graceful.

German and Austrian guns, on the other hand, almost always

have pistol grips. They often have cheekpieces and sometimes sling swivels. They are often relief engraved with animals, birds, oak leaves, and whatnot on the frame and the breech, and often the pistol grip and forend are decorated with carved oak leaves instead of checkering. Combs run thin and drop at heel is often excessive for modern American tastes. Central European shotguns have many admirers but in general they are not precisely my dish of tea. I don't think a cheekpiece has any place on a shotgun. I prefer scroll engraving to oak leaves and leaping stags.

The best Belgian guns look much like the good British product and the Spanish and Italian also tend to follow British models. The few Czech shotguns I have seen look much like the German and Austrian products. I have seen some very fine checkering on Belgian, German, and Italian guns, but often the checkering is not as good as that on the best British guns and on stocks turned out by a handful of fine American stockmakers.

In the early days of the breech-loading double gun, the straight or "English" grip was used on most shotguns, as the straight grip permits moving the hand slightly when the gunner shifts from front trigger to rear or vice versa. The single triggers on pump and automatic shotguns and on most American doubles have made the use of the full pistol grip almost universal in the United States. Such grips give a bit more control over the gun and put the wrist at a more natural and comfortable angle. The best pistol grips on shotguns are not quite as "full" as those on rifles, as the measurement from the edge of the grip cap to the center of the trigger is longer. Since the right hand of the shotgun user is more at the side of the grip than it would be with the large-caliber rifle, the pistol grip of the shotgun is generally oval in cross section instead of being nearly round, as most rifle grips are. There are freakish shotgun grips as well as rifle grips. One extremely close pistol grip had a run among trapshooters right after the last war, but to me it appeared ugly and it cramped the wrist uncomfortably.

The "half pistol grip" was at one time available on special order on any of the American double guns, and is now seen on the Browning guns. It has a more gentle curve and instead of being capped it is generally round on the end. Straight grips on the finest British,

Belgian, and sometimes Spanish doubles are often diamond shape to give a better hold and to keep the gun from twisting in the hand.

There is a slight tendency for the gun with the full pistol grip to shoot low because the firmer grip enables the shooter to hold the gun down. The gun with the straight grip has a slight tendency to shoot a bit high. However, I am inclined to believe that these differences are more theoretical than actual.

As we have seen, the combs of American stocks are generally fuller and more rounded. English combs are less thick and the combs on some Continental guns are quite thin. To some extent comb thickness can be substituted for comb height, and the low thick comb will put the eye in the same position as a higher but thinner comb. The comb is just about the most important component of the stock, as the comb is in effect the elevation mechanism of the rear sight of the shotgun. Actually, the eye itself is the rear sight. If a too high or too thick comb puts the eye too high, the shooter will see too much barrel and overshoot. If the comb is too thin or too low, the shooter cannot cheek his gun firmly, has a tendency to shoot low, and a tendency to become an arm swinger instead of swinging the gun with his whole body by rotating the hips.

Trap guns generally have high, thick combs (often as little as 1¼ inches drop at that point) as the trapshooter always shoots at a sharply rising target and wants a gun that shoots high. As can be easily seen, if the stock has more drop at heel than at comb, the farther back on the stock the face is placed the more drop in effect the shooter is using. This explains why sometimes the short-necked man with a full face is fitted with the same stock as a long-necked stock crawler with a thin face. The short-necked chap shoots with his cheek farther back and gets more drop. It is for this reason that trap guns have very straight stocks and that many of them have Monte Carlo combs—a type of comb that comes back with no drop whatsoever, so no matter where the cheek is placed the comb drop will always be the same. To me anyway, the Monte Carlo is no thing of beauty, but trapshooters love it.

Combs are generally higher and thicker and stocks are generally made with less drop both at comb and heel than they were a generation or two ago. Many old guns made for field use before World War I had comb drops of 2 inches and heel drops of 3 to 3½. Such old guns point sluggishly, and with heavy loads they kick like the devil. The straighter the stock, the easier it points, just as a ruler points more naturally than a T-square, and the less the recoil effect. Crooked stocks jam the comb up against the cheek. The hardest kicking of all shotguns is one with a sharp, high comb, excessive heel drop, and a small butt.

The length of pull should be as long as it can be and at the same time be easy to mount. If the butt catches on the clothes when the gun is mounted, it is too long. If the shooter gets bopped in the nose with his right thumb now and then when he shoots, the stock is too short. As we have seen, trap guns have stocks longer than field guns. Stocks for duck guns generally should run shorter than those on upland guns because the duck hunter is generally pretty well wrapped up in heavy clothing.

American repeating shotguns and cheap doubles are generally furnished with buttplates (heel plates to the British) of hard rubber, plastic, or some composition. Recoil pads are generally used on wildfowl guns to be shot with heavy loads, and of the recoil pads I prefer those of solid rubber faced with leather. To me such a pad is more pleasant since it does not give the excessive jump of some of the ventilated pads, and the leather facing keeps the butt from catching on the clothes. Many high-class doubles have butts of plain wood sharply checkered to keep them from slipping. In the past many high-class guns have had skeleton buttplates or heel and toe plates with checkered wood in between. These keep the stock from denting or splitting at heel and toe. High-grade Parkers were famous for their skeleton buttplates and Winchester Model 21 skeet guns usually had checkered butts. It should be remembered that wide flat buttplates seem to kick less than narrow ones, as the greater the area over which recoil is distributed the less the recoil effect.

The conservative British and Continentals generally cling to the little "splinter" fore-ends that do little more than cover up the fore-end irons and ejector mechanism. These give the gun a racy look, but they do not protect the hand from hot barrels and do not get the left hand far enough forward to enable the gunner to control his piece swiftly and accurately. The wider, longer, and flatter beavertail fore-end on the double gun is preferred in America. It gets the left hand forward for good control, protects the fingers from hot barrels. Like the Monte Carlo comb, the beavertail fore-end is a product of trapshooting. The first American pump guns had rather small slide handles, but for a good many years now these have been large and hand filling. These give gun control and make accurate pointing easy since they put both hands pretty much on the same plane.

Most foreign double guns are made with "cast-off," a term which means that the buttstock angles slightly to the right. This presumably makes the gun faster to mount and point, as the right eye does not have to be so far to the right in order to look down the rib. American guns are seldom made with cast-off, and actually cast-off doesn't amount to much, as it is generally only about a half inch. Some guns stocked especially for women have more cast-off at the toe than at the heel—and for obvious reasons.

An extreme type of cast-off is the "cockeyed" stock, with so much cast-off that the gun can be used from the right shoulder but aimed with the left eye. This same problem of the right-handed shooter with a bad right eye but a good left eye can be whipped by cutting down the comb of the stock so that the shooter can put his head across an otherwise normal stock until he can aim with his left eye.

Probably the slight cast-off given most stocks has little effect on recoil, but theoretically anyway cast-off increases recoil effect since it tends to drive the comb against the cheek. "Cast-on," which is seldom encountered, has the opposite effect.

The world's best gunstock material is good European walnut. It is harder and lighter than American black walnut. It has more contrast between light and dark. The pores are smaller and consequently the wood takes a better finish and takes and holds finer and sharper checkering. All European walnut comes from trees that produce thin-shelled nuts—the so-called English walnut. Good wood of this variety is grown in England, France, Italy, Spain, Yugoslavia, the Balkans, Turkey, Iran, the areas of Russia around the Black and Caspian seas, and northern India. Thin-shelled walnut trees are also grown in California, but these are generally in irrigated groves and the wood they produce when cut is not equal to the best European wood.

Probably more good wood comes from the Rhone valley of France than from any other area, and for that reason there is a tendency to call any good, well-marked European walnut "French." Good wood is good wood, no matter where it comes from. The best for shotgun use has the grain running parallel to the grip and shows a good figure in the butt. British makers prefer wood with long, sweeping, dark lines. Others prefer contrasting feather in the butt-wood which generally comes from portions where roots or branches join the trunk.

The best British makers select their wood carefully and take trips to France to go through hundreds of drying blanks. American stockmakers have a much more difficult time finding fine European wood. In the days when the American double-gun factories were operating, French walnut was generally used in the higher grades by Parker, Fox, Baker, Remington, and Syracuse Arms Company. So far as I know, Ithaca confined itself to the use of American walnut in the higher grades, but some of the crotch wood used was very handsome. For all I know Winchester never used French walnut in the Model 21, as I have never seen a gun so stocked at the factory, but wood for the 21 was generally pretty well chosen. Stocks for trap and other premium-grade repeating guns of most makes are generally figured American black walnut.

It is easy to tell European walnut from black walnut. The European wood is much finer grained, has more contrast, tends in color to dark brown streaks and whorls in contrast to light brown. American black walnut has larger pores, is softer, has less contrast, shows less of a sheen when finished, and has a sort of a liverish color.

Good wood of any variety is harder to get than it used to be since walnut groves all over Europe and America were chopped down and sawed up to make gunstocks during two world wars. Before the last war, it was possible to acquire a good short blank for a shotgun buttstock for about $10. Now a hard, dense, and fairly well-marked piece of wood will cost from $50 to $150 and really spectacular pieces cost even more. However, American custom stockers and good European gun builders still manage to get hold of good wood.

I have seen some of the cheaper European shotguns that have apparently been stocked in beech, and in the United States some custom stocks have been made of myrtle, maple, and other light-colored woods. Remington some years ago tried the experiment of stocking some repeating shotguns with maple. Before the last war, Stevens turned out a cheap shotgun with a plastic stock. However, to me light-colored wood looks like the devil and plastic stocks have a cold, greasy, and repellent feel about them. The only genuinely satisfactory stock material for the scatter gun is walnut with European the first choice, American black walnut the second.

Next to a hard and finely figured piece of walnut, the best decoration for the shotgun is plenty of fine, sharp checkering. I would much rather spend my money for good checkering and skimp on the engraving than have an elaborately engraved gun with large, flat-topped, sprawling checkering.

Good checkering should be sharp, precise, and every diamond should look exactly like every other diamond. I prefer rather long diamonds. And I prefer checkering patterns with no borders, as borders are generally used to conceal run-overs. I like large, continuous areas of checkering as I think small isolated areas of checkering tend to make the stock look cheap, and I think French-skip checkering looks cheap and showy. Many of the best checkerers recess the patterns into the wood about 1/32 inch, and this is very handsome. Most fine shotguns are checkered with diamond patterns, but the fleur-de-lis is also good.

In the days of the American double-gun companies the fineness and precision of the checkering and the elaborateness of the pattern were indicative of the grade of the gun. The field-grade guns usually had fairly small patterns of rather coarse checkering, but the top-grade guns had elaborate and extensive patterns of fine checkering that ran from 22 to 26 lines to the inch. No finer

The Parker "Trojan," the cheapest of the Parkers, was always made to standard stock dimensions with a length of pull of 14 inches, drop at comb of 1⅝ inches, drop at heel of 2½ inches, full pistol grip, hard rubber buttplate. The gun was never fitted with automatic ejectors, but a single trigger was available at extra cost. Though there was never anything fancy about these old Trojans, they were good solid guns.

The Parker AHE grade was a genuinely fine firearm with a superbly checkered stock and fore-end of European walnut. The stock was fitted with a gold name plate with name or monogram. Stock dimensions were to measure and any type of grip, Monte Carlo or cast-off, could be obtained. The guns could be fitted with regular pad or skeleton buttplate and the receiver was handsomely engraved. Automatic ejectors were standard but a single trigger was extra. The gun was made in 10, 12, 16, 20, 28, and .410 gauges.

The Parker single-barrel trap gun in a good grade, in this case a DHE.

The BHE grade Parker was custom stocked in French walnut; automatic ejection was standard. It was made in all gauges from 10 magnum to .410. A selective single trigger was extra.

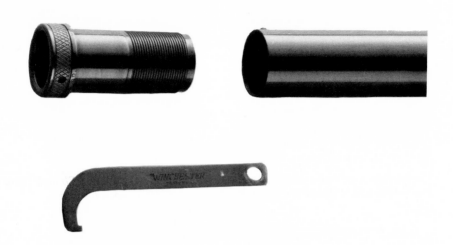

The Winchester "Winchoke" is a successful device which screws into the barrel.

A modern plastic wad column.

Most modern American shotshells are built like this one. They employ a plastic wad column which includes the shot protector. These shells are star crimped.

A Winchester Model 21 Trap gun with ventilated rib, beavertail forend and Monte Carlo comb.

A custom-made Winchester Model 21 double with fancy American black walnut stock with fancy checkering and elaborate engraving.

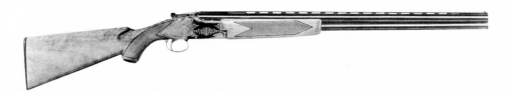

The Winchester Model 101 over-and-under shotgun is made in Japan by a Winchester affiliate and under Winchester direction.

Remington Model 1100 Automatic Magnum Duck Gun.

Remington 3200 Magnum over-and-under shotgun.

The Winchester Model 12 was one of the most widely used and dearly loved guns ever made in America.

Remington Model 1100 Deer Gun.

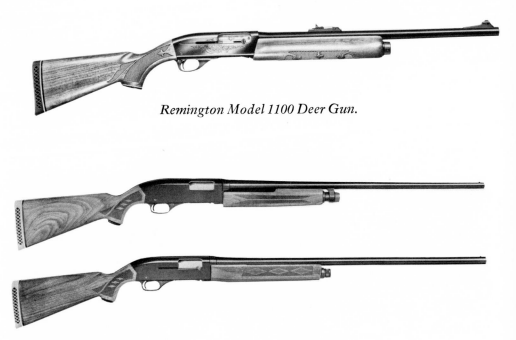

The Winchester Model 1200 Pump and 1400 Automatic. Both have been replaced to some extent, the 1200 by a revived Model 12 and the Model 1400 by the new Super X.

Two beautiful Holland & Holland sidelock doubles. These were part of a matched set and were in gauges from .410 to 12.

Fine English scroll engraving on a high class British sidelock double. (photo by Jim Carmichel)

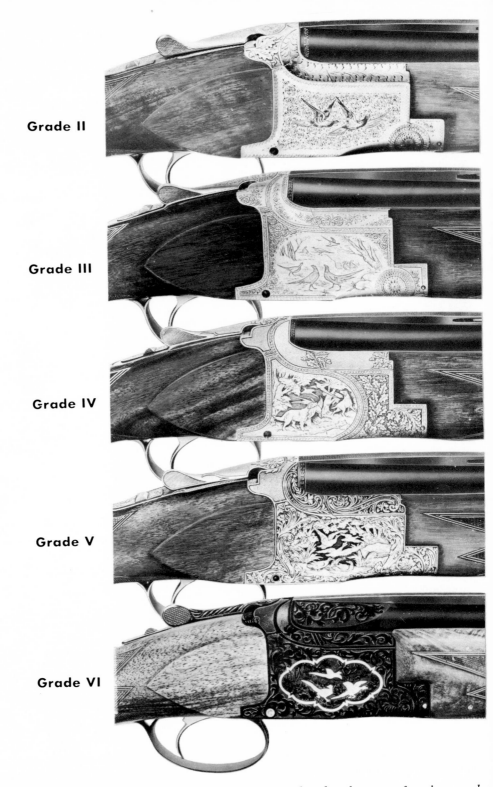

Grade II

Grade III

Grade IV

Grade V

Grade VI

The standard engraving on the Browning over-and-under shotguns of various grades

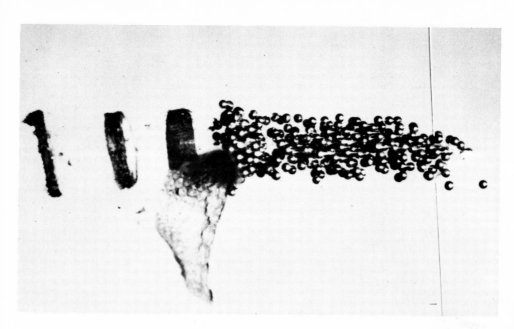

A 12-gauge Western Mark V trap load from a full-choke gun shown dropping the polyethylene collar at 36 inches from the muzzle.

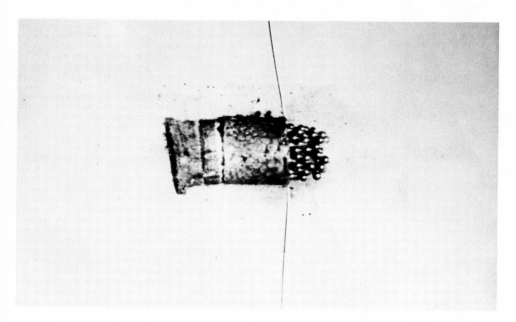

Western Mark V trap load with polyethylene collar 9 inches from the muzzle.

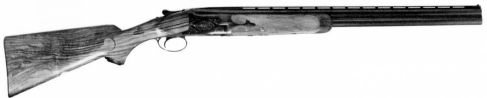

This Browning Superposed double was stocked by Al Biesen of Spokane, Washington, for Dr. Glen Carlson of Lewiston, Idaho.

The Winchester "Grand American" Model 21 is elaborately engraved with a fancy checkered stock of select walnut. The 21 is the only high-class double being manufactured in the United States today.

A high-grade Remington Model 870 pump gun.

The Fox shotguns made by Savage are now the only moderately priced American-made /doubles.

The Ithaca Model 37 Deer Slayer shotgun has rifle sights and a special cylinder bored barrel. It is very accurate with rifled slugs.

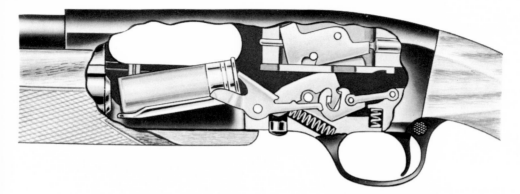

Cutaway view of the action of the Marlin Premier repeating shotgun.

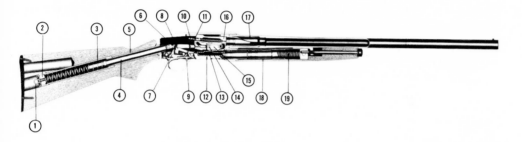

Cutaway view of the Winchester Model 50 and 59: 1. buffer plug lock; 2. buffer plug; 3. closing spring; 4. inertia rod; 5. receiver extension tube; 6. link and link pin; 7. hammer catch spring; 8. hammer; 9. safety; 10. ejector; 11. firing pin; 12. carrier; 13. carrier lock; 14. slide pin; 15. slide right; 16. bolt; 17. chamber; 18. magazine tube; 19. magazine spring.
—drawing George Fremault, courtesy Robinson-Hannagan Associates, Inc.

Cutaway view of a Winchester Model 12 pump.

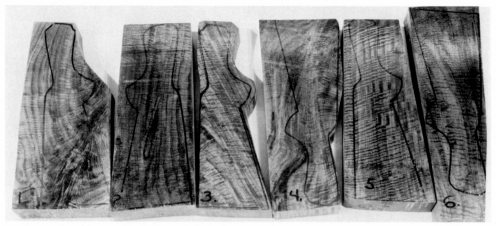

Some fine European-type walnut blanks for shotgun buttstocks. This wood was furnished by Frank Pachmayr, Los Angeles.

A Parker frame and barrels elaborately engraved by Pachmayr.

Checkering the pistol grip of a Winchester Model 21.

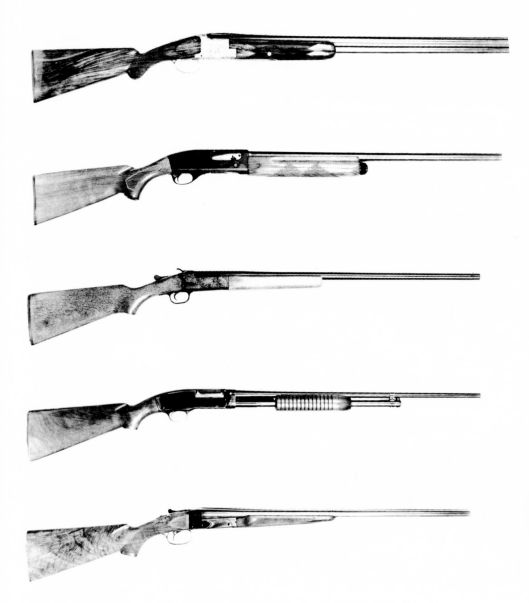

The common types of shotguns from the top down: a Browning over-and-under, a Remington automatic in 12 gauge, a break-open single shot with hammer, a Winchester Model 42 pump in .410 gauge, a Winchester Model 21, 20 gauge.

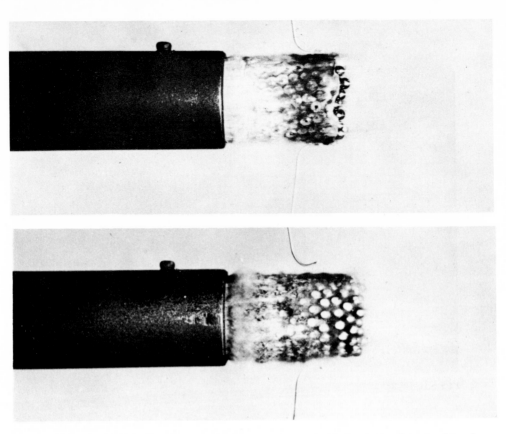

A shot charge, with and without plastic collar, emerging from shotgun barrel.

This very handsome and utilitarian forend is on one of Jack O'Connor's 12 gauge AYA model XXVSL's. It is neat, light, hand-filling.

Jack O'Connor inspects the breech of one of his AYA model XXVSL 12 gauge guns.

When mounting a shotgun, the shooter should lower his head, bring the butt out and back to his shoulder—put his gun to his face, not his face to his gun.

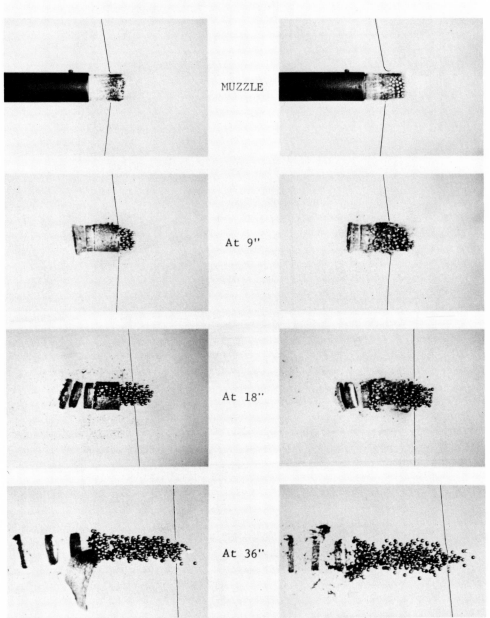

NEW MARK 5 LOAD
WITH PROTECTIVE COLLAR

CONVENTIONAL LOAD
WITHOUT PROTECTIVE COLLAR

MUZZLE

At 9"

At 18"

At 36"

Shot and wads, both with and without a protective collar, at various distances from the muzzle.

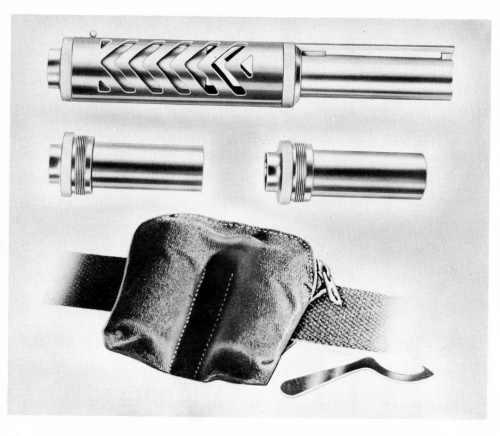

The PO Wer PAC was a variable choke device with tubes that screwed inside the cage. It was one of several variable choke devices which are no longer manufactured.

The Cyclone Choke is a collet-type choke with a ventilated sleeve. It is similar to the Poly Choke.

The standard Poly Choke has been one of the most successful and popular of the variable choke devices.

An aerial view of a Winchester franchise gun club showing trap fields at upper left, skeet fields below. Since finding a place to shoot a shotgun is a problem in these days of population explosion, Winchester embarked in 1964 on a program of establishing franchised trap clubs.

Shooting at hand-thrown live pigeons. This is a popular sport in Spain and Mexico.

This remarkable photograph shows the shot charge and wads leaving the muzzle of a Winchester Model 59 shotgun. The polyethylene collar is separating from the charge.

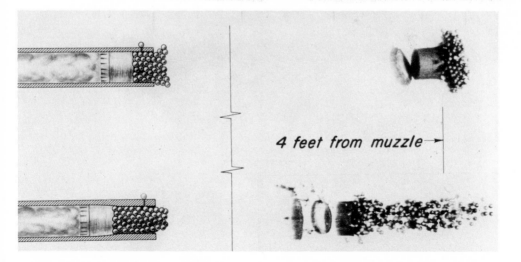

4 feet from muzzle →

The effect of cylinder bore and full choke on shot patterns at four feet from the muzzle. The shot charge from the cylinder bore has more speed and a shorter shot column.

Gunner shooting an over-and-under. Notice that his head is down and he is looking right along the rib.

Shooting whitewings near Tucson, Arizona. Notice that the gunner shoots with both eyes open.

The author's daughter Caroline with a pheasant rooster of which she is very proud.

Good style on a classic crossing shot.　　　　　—courtesy Winchester News Bureau

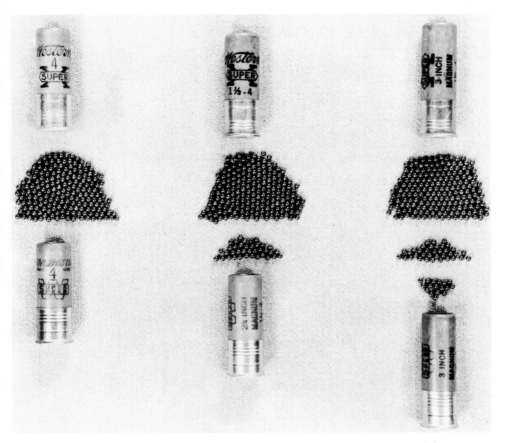

Winchester-Western photograph showing the amount of shot used in 1¼- and 1½-ounce loads, and in the 3-inch magnum with 1⅞ ounces.

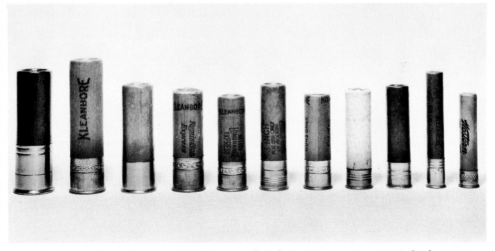

The shotgun gauges, left to right: the now illegal 8 gauge, 10-gauge 3½-inch magnum, standard 10 gauge, 2¾-inch 12 gauge, 16 gauge, 20-gauge 3-inch magnum, 2¾-inch 20 gauge, 24 gauge, 28 gauge, 3-inch .410, 2½-inch .410.

August Pachmayr, left, shows his son Frank, right, a double-barrel shotgun he built in Germany before he came to the United States which was incredibly brought back to the United States by a returning G.I.

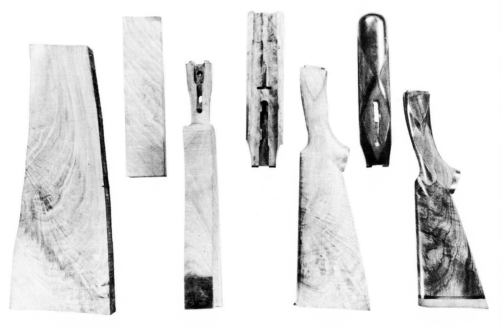

A shotgun stock from unfinished wood to finished buttstock and fore-end.

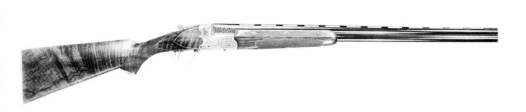

An excellent over-and-under shotgun imported from Belgium by Continental Arms Corp. of New York.

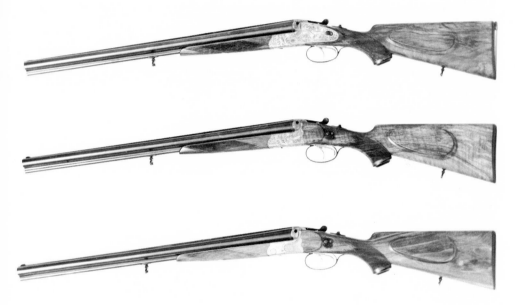

German three-barrel guns imported by Charles Leavell of South Carolina. The top gun is a sidelock, the two bottom guns box locks.

A classic upland gun imported from Belgium by Continental Arms Corp. with straight grip and scroll engraving. This gun has sidelocks, a short beavertail fore-end.

The Model 1897 Winchester shotgun was the first completely successful pump gun and was manufactured for half a century.

A Mossberg Model 185D 20-gauge bolt-action shotgun with interchangeable tubes and different degrees of choke.

This old Winchester 10-gauge lever-action Model 1901 is probably the ugliest repeating shotgun ever designed, but those who own those guns love them.

A Savage over-and-under shotgun, the Model 24 with a 20-gauge shot barrel and a .22 magnum rimfire rifle barrel.

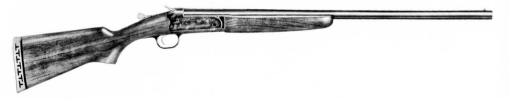

This little Savage single-shot hammer gun is made especially for the young shooter.

The Remington Model 11–48 shotgun is a streamlined version of the old Remington Model 11. It is made in 12, 16, 20, 28, and .410 gauges and most of the small-bore and sub-small-bore skeet being shot today is shot with this model.

The Mossberg Model 500 is a relatively new entry into the pump-gun field. It has a top safety and is a rugged, well-designed gun.

The Remington Model 31 was a very smooth-working, much-loved shotgun. It was discontinued after the war and its place was taken by the Remington Model 870 pump.

The Remington Model 11–48 skeet gun in .410 is probably the most popular of all repeating .410s for small-bore and sub-small-bore shooting.

A Model 21 Winchester 20 gauge handsomely restocked for the author in genuine Circassian walnut.

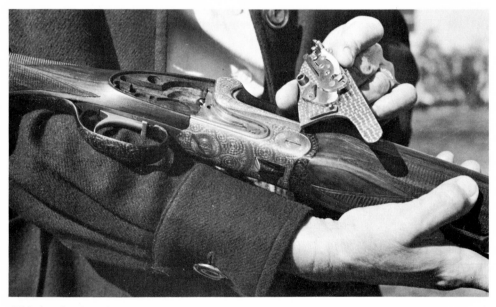

This is a back-action sidelock from an AYA over-and-under. The locks are beautifully polished and gold plated.

The Darne shotgun made in France has a novel breech system.

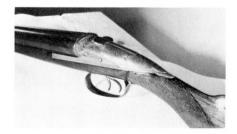

A Darne with the breech closed.

Turkey, the greatest upland game.
    —courtesy Winchester News Bureau

A possible double on pheasant.
    —courtesy Winchester News Bureau

What is the right lead?
    —courtesy Winchester News Bureau

A big pointer and two friends.
    —courtesy Winchester News Bureau

Jim Rikhoff, public relations direc-
tor of Olin Mathieson, demonstrates
the effectiveness of the Winchester
Model 59 autoloader.

The moment of release.

Ruffed grouse limit.

Safety and courtesy at the fence line.

A quail covey rise.   —courtesy Winchester News Bureau

It's hard to figure out what the dogs are up to, but the lady will be on the bird first.
—courtesy Winchester News Bureau

Shooting from a natural feather-grass blind. —courtesy Winchester News Bureau

Fully equipped for ducks. —courtesy Winchester News Bureau

Evaluating a shotgun pattern. This is a 12-gauge pattern shot with Federal trap loads from a full-choke barrel at 40 yards. Like most full-choke patterns, this one shows a dense center and a thin fringe.

The Choke-Chek pattern sheets are helpful in patterning a shotgun, particularly for the trapshooter.

In patterning a shotgun, one should use a piece of paper about four feet square and then inscribe a 30-inch circle to enclose the most shot.

A gimmick like this speeds up the inscribing of 30-inch circles on pattern sheets.

The sage grouse is the largest of the North American grouse and one of the slowest flying of all game birds.

The moment of truth on pheasants. —courtesy Winchester News Bureau

W. R. "Bill" Weaver, the scope manufacturer, shooting a shotgun equipped with his 1X shotgun scope and his Weaver Choke with a full-choke tube attached. The Weaver Choke has been discontinued.

A target shot at 40 yards with an Ithaca pump gun with rifle sights that is especially bored for rifled slugs.

A double and an automatic pass shooting at ducks.

—courtesy Winchester News Bureau

Three Labrador retrievers await the kill.

—courtesy Winchester News Bureau

Notice that the bird fired at by the gun on the left is already out of the picture.

—courtesy Winchester News Bureau

An example of good, tucked-in shooting form.

—courtesy Winchester News Bureau

checkering has ever been turned out than that seen on high-grade Parker and Fox guns.

But checkering has always been a headache to those who wanted to produce good serviceable guns at a moderate cost. The pattern on an A–1 Parker probably took a skilled checkerer a week to do, and that on medium-grade Parkers from one to three days. Today, a good job of hand checkering will cost from $100 to $250, depending on the fineness of the diamonds and the area to be covered.

Since the last war, checkering on mass-produced American shotguns has been done by operators using electric checkering machines or purely by machine. For a time Remington used machines for all checkering on the Model 11–48 automatics and the Model 870 pumps. Another concern used machine checkering with hand-finished borders. Checkering on prewar Winchester Model 21 shotguns was carefully done and extensive in area. For my taste the diamonds could have been longer, smaller, and sharper but on the whole the checkering was quite good. Model 21s that came out after the war were not noted for the excellence of their checkering, but now that the Model 21 is strictly a custom proposition, the checkering is not bad. It does not compare, however, with the checkering done before the war on custom-made Model 21s and on the Parkers of higher grades.

Today the best checkering in the world is being done by a handful of individual American custom stockmakers such as Lenard Brownell, Al Biesen, and Monte Kennedy. Excellent checkering is generally found on expensive Italian, British, and Belgian guns and occasionally on German and Austrian guns. But most European checkering is not carefully sharpened up with a finishing file, and much of it is square-topped and downright sloppy.

In the future most American repeating shotguns will probably be "checkered" by a process employing heat and pressure to press the pattern into the wood. Remington perfected the process in 1962 with the introduction of the Model 700 rifle and Model 1100 shotgun. Winchester and Savage also employ the method. Some of the patterns are very handsome and the guns on which it is employed look like a million dollars. However, since the checkering is in reverse with the diamonds recessed into the wood, they do not keep the hand from slipping. Such checkering will do for a mass-produced repeater, but it will never be seen on fine shotguns made largely by hand.

In the old days of guns largely made by hand, stocks on better grade guns were all finished with linseed oil. They were very carefully sandpapered with progressively finer grades of sandpaper used on a block so that the grit would not dig into the softer portions of the grain. Between sandings the stock was wetted, then dried quickly to raise the "whiskers" of the wood. The last sandpaper used was so fine that it actually polished the wood rather than sanding it. Then the stock was warmed and covered with hot linseed oil so that it would sink into the pores. When another application or two of linseed oil filled the pores and gummed on the surface, the finish was cut right down to the bare wood with fine wet-or-dry sandpaper used wet or with pumice used on a leather-covered stock.

The pores were then filled with oil. From then on, a few drops of linseed oil were put on the palm and carefully rubbed into the stock. After fifteen minutes or so of hand rubbing, the stock was carefully wiped off with a clean, dry rag. It was then set aside until the last thin coat was thoroughly dry. Then another microscopically thin coat was put on in the same manner. This method is expensive and time consuming, but it is still an excellent way to finish a piece of hard, fine-grained walnut.

If the wood is softer and more open of grain, the first coat can be spar varnish, which is left on until it is bone dry. Then it is cut down to the bare wood with wet-or-dry sandpaper used wet, and thin coats of oil are put on as described above. If only oil is used, soft wood will continue to absorb it with the result that the wood becomes too dark and the figure is lost. The chap who wants to refinish a factory stock should remove the old finish with varnish remover and then proceed as above.

Many cheap shotguns and some not so cheap have been finished with sprayed-on lacquer or cheap varnish. Mostly this stuff did not penetrate and a little use made the finish flake off in large chunks showing bare wood underneath. Today, the new plastic varnishes used by American gun factories are much better than the old ones used to be. Some custom stockmakers use several coats of spar varnish, sanding the stock down between coats. No American factory stocks are oil finished. For one thing that is an expensive finish slow to put on. For another the American gun buyer wants his new gun to shine in the display rack.

Some of the new varnishes are more waterproof than oil and some are pretty tough, but none of them are as handsome as oil, and the oil finish has the advantage of being renewable by rubbing on a few drops of oil with the palm and then polishing it off with a dry cloth. In time the loved and cared-for oil-finished stock builds up a deep, rich sheen which no other finish can duplicate.

The gun-lover who wants to individualize the stock of a fine gun should have a gold or silver crest plate put on the bottom of the stock about midway between the grip and the toe. Fine English guns and high-grade Parkers almost always had crest plates. The owner's name, initials, or indeed his crest, if he has one, can be engraved on the plate. This in turn can be of silver or gold, oval, or shaped like a shield.

CHAPTER **13**

Shotgun Fit

A SHOTGUN user can approach the subject of gun fit from two directions. He can fit himself to the gun or he can get the gun to fit him.

Within limits, most of us can fit ourselves to a gun and do a good job of it. Over many years American shotgun manufacturers have found that a gunstock with a drop at comb of 1⅝ inches, drop at heel of 2½ inches, and length of pull of 14 inches fits the average man well enough so that he can do good shooting with it if he in turn tries to fit himself to it.

We say average man. What do we mean? I have read that the average American male is between 5 feet 8 inches and 5 feet 9 inches tall and about 160 pounds in weight. If such a gunstock fits this lad exactly, it obviously won't fit Shorty Smith, who is 5 feet 1 inch, or Slim Jones, 6 feet 4 inches. If Shorty and Slim are exceedingly adaptable, they can fit themselves to the stock sufficiently and do creditable shooting, but they'd do better if they didn't have to work so hard at it.

Shorty can hold the gun with his left hand farther back on the fore-end, and Slim can hold it far forward, thus each can to some extent take the curse off the too long or too short stock. Shorty will have to get his head just right on the stock—the same stock will have more drop at comb for him than for Slim because his face will be at a different spot. Our standard factory stock has one inch more drop at heel than at comb. Slim will have to watch it or he'll crowd his nose up against his thumb and will get smacked. I can do pretty good shooting with the standard stock, but I'm a bit over six feet, fairly long of arm, square of shoulders, and thin of face. For me the standard stock is somewhat too short, too low of comb, and too crooked. I tend to shoot under with such a stock, which is all right for skeet where most targets are falling, but miserable for upland shooting where the birds are usually rising.

For instance, I like to shoot pheasants with a gun that throws its patterns a bit high. Then I hold right on a fast-rising bird and hit it. With most standard stocks I tend to hit pheasants low and wound them unless I make a conscious effort to shoot high.

I don't own a trap gun, but now and then I shoot a round of 16-yard rise with a Winchester Model 21 skeet gun using the Skeet No. 2 barrel. If in mounting the gun, before calling for the bird, I take pains to place my cheek against the stock so that I see a good deal of barrel, I can do fairly well. I once broke twenty-four out of twenty-five targets shooting that way. That's a case of the shooter who fits himself to the gun.

Gun fit, then, is a matter not only of fitting the gun to the individual, but also fitting the gun to the type of shooting it is intended for, and to the clothes he's wearing. As we have seen, the trap gun should throw its pattern high because the target is always rising rapidly, and the skeet gun should tend to throw it a bit low since the target is generally falling—particularly if the shooter is on the slow side, which I am.

I have a sweet little Winchester Model 21 in 16 gauge. I got it on a trade and its stock didn't fit me at all. I had it restocked in French walnut by a fine craftsman. The comb is a bit thicker than that of my 12-gauge Model 21, which is otherwise stocked to the same dimensions. Result is that the little gun shoots quite high. It's deadly on fast-jumping pheasants, but, alas, I tend to shoot over with it on the little flat-flying California valley quail.

A pal of mine who used to lease a shooting preserve in Scotland had a matched pair of 12-gauge doubles built for him by Boss of London particularly for driven birds. As I recollect, their dimensions are about as follows: drop at comb, 1¼ inches, drop at heel, 1¾ inches, length of pull, 14¾ inches. Grips are straight and the stocks are long—both factors tending to make a gun shoot high. Combs are high and thick, so the guns centered their patterns more than 2 feet high at 40 yards. With their built-in lead, the guns are wonderful on overhead incomers, as one can hold right on the birds, follow their flight, and knock them cold. They'd be fine on jumping mallards, too; and they might do all right on pheasants. But for all-around shooting, they just shoot too high.

Our one-gun man will use the same gun for pheasants as for ducks; the same gun for bowling over a cottontail as for taking a pop at a whitetail buck. For pheasants he wants a gun that patterns high; for deer, one that puts buckshot, pumpkin ball, or rifled slug right at point of aim. For cottontails the ideal gun patterns low. The stock that's just right for the lightly dressed pheasant hunter in early fall is too long for the bundled-up character freezing to death in a duck blind. We see, then, that there are a lot of aspects to this business of shotgun fit—not only the shooter's build, but also what he's going to shoot, and what he's going to wear.

Many never attempt to get a shotgun to fit them. Instead, they try after a fashion to fit themselves to the gun and let it go at that. Some write in to a gun editor and ask what stock dimensions should catch them. Others seek help from skilled shooters. In England it's the practice for custom gunmakers to fit their clients by means of try-guns which are adjustable for length of pull, drop, and pitch. They not only see them mount the gun but also watch them shoot and observe their habits. The sporting-goods house of Abercrombie & Fitch in New York City has a try-gun, and Winchester has a couple at New Haven. Whether there are any others in the country or not, I can't say, but they are a very good idea. Most of those who arrive at satisfactory stock dimensions do so under their own steam. That's what I did. It's generally a slow and expensive process, but if we know what to look for we can do a fairly good job of it, and a far better one than we can get by mail from a gun editor.

There's no great mystery about the function of correct stock dimensions. All they do is help a shooter mount the gun fast and put the shot charge where he wants it to go. Probably the most important dimension is drop at comb. The eye is actually the rear sight of the shotgun, and the comb acts as an elevator. If the comb is too high or too thick, the eye is too high, and as is the case with a too high rear sight, the barrel will be pointed up and the gun will shoot high. If the comb is too low or too thin, the eye wil be too low, and as is the case with a rifle with a too low rear sight, the gun will center its shot charge low.

The next most important dimension is length of pull, or the distance between the center of the trigger and the center of the

Special stock made for the man who must shoot from the right shoulder but use his left eye.

butt. If the stock is too long, it's slow and awkward to mount fast. It tends to catch on the clothing. If it's too short, the shooter will bang his nose with his right thumb.

Naturally, a length of pull that's exactly right for the man shooting doves in shirt sleeves is too long for the same man bundled in several layers of clothing in a duck blind. That's why the Winchester Model 12 heavy duck gun, chambered for the 3-inch magnum shell, has a stock length of 13⅝ inches, whereas the compromise stock on the field gun of the same make has a length of pull of 14 inches. Because the long stock tends to cut down on recoil, and because the trapshooter mounts his gun before he calls for his target, trap stocks run long. The standard Winchester Model 12 trap gun has a pull of 14⅜ inches, as does the Remington Model 870 trap gun. The tall man needs a longer-than-average stock to keep his thumb away from his nose, and the small man needs a shorter stock if he wants to mount his gun fast. Individual shooting habits make a difference, too. One man may shoot with his head fairly erect. Another may crawl his stock and need a longer one.

As a rule, the more a man shoots, the straighter he likes a stock. Fifty or sixty years ago, most American factory guns were made with a great deal of drop, both at comb and at heel. I have seen guns with a 2-inch comb drop and a 3½-inch heel drop. Even today, some people like such stock dimensions, but to me they're miserable. The crooked stock is usually liked by the beginners who haven't yet learned to get their heads down.

Not much can be said for the crooked stock, but a lot can be said against it. The gun fitted with one is more difficult to point. It also kicks more, for the more drop a stock has at heel the more it tends to bang the comb up against the cheek. The stock with little heel drop, on the other hand, brings the recoil back in a straight line as a push, rather than as a blow. Until you've tried guns of the same gauge and same weight with different stock dimensions, it is difficult to realize how much difference the stock makes in recoil effect.

I once had a foreign shotgun which apparently had been built for driven-bird shooting, for the comb was so high that the patterns centered about 3 feet above point of aim at 40 yards. I cut the comb down until it was right for me, and by then the heel was about ¼ inch higher than the comb. Sounds cockeyed, but the result was a fast-handling gun that was very pleasant to shoot. As the gun recoiled, the comb was pushed away from instead of against the face.

Within limits, drop at heel doesn't make too much difference. A difference in drop at comb of ¼ inch would entirely alter the shooting. Even a difference of ⅛ inch would be noticeable. But ¼ inch difference in drop at heel isn't important. The man who shoots a lot and has learned to put his gun to his face, as he should, rather than his face to his gun, will take a straighter stock than the beginner who mounts his gun and then puts his head down. The square-shouldered man will take a straighter stock than the man with sloping shoulders.

Anyone should shoot as straight a stock as he can handle, though. As we have seen, a staight stock points faster, kicks less, and shoots more consistently, for slight differences in cheek placement don't make much difference in the elevation of the shot charge. With a crooked stock, the placement of the face against the comb at different points makes a good deal of difference in elevation. That's one reason that stocks for trap guns are straight and that many trap guns are made with Monte Carlo combs, which for several inches have no drop at all.

Drop at comb should be such that with the cheek pressed hard against the comb, the eye looks right down the rib. If, instead, the eye loses sight of the rib and sees only the breech, the comb is too low. The gun will then tend to center its pattern low, and because the gun doesn't have the support of the cheek, the man behind it

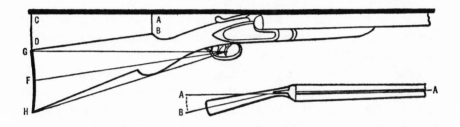

Showing how to give dimensions for a shotgun stock. TOP: A-B is drop at comb; C-D is drop at heel; F is length of pull. If measurements at G and H are given, the pitch will be right. BOTTOM: Difference between A and B is cast-off.

will tend to swing with his arms instead of pivoting his whole body. The too low comb also tends to make the shooter an aimer who lines up front bead and receiver on the target as if he were using the two sights of a rifle. The too high comb, on the other hand, is no good for all-around use because it causes the gun to center its patterns high. That's all right for high-bouncing pheasants and for traps, but poison for use on deer with ball, slugs, or buckshot, or for smacking cottontails. But if the gun is so stocked that when the cheek is hard against the comb the eye is right in line with the rib or the top of the barrel, the gun tends to shoot a bit high anyway; for in the field one doesn't ordinarily get his cheek down hard on the comb. Instead he places it firmly and easily, sees his barrel foreshortened a bit, the bird above it—and he hits. If he wants to, though, he can bear down hard on the comb and shoot his charge of buckshot right at the deer at 40 yards or aim under a scurrying rabbit.

The term "pitch" referring to a gunstock simply means the angle at which the butt is cut. A simple way to measure it is to set the gun against the wall with the butt flat on the floor and the breech against the wall. Pitch is the measurement from the muzzle to the wall. As can be seen, a slight difference in the angle of the butt makes a good deal of difference in the measurement at the muzzle—and the longer the barrel, of course, the greater this difference will be. Actually the function of pitch is to keep the gun comfortably at the shoulder. If the stock has zero pitch or even up pitch, the butt tends to slip down under the armpit and the gun tends to shoot high. If there's too much down pitch, the butt tends to slip up and throw the shot low.

Few American shotguns are made with what is known as "cast-off," but most foreign shotguns are. As mentioned before, the term means a slight bend of the stock away from the line of sight toward the shoulder. Some think this cast-off makes a gun easier to mount. I doubt if it makes any difference. Cast-off does, however, tend to drive the gun against the face and hence increases recoil effect. The more the cast-off, the greater the push. Its opposite, "cast-on," tends to push the comb away from the face and hence may slightly diminish recoil.

I arrived at my own correct set of stock dimensions by the long slow process of owning and shooting a lot of guns, changing their stock dimensions, and hitting and missing with them. Eventually I found that for all-around use these are about right for me: Length of pull, 14¼ inches; drop at well-rounded and fairly thick comb, 1½ inches; drop at heel, 2¼ inches; pitch down from 26-inch barrels on double-gun, 1 inch. With any gun so stocked, be it pump or automatic, side-by-side double, or over-and-under, I shoot pretty well. If these dimensions are changed to any great extent, my shooting falls off. A man with sloping shoulders would take more heel drop, and with shorter arms would take less length of pull. If the shooter is wide between the cheekbones, but otherwise my size, he'd take a rifle with a lower comb.

Probably the easiest and quickest way to get good stock fit is to go into session with a try-gun, knowing what to look for, and having the assistance of a skilled fitter. However, any man can fit himself if he is willing to do a little experimenting and to give the subject some intelligent thought. Length of pull is sometimes about right when the butt fits into the crook of the forearm with the finger on the trigger, but the acid test is how the gun comes up.

Remember these things: If the butt of your gun catches your clothes and hangs up under your armpit when you mount the gun rapidly, its stock is too long. If your thumb tends to bump your nose when you shoot, the stock is too short.

If the butt tends to slip down under the armpit when you shoot, the stock has too little pitch down. If the butt tends to slip up, the stock has too much.

If when you press your cheek hard against the comb, you see only the breech, your gun has too much drop at comb. You'll tend to be an arm swinger and to shoot low. If under the same circumstances you can't look right down the barrel, but instead see it foreshortened, you have too little drop at the comb and you'll shoot high.

If the gun seems to kick excessively, it may well be too crooked.

A good deal can be done to change stock dimensions by the gun owner himself, and also by the gunsmith. The comb can be rasped or scraped down if it's too high. The stock can be cut off if it's too long and lengthened by adding a recoil pad if it's too short. A piece of wood can be inletted into the stock and shaped up to give a higher comb or a Monte Carlo. Gunsmithing firms like Griffin & Howe of New York City and Pachmayr Gun Works of Los Angeles can bend a stock up to give it less drop at comb and at heel, or down to give it more. And the gun owner who thinks his pitch is wrong can loosen the screws which hold the buttplate to the stock, then insert a piece of cardboard at the toe to give less pitch down—or at the heel to give more.

Actually, there's nothing mysterious about gun fit, and once a man has learned to shoot he's a better authority on what fits him than anyone else. A well-fitting gun doesn't make a crack shot out of a dub, a poor fit doesn't make a dub out of a slicker, but everyone does his best shooting with a gun stock that fits.

CHAPTER **14**

Shotguns

for Various Purposes

The All-Around Gun

THE average man doesn't have the inclination, space, or money to hoard a whole battery of smoothbores and he generally does all of his gunning with one weapon. Sometimes he chooses this wisely, but sometimes he does not.

And what does our one-gun man use his smoothbore for? He'll undoubtedly knock off some cottontails with it, as the cottontail is America's No. 1 scatter-gun target. If he lives north of the Mason-Dixon Line, chances are that he'll take a crack at a few pheasants, and if he lives south of it, he'll probably do some dove shooting and catch himself a few quail. A minority of these hunters may also go out for ruffed grouse if they live in the north or for wild turkey if they live in Pennsylvania or in some of the Southern or Southwestern states. Our average hunter probably never pops a primer at a clay target, but some of these one-gun men will shoot a few clays for practice—maybe at a trap or skeet layout or maybe with a hand trap.

I am the last person in the world to say that there is any one gun that is ideal for all this shooting. There isn't. To be happy and well armed, the chap who does a variety of gunning should, I believe, have two guns—one for upland game and one for geese, for pass-shooting at ducks, and for wild turkeys. The upland gun can double at skeet and the wildfowl gun at traps, although they will do only fairly well, as both the trap and skeet gun for those who shoot competitively are pretty specialized instruments. The gun for long-range pass-shooting at ducks and geese is almost as specialized an instrument as a vaulting pole. However, by making some compromises it is possible to acquire a gun that will do reasonably well for most of these jobs, not perfectly but not too badly either.

Thirty or forty years ago, the one-gun man in the great majority of cases would, if he bought a double, get one with 30-inch barrels bored modified and full. If he bought a pump or automatic, it would be full choke and have a 30-inch barrel. In any case, chances are that his all-around gun would be a 12 gauge. Approximately half of the shotguns sold in the United States are still in 12 gauge and so are about half the shot shells. Yet, I am conscious of a slow, very gradual, shift away from the 12 toward the smaller gauges. From figures I get from the various arms companies, the 12 is still the best seller but not quite the overwhelming favorite it used to be in past years. The smaller gauges are coming up. There is also a shift away from long barrels and the full-choke boring. Once 32-inch barrels were very common, but they no longer are. Even the 30-inch barrel does not rule the roost as it once did. Slowly the word is getting around that a 30-inch barrel shoots no "harder" than a 28-inch barrel and that it produces so little more velocity than a 26-inch barrel that no one can tell the difference.

Not too many years ago, anyone considering the purchase of an all-around gun would pretty well be confined to the 12 gauge, as only the 12 gauge could handle 1¼ ounces of shot for 50 to 60-yard wildfowl shooting. Today I am not so sure that the 12 is the only choice, and if the one-gun man has a leaning toward a 16 or a 20, he can make a pretty good case for his favorite. The 16-gauge 2¾-inch magnum shell now handles 1¼ ounces of shot and generally does a pretty good job of patterning it. The 20-guage magnum chambered for the 3-inch shell also handles 1¼ ounces of shot. A modified barrel in any of these three gauges will kill single ducks very dead with 1¼ ounces of No. 4 or No. 6 shot at 45 yards and maybe a bit farther. A 70 to 75 percent full-choke barrel with the same amount of shot will turn the trick at 50 yards—and maybe, with luck, a bit farther.

Nevertheless, a very good argument can be made that the first choice of the one-gun man should probably be the 12 gauge. The popular 12 has its advantages. For one thing, the 12-gauge shells are most widely distributed, and one gets more shot for his money in the 12 than in any other gauge. A 12-gauge shell with 1⅛ ounces of shot costs less than the same amount of shot in a smaller gauge. Theoretically anyway, the 12 gauge will throw a better pattern with the same amount of shot than any of the smaller gauges because the shot column is shorter and fewer shot are deformed by friction against the barrel or by battering against the forcing cone of the chamber or against the cone of the choke. The 12 also handles large shot better than the smaller gauges. If the all-around gun is to be used on deer, the 12 patterns buckshot better and uses heavier slugs that deliver more energy.

On the other hand, 12-gauge shells are heavier, bulkier, and 12-gauge guns average a bit heavier than guns in the smaller gauges. They are also less trim. The 12 gauge, even with the same amount of shot, is a noisier gun than those in smaller gauges. The only real advantage the 12 has over the 16 and the 20 is at extreme ranges on ducks and geese or with its denser patterns at trap or skeet.

At the turn of the century, chances were that the one-gun man would buy a double-barrel gun, but by the time World War I broke out, probably as many single-barrel repeaters as doubles were sold. Now the overwhelming majority of shotguns sold are pumps or automatics, and in this country the double of American manufacture is pretty dead.

A good double is a very fine gun. It is the handsomest of all guns, probably the best balanced, and certainly the safest, as opening up the double to expose the breech will tell instantly whether the gun is loaded or not. It also handles handloaded shot shells somewhat more reliably than do repeaters. There are still many lovers of the double gun in the United States, but the manufacture of a first-rate double with selective single trigger and automatic ejectors is tremendously expensive because of the great amount of handwork necessary. During the depression a generation ago, it was possible to purchase a first-quality double for around $100. I bought a Winchester 21 in 1939 or 1940 for, if I remember correctly, $116. The good Remington Model 32 over-and-under sold for a little more. The Browning over-and-under was somewhat cheaper. One of the famous Parkers with automatic ejectors and single trigger cost about $150. A good grade Ithaca or L. C. Smith sold for less.

Today, the Remington Model 32, the Parker, the Ithaca double, and the L. C. Smith are no longer made. The Winchester Model 21 is now strictly a custom gun and the cheapest sells for $4,000. The Winchester Model 101 over-and-under introduced in 1963 and selling for about $250 is made in Japan, where wages are a fraction of those paid in the United States. The Belgian-made Browning Superposed today has the lion's share of the quality market.

As compared to the market for repeating shotguns, the demand for doubles in this country doesn't amount to much, but by European standards it is tremendous. To meet it, doubles are imported from Belgium, France, Spain, Italy, Germany, and Austria. Some are very fine guns, but many are shoddy and unreliable. Generally speaking, the foreign double that sells in this country for the same price as an American pump gun is apt not to be the world's greatest bargain.

But a good double with 26 or 28-inch barrels bored about 50 and 60 percent (tight improved cylinder and modified) or, still better, one with two sets of barrels, one improved cylinder and modified (45–50 and 60) and one modified and full, is hard to beat for all-around use. I have a Model 21 12 gauge with two sets of barrels, one Skeet No. 1 and No. 2 (about cylinder and modified) and the other modified and improved-modified. I got the gun right after the war before the price of the Model 21 had skyrocketed. I couldn't afford it now. Someday I'll sell it and use the dough to put my grandson through college.

The pumps and automatics are the guns most of those looking for an all-around shotgun will buy. Although single-barrel repeaters are now manufactured in Europe, they are an American invention, an American specialty, and a manufacturing marvel. Neither type is quite as well balanced as a good double—although more of that later. Neither is quite as safe, for it is more difficult to tell if one is loaded. For obvious reasons the automatic is probably less safe than the pump. Beauty is pretty much a matter of taste, but to my own way of thinking, no repeater is as handsome as a good double. The better finished ones are by no means ill-favored. A legitimate criticism of many repeaters in the past has been that they were too long, too muzzle heavy, and consequently the point of balance lay too far forward. A pump or automatic with a 26-inch barrel is about the same overall length as a double with a 30-inch barrel, and a repeater with a 30-inch barrel is about the same overall length as a double with a 34-inch barrel! But today, the repeating shotgun is quite a different instrument from what it was a generation ago. The use of light alloy steels and even of Duralumin in repeating shotguns has made them lighter and handier, and self-loading shotguns employing the short-recoil system or gas have cut down on the apparent recoil in light weapons with heavy loads.

A pump or automatic with a 26 or 28-inch barrel bored modified and in 12 gauge is a pretty handy weapon for about everything. Still better would be to get such a gun with two barrels—one bored improved cylinder for use on upland game and the other modified or full choke for doves, waterfowl, and possibly occasional trapshooting. Another solution would be to have this all-around repeater fitted with one of the variable choke devices discussed in Chapter 9. If the gun is to be used primarily in the uplands, one of the lighter repeating shotguns should be chosen. The Browning double automatic with the dural receiver was as light an upland 12 gauge as anyone could want, yet it handled plenty of shot for wildfowl if the need arose. The Winchester glass-barrel Model 59 was another very light 12-gauge automatic. The Ithaca and the Marlin are very light pumps. If, on the other hand, the gun is to be used more on waterfowl than on upland game, one of the heavier repeaters is the best idea.

The Upland Gun

The upland gun is something I write about with considerable enthusiasm since as far as scatter-gun sports go, I am a congenital upland hunter. Give me a good pointing dog, a light upland gun, and put some pheasants in the wheat stubble and some quail in the draws and I am a happy man.

The upland gun should be light since generally the upland hunter does a lot more walking than he does shooting. An Eastern ruffed-grouse hunter of my acquaintance tells me that he walks an average of three miles for every shot he gets at grouse. I imagine that in the Northwest where I live I walk at least a mile for every pheasant I bring to bag, and woodcock hunters probably put more mileage behind them than that.

Upland game is shot at short range. Most quail are killed at 25 yards or under, and most pheasants at under 30. Ruffed grouse and woodcock are generally taken at under 20. Chukar and Hungarian partridges are generally shot at somewhat longer range than quail, or even pheasants, and the Western varieties of quail (valley, Gambel's, and scaled) tend to flush somewhat wilder than bobwhites. Nevertheless, with any upland game more birds will be killed at under 30 yards than over. For that reason, the repeating shotgun used in the uplands should be bored no tighter than modified, and in most instances improved cylinder is better. There is nothing whatsoever wrong with a light 12 gauge as an upland gun, but with lighter report and recoil, lighter ammunition, and generally lighter weight, the 16 or the 20 gauge is generally preferable.

In the 12-gauge gun, skeet boring, which will generally give about a 40 percent pattern at 40 yards, is exceedingly deadly, but the standard improved cylinder boring will reach out a bit farther. In the 16 and 20 gauge with 1 and 1⅛ ounces of shot, a tight improved cylinder (sometimes called quarter choke) that patterns about 50 percent is about right. Now that 28-gauge shells can be obtained with 1 ounce of shot, one of the little guns bored about 50 to 55 percent is a wicked little upland gun. I have two—a handsome little Spanish Arizaga double and a Remington Model 11–48 with two sets of barrels—one bored skeet and the other bored modified.

To me the ideal upland gun is a 16 or 20-gauge double with 26-inch barrels bored improved cylinder and modified. Such guns are almost universally used in the quail country of Georgia and South Carolina where bobwhite hunting is almost a religion. These light, fast-handling doubles also do beautifully for grouse and woodcock, and are even exceedingly useful on decoyed ducks.

When the pheasant is the principal game bird I think the average gunner, who is not the world's fastest shot, should get a repeater bored modified, a double bored modified and full. He will be slow on the target and will have many 35–40-yard shots. I have had many favorite pheasant guns. I killed many with a Winchester Model 21 12 gauge with 26-inch barrels bored modified and full, many with a Model 21 20 gauge with same boring and barrel length. Today I seldom use more than 1 ounce of shot in 20 or 12 gauge. My beautiful sidelock Beretta side-by-side with 26-inch improved cylinder and modified barrels is the reigning favorite.

Since most upland game birds are rising when shot at, I think a slightly high-shooting gun is indicated—and that means a rather straight stock. The pheasant particularly rises sharply when flushed and most pheasants are missed because gunners shoot beneath them. Because the upland gunner generally shoots fast at rising targets he should use a short-barreled gun. The upland double is about right with a 26-inch barrel. The repeater should not have a barrel over 26 inches in length, and many upland gunners are having variable choke devices attached to give overall lengths of 24 and even 22 inches. I have never known anyone who used one of these short barrels in the uplands who did not swear by it.

Light weight, short barrel, open boring, straight stock—this is the recipe for upland success!

The Wildfowl Gun

The average duck and goose hunter fancies himself taking his waterfowl at extreme ranges, but actually more birds are killed at under 40 yards than over. For decoyed ducks and geese, the open-

SUGGESTED SHOTGUN LOADS FOR VARIOUS GAME

	SHOT SIZE	OUNCES OF SHOT				
	By Number	12 Gauge	16 Gauge	20 Gauge	28 Gauge	.410 Gauge
Turkey, Geese, Fox	2 or 4	1¼, 1⅜, 1½, 1⅝, 1⅞	1¼	1 3/16, 1¼		
Ducks (Pass Shooting)	4 or 5	1¼, 1⅜, 1½, 1⅝	1¼	1 3/16, 1¼		
Ducks (Over Decoys)	6 or 7½	1⅛, 1¼	1, 1⅛	⅞, 1, 1⅛		
Pheasant	6	1⅛, 1¼	1, 1⅛	⅞, 1, 1⅛		
Sage Grouse, Crows	6 or 7½	1⅛, 1¼	1, 1⅛	⅞, 1		
Squirrel	5 or 6	1⅛, 1¼	1, 1⅛	⅞, 1		
Rabbit	5 or 6	1⅛, 1¼	1, 1⅛	⅞, 1	¾, 1	¾
Grouse, Partridge, Prairie Chicken	6 or 7½	1, 1⅛	1, 1⅛	⅞, 1	¾, 1	
Quail, Doves	7½ or 8	1, 1⅛	1, 1⅛	⅞, 1	¾, 1	¾
Woodcock, Jacksnipe, Rail	8 or 9	1	1	⅞, 1	¾, 1	½, ¾
Trap	7½ or 8	1⅛				
Skeet	9	1⅛	1	⅞	¾	½, ¾
Deer	Rifle Slug or	1	⅞	⅝		
	00 to 0 Buckshot	9 to 15 Pellets				

bored upland gun used with suitable shot size does quite well. At 40 yards a modified 20 gauge will kill a duck just as well as a magnum 10 and unfortunately most of us are better 40-yard shots than we are 60-yard shots. The best shooting on decoyed ducks I ever did in my life was with a Winchester Model 21 double with barrels bored Skeet No. 1 and No. 2 and using 1½ ounces of No. 6 shot. With the big even patterns, I could not miss and neatly wiped the eyes of my companions who were using 30-inch full-choke barrels.

Most duck hunters greatly overestimate the distance at which they kill ducks. Once in northern Arizona I made myself quite a reputation by knocking off passing ducks that flew from one lake to another right over a particular pine tree. I was using a 20-gauge L. C. Smith at the time, and the natives used to marvel at what a "hard shooter" it was. Then a mechanically inclined character figured out the height of that pine tree by triangulation and decided I was killing those ducks at between 30 and 35 yards—well within the reach of a modified 20.

However, there is such a thing as pass-shooting, and a skillful shot who is properly armed and knows how to lead can reach out and bring down ducks and geese at surprising distances. For this work, I think the medicine is a pump or automatic with a 28 or 30-inch 12-gauge full-choke barrel with a ventilated rib and using anything from the 1½-ounce load of the 2¾-inch magnum shell to the 1⅞-ounce load of the 3-inch 12-gauge magnum. Because heavy loads are used, the gun should be fairly heavy. It should for the same reason wear a recoil pad, and since the wildfowler is generally pretty well bundled up, the stock should be about ¼ inch shorter than the one on his field gun. The automatics that are operated by gas or use the short-recoil system give less apparent recoil than pumps or long-recoil automatics and are consequently somewhat more pleasant to shoot with heavy loads.

Properly led, a duck can be killed at something over 50 yards with 1¼ ounces of No. 4 shot, at close to 60 yards with 1½ ounces of No. 4 in the 2¾-inch magnum load, and to perhaps 65 yards with the 1⅞-ounce loads in the 3-inch 12-gauge magnums or the 2 ounce in the magnum 10s. Lucky hits will often knock down ducks at considerably greater ranges than these, but such kills come by chance and not by skill. Duck hunters tend to shoot at birds much too far away. Many times I have seen citizens blaze away at large ducks at least 200 yards from the gun. The man who waits until the birds are within 40 yards is a better sportsman and has better luck.

Geese, because they are big birds, are often shot at so far away they'd be difficult to bring down with a rifle. Often the goose hunter must try to take his birds at 60 to 65 yards or not shoot. Then the best advice I can give is to get ahead of the bird about twice as far as you think you should, to pick one bird out of the flock, and to keep pouring it on him until he goes down.

The Trap Gun

The trap gun is always a 12 gauge, since trapshooting is a highly competitive sport and is shot for money. There is no law against shooting traps with a 16 or a 20 gauge, but there are no special classes for the small gauges and as a consequence they are almost never used. The clay targets shot at are always sharply rising, and since the gun is mounted before the target is called for, the trap gun has a longer and straighter stock than the field or skeet gun.

The fast shot breaks his targets from a 16-yard rise at about 30 to 35 yards, and hence he is probably better off with a modified or improved-modified boring than with a full choke. I am no trap-shooter and have never owned a trap gun but I once broke 24 straight targets at 16 yards with the Skeet No. 2 barrel of a Winchester Model 21 skeet gun. No. 2 Skeet is about like modified.

The typical trap gun is an especially stocked Winchester Model 12 or Remington Model 878 pump with 28 or 30-inch full-choke barrel and ventilated rib. Automatics are almost never used at trap because they toss their shells out to the side to the annoyance of other shooters on the line. Ventilated variable choke devices are never used, since the high-pitched report bugs the other shooters. Actually, variable choke devices of any sort are almost never seen as they tend to make guns shoot low and a low-shooting gun is the last thing one wants for traps.

At one time, many side-by-side double-barrel trap guns with ventilated ribs were seen but they seldom turn up any more except for doubles shooting. Browning over-and-under trap guns are quite popular. Many like single-barrel trap guns for 16-yard and handicap shooting, and old Parker and L. C. Smith single-barrel trap guns are greatly prized. Ithaca still builds a good and quite expensive single-barrel trap gun.

A typical stock on a trap gun would have about the following dimensions: drop at comb, 1⅜; drop at heel, 1¾; length of pull, 14⅝; pitch down, 1 inch. However, trapshooters are always fiddling with their stocks, fitting them with adjustable buttplates, rasping the combs down, building them up, changing the pitch.

The Skeet Gun

Just as traps and skeet are entirely different games, the skeet gun and the trap gun are entirely different instruments. The trap-shooter shoots at rapidly rising targets and breaks them at from 33 to 40 yards. The skeet shooter shoots at targets which are for the most part falling and breaks them at from a few feet (as is the case with the incoming No. 8 station birds) to about 22 or 23 yards. Whereas the trapshooter needs considerable choke—nothing less than modified and generally improved-modified or full—the skeet shooter wants all the pattern he can get—nothing less than improved cylinder and generally full cylinder or one of the special Skeet No. 1 or "Skeet In" chokes. Even a Skeet No. 2 or "Skeet Out" choke is a mistake in a skeet gun as it throws too small a pattern. Actually, these chokes are generally about modified.

The first skeet guns were generally side-by-side doubles with the barrels sawed off to give a length of 25 or 26 inches and no choke whatsoever. The double-gun makers—Parker, Winchester in the Model 21, L. C. Smith, and Fox all brought out special skeet guns with automatic ejectors, non-automatic safeties, selective single triggers, 26 and sometimes 28-inch barrels with special skeet borings. Today, side-by-side doubles are seldom seen on the skeet range, as most skeet shooters think they do better with the single sighting plane of the pump or automatic. Browning Superposed skeet guns are popular, and the old Remington Model 32 over-and-under skeet gun brought out thirty years ago is still liked for skeet, and one in good condition will bring four or five times its original cost.

Today most skeet shooters use pumps or automatics with 26-inch barrels bored Skeet No. 1 and with ventilated ribs. It is my observation that automatics are gradually displacing the pumps. They are more convenient as the slide handle does not need to be operated. Before the war most pump and automatic skeet guns were fitted with Cutts Compensators and shot with the spreader tube, but today it is rare that any variable choke device is seen on the skeet field.

Various classes are shot at skeet: All Bore (16 and 12 gauge) 20 gauge, Small Bore (.410 and 28-gauge guns used with ¾ ounce of shot) and Sub Small Bore (the .410 used with the 2½-inch shells with ½ ounce of shot).

Competitive skeet shooters who compete in all classes go to great lengths to maintain the same balance in guns of different gauges. Often, the serious skeet shooter will have one over-and-under gun (generally a Browning) made up with several sets of barrels, each set giving the same balance. If he doesn't do that, he will have a set of automatics with identical stocking. All the Remington skeet guns, for example, are stocked alike.

Skeet guns are generally stocked about like field guns. A typical stock would be about as follows: Drop at comb, 1½–1⅝; drop at heel, 2¼–2½; length of pull, 14; pitch down, 2 inches from 26-inch barrel of repeater.

Skeet is a game of smooth, fast, uniform swings, and therefore it is easy to get a skeet gun too short of barrel and too light. Generally, the dainty 6¼-pound upland gun will be found to be so light it is difficult to control. A double with a 28-inch barrel probably swings a bit steadier than a gun with a shorter barrel. For the pump or automatic, a 26-inch barrel is about right. In 12-gauge the guns using the short-recoil system or gas operation are more pleasant to shoot than those using the long-recoil system. Ideal weight for a 12-gauge skeet gun is 7½ to 7¾ pounds.

Skeet guns do pretty well as upland guns, particularly in the smaller gauges. A skeet-bored 16 or 20-gauge double is just about ideal for bobwhite shooting, and a skeet-bored 20 or 28-gauge automatic is also very handy in the uplands.

Skeet is a more relaxed game than traps, and for my money better practice for the bird shooter since it offers a greater variety of angles.

The Slug Gun

The repeating shotgun designed especially for the use of rifle slugs on deer is a relatively new development brought about by laws prohibiting the use of rifles for deer in many areas. These guns are made with barrels from 20 to 26 inches in length equipped with front and rear sights like a rifle and especially bored to handle slugs accurately. These barrels may also be obtained as extras and fitted to the regular game gun. They are bored straight cylinder throughout and the bore diameter is generally somewhat smaller than that of a barrel with constriction at the muzzle. These cylinder slug barrels incidentally throw excellent 20 to 25-yard patterns for skeet or short-range upland shooting. I once shot quail in Georgia with a chap who used an Ithaca Deerslayer and he did very well indeed.

Some of these slug specials are equipped with receiver sights and some even with scopes of from 1 to 2½. Accuracy obtainable with these guns is surprising. From a rest, most of them will shoot into 3 inches at 50 yards, and some will group smaller. One of the most accurate guns with slugs I have ever seen was a Remington Model 1100 skeet gun with ventilated rib and middle bead as well as front bead. By aiming with the two beads and shooting from the sitting position, I could keep almost all shots in a 6-inch bull at 100 yards. This baby shot *exactly* to the point of aim.

The rifle slug is a deadly missile that makes a wicked wound and has a lot of knock-down power. If the slug is used in a properly bored gun with rifle sights, most hunters can do about as well with it to 100 yards as they can with a rifle.

The Riot Gun

Most repeating shotguns have appeared in riot-gun form—simply guns with short (generally about 20-inch) barrels bored cylinder. These guns are the descendants of the sawed-off double-barrel shotguns used by express messengers in the West and by some gunmen like Doc Holliday, of Tombstone, Arizona, fame, who preferred to do his serious social shooting with a shotgun. Riot guns are used by police, by bank messengers, and prison guards. They have also been used for close-range trench and jungle fighting and to 50 yards or so they are far more dangerous than rifles. Many have come on the surplus market since the war. As they stand they are too muzzle-light and they scatter their shot too much for anything except very short range shooting. They can be civilized by attaching one of the longer variable choke devices to give better balance and to furnish some choke.

CHAPTER 15

The Shotgun Gauges

In the days of the muzzle-loading shotgun, the shooter could have a hole of any size he fancied through the barrel of his gun, as there was no such thing as fixed ammunition. The gunner simply dumped his powder, shot, and wadding down the muzzle, rammed it home, put a cap on the nipple, and that was that.

The advent of the breech loader and fixed ammunition quickly brought on standardization of shot shells and limitation of bore sizes. At the present time in the United States, shot shells are manufactured in six gauges: 10, 12, 16, 20, 28, and .410. Several have been dropped. The 8 gauge was killed off when guns of that caliber were prohibited for use on waterfowl by the Federal Firearms Act. The 4 and 6 gauges were simply too much gun and were never popular. I have never even seen a 4-gauge shell and only one 6 gauge. The 14 gauge was something the world could live without, but in recent years one of the major American manufacturers gave serious consideration to bringing out a 14-gauge gun and I did considerable shooting with a pilot model. I have never laid eyes on a 24-gauge shotgun, but I do have a Winchester-made 24-gauge shell and such ammunition was advertised in Winchester catalogs before World War I. I have never seen a 32-gauge gun, but such things were made and I have been told that it is still possible to have 32-gauge guns built and to buy 32-gauge ammunition in Belgium.

Winchester at one time made a 9-mm. bolt-action rimfire shotgun, and the ammunition has been loaded in this country and is still loaded in Europe. The .410 (which is properly a caliber, not a gauge) evolved in this country from cartridges like the .44 XL, which were shot shells in rifle cases and used to pot small game when shot from rifles and from the old Marble game getter.

The gauges are named from the number of balls of the particular bore diameter it takes to weigh a pound. For example, ten 10-gauge round lead balls weigh a pound, 12 spherical balls of 12 gauge, and so on. The .410 is about a 67 gauge. In the black-powder days, there were 8, 10, and 12-gauge rifles as well as shotguns. A 10-gauge rifle shooting both conical and spherical bullets was considered pretty good rhino and elephant medicine, and smoothbores of large caliber were very popular for elephants until the advent of the high-velocity nitro-express rifles using jacketed bullets and smokeless powder. Frederick Courteney Selous, the famous ivory hunter, museum collector, and writer who hunted the game fields of South Africa in the 1880s and 1890s, used at first a single-shot smoothbore 4 gauge on elephants. Sir Samuel Baker, a powerful and ebullient Englishman who explored the headwaters of the Nile accompanied by a beautiful blonde wife back in the 1870s, had a 2-bore single-shot elephant gun using an explosive shell. Imagine a gun firing a bullet weighing a half pound! This monster, Baker wrote, always spun him around two or three times and gave him a nosebleed and a violent headache when he fired it.

Here are the bore diameters of the gauges with which Americans are familiar. Round (pumpkin) balls loaded into shells of these gauges are of course smaller, since they have to be made small enough to get through the tightest of full chokes. As an example, the round (pumpkin) balls loaded in 12-gauge shells are about 14 gauge. But here are the bore diameters of the various gauges:

> 10 gauge—.775 in.
> 12 gauge—.729 in.
> 16 gauge—.662 in.
> 20 gauge—.615 in.
> 28 gauge—.550 in.
> .410 bore —.410 in.

The 4, 6, and 8 gauges were always used on wildfowl, as even the smallest of them, the 8 gauge, is a pretty ponderous weapon. I have hefted and pointed an exceedingly handsome 8-gauge Parker with 36-inch barrels, and although I would like to own it just for kicks, I'd hate to have to hit anything with it, as it swings about as handily as a vaulting pole. Back in the early days of breech loading the 10 was the all-around gauge and very popular. Those who hunted with the "little 12-gauge guns" were considered to be on the racy and exhibitionistic side—a bit like those who hunt with .410s and 28s today. I have run across many dozens of old 10-gauge hammer guns with twist barrels made in the 1880s. However, along in the 1890s the 12 began to cut into the popularity of the 10 and to replace it as the all-around gauge. In this century the 10 has always been considered a wildfowl gun exclusively.

The versatile 12 gauge is the all-around gauge in the United States and in England. It is the most widely used and it is furnished with the greatest variety of loads and with the greatest variety of shell lengths—from 2 inches in Britain to 3 inches in both the United States and Britain. The 16 gauge is used to some extent as an all-around gauge in the United States and is *the* all-around gauge on the Continent. However, in the United States it is generally considered an upland gauge.

The 20 gauge is considered the upland gauge in the United States, but since the advent of the 2¾-inch magnum 20-gauge shells with 1⅛ ounces of shot and the 3-inch 20-gauge magnum with 1¼ ounces, it is being used more and more as an all-around gauge on ducks as well as upland birds.

The 28 gauge is a very pleasant little gun to take into the uplands and is growing somewhat more popular since in magnum form it is being loaded with ⅞ and a full ounce of shot. For a long time though, it was kept alive only because it was legal for small-bore skeet shooting with ¾ ounce of shot and did a better job of patterning it than did the .410. The .410 is a kid's gun, a woman's gun, a pot gun for the farm and camping trip, a gun for small-bore and sub-small-bore skeet shooting and NOT a man's gun.

A survey made by the *American Rifleman* some years ago showed that approximately 50 percent of the shotguns sold in the

United States were in 12 gauge. About 25 percent of all guns were in 16 gauge. The 20 gauge accounted for about 17 percent of the sales, the .410 about 4 percent, and the 28 and 10 gauges about 2 percent each. From corresponding with manufacturers, I gather that sales of the 12 gauge have declined a bit to less than 50 percent. The 20 and 16 gauges now each have about 20 percent of the market but the 20 gauge seems to be slowly gaining on the 16. The .410 has increased its share of the market to approximately 10 percent. The balance is shared by the 28 and the 10 gauges. The 28 is gaining a bit and the 10 declining. All of the 10-gauge guns sold are made in Europe.

The various gauges have their advantages and disadvantages. The guns in the larger gauges are generally heavier and bulkier, and guns in the smaller gauges lighter, trimmer, neater looking. However, all guns are getting lighter with the use of new materials and some 12s are now lighter than some 20s. Even when they use the same amount of shot, shells for the smaller gauges are lighter and less bulky. The larger the gauge the louder the report and generally the more severe the recoil.

The greatest advantage of the larger gauges is that the larger the bore the shorter the shot column. The short column means that fewer shot are deformed by contact with the cone of the choke, the forcing cone of the chamber, and by friction against the sides of the barrel. An ounce of shot in a 10-gauge gun has a column only .610 inch long, for example, whereas the same amount of shot in a .410 is contained in a column 2.175 inches long. A 1-ounce shot column in the various other gauges are as follows: 12 gauge—.690, 16 gauge—.837, 20 gauge—.968, 28 gauge—1.210.

There is no doubt but that the 12 gauge will pattern somewhat better than the 20 gauge with the same amount of shot. However, with plated shot or for that matter with modern chilled (hardened) shot, the difference is not important under modern field conditions. Not many full-choke 12-gauge guns will regularly pattern much over 70 percent with any load but many 20-gauge guns for the 3-inch magnum shell using 1¼ ounces of shot will pattern almost as well as a 12 gauge at 40 yards. Still, there is no doubt that a trapshooter will break a few more birds, particularly at handicap ranges, with a 12 gauge shooting 1⅛ ounces of shot than he would with a 16 gauge using the same charge, and that the duck hunter will get a few more birds at extreme ranges with a 12 than with a smaller gauge.

Guns in .410 are patterned at 25 yards, but the standard patterning distance for all other guns is 40 yards. There is nothing to the old wives' tale that the smaller gauges throw smaller patterns and are hence harder to hit with. Guns in 12, 16, 20, and 28 gauge are all bored to put 70 percent of their shot in a 30-inch circle at 40 yards, 60 percent if modified, about 45 to 50 if improved cylinder. The 20-gauge pattern is just as big as a 12-gauge pattern with a given choke and given range, but because it contains less shot it is thinner. The thinner pattern is no more difficult to hit with but more difficult to make clean kills with. In clay target shooting, patterns of 20 and 12-gauge skeet guns cover about the same area, but the 20-gauge pattern is thinner and targets sometimes slip through such a pattern when they would be broken by the thicker pattern of the 12 gauge.

The guns of smaller gauge have trimmer lines, are more pleasant to shoot, and as they generally handle faster, they make up in speed what they lack in range. If, for example, and upland gunner is able to get on a bird and shoot at 25 yards, he would hit the bird with as thick a pattern as if he had fired at 30 yards with the slower 12 gauge.

As we have seen, the 10 gauge was the standard and popular all-around gauge in the 1880s and into the 1890s, at which time the 12 began to replace it. In those days, the 10 was not loaded very heavily. A charge of 1¼ ounces of shot was considered a right hefty load and some 10-gauge shells were loaded with as little as 1 ounce of shot. When the 10 gauge was in its heyday, handloading with brass shells was very popular. Duck hunters used to take their loading tools, primers, powder, and shot with them into duck blinds and put together shells between flights.

Winchester brought out the only 10-gauge repeater ever made when the Model 1887 lever action was introduced in the year for which it was named. Later it was redesigned a bit and called the Model 1901. It was not discontinued until 1920. All of the compa-

SHOTGUN BORES

| 10 GAUGE | 12 GAUGE | 16 GAUGE |
| BORE=.775 | BORE=.729 | BORE=.666 |

| 20 GAUGE | 28 GAUGE | 410 GAUGE |
| BORE=.613 | BORE=.550 | BORE=.410 |

Here are the sizes of the holes in shotgun barrels of the various gauges. Many think that the smaller the hole in the end of the barrel the smaller the pattern. Actually 28-, 20-, 16-, and 12-gauge guns with the same choke throw patterns of the same size. With any luck, a full-choke gun should pattern 70% of its shot charge in a 30-inch circle at 40 yards. The .410 should do the same at 40 yards. In the smaller gauges the patterns are not smaller—only thinner.

—courtesy Browning Arms Co.

nies manufacturing double guns made them in 10 gauge.

For many years the standard 10 gauge load was 1¼ ounces of shot in front of 4¼ drams of black powder or its equivalent in smokeless in a 2⅞-inch case. When heavier loads of shot in front of progressive-burning powder came along in the 1920s, the 10-gauge "high-velocity" load came into being under the Super X (Western) brands and Nitro Express (Remington). These were also in 2⅞-inch cases but contained 4¾ drams of powder and 1⅝ ounces of shot. The range of the 10 was extended somewhat and the companies making double guns turned out beefed up guns for the new load. Human nature being what it is, a lot of chaps with ancient 10s with outside hammers and twist barrels shot this hot stuff in them and blew them up.

In 1932, Western Cartridge Company under the direction of John and Spencer Olin, duck and goose-hunting aficionados both, developed the 10-gauge magnum shell in a 3½-inch case with a potent load of powder and 2 ounces of shot. Ithaca made one thousand double-barrel guns of various grades for these roman-candle shells, and Parker followed suit with a big double chambered for them. How many Parker made I have no idea. Neither of these great guns survived the war and they are now collector's items.

Ammunition for 10-gauge guns is still manufactured in the United States with the regular 2⅞-inch cases and also with the 3½-inch cases. Some double guns (mostly Spanish and mostly cheap) are imported in 10-gauge magnum and one single barrel for the monstrous 3½-inch shells. However, since the 3-inch, 12-gauge magnum shell is now loaded with 1⅞ ounces of shot, there isn't much a 10 gauge will do that a 12 will not do. What popularity the 10 retains comes from the superstition that the reason people miss wildfowl is that they don't throw enough shot at them. Sales of both guns and ammunition in 10 gauge have just about reached the vanishing point.

Over most of the world the 12 is the most popular of gauges and 12-gauge ammunition can be obtained in shops from the fly-specked Indian duccas of Tanganyika to the suave and walnut-paneled gunmakers' shops of London's plush West End. In Britain 12-gauge shells are loaded with cases as short as 2 inches and with ¾ or 1 ounce of shot and in the United States in cases as long as 3 inches and with 1⅞ ounces of shot.

For many years the standard 12-gauge shell was 2⅝ inches in length but beginning in the early 1920s, all 12-gauge guns made in the United States were chambered for 2¾-inch shells. In England the standard chamber is 2½ inches (65 mm.) long and so are the standard shells. But the British make both shells and chambers in 2¾-inch (70 mm.) lengths, as well as some special wildfowl guns for 3-inch shells.

In the United States 12-gauge shells in 2¾-inch cases are still loaded with as little as 1 ounce of shot and 3 drams of powder, but the standard light field load is 3¼ drams of powder with 1⅛ ounces of shot. The old "high-velocity" duck load of 3¾ drams of powder and 1¼ ounces of shot is still very popular, but in recent years the 2¾-inch magnum load with 1½ ounces of shot has come along.

Back in the 1920s there was much whoopla about the 12-gauge 3-inch magnum loads with 1⅜ ounces of shot in 3-inch shells. All the double companies built special long-chambered and generally over-bored guns for these, and in 1935 Winchester brought out the Model 12 heavy duck gun for the 3-inch shells. Now it is possible to obtain doubles, pumps, and automatics for the 3-inch shell. The load itself has been stepped up gradually from 1⅜ ounces of shot to 1⅝ ounces and then finally to 1⅞ ounces—or almost the equivalent of the magnum 10 gauge. Incidentally, 2¾-inch shells can be used in any gun chambered for the 3-inch shells. For years the story went around that using short shells in long chambers opened up the pattern, but I did some extensive experimenting with them some years ago and I could find little if any difference.

Many writers have said that the 16 gauge was on its way out, but year in and year out it does a pretty good job of holding its own. For a few generations it outsold the 20 gauge but as far as I could find out in the fall of 1963 it was just about running neck and neck with the 20 gauge. In the Northwest, so few 16s are sold that many small-town stores do not stock the ammunition, but in other areas, particularly in the South, it is far more popular than the 20.

Actually, the 16 is a fine choice as an all-around gun, as it patterns about as well as the 12, kicks less, handles enough shot for most purposes, and makes up into a trimmer gun. The 16 is the standard gauge on the Continent and most German, Austrian, and Belgian doubles made for Continental consumption are 16s. The standard chamber on the Continent is 2⁹⁄₁₆ inches (65 mm.) and this was the standard in the United States until 1929 when the 2¾-inch chamber was adopted by the Sporting Arms and Ammunition Manufacturers Institute. The 16 is a particular favorite for the shotgun barrels of Continental three-barrel and over-and-under rifle-and-shotgun combinations. The standard 16-gauge low-brass field load uses 3 drams of powder and 1 ounce of shot, but 3¼ drams and 1⅛ ounces are also available in low-brass shells as well as in high brass. The 16-gauge 2¾-inch magnum shell uses 3⅓ drams of powder and 1¼ ounces of shot—as much shot as what used to be called the "heavy duck load" in the 12 gauge. Down South, where thousands of deer are killed annually with 16-gauge guns, the favorite buckshot load No. 1 is with 12 pellets.

A factor in popularizing the 20 gauge was the introduction of the Model 12 Winchester shotgun in 1912 in that gauge. It was a cute and handy little gun. It was chambered for 2½-inch shells using ¾ ounce of shot. However, fine doubles were made in 20 gauge before that. In the period just before World War I, the 20 was loaded with both black and smokeless powder with as little as ½ ounce of shot and as much as ⅞ ounce. When the high-velocity shells were developed with progressive-burning powder after World War I, the 20 gauge was loaded in 2¾-inch cases with 1 ounce of shot. In 1926 the chamber length of American 20-gauge guns was changed to 2¾ inches but there are still some 20-gauge guns around with the short chambers, and using long shells in short chambers raises pressures. Latest goat glands for the standard 20 gauge has been the 2¾-inch magnum shell loaded with 1⅛ ounces of shot.

In the days of much handloading for double-barrel guns, a few 20-gauge guns were made with 3-inch chambers but the universal popularity of the repeater killed off the long 20s. The idea, however, did not die. It came to life again because duck-hunting officials of Winchester-Western got Model 21 Winchester shotguns made up with 3-inch chambers and used specially loaded lots of ammunition with 3-inch cases. At first those 3-inch 20-gauge magnum cases were loaded with 1⅛, then with 1³⁄₁₆, and finally with 1¼ ounces of shot. I borrowed a Model 21 for these long shells from an official of the Winchester company, liked it, and ordered a Model 21 for the long chamber. But I specified 26-inch barrels, much to the shocked surprise of my friends at Winchester. I have never regretted my choice and have killed a lot of game with the little gun using 2¾ as well as 3-inch shells. Now pumps as well as doubles are made for the long shells.

A few years ago a gun writer said the 28 gauge was a real bastard and in many ways he was right. Actually, there isn't much excuse for it, and it has been kept alive only because it is legal for small-bore shooting at skeet with ¾ ounce of shot. Because of the shorter shot column, it patterns better with that amount of shot than the .410. The 28 was introduced in 1903 by Parker, a company which made beautiful little doubles for it. The first load was ⅝ ounce of shot. Then it was stepped up to ¾ ounce. For a time the 28 was loaded in 2⅞-inch cases but they are now the 2¾-inch standard length. In the late 1950s Federal Cartridge Company kicked over the traces and loaded a 28-gauge magnum shell with 1 ounce of shot. The other companies followed suit. This makes the 28 a good all-around upland gun. I have shot many doves, pheasants, Huns, and chukar partridges with my little 5¾-pound Spanish Arizaga double. I also own a Remington Model 11–48 in 28 gauge and have shot a lot of skeet with it. Winchester made the Model 12 in 28 gauge for years and has turned out some 28-gauge Model 21s. One can get a 28-gauge Browning over-and-under on a 20-gauge frame on special order.

The .410 is the direct descendant of the .44/40 rifle cartridge. At first the standard .44/40 case was used, bottle neck and all, and the shot was in a paper container. Then 2-inch straight brass cases were used, then 2-inch paper cases, then 2½-inch cases. At one time the shell was known as the .44 XL. It was loaded with ⅜, then ½ ounce of shot in 2½-inch cases. Then in the early 1930s Winchester-Western pioneered the 3-inch .410 shell with ¾ ounce of shot and brought out the Model 42 Winchester pump shotgun for it. The Model 42 was discontinued in 1963, but Remington makes the excellent Model 11–48 and the Model 1100 in .410. Noble introduced a .410 automatic in 1963 and various single shots, bolt-action, and slide-action guns are made for it. It is the only gun to be used in sub-small-bore skeet shooting with 2½-inch shells and ½ ounce of shot. It is fun to break clay targets with and it is a fair enough meat gun on a pack trip. Outside of the skeet field, it is most popular as a woman's and beginner's gun in cheap single shots and bolt actions.

CHAPTER 16

Guns and Loads

for Pheasants

MANY won't agree, but to me the pheasant is king of the upland gamebirds. He is big, gorgeous, wonderful eating, and as smart as a whitetail deer. Under some conditions he is very easy to hit, and under some conditions exceedingly hard to hit. He is almost always hard to get a shot at and always hard to kill.

I grew up and lived most of my life in Arizona, and I was a middle-aged man when I shot my first pheasant. Two friends and I crossed a cold, knee-high creek in south Idaho to hunt an island where many smart pheasants had fled from the gunning in nearby fields. We had to roll up our pants and take our shoes off to wade across. I stood on the bank, barefoot, with my shoes in one hand and an unloaded, double-barrel shotgun in the other. Suddenly, in the tall grass under my feet, there was a thrashing and a shrill cackling, and a beautiful cock pheasant shining in all his glory came boiling out. I dropped my shoes, opened my gun, dropped a shell into one barrel, and managed to cut the cock down while he was still in range. As I fondled the bird I knew this was for me—all the excitement of a fast-jumping whitetail buck without the fuss and trouble of dressing it and lugging it in.

I had some difficulty those first few days of pheasant hunting. I made some pretty fancy misses before I found out how slow a pheasant is when he first takes off and how fast he is once he's got his steam up. I tended to overlead the short-range, right-angling shots and to underlead crossing birds that had had 50 to 100 yards to get under way or were flying down from a hill. I also wounded close-rising birds because I didn't realize that pheasants rise at a very sharp angle when they are flushed. I hit many low and behind. But after a week or so of performing indifferently on pheasants, I began to get the knack of how they should be shot, and on several occasions since that time, I have killed twenty and more pheasants straight without a miss. These were mostly birds that had been pinned by a good dog and which got up within 35 yards and were killed within 40 yards. Mostly they were killed within 30.

On the other hand, the pheasant that has got under way is a tough baby to hit. Once in Idaho I was hunting with one of the finest shots in the United States, a man I have seen make a triple on rising Huns, break 100 straight at skeet, and kill ten quail with fifteen shots, taking everything that got up within 40 yards. For some reason, cock pheasants were flying off a ridge in late afternoon and were coming over us. They were passing within 40 yards, but very high, and my pal shot five times before he managed to bring one down. He averaged about four shells for each pheasant in the bag, and before he hit that first bird he was roaring with frustration.

In England, the classiest way to shoot pheasants is to have a group of drivers push them so they fly over a row of high trees. The "guns" then take them as high, overhead incomers, and they are really moving. I would call this shooting more difficult than driven grouse because the pheasants come in higher and, I believe, just as fast.

When I first started hunting pheasants, I used a 12-gauge double most of the time. I also swore by the maximum loads with 3¾ drams of powder and 1¼ ounces of shot. I wounded a good many birds that first year, and I thought I needed heavy loads to bring them down. I found, however, that I was wounding them not because I wasn't throwing enough shot but because I was not centering them. Instead, I was under- and overleading and catching them on the edge of the pattern.

The average pheasant hunter goes out with a 12-gauge pump or automatic with a 30-inch barrel bored full choke. The long-barreled gun is sluggish. His swing is slow. He tends to shoot right at the rising birds and at their tails instead of their heads. He shoots too soon for the choke he is using, and at short range the small, dense pattern greatly handicaps him.

The pheasant gun (like all upland guns) should be short of barrel, light, and lively. The double should have 26-inch barrels and the repeater barrels should be no longer. Actually, for the upland repeating gun, I think it is smart to put on a variable choke device of some sort for an overall length of 24 inches. Many dozens of hunters have written me about the idea and then, with some misgivings, have had the operation performed. Most have written later that they shot far better with the amputated barrels.

As long as the gun itself is relatively short of barrel, fast to handle, and easy to mount and carry, the gauge doesn't make too much difference. For several years my pet pheasant gun was a Winchester Model 21 in 12 gauge. It has two sets of barrels, one set bored Skeet No. 1 and No. 2 (about improved cylinder and modified) and the other bored modified and improved-modified. The gun weighs 7¾ pounds and is handsome and delightful.

I also have two other Model 21s, and all three of these good doubles are stocked to the same dimensions. One is a 16-gauge bored improved cylinder and modified, the other a 20 gauge bored modified and full and chambered for the 3-inch 20-gauge magnum shell. The 16 and the 20 each weighs 7 pounds and have 26-inch barrels.

For the past three years I have shot more pheasants with a beautiful side-by-side Beretta 12-gauge that with two sets of barrels and an oak and leather case cost me about $1,000 in Italy in the middle 1960s. I use it with 1 ounce of No. 6 shot. It is bored improved cylinder and modified.

Another gun I have enjoyed shooting pheasants with is a dainty little Arizaga sidelock double 28 gauge from Spain. It has 25-inch barrels bored modified and full, a single trigger, and an automatic ejector. It weighs only 5¾ pounds and handles like a flash. I have killed many pheasants with it, many quail, some Huns, and chukar partridges. Incidentally, the 28 gauge is by no means a toy when used with the 28-gauge magnum load with 1 ounce of shot.

For most pheasant hunting with pointing dogs, a gun bored improved cylinder or Skeet No. 1 is right. Kills are usually within 30 yards, and at that distance an improved cylinder will kill just as well as a full choke and will chew up less meat.

I have often used the skeet barrels on my Model 21 on pheasants, and on close-rising birds it is almost impossible to miss with the more open barrel. I have shot pheasants over two weekends on the Nilo Farms, owned by the Olin Corporation.

I used the now-discontinued Winchester Model 59 automatic with a fiberglass barrel wrapped around a steel liner. I did very well with it. Out of around thirty pheasants I don't think I missed a one. I fired twelve shots at bobwhite quail and put eleven down. However, the birds were all pen-raised. They were shot in the open and were tamer and less speedy than the wild birds. The pheasant is a hard bird to get a shot at, an easy one to hit once he is airborne.

In the past thirty years I have shot a lot of pheasants, mostly over a line of great Brittany spaniels that began with my dog Mike. My ideas have changed. As of 1976 I use the 7-pound 12-gauge Beretta sidelock double and an Arizaga sidelock 20-gauge, and another 20—a Winchester Model 21. With my good dog Dick I use 1 ounce of shot. I almost never lose a bird!

Best all-around boring for a pheasant gun, particularly if it handles less than 1¼ ounces of shot, is modified. Nine out of ten times improved cylinder is all the pheasant hunter needs, but when a wild flush comes along, the open boring is apt to result in a feathered bird that gets away. Many times a wise old cock simply will not sit down in front of a dog. Even if a bird does sit, he'll often flush wild when he hears the footsteps of the approaching hunter. Then the bird must be shot at 40 to 45 yards, and the Skeet No. 1 choke or improved cylinder boring simply will not put enough shot into him.

In the fall of 1960, I was hunting pheasants in the Sacramento Valley of California. The first day I took my 12 gauge with the modified and improved-modified barrels. My hosts had good dogs and all shots were close. The second day I put the Skeet No. 1 and

No. 2 barrels on but regretted it as the shots were much longer. Birds were hunted by parties approaching each other in four directions in an enormous rice field. Birds came over as high and fast as ducks and had to be taken at 45 and 50 yards. The Skeet No. 1 barrel would feather them but not nail them. I switched the selector button to fire the Skeet No. 2 barrel (about 60 percent or modified) first, and with it I dumped the big birds quite neatly.

If by chance the pheasant hunter could pick up a gun bored 50 percent, or what used to be called quarter choke, I think he would find it ideal as the first barrel in a double or the only boring in a repeater. I had a fine No. 4 Ithaca so bored at one time. It patterned right at 50 percent with 1¼ ounces of No. 6 shot. It was easy to hit with and deadly at 40 yards. The man who wants to use 1 ounce of shot in a 20 or 28-gauge gun should usually have it bored modified rather than improved cylinder. The improved cylinder pattern in these little guns is just as large as that of the 12 but thinner. One needs a tighter but somewhat denser pattern.

I had this lesson strongly impressed on me eight or nine years ago on the last Sunday of the pheasant season in Idaho. I was out with a little Ithaca 20-gauge double bored improved cylinder and modified and found a stubble field full of cock pheasants that had been driven up by heavy hunting from brushy draws below. The stubble had been heavily pastured, was thin, and the birds would not hold tight for my Brittany spaniel. I feathered three cocks with the improved cylinder barrel and 1 ounce of No. 6 before I switched to the modified barrel.

Ideally, the pheasant gun should center its pattern high, since the pheasant rises sharply on take-off, and the straight-stocked, high-shooting gun has a built-in lead. My guns are stocked with a drop at comb of 1½ inches, drop at heel of 2¼, length of pull of 14¼, and pitch down of 1 inch from 26-inch barrels. Combs are thick, and I see the barrels foreshortened with the bird above them. When I shot fast, they center their patterns about 9 inches high at 30 yards. This built-in lead, combined with fast-rising barrels, centers the patterns high enough so that I hold right on a jumping cock and kill him.

When the odd pheasant takes off and flies low along the ground, however, I am apt to miss him with these high-shooting guns if I shoot without thinking and do not see the muzzles well beneath the bird. With standard American stock dimensions of 1⅝-by-2½-by-14 inches, I am apt to shoot low on rising birds.

Under most conditions, 1 ounce of shot is plenty for pheasants. I have shot many dozens with the 1-ounce load in the 20 gauge. Often when I go afield with my 20 double I put a 2¾-inch shell with 1 ounce of shot in the modified barrel, a 3-inch magnum shell with 1¼ ounces in the full-choke barrel in case I miss or wound with the first. For the 12 gauge, the ordinary field load with 3¼ drams of powder and 1⅛ ounces of shot is sufficient. The British 12-gauge field load uses only 1¹⁄₁₆ ounces of shot and kills pheasants well. In the 16 gauge, either the 1 or the 1⅛-ounce load does the job very nicely.

Many excellent pheasant hunters with more experience than I have had like No. 7½ shot for pheasants. I do not. On a crossing bird, where the shot can drive into the lung area from the side, No. 7½ is deadly. It is also deadly if the hunter can shoot high and fast and get shot into the head and neck. But more often than not, the pheasant hunter puts his shot into the rear end of the bird. He must break heavy wing bones, and he must drive the shot up into the vitals. For this, No. 7½ is too light, it seems to me, and I have lost entirely too many pheasants with it to make me happy.

The choice of most pheasant hunters is No. 6. It has sufficient weight to smash wings and drive up into the vitals from the rear; yet it gives sufficient pattern density. I was interested to note that Alex Kerr, the famous skeet shot, has reached exactly the same conclusion on shot size for pheasants as I have. We had a session on the subject of shot size about a year or so ago.

Another load which I tried in the 12 gauge and found superior to No. 7½ was the old live-pigeon load of 1¼ ounces of No. 7, but it is seldom encountered these days. A very good friend of mine who shoots a double bored improved cylinder and modified swears by No. 4. I have patterned his improved cylinder barrel with his favorite shot size, and at 35 yards the patterns have holes that you could throw a cocker spaniel through. Odd thing about it is that this chap is one of the best pheasant shots I have ever seen. By all logic he should wound many birds, as he shoots at everything that goes up to 40 yards. But somehow he just doesn't.

One fall, I kept notes on every pheasant I shot. I marked those which the dog had to chase and those which came down dead. Then when I dressed them I noted how many No. 6 shot they had taken. Of those that were killed dead and didn't move when they hit the ground, nearly all had five or more shot in them, and almost all had broken wings. Of those the dog had to hunt up, almost all had less than five shot in them, and many did not have broken wings. In many cases where birds that were plainly hit and had flown on and landed but either had been recovered by my dog or had been pointed again, from two to four shot had been taken through the body. For this reason I think the breaking of a wing is very important if one wants a high percentage of recovered birds. The fall seems to hurt and confuse the birds and give time for the wounds to have effect. Then the dog can grab them.

One season I was hunting a big stubble field. My dog was working a running pheasant, racing and circling and trying to pin it down. The bird flushed ahead of the dog at about 40 yards. I shot, saw feathers fly. The bird went over a hill and out of sight, my dog right after it. When I came over the hill, I saw my dog on point about 400 yards away. He had the cock under his nose. The bird was well hidden in thick stubble and was very sick. I grabbed it. It had four shot through the body. If a wing had been broken in addition, I do not think it would have moved.

The recipe for pheasants, then, is a light, fast-handling gun bored from 50 to 60 percent using at least 1 ounce of No. 6 shot. Barrel should be short, stock relatively straight. Pumps, doubles, or automatics are all good for this type of hunting.

Far fewer wounded birds would escape if pheasant hunters never shot at birds over 45 yards and seldom over 40 yards. It has been my experience that at 40 yards a pheasant can be killed nicely with a quarter-choke 12 or a modified 16 or 20, but at over 45 yards it is difficult to kill a pheasant with any load or any boring. The bird is as tough as a boot and has as many lives as the proverbial cat. If you don't put at least five No. 6 shot into him, you probably won't get him, and if you don't have a good dog, you're pretty sure not to get him.

CHAPTER 17

Quail Guns and Loads

WHEN I was a kid I lived in a little town within a few miles of Phoenix on the Salt River in Arizona. This was long before what passes for progress had caught up with Arizona. Phoenix then had a population of from ten thousand to maybe twenty-five thousand. Today Phoenix is an enormous sprawling city of well over a half million. In those days just before and after World War I, the Salt River always had water in it. Now every drop is taken out to be diverted to raise cotton and vegetables. The bed of the river where we kids used to swim, shoot ducks, and catch catfish is now a dry and dusty wilderness of garbage dumps, rusting automobile bodies, and discarded tires.

But in these days of long ago there were always swimming holes in the river. Mourning and whitewing doves nested in the trees along the banks and watered in the stream. In the fall thousands of ducks flew in from the north, rested in the river, and fed out in the fields. I used to cut classes to pester them with my old Winchester Model 97 pump with its 30-inch full-choke barrel. With that old gun I wasn't too bad a shot if what I was shooting at was against the sky and I had plenty of time. The long-barreled Model 97 was so muzzle heavy that once I got it rolling, it was so hard to stop that I seldom slowed or stopped my swing. My mother was an underpaid normal-school teacher and the doves and ducks and the occasional goose I brought in were welcome additions to the menu.

But quail were my Waterloo. North of the Salt was a scrubby forest of mesquite and cottonwood trees from a half mile to a mile wide. Beyond that were wheat and alfalfa fields. Today my old quail-hunting country is one solid housing development filled with hundreds of houses all exactly alike and owned by citizens each with an I.Q. of exactly 100 and each exactly 5 feet 9 inches tall. But then the brush was full of quail, and in the middle of the day when the ducks weren't flying, I used to try to get myself some birds. My duck hunting paid off in meat on the table but I really ran up a deficit on quail. I simply could not get on the little devils quick enough and most of my shots knocked off mesquite and greasewood leaves and twigs behind them or simply blew holes in the desert air. I concluded that for whatever the reason I simply was not destined to be a quail shot. Most of my acquaintances also considered quail on the wing a pretty rough target, and probably the majority of the quail that were brought to bag were ground sluiced. Almost everyone used a 12-gauge shotgun in those days. A typical double had 30 or 32-inch barrels, about 2 inches drop at the comb and 3½ inches at the heel. The typical pump gun was also long of barrel, had plenty of drop. The pumps were all bored full choke and the doubles modified and full or full and full. The way we patterned shotguns in those days was to put a tin can on a fence post, pace off forty steps, and shoot. If the can was as full of holes as the business end of a salt shaker, we were happy and knew we had a strong shooting gun.

After I got married I lived for a time in West Texas. The quail there were locally called "blue" quail, but they are more generally known as scaled quail or cottontops. I had a Winchester Model 12 pump in 12 gauge at the time. It had a 30-inch barrel and was bored full choke. With it I got perhaps one quail with six or seven shots. Because my wife is a little gal who stands 5 feet 2 inches high and begins to worry about being overweight when she tips the beam at 115 pounds, I bought her an Ithaca 20-gauge double with 26-inch barrels.

One day the storm and strife wasn't feeling too pert so, just to see how I would do with the little Ithaca, I laced on a recoil pad to lengthen the stock, got into the family jalopy, and drove out to a nice grassy area where I knew several coveys of scaled quail hung around. For the first time in my life I found myself shooting quail fairly well, and a great light dawned on me. The reason I had been missing those birds with my long-barreled, tightly choked, slow, and muzzle heavy 12 was I had been using a gun completely unsuited to the task. I had always been a rifle nut of the most depraved sort. Since I had been knee high to the traditional duck, I had been able to quote rifle ballistics by the yard. Instead of dreaming about money and lovely maidens as normal young men do, I dreamed about rifles. Shotguns, though, I'd pretty much taken for granted.

But this experience with the 20 gauge started me thinking. I paced off the distances at which I killed quail, and I found that even with the rather wild flushing Western quail I killed far more at under 30 yards than over, some as close as 10 yards and few at over 35. I got myself a roll of heavy paper about 36 inches wide and shot some patterns at 10, 15, 20, 25, 30, and 35 yards as well as at 40 yards.

Until that time I had been pretty vague about the size of patterns that shotguns threw at various distances. It dawned on me that it was a lot easier to hit a quail at 20 yards with the 26-inch pattern of an improved cylinder than it was with the 16-inch pattern of a full choke. At 10 yards the 15-inch pattern of an improved cylinder was certainly less tricky to handle than the 9-inch pattern of a full choke. The 19-inch pattern of a skeet No. 1 boring at 10 yards was even better for such shooting. Even the 20-inch patterns of a modified barrel give more room for error at 20 yards than the 16-inch pattern of the full choke.

The speed with which the quail gun can be handled is possibly just as important or even more important than the degree of choke. A quail isn't the fastest bird that has ever flown, but he takes off like a rocket and by the time he has flown a few feet he is flying about as fast as he ever flies. This quick getaway combined with his sudden appearance and the noisy whir of his wings makes it seem that he is traveling at 100 miles an hour. Actually, he is probably flying at about 35.

The classic quail of the United States is the bobwhite, one of the most beloved of all game birds. He lies beautifully to a dog. He is a strong flier, and he is good to eat. I have shot bobwhites in Missouri, Arkansas, South Carolina, Illinois, New Jersey, Georgia, and Idaho. He is a great bird and I love him dearly, but I do not think he is as smart a bird as the valley and the Gambel's quail. Nor do I think he flies as fast or is as hard to hit.

In the South, the bobwhite is almost as much of an institution and an industry as the red grouse is in Scotland. There the wealthy owners of plantations hunt the birds with ceremony and style. They use fast and wonderfully trained dogs (mostly pointers) and follow them on horseback or in hunting wagons built to run softly on automobile tires and drawn by matching mules. Sometimes the dogs are followed in four-wheel drive automobiles with special bodies. However the birds are followed, the moment of truth comes when the hunters get out of their car or wagon or off their horses and walk in to flush the covey. Sometimes they don't even have to walk in, as they may have a dog handler who will flush the birds for them.

The classic bobwhite gun in the South is a double in 16 or 20 gauge bored improved cyclinder and modified and with 26 or 28-inch barrels. When I was shooting quail in Georgia in the fall of 1963, I saw a great many Winchester Model 21s. Almost all had 26-inch barrels. Some were bored skeet No. 1 and No. 2 (about cylinder and modified) but most were bored improved cylinder and modified. A good many Parkers are still being used in the South and now and then one runs into a bird hunter who shoots a Purdey or a Boss, both prestigious British guns. Among the flossier quail hunters, it is considered something of a social error to hunt bobwhite with a repeater or with a 12 gauge.

Southern hunters like to have two shotguns—the light, open-bored double for quail, and a heavier more closely choked gun for wild turkeys and for waterfowl. Often they use their 16-gauge bird guns with No. 1 buckshot for driven whitetail deer.

Much of the shooting in the famous bobwhite country of South Carolina, Alabama, and Georgia is on coveys in tall grass among scattered pines. The birds are then not too hard to hit, and with a light, open-bored gun it isn't too difficult to make a pretty fair average of doubles. The first bird will probably be killed at 18 or 20 yards, the second at 27 to 30 yards.

I have been told that the pure and aristocratic blood of the Southern bobwhite quail has been corrupted by the genes of Mexican bobwhites which were trapped below the Texas border in northern Mexico and turned loose in the Southern states. I get many letters on the subject every year. According to my correspondents, the resulting hybrid bird is smaller than the old-fashioned, pure-blooded bobwhite. He flies faster, they say, lies less well to a dog, likes to hang out in brush and timber, and when he isn't feeding he likes to sit around and think up dirty tricks to play on dogs and hunters.

Not knowing much about this I have wondered just how true this all was. It has occurred to me that perhaps all the fault does not lie with the infusion of Mexican bobwhite blood. Maybe the birds are just getting smarter and have found that they were safer in brush than in open grass and stubble. Perhaps they really don't fly faster. My correspondents are generally in their late fifties and sixties. Possibly they just think the birds fly faster. I am not as young as I used to be, and it seems to me that birds and clay targets travel about twice as fast as they did thirty and forty years ago.

All southern bobwhites are not shot by rich plantation owners with fancy double guns, pairs of highly trained pointers, dog handlers, and blooded horses. One of the best bobwhite hunts I ever had was with an Arkansas farm boy. We were strictly on foot, and we had but one dog—a very homely but very smart pointer who looked as though his mother had been frightened by a bloodhound. The lad used an old Winchester Model 97 pump in 16 gauge. It had at one time been run over by a wagon, and the barrel had been amputated to about 22 inches. It had no choke whatsoever, but that kid could knock down a couple of birds with it while I was thinking about killing one.

Because a double does not have the long receiver of the pump or automatic, one with a reasonably short barrel puts the weight more between the hands and is faster and livelier to handle than a repeater. For quail, a 16 or 20 with 26-inch barrels, bored to throw about 45 and 55 percent patterns (improved cylinder and modified), and with a single trigger, is just about ideal. But doubles are hard to come by in this country today unless the gunner is willing to part with considerable scratch.

A Browning Superposed 20 gauge bored for skeet or improved cylinder and modified is a very fine quail gun and so is a similarly bored Winchester 21 in 16 or 20 gauge if the gunner has one, has inherited one, or can afford one.

Many foreign doubles come into this country. They run all the way from sad to excellent, from cheap Spanish jobs that retail with double triggers and extractors for about $100 to Purdeys that cost about $7,000. Some good foreign doubles made in Belgium, Italy, and Spain can be had for a lot less than the Purdey.

Probably the most sensible solution for the quail-gun problem is a pump or an automatic. I am a double man myself, but if I had to choose between the two types of repeaters I'd pick the automatic. Many, I know, will disagree with me. I have a Remington Model 11-48 in 28 gauge with two barrels with ventilated ribs—a skeet barrel 25 inches long and a modified barrel 26 inches long. With ⅜ ounce of shot and the skeet barrel, it is a deadly quail gun.

As long as the hunter is getting an automatic and doesn't want two barrels as I did, he can install such a variable choke device as the Poly Choke and with a 24- or 25-inch barrel he will find he has a livelier gun.

For my part, I am a traditionalist. I can see a repeater for waterfowl, but I cannot muster much enthusiasm for using them in the uplands.

The Western quail tend to be quite a different proposition from bobwhites. They are found in country with much less ground cover, often in overgrazed cattle country that wouldn't conceal a healthy flea. Then all a quail with any instinct for survival can do is to run. If he didn't run or flush wild, he'd be half-witted. I have shot far more Gambel's quail than quail of any other variety. I have heard the Gambel's denounced as a runner, a bad actor who won't lie for a dog.

Give him something to hide in and the Gambel's, the scaled quail, or the valley quail will all do a pretty good job of staying put. Some of the finest quail hunting I have ever had was north of Oracle, Arizona, in a year of good grass. A friend of mine had a rangy, homely cocker spaniel. He would find the close-lying singles and push them into the air with his nose. Every year I hunt California valley quail and sometimes mountain quail with a pointing Brittany spaniel, and given cover they all lie very well.

The Western quail seem to me harder to kill than bobwhites. When they are wounded they run off to go down a badger hole or hide in a packrat's nest. Almost all of my Gambel's quail hunting was done without a dog, as few dogs can stand the thorns and the thirst of typical Gambel's quail country. I made it a practice to mark well where every bird fell and go at once to the spot. Unless he is retrieved immediately a fatally wounded Gambel's will gather his last strength, find a hole to crawl into, and will be lost. The same thing is true of the scaled quail and to a lesser extent the valley quail.

If one is able to find Western quail under ideal conditions in good cover, the same gun that works nicely for bobwhites will do well for them. However, because Western quail are generally shot in barren, chewed-over cattle country, they are shot at longer average range than bobwhites are. As good a gun as I have ever had for Gambel's quail was a 20-gauge L. C. Smith Field Grade double bored modified and full. It had automatic ejectors and it came with a leather leg-of-mutton case. I bought it secondhand right in the worst part of the depression for $17.50 and for weeks my conscience hurt me for throwing my money around like that!

Just before World War II, I got a Winchester Model 21 skeet gun, a fowling piece that does very nicely for bobwhites. I found it too open for Gambel's quail, as too many birds will rise at 25 to 35 yards. With these wild rises, the skeet boring either let them fly off feathered or fall wounded. For Gambel's and scaled quail under typical desert conditions I think a 16 or a 12 should throw about a quarter-choke (50 percent) pattern and a 20 gauge should throw nothing less than a weak modified or about 55 percent. Using guns bored like these, the hunter of scaled and Gambel's quail has to learn to let the close birds get out to around 20 to 25 yards before he lets them have it. When he shoots them at 10 or 15 yards with a modified boring, he tears them up pretty badly.

I may be wrong, but I don't think the California valley quail is as tough a bird and as hard to kill as a Gambel's, and for these birds I do very well with 16s or 20s bored improved cylinder. But maybe this is because I have always hunted valley quail with dogs and get birds I would have lost if I had not had a dog. On the other hand (and again I may be wrong), I think the valley quail flies faster than either the scaled or the Gambel's and is harder to hit.

The hunter of bobwhites may be able to carry his shotgun in a saddle scabbard and follow the dogs on a well-trained and glossy thoroughbred or in a quail wagon, but the poor hombre who is out after scaled and Gambel's quail does it on foot. Lazy road hunters won't go after any coveys they don't see from an automobile, but the real quail hunter isn't afraid to walk. The Gambel's quail hunter who has only walked ten miles or so can hardly be said to have worked up a sweat. Many times I have covered fifteen miles in a day's hunting and not a few times I have gone twenty. One year in the very depths of the depression I used to leave my car on a desert road on the lower Verde River in Arizona and hunt to a chain of hills that was seven miles away by a forest service map. Since I was my own bird dog I covered a lot more than fourteen miles before I got back to the car. There were tens of thousands of quail at that time, but everyone was broke and even on Sunday I seldom heard a shot or saw another hunter. The limit in those days was twenty-five birds and I never went after a limit but what I got one.

On those long walks after desert quail, a light gun and light ammunition are twice blessed. You can make mine either a 16 or a 20, just so long as you make it light.

I think the medicine for bobwhites under most conditions is 1⅛ ounces of No. 8 shot, but some swear by No. 9 and I doubt if anyone could tell much difference if he used No. 7½. For the tougher Western quail I'd want no less than 1 ounce of No. 7½, as I think one needs shot a bit bigger than No. 8 for penetration at 30 to 37 yards. Given that much shot it doesn't make much difference what you shoot it out of—a 16, a 20, or even a 28 gauge!

CHAPTER 18

Combination Guns

ON the first day of the quail season some years ago, my wife and I were out on the Arizona desert, ready for action just as the sun came over jagged mountains. Suddenly I spotted a big covey of topknotted Gambel's quail scurrying across the ranch road just ahead. I pulled the car off to the side, and grabbing our shotguns, my wife and I jumped out and took after them. The covey flushed and disappeared over the crest of a little hill about 100 yards away.

The quail weren't too spooky, and we felt sure they'd scatter out and give us some shooting at singles if we followed them up. We found them all right when we topped the rise, but we saw something else, too. Standing in a sandy arroyo about 125 yards away were three desert mule deer, all bucks. One was a forkhorn, one a run-of-the-mine four-pointer, and the third a patriarch with a many-pointed head that would knock your eyes out.

"Don't move!" I hissed to my wife. "I'll scram back and get the rifles."

I returned shortly with the .257 and the .270 that we'd put in the car for just such an emergency, but my wife told me that the bucks had disappeared over a rise into a patch of cholla, mesquite, cat-claw, and ocotillo. With quail flushing all around us, we took the rifles and pussyfooted through the thin brush, trying to spy a buck before it saw us.

But no luck that sad day! We found where the deer had finally gone off in long, plunging bounds. They'd probably heard or smelled us.

We exchanged our rifles for shotguns, but the single birds had joined up to fly off for parts unknown. We moved on, eventually collected a few quail. Presently I saw another buck. Once more I dashed for the car, but again the buck was long gone by the time I got back. For the rest of the day I hunted quail with my shotgun, but carried the .270 strapped over my back. With this clumsy outfit I managed to do away with one unfortunate coyote, but no other deer did I see.

This is a sad tale with an unhappy ending, one of several incidents in my frustrated life which have convinced me that a weapon able to take large and small game at both short and fairly long range would often be very useful to have around.

Many attempts have been made to perfect such a weapon. Pumpkin balls and rifle slugs turn ordinary shotguns into makeshifts that will do for birds yet will kill deer and larger animals at short range. For many years the British built guns that were smoothbores except for a few inches of rifling at the muzzle. They are reputed to have given rifle accuracy to 150 yards or so with balls and special slugs. With shot they threw what their makers used to describe as "regular cylinder-bore patterns." From a couple that I patterned, though, I'd say that they scattered their shot pretty badly and that the killing range wasn't over 25 yards.

These ball-and-shot guns were known by various names, including Paradox and Explora. A common pothunter's gun on the Continent has one barrel conventionally choked and the other rifled at the muzzle in the Paradox manner. This is the French farmer's one gun, and with it he can knock over a pheasant, pot a rabbit, or lay low a raiding wild boar.

In many cases a double of the Paradox type or the crossbreed Continental shotgun with one barrel rifled at the muzzle is about all the weapon one would need. Sportsmen in India tell me that a British Explora or Paradox with special slugs is adequate for about any situation in the jungles.

Tigers and leopards (called panthers in India) are shot at close range from a machan (tree platform) or on occasion from the back of an elephant, and a 12-gauge Paradox slug at 30 yards or so has worlds of knockdown power and penetration. The missile is also accurate enough when fired from a Paradox to hit other jungle game well up to 150 yards or so—and anything over 100 yards is a long shot in the jungle.

The British version of the pumpkin ball is used in Paradox-type guns as well as in ordinary shotguns, but they have astonishingly little penetrating power. When my first tiger was lying dead in a nullah, one of the drivers on an elephant rode up and put a ball in the cat's heavy rump muscles. I dug it out and found that it had penetrated only about 2 inches. A similar ball in the chest muscles of Lee Sproul's tiger showed only slightly more penetration.

I'd hate to have to defend myself against a really indignant tiger if armed only with those balls, and I'd hate even more to have to stop a giant Indian water buffalo. But with the slugs they have good killing power, and with bird and buckshot at short jungle ranges they do well on peacocks and jungle fowl, and even on small deer like the hog and barking deer.

In many parts of the globe the weapon that combines the virtues of rifle and shotgun is worth a lot. On the Southwestern deserts where I grew up, quail and desert mule-deer seasons often overlap. They always do in Mexico. In the far north the big-game hunter who likes to change his luck with a spot of wing shooting on blue grouse or ptarmigan may run into a moose or even a grizzly.

Early one fall I was scouting for pheasants in eastern Washington, and in the course of the day my Brittany spaniel put out three fine whitetail bucks. Since both seasons are open at the same time, I cannot imagine anything better for the area than some sort of shotgun-rifle combination. Most of the wild turkeys I shot in Arizona were taken with a rifle, but on many occasions I missed running shots at close range in the brush—shots that I could have made with a shotgun.

The real home of the combination gun that is part rifle, part shotgun is Central Europe, where shooting preserves may produce hares, pheasants, wild boar, or roe deer all in one day. Before the war most German and Austrian sportsmen owned combination guns of various kinds, and American soldiers returning from abroad brought thousands of the guns into this country. These weapons aren't makeshifts like the Paradox and the Continental double with the rifled muzzle, but instead combine at least one genuine rifled barrel with one or more shotgun barrels. The most common form is the three-barrel gun, or "drilling" as it is called in German, with a barrel for a rifle cartridge beneath two shotgun barrels. Another is the over-and-under, with the top barrel for a shotgun shell and the bottom one for a rifle cartridge.

But this isn't all, as these combination guns are handmade by some of the world's cleverest craftsmen who are capable of turning out about anything the customer can dream up. Now and then one runs into a double rifle with a shotgun barrel underneath, or an over-and-under shotgun and rifle combination with a third small-caliber rifle barrel at the side. The ultimate, I suppose, is the four-barrel gun with two shotgun barrels side by side and two rifle barrels, one above the other, underneath. (One of these was for a small caliber like a .22.) Still another variation puts the small-caliber barrel in the rib above and between the two shotgun barrels.

Darndest weapon of this type I've ever seen was in the second-hand rack of a New York sporting-goods store. It had two 16-gauge shotgun barrels side by side, a 7 x 57–R barrel beneath them, and a .22 Hornet barrel in the rib.

Various combination guns are imported. They sell for up to almost $3,000, as in the case of a four-barrel job built in Ferlach, Austria.

The German and Austrians will make combination guns for almost any cartridge to special order, even for rimless cartridges like the .257, 7 x 57 mm., .270, and .30/06. It's much more difficult to make an extractor to yank out rimless cartridges than it is to build one for those with rims, particularly if the rimless cartridge is a hot number like the .270. However, many combination jobs for rimless ammunition have been imported and they seem to be satisfactory.

Among the thousands of German combination guns brought into this country, the 16 gauge is the favorite for shot barrels. I'd say offhand that I've seen literally dozens in 16 gauge for every one I've seen in 12. Among the older jobs, the most common rifle barrel was for the 9.3 x 72–R cartridge, an old straight-taper job for black powder. Ballistically it's similar to our .38/55, and ammunition loaded in Europe is stocked by big sporting-goods stores and by specialty outfits like Philip J. Medicus of New York.

Another old cartridge is the 8 x 58–R, which as I get it is a straight-taper cartridge of moderate power. The 8 x 57–JR, on the other hand, is the rimmed version of the 8 x 57–J, or infantry cartridge. One occasionally sees a drilling with a barrel for the 8.15 x 46–R—the favorite German mid-range target cartridge, which is generally adapted to single shots—or for the powerful 9.3 x 74–R, a rimmed cartridge about as powerful as our wildcat .35 Whelen. Now and then one runs into a drilling barrel marked 7.62 x 51— none other than our old friend the .30/30.

As a general thing, one can usually find a rimmed counterpart of the rimless cartridges intended for Mauser repeating rifles. As we've seen, the 8 x 57–JR is the rimmed version of the military rimless which we call the 8-mm. Mauser here, and ordinary 8-mm. ammunition will chamber and fire in an 8 x 57–JR barrel. The case has to be punched out, however. The 7 x 57–R for single shots, combination guns, and even doubles, is the rimmed version of the 7 x 57-mm. "Spanish" Mauser.

Outdoor Life once carried a piece about a huge black bear shot in New York State with a three-barrel gun made in the United States. I've had many letters about those home-grown drillings. They were made by one concern which operated around Wheeling, West Virginia, but which used various names—Wheeling Gun Co., Hollenbeck Gun Co., Three-Barrel Gun Co., and finally Royal Gun Co., which folded in 1911. Those interesting guns sold for from $75 to $500. Most were in 12 gauge, and favorite rifle barrels were .32/40, .38/55, and .30/30.

Another American combination gun that's been made for many years is the over-and-under Stevens .410/.22, and, in 20 gauge and .22 WRF magnum, probably as fine a little weapon for pothunting as was ever made. It is in 12 gauge/.308 too. I've never owned one, but I have used a couple on big game. Once in the Yukon I had some sweet wing shooting with the .410 barrel of one that belonged to Myles Brown of Cleveland, an old sheep-hunting pal, and another time in Mexico I kept four of us in quail, doves, and cottontails with the same gun.

Just before the last war, Marlin made some beautiful little over-and-unders with, if I remember correctly, 20, 16, and 12-gauge shotgun barrels and .22 rimfire, .22 Hornet, and .218 Bee rifle barrels. I played with one for the 20 gauge and .218 Bee and it was a dandy. Savage has produced a shotgun with interchangeable rifle barrels and forends. I had one once—a 20-gauge shotgun barrel with a Weaver Choke on it along with an extra .30/30 barrel and fore-end. I used to take the outfit into Mexico, shoot quail and doves with the shotgun barrel, deer with the .30/30 barrel. I wish I still had it. Another odd rifle formerly made here was a Model 99 Savage takedown in .300 caliber with an interchangeable .410 gauge barrel.

Some of the German three and four-barrel guns are mechanical marvels and a delight to play with. The commonest type has two triggers like a double-barrel shotgun, but when a button on the tang is pressed forward, a rifle sight goes up on the rib and one of the triggers is then ready to fire the rifle barrel. Such drillings usually have Greener safeties on the side of the stock. Many three-barrel jobs are fitted with scope sights, and, with surprising accuracy, will pick a buck off nicely at 200 yards or more.

Even with the high American labor costs, I believe over-and-under combination guns can be built at prices to interest the ordinary consumer. It might not be too dreary an idea for Marlin to revive the one it made. But three and four-barrel guns are something else again. There is so much handwork on them that they'd have to cost as much as a good automobile.

But one can often pick up surprising bargains in secondhand European combination guns. I've seen beautiful drillings with good engraving, excellent checkering, and superb hand fitting go begging for not much more than $100—guns that would cost $1,000 to duplicate, even at European wage scales.

A gun nut who passes up one of these will probably live to regret it. The combination gun is not only a fine example of the gunmaker's art, but under many conditions it's one of the most useful of all firearms.

CHAPTER 19

The Shot Shell

and Its Components

SHOTGUN shells have been made of brass, of paper tubes with brass heads, of aluminum, of plastic, and of plastic in combination with brass or copper-plated steel bases.

For many years, the changes in shot-shell manufacture were both gradual and mild, and essentially the shot shell of 1940 was not very different from that of 1885. But since the end of World War II, as we shall presently see, the components of shot shells and the techniques of putting them together have really been in a state of flux.

As the illustration on p. 219 shows, the classic shot shell is a tube of strong paper, generally impregnated with wax to make it moisture and water resistant but sometimes shellacked. At the breech end of the tube is a brass head with a recess for the battery cup primer. The head of the case is reinforced with a base wad of paper strip wound in a spiral. Above the primer and the base wad is the powder charge. Over it is a thin wad known as the "overpowder" wad. Then in the classic shell there are a couple of filler wads generally of felt and greased to clean out the bore and to help make the wads gas tight. Then comes the shot charge and above it in the classic shot shell was the thin top wad held to the unit by a crimp in the end of the paper tube.

The standard shell length given is that of the tube before it has been crimped. The standard American shell in most gauges is 2¾ inches long before crimping. Some .410 shells and 12 and 20-gauge 3-inch magnum shells are three inches long before crimping. The British shell or "cartridge" for upland hunting is 2½ inches long before crimping, and many guns made on the European Continent are chambered for 65-mm. (2%₁₆-inch) shells. However, British and Continental guns made for export to the United States are chambered for 2¾-inch shells and are marked either "2¾ in." or "70 mm.," the metric designation for the same thing. Many guns made for export to the United States are chambered for 3-inch magnum shells in 12 and 20 gauge and are so marked—3 in. or 75 mm. All Browning Superposed (over-and-under) 20-gauge guns, for example, now have 3-inch chambers, but for many years Browning 16-gauge guns had 2%₁₆-inch chambers and until along in the 1920s most American 20-gauge shotguns had 2½-inch chambers, as did all .410-gauge guns until the early 1930s when Western Cartridge Company introduced the long .410 shell with ¾ ounce of shot.

A 2¾-inch loaded shell does not measure 2¾ inches overall, nor does a 3-inch loaded shell measure 3 inches. A 2¾-inch shell measures 2¾ inches before it is loaded and crimped and after the crimp has unwound when the gun is fired. The chamber must be cut to fit the fired shell. It is perfectly feasible to fire a 2¾-inch shell in a 3-inch chamber. In fact, short shells pattern about as well in long chambers as do long shells. A 3-inch shell will go into a 2¾-inch chamber and can be fired. But the use of the long shells in short chambers is not a good idea. The practice raises pressures, for the long shell as it unfurls goes past the forcing cone into the barrel and the wads must be compressed to get past the mouth of the case. When a long shell is fired in a short chamber, the mouth of the ejected case usually looks bitten off and chewed up.

Many years ago some American shotgunners preferred cases of drawn brass. These required a different type of forcing cone in specially chambered guns as the mouths of the brass cases were thinner than those of the paper cases, These thin brass cases were crimped by "puckering" the mouths to hold the top wads in. Since the cases were thinner than paper cases, the wads had to be larger. Today some brass cases turned from solid brass are in use. However, these have the same thickness as paper cases and the top wads, I understand, are held in by friction.

The manufacture of the conventional paper shot shell with the cardboard tube and the brass head is an expensive and complicated business.

According to a photo story some years ago in *Outdoor Life*, it took 212 operations to make and put together the 14 components that made up the loaded shot shell. These components of the classic shot shell are brass head, the five components of the primer, top wad, two filler wads, overpowder wad, base wad, paper case body, shot charge, powder charge.

The manufacture of the classic shot shell is necessarily expensive because of the many operations and the investment in the many and complicated machines necessary. It is difficult to save much money in producing such a shell. Relatively small savings can be made by using cheap cardboard for the tubes and making no attempt to waterproof it by impregnating it with wax. A little money can be saved by using less shot and, of course, a shell containing one ounce of shot is cheaper to load than one containing 1¼ ounces. Plain "chilled" shot is cheaper than shot plated with copper or nickle. Using cheaper powder and less of it will also cut the price of the finished product, as will the use of cheaper material for wads.

American shot shells are the world's best. They are the most carefully made with the most highly developed automatic machines. They use the best materials, pattern the best, and give the most reliable performance. Velocities and pressures of American shot shells run very uniform. It is almost unheard of for an American factory-loaded shot shell to fail to fire, or to give a "blooper" (an exceptionally loud report showing non-uniform pressures), as is the case with some handloaded and foreign ammunition.

German shot shells, like German centerfire metallic cartridges, have a good reputation. I have used the British "game loads," which in 12 gauge in 2½-inch cases and with 1 1/16 ounces of shot are lighter than shells generally used for upland shooting in the United States. I found them reliable and satisfactory. Belgian shells also have a good reputation. French, Italian, and Spanish shot shells I have used appear cheaply made. With them bloopers, "punk" shots, and misfire are not uncommon, and they tend to give trouble in automatic guns. However, it may be that American shot shells are too good for many purposes, and because they are unnecessarily good they are unduly expensive.

The paper shot shell with the brass head has been in use in approximately its present form ever since the early days of breech loading and fixed shotgun ammunition. It has been quite satisfactory but it is by no means perfect. As we have seen, it is complicated to manufacture. The paper body is difficult to make waterproof, and even the best shells if stored long in a damp climate swell so they are difficult to chamber and eject. Paper tubes of poor quality often burn through when fired and sometimes separate (cut off) at the point where the brass head ends. Paper does not contract once the shell is fired as well as certain metals, nor does it resize as well. The best paper shells can be reloaded no more than five or six times.

The ideal shot-shell case should be cheap and easy to manufacture. It should be strong, springy, should be reloadable fifteen or twenty times, should not shrink or swell, and it should not absorb moisture.

The conventional shot shell has served well in the past and will serve well in the future. If it is stored in a relatively cool place at a temperature of about 70 degrees and a relative humidity of around 70 percent, shells will perform satisfactorily for many years. If shells are stored where they alternately dry out and absorb moisture, the wads may become loose and the shell may give erratic pressure, pattern less well than a properly stored shell, and give "punk" shots. If shells are stored near a hot radiator or left out in the sun, the wax in the paper tubes may liquefy, spill out on the powder, and weaken it.

Various materials have been used for the filler wads—leather, cellulose composition, cork, paper, linoleum, felt. Of all these, felt has in the past been the most widely used but of recent years it is being replaced by composition wads made of cellulose. Wads between the powder and the shot have a double duty to perform. They have to seal off the hot powder gases and they also have to soften the blow of the expanding powder gases against the shot. At the same time the wads should remain square with the bore to keep gas from leaking past and fusing, balling, and disrupting the shot charge. A thick, heavy wad has a tendency to smash into the shot charge and break it up. Lighter and thinner wads have a tendency to tip. Incidentally, one of the theories as to why chokes in the ends of the barrels work as they do is that the heavier shot outrun the lighter wads. The more the constriction, the more the wads are held up and the tighter the pattern.

Good wadding in the shot shell is all important. The wad column acts as a piston to push the shot out of the muzzle and to protect the shot from the hot powder gases. If the gas leaks past the wads because they have tipped or are undersize, or for any other reason, the shot pattern is blown apart and some of the shot fused.

As we have seen, the typical wad column in the classic American shot shell consisted of an overpowder wad, two felt or composition filler wads, and a top wad. British wad columns are similar except that British shells usually have an overfelt wad between the felt wad and the shot charge.

The length of the wad column is determined by the height of the base wad, the density of the powder charge, the amount of shot loaded, the length of the case, and the length of the crimp. The loading companies have been able to load 2¾-inch magnum shells with heavy charges of shot at approximately standard velocity by using low base wads, denser powders that burn slowly, a shorter wad column. In that way there is room for more shot. "Magnum" shells 2¾ inches long now carry 1½ ounces of shot, 16-gauge 2¾-inch magnums 1¼ ounces of shot, 20-gauge 2¾-inch magnums 1⅛ ounces of shot, and 28-gauge magnums 1 ounce of shot.

In *Smokeless Shotgun Powders*, a 1933 Du Pont publication, Wallace H. Coxe, ballistic engineer at the Du Pont Burnside laboratory wrote: "Experience has indicated that the length of the wad column should not be less than half the bore diameter nor greater than the bore diameter of the gauge."

Shooters refer to "low-brass" and "high-brass" shells, and the notion has got around that the high-brass shell is a real hell-bender and the low brass pretty mild stuff. This has come about because the so-called "high-velocity" shells like Western Super X and Remington Nitro Express are high-brass shells with low base wads. The low base wads give more room for more powder and heavier charges of shot. Most shells loaded for trap and skeet are low-brass–high-base wad shells. Canuck (Canadian) and Federal trap shells have low or medium brass heads and low inside bases.

For many years the principal ingredient of the primer compound for shot-shell primers was potassium chlorate, a substance which turned into potassium chloride (a compound similar to table salt) when fired. It was this primer ingredient which caused rust in rifle bores in the old days, which made it necessary to clean rifle bores with hot water, and which was responsible for the short barrel life of .22 rimfire rifles and of rifles in such calibers as .25/20. This corrosive priming mixture was never so much of a problem with the shot shell because the primer mixture was well diluted with the powder charge. Given reasonable care, a shotgun bore did not generally rust. Yet, the primer residue did attract moisture, just as it did in a rifle bore, and the fact that many shotguns made before the invention of the non-corrosive primer have pitted barrels shows that trouble was not entirely absent. But non-corrosive shotgun primers followed non-corrosive rifle primers, and now nothing in the residue in a shotgun barrel attracts moisture. As a result the bore of a shotgun does not have to be cleaned as often as it used to if rust is to be avoided.

All American shot shells now take the same size primer. Until a few years ago Remington took a special size, but Remington primers are now interchangeable with the others. The old Remington primer was called the No. 57. The present standard Remington primer, the No. 97, is the same size as the Winchester No. 209, the Federal No. 209, and the C.C.I. No. 109.

American shot-shell primers are very reliable, so reliable that a misfire is almost unknown. However, misfires can occur if the gun has a broken firing pin, a weakened spring, a poorly shaped firing pin, or excessive headspace. Some foreign-loaded shot shells have given misfires when used in over-and-under shotguns where the firing pin for the bottom barrel strikes at an angle. Primer failure can come about through improper priming mixture, non-uniform priming charge, a loose anvil, too hard metal in the primer itself, or improper seating of the primer.

Before the last war, shot shells were available loaded with "drop shot," which were made of pure lead with a little arsenic added to help the molten lead to form into spheres as it streamed out of the shower pans in the shot tower. Drop shot was soft, deformed easily, and tended to lead the barrel. It is no longer loaded in the United States. Instead so-called "chilled" shot is used. This actually is shot made hard by the addition of arsenic and antimony. It got the name "chilled" because in the early days in England some manufacturers blew cold air across the shot as it fell past the bottom of the tower. It was thought that this hardened the shot. Actually, it had no effect. In some premium loads the shot are coated with copper by electroplating. This increases the strength and elasticity of the shot pellets. They are less subject to deformation and give more even patterns.

All the loading companies put together "brush" or "spreader" loads to give open (about improved cylinder) patterns in full-choke guns. One way this is done is to divide the shot charge into segments by loading two thin wads parallel to the end of the shell in order to divide the shot charge into three portions. Another way is to quarter the shot charge by the use of a cruciform spreader made of two pieces of cardboard slotted and fitted together. By this means the diameter of the total shot pattern at 20 yards can be opened up from about 16 to about 26 inches in a full-choked gun.

On a box of shot shells one sees a cabalistic set of figures such as this: 3 drams. equiv., $1\frac{1}{8}$, 8 shot—or simply $3\frac{3}{4}$–$1\frac{1}{4}$–6. The first figure stands for a powder charge sufficient to produce the same velocity as an equivalent amount of black powder.

But let's have Du Pont explain this dram-equivalent business:

"A dram is a measure used for black powder and is normally

used as a volume measure (although strictly speaking it is a weight measure equivalent to ⅟₁₆ oz. or ⅟₂₅₆ lb.). A certain dram charge of black powder imparts a certain velocity to a given weight of shot. For example, three drams of black powder with 1⅛-oz. shot in 12 gauge gives about 1200 ft./sec. muzzle velocity. When the change to smokeless powder was made, the dram equivalent designation was used as a measure of the approximate power of the load regardless of the actual powder charge. For example, in 12 gauge, a 3 dram equivalent load with 1-⅛ oz. shot gives a muzzle velocity of about 1200 ft./sec. A scheme was devised to relate velocity and shot weight of commercial loads to the dram equivalent system, but modern loadings depart from the system in a number of instances.

"Some shooters mistakenly believe a low dram equivalent is synonymous with low pressure. This is not so, as all modern shotshells regardless of dram equivalent marking, gauge, brand, powder or shot charge are loaded to approximately the same pressure level. Therefore, those who attach significance to the term 'dram equivalent' in respect to chamber pressure are in error.

"The main problem is that people still confuse a 'dram equivalent' designation with a 'dram measure' of powder and this may be serious in the case of modern fast shotshell powders. Taking the density of black and smokeless powders into account, a volumetric 3-dram measure of such modern fast powders is approximately 40 grains (where a grain equals 1/7000 lb.) or about a double charge."

The reason the term "dram equivalent" was originally used was that in the early days of smokeless powder and fixed shotgun ammunition, a great many shooters were used to loading black powder in muzzle loaders and in their own shot shells. They knew, let us say, what a 3-dram charge of black powder would do with 1⅛ ounces of shot. In the early smokeless days, powders were turned out that could be loaded "bulk for bulk" with black powder and which were designed to give about the same pressure and the same velocity without the smoke. Then the handloaders could use these "bulk" powders with their dip measures. They were known as "bulk smokeless." The other powders which could not be measured bulk for bulk with black were known as "dense powders." Today only one bulk powder is made in the United States and that is Du Pont bulk Smokeless. It cannot be substituted for black powder in old guns designed for black powder only.

Shotgun powders, like rifle powders, are made as both single base (nitrocellulose) and double base (nitroglycerin and nitrocellulose) powders. Excellent shotgun powders are manufactured in England, Sweden, Germany, Belgium, and Italy. Suitable powder is also turned out for shotgun use in Spain, France, Czechoslovakia, and Russia. Some foreign shotgun powders are imported into the United States for the use of handloaders.

Shotgun powders must burn efficiently at relatively low pressures, as shotgun pressures are much lower than rifle pressures. Many modern centerfire rifle cartridges are loaded to mean pressures of around 54,000 pounds per square inch, whereas shotgun pressures run 8,000 to 11,000 p.s.i. Some shotgun powders are designed to burn relatively quickly to propel light charges of shot as in skeet and trapshooting. Other powders are designed to sustain their pressure peak longer, to burn more slowly, and to push heavier charges of shot and longer shot columns.

To some slight extent it is possible to use certain shotgun powders in rifles and certain rifle powders in shotguns. Light, low-pressure loads with lead bullets are sometimes made up for rifles with shotgun powders. Some of the faster-burning rifle powders are used to load shells for small-bore shotguns that use long shot columns. Two fast-burning (for rifles) powders have been used in the .410 and 28 gauge—No. 2400 (Hercules) and No. 4227 (Du Pont). At one time there were a number of small powder maufacturers in the United States, but now the firms making powder are Du Pont (which largely specializes in single-base powders), Hercules (which specializes in double-base powders), and Western (which specializes in ball). All loading companies buy powder from Hercules. Western buys certain powders from Du Pont (which owns Remington) and Remington buys some ball powders from Western. Alcan, a concern which specializes in furnishing shotgun components for the handloader, imports powder from

Sweden, and B. E. Hodgdon, who also caters to the handloader, sells government-surplus powders.

The 2¾-inch magnum loads in 28, 20, 16, and 12 gauge have been made possible by the development of dense, slow-burning powders which can propel extra-heavy charges of shot without raising pressures beyond the limit of safety and pattern efficiency. For more discussion of shotgun powders, see the chapters on the handloading of shot shells and shotgun ballistics.

The present generation has seen many changes in the classic shot shell and its components—and as this was first written in 1964 the changes probably were not over. Progressive-burning powders which made possible the loading of heavier charges of shot at standard velocity and also, I understand, shorter shot strings were introduced in the early 1920s. Non-corrosive priming came out in the early 1930s.

About the time World War II began, some shells appeared without top wads. These had the "pie" or "star" crimp, which is now pretty universally used, not only in this country but abroad. The theory was that the top wad, held to the front of the shell by a roll crimp, caused erratic patterns because the top wad interfered with the shot charge and sometimes scattered it unduly. Federal developed a "frangible" top wad of thin cardboard made brittle by chemical treatment. This disintegrated under the impact of the shot, did not disrupt patterns. However, the advertising of the other manufacturers had so brainwashed the consumers that they looked upon any shell with a top wad and a roll crimp as old-fashioned and somehow inferior. Federal was forced to go to the star crimp.

Another innovation which came along not long after that was the use by Winchester-Western of an overpowder wad that was shaped like a little cup. This was supposed to, and undoubtedly did, act as a gas seal. Remington used a wad designed for the same purpose, a plastic "H" wad. This was, I believe, the first of the plastic wads to be loaded commercially, but Alcan was selling a similar wad to handloaders two years or so earlier.

One of the next innovations in shot shells was the use by Winchester-Western of a polyethylene collar to enclose the shot charge. As is well known, a good many of the shot are deformed by friction with the barrel and by being jammed together by the forcing cones of the chamber and the choke. These deformed shot lag behind the shot that have retained their spherical form, and lend little to killing powder. If they hit the pattern sheet at 40 yards, they are usually outside the 30-inch circle. By protecting these pellets from deformation, the collar thickens the pattern in the bird-killing, target-breaking area. The loading-company technicians say these collars (and similar gimmicks used by other outfits) make the patterns thicker but not smaller. In a couple of 12-gauge guns I have, the Mark V Western ammunition with protective collars and Remington trap loads with the Power Piston definitely shoot smaller skeet and improved cylinder patterns than do shells with unprotected shot charges. From the patterns I have shot and evaluated I'd say that shells with shot columns protected by polyethylene make good 30 to 35-yard killers out of barrels bored Skeet No. 1.

Remington brought out a combination wad column and shot protector called the "Power Piston." This gimmick is made of plastic. It serves as a gas seal, substitutes for overpowder wad and filler wads, and as a shot protector. The forward portion, which holds the shot, is slotted so that it opens up and falls away when it strikes the air. Winchester-Western makes and sells to shot-shell handloaders, and in 1965 also loads, a similar combination plastic shot column and shot protector called "Win-Wad." Federal is now selling, as well as loading in 12-gauge trap and skeet shells, a plastic protector and wad column that looks much like the Remington Power Piston. Presumably in all of these plastic wad columns, the wad portions contract when struck by the blow of the expanding powder gases and hence cushion the shock to the shot pellets and give minimum deformation, just as the conventional and classic greased felt filler wad used to do. The grease on these wads was supposed to clear the crud out of the barrel and to cut down on leading. The plastic wad columns are not greased, but the shot do not touch the barrel when they are used and hence can't lead. Plastic wad columns are sold by various dealers in reloaders sup-

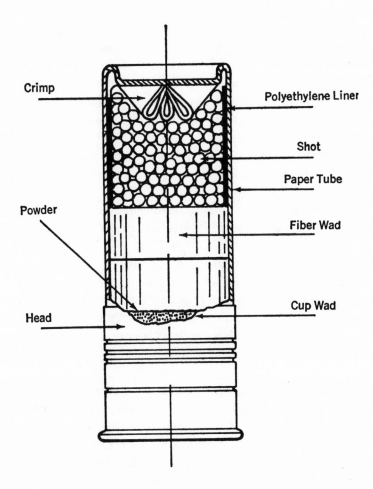

Crimp

Polyethylene Liner

Shot

Paper Tube

Powder

Fiber Wad

Head

Cup Wad

SHOT SHELL WITH POLYETHYLENE LINER
(Partial Sectioned View)

The construction of a Winchester Mark V shot shell.
—*courtesy Winchester Arms*

plies. So are the thin card overpowder wads and various types of filler wads (felt, cork, plastic, fiber, cellulose composition). Overshot or top wads are also available, but most shells reloaded today use the star or pie crimp which takes no top wad.

Right after the war there was much experimenting in the manufacture of shot-shell cases. For a time Continental Arms Company of New York imported 12-gauge shells with aluminum cases from the Netherlands. I believe shells with aluminum cases were made in Belgium as early as the 1930s. I have in my possession a shot shell made somewhere in Europe of transparent plastic, and for some years the loading companies and plastic manufacturers were experimenting with plastic shot shells.

Remington was the first American manufacturer to put a shot shell with a plastic tube on the market—green in high-brass Remington Express brand, red in Shur Shot, and blue in Peters. The shells had copperplated steel bases and rims. It is perfectly possible to make plastic shot shells with integral plastic rims and base wad portions, but the manufacturers have felt that consumer acceptance demanded a base that looked like brass. At the time Remington introduced their plastic shot shells, it was pretty generally known that Winchester-Western was also working on the same problem.

The Winchester-Western plastics were introduced to the gun writers in November 1963, and were on the market early in 1964. They are of two types. The high-brass hunting-type shells (Super X and Super Speed) are injection molded and the "base wad" is actually integral. It uses a high-brass base, a cup-type overpowder wad, two fiber filler wads, and a polyethylene collar around the shot charge. The other plastic shell is the low-brass (Winchester Ranger and Western X-Pert). It is made of plastic tubing, has a brass head, paper base wad, and the shot charge is enclosed in a plastic collar. All Winchester-Western shells with the plastic collar to protect the shot column are known as "Mark V."

I am convinced that the plastic shot shell, probably molded with integral rim and base wad, is the shot shell of the future. Such a shell does not scuff, does not swell, and can be perfected so that it can be reloaded many times. Furthermore such a shell, once the necessary machinery is written off, should be cheaper and far less complicated to make than the classic shot shell of wax-impregnated cardboard tube with brass head and paper base wad.

When I completed the first edition of this book, Federal had not yet come on the market with a shot shell in a plastic case. Today almost all of the Federal production of the various gauges is in plastic cases. An exception is a skeet shell with a paper case which some enthusiasts say throws the best skeet patterns of any skeet shell.

In fact, plastic components have taken over the shot shell field and plastics have greatly simplified shot shell manufacture. The new plastic shells are cast in one piece and need no base wad. Instead of the conventional wad column they use one-piece wad column shot protectors. Because the shot protector protects the shot from deforming in the barrel and against the forcing cones and also because of the light weight of the plastic shot column, shells with plastic components tend to pattern more densely than the older shells with the conventional wad columns. The heavy shot charge outruns the light plastic shot column more easily. Because of the plastic shot protectors, leading of shotgun barrels is about a thing of the past. Some plastic rubs off against the bore, but I have found it easy to remove with a brass brush dipped in light solvent.

The plastic shells have one fault: when dropped on the ground, they just about last forever. In times when a lot of attention is being paid to the environment, this is bad. A good sportsman should pick up his empties, carry them away, and dispose of them.

CHAPTER 20

Ballistics

of the Shot Shell

THE shot shell came into common use along with the breech-loading shotgun in the 1880s. In the more than eighty years that fixed shotgun ammunition has been in use, shotgun ballistics have not changed to anything like the same extent that rifle ballistics have changed. In the 1880s the United States military cartridge was the .45/70. Big-game cartridges were those used in the Sharps, Remington, and Winchester rifles and the British double-barrel and single-shot express rifles. Like the shot shells of the 1880s, the rifle cartridges were loaded with black powder.

The introduction of smokeless powder in the late 1880s and early 1900s immediately jumped velocities of rifle cartridges from 1,300–1,500 feet per second to 2,000–2,300. Range was increased enormously since smokeless powder made possible the use of long, jacketed bullets with better ranging qualities. Whereas a 150-yard shot at big game with a rifle using one of the old black-powder cartridges was a long one, shots at twice that distance became possible with the flatter-shooting smokeless-powder cartridges with their higher velocity.

Ballistically, the shot shell has made no such strides. Before the invention of fixed ammunition and breech-loading shotguns, a cylinder-bored muzzle loader using 1⅛ ounces of shot and 3 to 3¼ drams of black powder was about a 35-yard killer, with many kills at 40 yards. This is about the range of a cylinder-bored shotgun with 1⅛ ounces of shot today.

Shotgun velocities have not increased a great deal because a spherical shot pellet is ballistically a pretty inefficient projectile which loses its velocity rapidly. Speeding up the velocity of the shot charge at the muzzle of the shotgun would make little difference out at 40 to 60 yards where ducks are taken. Working pressures of centerfire rifle cartridges have been increased about 30,000 pounds per square inch since smokeless powders came into use, from about 25,000 p.s.i. to 55,000. No such increase had occurred with shot-shell pressures because high pressures would result in poor patterns. What hairsplitting accuracy is to the rifle, uniformity and consistency of pattern is to the shotgun. This is best achieved with pressures which compared with rifle pressures are very moderate indeed.

Actually, the greatest improvement in shotgun ballistics came with the invention of choke boring along in the 1870s. Choke boring changed the shotgun from a 35 to 40-yard weapon to a 50 to 65-yard weapon. Compared to choke boring, most of the other changes in the shotgun and the shot shell have been in the nature of refinements. Smokeless powder gives less recoil than black powder and is much more pleasant to shoot. Progressive-burning dense powders have enabled the loading companies to use heavier charges of shot and thus increase sure killing range somewhat without exceeding permissible pressures. The use of star crimps, various types of cup wads and "H" wads, and plastic wad columns have improved patterns and have cut down on recoil a bit. Plastic collars for the protection of the shot column have also resulted in some pattern improvement. Plastic shot shells do not swell when they get damp or wet and non-corrosive priming makes it easier to take care of a shotgun bore. But again, these are all minor improvements as compared to choke boring.

Pressures for shot shells loaded with black powder ran from 5,000 to 7,000 p.s.i. Pressures with today's shot shells run from

10,000 to 13,000 p.s.i. American pressures are always given in pounds per square inch, incidentally. British pressures are given in long tons per square inch. The British long ton is 2,260 pounds. The so-called "high-velocity" "long-range" loads give little if any more pressure than field or trap loads. However, their pressure peak is of longer duration and comes farther down the barrel. These progressive-burning powders with heavier charges of shot were pioneered by the Western Cartridge Company right after World War I and John Olin was the driving spirit behind their development. Most gunners thought that such loads as Western Super X, Remington Nitro Express, and Federal Hi-Power gave the shot charge much higher velocity than did ordinary "field" loads like Remington's Shur Shot and Winchester's Ranger. They also thought that because of the supposed higher velocity less lead would be needed. Actually, the velocity increase is minor, so little that no difference in necessary lead can be detected.

Pressures run higher in the small gauges than in the large. In a table of loads compiled with Du Pont powders by the Du Pont Company and giving velocity and pressure, the highest pressure listed for the 10 gauge is with a load for the monstrous 10-gauge magnum 3½-inch shell with 49 grains of SR 7625 behind 1⅞ ounces of shot. Pressure is 10,500 p.s.i. The highest pressure listed for the 12-gauge magnum shell with 1⅝ ounces of shot is 10,700. The highest pressures listed for 20-gauge loads go to 11,000, and for the .410 and 28 gauge to 11,700.

With the same powder charge, an increase in weight of shot charge raises pressure. An increase in the weight of the wad column raises pressure as does an increase in wad pressure, the tightness of the crimp, or a decrease in the size of the shot. With the same powder charge, for example, pressure with 1¼ ounces of No. 7½ shot will run about 500 p.s.i. higher than with the same amount of No. 4.

For many years shot-shell velocities were taken with a Le Boulengé chronograph. One disjunctor was set up at the muzzle and the other at 40 yards. The average velocity over 40 yards was registered and that was how velocities for shot shells were quoted.

In a pre-World War II Winchester catalog, I see the following mean velocities over 40 yards quoted for various types of shot shells:

12-gauge trap load	1⅛ oz. No. 7½	850 f.p.s.
12-gauge Super Speed	1¼ oz. No. 6	975 f.p.s.
12-gauge 3-in. Magnum	1⅝ oz. No. 6	965 f.p.s.
12-gauge field load	1⅛ oz. No. 6	935 f.p.s.
16-gauge Super Speed	1⅛ oz. No. 6	925 f.p.s.
20-gauge Super Speed	1 oz. No. 6	900 f.p.s.

Since electronic chronographs came into common use after the last war, shot-shell velocities are now quoted at the muzzle. Here are the muzzle velocities for the same loads as above:

12-gauge trap load	1⅛ oz. No. 7½	1200 f.p.s.
12-gauge Super Speed	1¼ oz. No. 6	1330 f.p.s.
12-gauge 3-in. Magnum	1⅝ oz. No. 6	1315 f.p.s.
12-gauge field load	1⅛ oz. No. 6	1225 f.p.s.
16-gauge Super Speed	1⅛ oz. No. 6	1295 f.p.s.
20-gauge Super Speed	1 oz. No. 6	1220 f.p.s.

The small gauges deliver their shot with somewhat higher pressures and with somewhat lower velocity. In addition, their shot columns, in proportion to their weight, are longer and a higher proportion of their shot pellets are deformed by contact with the barrel and with the forcing cone. The results of the long shot columns are particularly noticeable in the case of the .410 using the long shell and ¾ ounce of shot and to a much lesser extent with the 28 gauge. Generally, a full-choke pattern from a .410 will look pretty good at 30 yards, but at 35 yards, where the results of the high proportion of deformed shot can be seen, the pattern will generally go to pieces.

Many notions held dear by shooters originated back in the days of black powder. Today, for example, most trapshooters open their guns when they have fired a shot on the line and solemnly blow into the breech. A little puff of smoke comes out of the muzzle and then they are happy. I have asked many of them why they do this and they cannot give a sensible answer. Actually, the origin of this curious tribal custom was that in muzzle-loading days all hell broke loose if a bit of smoldering wadding remained in the bore when the powder was dumped in. Gunners used to blow through the flash hole to blow such bits of wadding out before they reloaded. Some gunners still do it today when they have time, but they do not know why. Another holdover from black-powder days in the American shotgunner's credo is the belief that the longer the barrel of the shotgun the "harder" it shoots. Precisely what is meant by "harder" I cannot say. Whether our gunners mean the long-barreled guns throw denser patterns or give higher velocity I am not sure. Perhaps they mean both. In the days of black powder and before choke boring was perfected, a long barrel was needed to burn large amounts of black powder as it burns at the same rate confined or unconfined. The very long cylinder barrels gave not only higher velocity but also denser patterns since the long barrel gave the shot the opportunity to outrun the wads.

Today the more unsophisticated gunners are still convinced that the longer the gun barrel, the harder it shoots and the farther away game can be killed. I get many letters from those who in their youth had long-barreled single-shot guns sold by mail-order houses and called "Long Toms" or "Long Range Wonders." They remember these clumsy old cannons with great fondness, tell me of the fantastic ranges at which those monstrosities would kill ducks. It is impossible to find anything nearly as effective today, they say. Along in the late 1950s, Savage made up a lot of single-barrel guns with 36-inch barrels. They sold very well indeed to those wanting "hard-shooting" guns.

A rule of thumb which used to be quoted quite often was that the velocity of a shot shell dropped 7½ feet per second for every inch the barrel was chopped off below 30 inches. The old rule for rifles was that velocity fell 25 f.p.s. for every inch of barrel amputated. Neither of these rules is of much use any more. Velocity loss varies with pressure and also with the composition of the powder. An increase in pressure makes the powder burn faster and hence exert its push in a shorter space and lose less velocity when fired in a short barrel. The slower-burning powders lose more velocity than the quick-burning ones. However, by rifle standards any shotgun powder is pretty quick burning.

Some years ago I obtained from Winchester some data on velocity loss in barrels of various lengths with the 12-gauge Winchester Super Speed shell loaded with 3¾ drams equivalent of powder and 1¼ ounces of No. 6 shot, a load which is a favorite with many gunners for ducks and pheasants. The load has reached its maximum velocity in a 28-inch barrel, where it is traveling at 1,351 f.p.s. In a 30-inch barrel the average velocity has actually dropped slightly to 1,350. In a 23-inch barrel, the velocity is 1,328, a loss of less than 25 feet! Even with this load, which uses a progressive-burning powder, velocity loss is insignificant until a barrel length of 20 to 21 inches is approached. Long barrels may have their advantages in a longer sighting plane and lessened muzzle blast but added velocity and denser patterns are not among them.

A 28-gauge load of 2¼ drams and ¾ ounce of shot gave a velocity of 1,318 from a 26-inch barrel, 1,236 from a 15-inch barrel. The heavy 3-inch .410 load with ¾ ounce of shot registered 1,195 from a 26-inch barrel, 1,113 from a 15-inch barrel. Of course, no one wants to use a 15-inch barrel, but he could do so without losing important velocity. Many gunners write to me in my capacity as a shooting editor and want to know how short they can have the barrels of their shotguns when they install variable choke devices. The answer is that for all practical purposes they can have them as short as the spirit moves them. A pump or automatic shotgun fitted with a variable choke device to give an overall barrel length of 22 to 24 inches makes a very handy upland gun which handles about like a double with 26-inch barrels.

The superior ranging qualities of large shot give them a higher terminal velocity over 40 or 50 yards and a higher average velocity over 40 yards. Although they start out at about the same velocity, No. 2 shot averages in the 3¾ dram equivalent loads a velocity of 1,040 over 40 yards, whereas No. 4 averages 1,010 and No. 7½ shot 935. Since the larger shot do a better job of retaining velocity than smaller shot, they give sufficient penetration to a greater distance. At the same time they give less dense patterns. As is said elsewhere in this book, the selection of shot sizes for various purposes is always a compromise between ranging quality and pattern density.

The question of how far shotguns are dangerous is constantly coming up in these crowded times. A few months before this was written the gun club in the town where I live was to be relocated near the airport. The C.A.B. protested the location. The area board contained one self-nominated expert who told the others that the new magnum shells give shotguns twice as much range as they formerly had, and that if the gun club were located anywhere near the airport some slob would sooner or later shoot down a plane.

Actually, exhaustive tests have shown that the maximum range for No. 7½ shot commonly used in trapshooting is 209 yards and that the maximum range of No. 8 shot is 198 yards. Even if some citizen made a mistake and shot off a load of No. 2s at a clay target, the shot could travel no farther than 330 yards. If two or three shot fused together for any reason, they would fly somewhat farther. However, any club with a safety zone of 440 yards should be entirely in the clear.

Most of us have had the experience of being sprinkled with spent shot fired at a high angle by some other gunner. Larger sizes may sometimes sting bare skin, but seldom do they do even that. The resistance of the air slows down any free falling body. If it were not for this, a rain drop would fall fast enough to knock one's head off. Large rain drops fall faster than small ones, just as the terminal velocity of large shot pellets is greater than that of small. The terminal velocity of No. 10 shot never exceeds 80 f.p.s., whereas that of No. 2 never exceeds 130 f.p.s.

One often hears the advice to hold high for a long shot at waterfowl with a shotgun. It doesn't hurt anything to hold a bit high. On the other hand, it doesn't do much good, since the spread of the shot charge pretty well takes care of the drop of the shot. At 60 yards a No. 2 shot will drop only about 7 inches and a No. 4 pellet only 7.7 inches. At that distance the shot pattern will have a diameter of at least 6 feet. Smaller shot have somewhat more drop, but nothing smaller than No. 4 should ever be used at 60 yards.

One of the most interesting developments in the shot shell in recent years has been the increase in the amount of the charge of shot. This is made possible by the development of dense, progressive-burning powders which enable the loading companies to use more shot at standard velocity or with only slight decrease in velocity. This trend has been going on ever since the early 1920s when Western Cartridge Company pioneered heavier charges of shot in front of charges of progressive-burning powder. The first powder used by Western in the Super X loads was imported from Germany. Today Herco, a progressive-burning powder turned out by the Hercules Powder Company, is widely used for loads of this sort. A Du Pont powder of the same class is No. 4756, which is often used in the 2¾-inch magnum loads in all gauges.

The use of these and other slow-burning powders has enabled the loading companies to increase the amount of shot, to thicken up the patterns at ordinary ranges, and to maintain killing-pattern density at greater distances. When I started using the shotgun, the standard load for the 20 gauge was ¾ ounce of shot. The load was increased to ⅞ ounce, then to 1 ounce, and now 20-gauge 2¾-inch magnum shells are available with 1⅛ ounces of shot and 20-gauge 3-inch magnum shells with 1¼ ounces—as much shot as was once used in "maximum" duck loads. The shot charge in the .410 has been stepped up from ⅜ ounce in a 2½-inch case in the 1920s to ¾ ounce in a 3-inch case. The powder used for this .410 load is No. 2400, a rifle powder developed originally for the .22 Hornet cartridge. As a rifle powder it is quick burning, but as a shotgun powder it is very slow burning.

By using a dense slow-burning powder and a shorter wad column, Federal Cartridge Company was enabled to load 1 ounce of shot in the 28 gauge, and made of that little gauge a fine bet for the uplands and a 40-yard killer in a full-choke barrel. The 2¾-inch magnum shells in 12 gauge are a postwar development. They throw 1½ ounces of shot—a charge which was considered about right for a 3-inch 12-gauge magnum not many years ago. The 3-inch magnum 12-gauge shell is loaded not only wtih 1⅝ ounces of shot but also with the super charge of 1⅞ ounces—almost as much as is stuffed in the 3½-inch 10-gauge magnum shell and what once was considered proper for an 8 gauge.

These heavy charges of shot extend the range of the shotgun, but possibly more important is that they thicken up the pattern and increase the effectiveness of an open-bored gun at ranges where it ordinarily would not be used. I know an ardent duck hunter who always uses a skeet-bored automatic 12 gauge with 2¾-inch magnum loads over decoys. He claims that he simply cannot miss to 40 yards.

Some years ago I went out one afternoon with the skeet barrels fitted to my 12-gauge Winchester Model 21. Using the magnum loads of 1½ ounces of No. 6, I knocked off a limit of quail and a limit of Huns. Maybe I missed a shot or two, but if I did so I cannot remember it. These magnum loads, however, kick like the devil in a 7½-pound double gun.

All the loading companies put together three principal types of loads. The first consists of long-range and magnum shells with large charges of shot in front of progressive-burning powder. Typical of such premium loads are Western Super X, Remington Express, and Federal Hi-Power. For many years the standard 12-gauge load of this class was the "heavy" or "high-velocity" load with 3¾ drams equivalent of powder and 1¼ ounces of shot. In the 16 gauge, 1⅛ ounces of shot was loaded, in the 20 gauge 1 ounce. The magnum loads of this class use heavier charges of shot but at slightly lower velocity than that delivered by standard long-range loads.

The second class of load is the "field" load. Of this type the most widely distributed 12-gauge load is with 3¼ drams equivalent and 1⅛ ounces of shot; but 12-gauge field loads are also available with 3 drams and 1 ounce and with 3¼ drams and 1¼ ounces. Field loads for the 16 gauge contain 1 dram and 1⅛ ounces of shot and for the 20 gauge ⅞ dram and 1 ounce.

The third type of shell is loaded for trap and skeet—from 2¾ to 3 drams equivalent in the 12 gauge and 1⅛ ounces of No. 7½, 8, or 9 shot, 1 ounce in the 16 and ⅞ ounce in the 20. The 16 and 20 gauge are almost never used for trapshooting and no special trap loads are made for them. For skeet the 16 gauge is loaded with 1 ounce of No. 9, the 20 with ⅞ ounce, the 28 with ¾ ounce, the .410 with ½ ounce (sub-small bore) and ¾ ounce (small bore).

In addition, all the loading companies turn out scatter loads to throw wider patterns in choke-bored guns, buckshot loads, and shells loaded with rifled slugs.

The following list of loads was taken from a Remington catalog, but the lists of the three big loading companies pretty much duplicate each other and all shells are loaded to S.A.A.M.I. standards.

	GAUGE	LENGTH OF SHELL IN INCHES	POWER EQUIV. DRAMS	OUNCES OF SHOT	SHOT SIZES
	10	2⅞	4¾	1⅝	2
	10	2⅞	4¾	1⅝	4
	12	2¾	3¾	1¼	BB,2,4,5,6,7½,9
	16	2¾	3	1⅛	2,4,5,6,7½
	16	2⁹⁄₁₆	3	1⅛	2,4,5,6,7½
Long Range	16	2¾	3¼	1⅛	2,4,5,6,7½,9
	20	2¾	2¾	1	2,4,5,6,7½,9
	28	2¾	2¼	¾	4,6,7½,9
	410	2½	—	½	4,5,6,7½,9
	410	3	—	¾	4,5,6,7½,9
	10	3½	5	2	BB,2,4,(Mag.)
	10	3½	5	2	2,4 (Mag.)
	12	2¾	4	1½	2,4,6 (Mag.)
	12	3	4½	1⅞	BB,2,4 (Mag.)
Magnum	12	3	4¼	1⅝	BB,2,4,5,6 (Mag.)
	16	2¾	3½	1¼	2,4,6 (Mag.)
	20	2¾	3	1⅛	2,6,7½ (Mag.)
	20	3	3¼	1¼	2,4,6,7½ (Mag.)
	12	2¾	3¾	—	oo Buck-9 Pellets
	12	2¾	3¾	—	o Buck-12 Pellets
	12	2¾	3¾	—	1 Buck-16 Pellets
Buckshot	16	2⁹⁄₁₆	3	—	1 Buck-12 Pellets
	12	2¾	4	—	oo Buck-12 Pellets
	12	3	4½	—	oo Buck-15 Pellets
	12	2¾	3¾	1	Rifled Slug
Rifled Slug	16	2⁹⁄₁₆	3	⅞	Rifled Slug
	20	2½	2¾	⅝	Rifled Slug
	410	2½	—	⅕	Rifled Slug

	GAUGE	LENGTH OF SHELL IN INCHES	POWER EQUIV. DRAMS	OUNCES OF SHOT	SHOT SIZES
Field	12	2¾	3	1	4,5,6,8
	12	2¾	3	1⅛	4,5,6,8,9
	12	2¾	3¼	1⅛	4,5,6,7½,8,9
	12	2¾	3¼	1¼	7½,8
	16	2⁹⁄₁₆	2½	1	4,5,6,8,9
	16	2¾	2¾	1⅛	4,5,6,7½,8,9
	20	2¾	2¼	⅞	4,5,6,8
	20	2¾	2½	1	4,5,6,7½,8,9
Scatter	12	2⅝	3	1⅛	8
	16	2⁹⁄₁₆	2½	1	8
	20	2½	2¼	⅞	8
Trap and Skeet	12	2¾	3	1⅛	7½,8,9
	12	2¾	2¾	1⅛	7½,8,9
	16	2¾	2½	1	9
	20	2¾	2¼	⅞	9
	28	2¾	2¼	¾	9
	410	2½	—	½	9
	410	3	—	¾	9

Just as the average gunner uses too much choke, he also has the tendency to use too much shot shell. Citizens who lack the skill to lead a duck or a goose properly at 40 yards use 2¾ and 3-inch magnum shells and blast away at birds that would be out of the range of a 4 gauge. An old hunting companion of mine in South Idaho used to shoot 3-inch magnum 12-gauge shells with 1⅝ ounces of shot at pheasants and I am sure that now that they are available he is using the super-bump load with 1⅞ ounces. Many gunners use the premium long-range loads like Super X and Nitro Express in the field when the cheaper field loads or even trap loads would do just as well and kick less. The British standard field load for the 12 gauge is in a 2½-inch case and contains 1¹⁄₁₆ ounces of shot. It is a pleasant load to shoot and seems adequate for any upland hunting.

Killing Range of the Shotgun

It is always easy to start an argument about the killing range of the shotgun, as those who argue on the subject are long on testimonial evidence and short on facts. One hunter will swear that if he leads right he can kill single ducks to 85 yards with his 12-gauge magnum and another is convinced he has knocked off many geese at 100 yards with a 10-gauge magnum. In arriving at such figures few people actually measure distances from where they shoot to where the birds fall. Even if they pace off the distance, they don't take into consideration the fact that 60 paces in hip boots over soggy ground is seldom 60 yards. Neither do they take into consideration that the distance where the bird fell was the same as the distance at which it was shot. They also tend to take the exceptional as the typical. Now and then a lucky hit or two will knock down a duck at far beyond normal range, or a fortunate cluster of shot will do the same thing. Inexperienced hunters tend to shoot at birds (particularly waterfowl) at far too great a range. The result is that every year tens of thousands of ducks and geese fly off to die slowly and miserably of peritonitis from a shot or two in the guts. It is a common experience to go to a public duck marsh and never get a shot because over-optimistic gunners blast away at everything that comes within 150 yards.

The notion of a long-range shotgun that will down ducks and geese at from 75 to 100 yards is an exceedingly seductive one, but there simply is no such animal—at least in the United States. I have never shot a 4-bore gun, and such a cannon loaded with 3 or 3½ ounces of No. 2 shot or BB's might kill geese to around 100 yards, but a gun for such a load would be so heavy, so clumsy, so slow that it would be almost impossible to do wing shooting with it. Anyone who doesn't believe these gloomy words should try patterning at 70, 75, and 80 yards a 12-gauge magnum throwing 1⅞ ounces of shot or a 10-gauge magnum with 2 ounces.

Many of the executives of the Western Cartridge Company at East Alton, Illinois, are enthusiastic and expert duck hunters. They have kept records of the ducks they shot, counted hits, put down the distances at which they were killed. They have found that it takes on an average 5 pellets of No. 4 shot to make a clean kill on a duck. Used in guns that will give 70 percent full-choke patterns at 40 yards, a 1-ounce load will put on the average 5.6 pellets into a duck at that distance, a 1⅛-ounce load will hit him with 6.3 pellets, a 1¼-ounce load with 7 pellets, a 1⅜-ounce load with 7.7, a 1½-ounce load with 8.3, and a 1⅝-ounce load with 9.1.

The Western people consider that 1 ounce of No. 4 shot in a full-choke gun is a 43-yard duck killer. The 1⅛-ounce load is a 46-yard killer, the 1¼-ounce load a 49-yard killer. The old 3-inch magnum load of 1⅜ ounces stretches the range to 52 yards and the 1½-ounce 2¾-inch 12-gauge magnum load is good for 55 yards. The "light" 3-inch magnum 12-gauge load with 1⅝ ounces is a 58-yard load, and the 1⅞-ounce 3-inch magnum load and the 2-ounce 3½-inch magnum 10-gauge load stop at about 65 yards. Of course, birds are killed dead at ranges longer than this by lucky hits. Either the birds runs into a chance cluster of shot or gets smacked in a vital spot by a lucky pellet. But for every bird lucked down several fly off wounded.

Using the criterion of three No. 6 shot in a duck-size profile, the late Maj. Charles Askins came up with the following results: a 20 gauge with 1 ounce of shot was through at 45 yards, a 16 with 1⅛ ounces was through at 48, a 12 gauge with 1¼ ounces at 54, and a 12-gauge magnum with 1⅝ ounces at 65. Whether three No. 6 shot will consistently kill a large duck or not is open to question. The experimenters at Western did not think so.

My own criterion is that a 12-gauge gun can be counted on to kill cleanly to the distance where it will put 50 percent of 1⅛ ounces of shot of suitable size in a 30-inch circle. If it will put 50 percent of its charge of No. 8 shot in a 30-inch circle at 45 yards, it will kill quail at that distance. If it will put 50 percent of its No. 4 shot into that 30-inch circle at 49 yards, it will kill mallards. On the other hand, if it can throw a 50 percent pattern at only 35 yards, it is a 35-yard gun. The same gun used with heavier charges of shot will of course give the same pattern density at greater distances and will hence kill somewhat farther.

It is for this reason of pattern density that the 12-gauge gun can be opened up more than a 20 gauge. A 12 gauge throwing a 50 percent pattern (tight improved cylinder or quarter choke) with 1¼ ounces will give a slightly denser pattern at 40 yards with shot of the same size than a 20 gauge bored improved-modified (67½ percent) with 1 ounce of shot. On the other hand, a full-choke 20 gauge using the 3-inch magnum load of 1¼ ounces of shot will kill as far as a 70-percent 12 gauge.

Possibly the man behind the shotgun limits the practical range more than the load of shot in the shell and the amount of choke in the muzzle. The farther away a bird is the harder it is to hit and the more the pattern thins out. The average good shot who does a lot of shooting should kill the majority of the birds he gets routine shots at up to 40 yards—and he can do this neatly with a 50-percent 12 gauge. Beyond 40 yards with any amount of shot and any gun, our good average shot runs into difficulties. He begins to miss and cripple. Few hunters have enough skill to use a 12-gauge 3-inch magnum at 55 to 65 yards. For most purposes the shotgun is still a 40-yard weapon for most gunners, a 50 to 60-yard weapon for only a few experts.

Recoil of the shotgun

It is a curious fact that most shooters seem to be able to take more recoil from a shotgun than they can from a rifle. Part of the reason is physical: the shotgun is fired at a moving target by a relaxed man whose attention is focused on the target. The rifle more often than not is fired at a stationary target by a person who knows he is going to be belted. The "Heavy" trap load of 3 drams equivalent and 1⅛ ounces of shot fired from an 8-pound gun gives slightly more recoil than does a .270 cartridge with the 130-grain bullet fired in a rifle of similar weight. Most people would say the .270 had the greater recoil. The ordinary duck load with 3¾ drams and 1¼ ounces of shot fired in a 7¼-pound gun gives about the recoil of the .375 Magnum with the 235-grain bullet. Nevertheless, most people who would never think of firing twenty-five .375 Magnum cartridges at a sitting will shoot twenty-five shells at ducks in a morning and wish they could shoot more.

Today there are two tendencies in the world of the shotgun that together cause a lot of people to get shaken up by recoil. One is the development of heavy loads, which cause more recoil. The other is the development of light shotguns. Put a 2¾-inch magnum shell in a 6½-pound 12-gauge pump gun, and you have a combination that would loosen the fillings in the teeth of Gargantua.

The heavier the charge of shot, the heavier the wads, the heavier the powder charge, the greater the speed at which shot and wads are moved up the barrel, the greater the recoil. The lighter the gun, the greater the recoil, as the light gun comes back faster (kicks more) than a heavy gun. If the gun weighed the same as the shot charge, wads, and powder, it would come back as fast. On the other hand, if the gun weighed 50 pounds the heaviest loads could be fired and the recoil hardly felt.

In the days of double guns that were more or less custom-made gunners ordered duck guns to weigh 8½ or 9 pounds in 12 gauge, to have 30 or 32-inch barrels, and to be made with stocks somewhat shorter than normal to compensate for the heavy clothes they wore for duck and goose shooting on wet and chilly mornings. If a man had but one gun, it tended to be of the wildfowl type. Back in the 1920s and early 1930s the standard "high-velocity" duck load with 3¾ drams equivalent and 1¼ ounces of shot was considered a real hell-bender, and people talked with bated breath about the special Fox and L. C. Smith overbored duck guns that weighed 9 pounds and handled 3-inch shells with 1⅜ ounces of shot.

Nowadays, the typical all-around gun is a 12-gauge pump or automatic. Some 12-gauge pumps weigh as little as 6½ pounds. A typical one, the Remington Model 870, weighs between 7 and 7½ pounds. The Remington long-recoil operated Model 11–48 and the gas-operated Model 1100 weigh about 7½ to 7¾ pounds in 12 gauge. Into these light guns, the boys stuff some fearful loads and the result is that they get most roundly kicked. According to some old figures released by Du Pont, the old load of 3½ drams with 1¼ ounces of shot fired in a 6½-pound gun gave 34.5 foot-pounds of recoil. With 1½ ounces of shot as in the 12-gauge 2¾-inch magnum shell, the recoil in a 6½-pound gun must be up around 40 pounds. However, the 3½-dram–1¼-ounce load fired in a 9-pound gun gives only 24.8 foot-pounds of recoil. The moral is that those who want to use big bump duck loads should get a heavy gun to go with the heavy load, and those who like light upland guns should stick to upland loads. A 6½–6¾-pound 12-gauge gun and the standard field load of 3¼ drams and 1⅛ ounces of shot go very well together.

The table on p. 238 shows the correlation of gun weight and recoil. It is from Du Pont.

This combination of heavy loads and light guns has turned many to thinking of ways to reduce recoil effect. One method, of course, is to attach a recoil pad. This does not make the gun kick less but it reduces the recoil effect in that the rubber softens the blow and the shooter does not get bruised and hurt. Yet another method of reducing recoil effect without reducing recoil is to use a relatively straight stock. The greater the difference between drop at comb and drop at heel, the greater the recoil effect since the crooked stock bangs the comb up against the cheek. With the straighter stock the recoil comes more nearly straight back. Some trap guns are built with the same drop at heel as at comb, and once I had a European over-and-under with slightly more drop at comb than at heel. I have rather wide, square shoulders and a long neck. I tend to be a stock-crawler and I can shoot a very straight stock. I found this oddly stocked over-and-under quick-pointing, fast-handling, and pleasant to shoot. If a gun has a substantial fore-end, the left hand will take up some of the recoil, and a wide, flat buttplate distributes the recoil over a wider area.

The ventilated cage features of the various choke devices cut down on recoil by diverting the powder gases. If all the gases could be diverted straight back, the braking effect would be very great, but the shooter could not stand the blast. As it is, the blast and report are most unpleasant to others standing beside the shooter. Some manufacturers of recoil-reducing variable choke devices have made some pretty generous claims for them—recoil reduction of up to 40 percent. Probably reduction of recoil is more in the nature of 10 to 25 percent with the various gadgets which have been on the market or are still on the market.

A truly amazing device to reduce recoil is the Hydro-Coil. It is a recoil-reducing device fitted inside a hollow, plastic gunstock. It is

RECOIL IN FOOT POUNDS OF 12-GAUGE DU PONT SMOKELESS LOADS

Recoil in Foot Pounds with Guns of Different Weights

Load	Muzzle Velocity Ft. Sec.	6-lb. Gun	6¼-lb. Gun	6½-lb. Gun	6¾-lb. Gun	7-lb. Gun	7¼-lb. Gun	7½-lb. Gun	7¾-lb. Gun	8-lb. Gun	8¼-lb. Gun	8½-lb. Gun	8¾-lb. Gun	9-lb. Gun
3–1	1218	20.5	19.9	19.0	18.2	17.6	17.2	16.5	16.2	15.6	15.2	14.9	14.4	13.7
3¼–1	1314	24.0	23.0	22.2	21.0	20.4	19.8	19.0	18.9	18.3	17.7	17.2	16.7	16.0
3½–1	1424	28.0	27.2	26.0	24.8	24.2	23.5	22.5	22.0	21.4	20.8	20.1	19.6	19.0
3–1⅛	1180	24.0	23.0	22.2	21.0	20.4	19.8	19.0	18.6	18.0	17.2	16.7	16.4	16.0
3¼–1⅛	1278	27.9	26.8	26.0	24.8	24.2	23.5	22.5	21.6	21.0	20.4	19.7	19.2	19.0
3½–1⅛	1376	32.3	31.2	29.9	28.9	28.0	26.8	26.0	25.0	24.4	23.6	22.9	22.2	21.9
3–1¼	1148	27.6	26.2	25.2	24.2	23.5	22.9	21.8	21.0	20.4	19.9	19.6	19.2	18.6
3¼–1¼	1240	32.3	30.9	29.5	28.6	27.6	26.8	25.6	24.7	24.1	23.4	22.8	22.1	21.5
3½–1¼	1338	37.4	35.8	34.5	33.3	32.2	31.0	30.0	28.6	28.0	27.0	26.6	25.8	24.8

The Du Pont ballisticians who recorded the above recoil data are of the opinion that "recoil heavier than 28 foot pounds cannot be endured for any considerable time"—an opinion that experience proves reasonably conservative, we'd say.

a three-part unit similar in operation to an automobile shock absorber. It uses a pneumatic cylinder preloaded to 40 pounds of air pressure to absorb recoil. When a gun equipped with a Hydro-Coil buttstock is fired, the forward portion of the two-piece stock remains stationary while the butt portion recoils against the Hydro-Coil unit inside the stock and seated against the buttplate. Makers say the device absorbs 85 percent of the recoil and I can well believe it. It never caught on. The company folded.

Shooting a gun equipped with Hydro-Coil is a spooky experience. You can blast away with a 2¾-inch magnum 12-gauge shell expecting to be belted. But you are not. The recoil is as gentle as the caress of a lovely maiden. It is downright disconcerting. I have never shot a .458 Winchester so equipped but from my experience with shotguns I'd say the Hydro-Coil would make that wicked monster kick about like a .243. You have to try the gimmick to believe it.

Stocks are available for Winchester Model 12 and Browning Superposed shotguns. They are good-looking, made of a durable plastic called Cycolac in walnut and (ugh!) ivory and in trap and field-skeet models. The complete buttstock unit cost $80 in 1964. This was a useful gadget, but trouble to have installed.

The autoloading shotguns operated by the short-recoil system, such as the Browning Double Automatic and the Winchester Model 59, are definitely more pleasant to shoot than the autoloaders operated by the long-recoil system—the Remington Model 11–48, the Browning, and the Savage. In these the slam of the barrel coming back against the breech actually increases recoil. The gas-operated autoloaders like the High Standard, the Remington Model 1100, and the new Winchester Model 1400 soften the recoil considerably, as they distribute the recoil over a longer interval. I shot geese in Maryland with a Model 1100 using 2¾-inch magnum shells loaded with 1½ ounces of shot and found the recoil not unpleasant.

CHAPTER **21**

The Shot Pellet

W HEN I was a lad, it was the practice of my friends and me to carry, whenever we went duck hunting, a few shells loaded with No. 2 shot in a separate pocket. Then, when an especially long shot showed up, we would remove the No. 4s and No. 6s from our guns and fire a salute with the No. 2s. Now and then we actually killed a bird with the big shot, often at a fantastic distance. I can still remember a mallard drake that I must have downed at from 80 to 90 yards. One pellet had cracked him squarely in the head.

Our average on these long shots with No. 2s was perhaps one bird in 20 or 25 shots, and for a long time we humbly shouldered the blame, thinking we had not led correctly. Then one day, in a burst of curiosity, we did some patterning at 75 yards with our No. 2s, and we found that any duck we chanced to kill at the ranges at which we had been shooting was a very unlucky bird indeed. At that distance a duck might possibly be hit with a shot or two, but the patterns we got were so thin that a stork carrying quintuplets could fly through them time and again without a scratch.

Most hunters do not bother their pretty heads about shot, except to assume that the loading companies put some in the shells they buy. I doubt if more than one hunter in five ever patterns his gun on paper. Nevertheless, the man who does not spend some time patterning doesn't know much about his gun.

Because so few gunners ever use a smoothbore on anything unless it has hair or feathers on it, the whole subject of shot has a good deal of folklore connected with it. One chap I know hunts grouse with No. 4s and claims the big pellets smash through brush and twigs better than any smaller ones. Another uses No. 9s on grouse and claims the smaller pellets, because there are more of them, are most likely to get through the holes in the foliage. Both explanations sound logical, and both methods kill grouse. So far as I know, neither man has ever put up paper behind some foliage to find out if he's right.

Shot is made of lead because lead is heavy and fairly cheap. It is also soft and does not mar the relatively soft steel of shotgun barrels. Now and then someone removes the shot from a shell and reloads with steel air-rifle shot when he thinks he wants larger shot than is locally available. For two reasons this is a sour idea. For one thing, the steel pellets are less dense (weigh less for their size) than lead and lose their velocity more rapidly. For another, they are hard and often score the barrel badly.

"Soft" or "drop" shot has been obsolete since loading sporting ammunition was resumed after the last war. It was pure lead with a bit of arsenic added. Formerly, many hunters, particularly quail hunters in the South, swore by it, as they felt that it expanded like an expanding bullet when it struck the bird and hence had greater killing power. This is an old wives' tale. It is true that an examination of a bird killed with drop shot will show some deformed or upset pellets, but they were probably deformed by the forcing cone of the chamber or by the cone of the choke and *not* after they struck the bird. Drop shot throws a somewhat wider pattern because of this high percentage of deformed pellets, and hence it may be somewhat easier to hit with; but it patterns less reliably than harder shot and in the long run probably lets a higher proportion of cripples get away.

"Chilled" or "hard" shot is hardened by the addition of antimony. This not only assists the lead globule to form a sphere, but because it is harder, such shot does not give so high a percentage of deformed pellets and hence throws better and more even patterns. It also leads the barrel less, and produces a shorter shot string because of less shot deformity. Chilled shot is now standard.

Still harder, still less liable both to deformation and to the leading of the barrel, is copperized or copperplated shot, which is used in some premium loads. Shot is also coated with nickel.

Shot is manufactured in a tower of considerable height by pouring molten alloyed lead through a perforated "shower pan" with uniform holes whose size depends on the size of shot wanted. The falling trickles of lead form into spheres which are cooled by striking water below. Then the shot is gathered up and sent down a series of inclined planes. The round pellets run true, but the lopsided ones run cockeyed and fall off at the side, to be collected, remelted, and given another chance.

"Bird shot" was formerly manufactured in all sizes from No. 12 or "dust" (which, I believe, is the size still loaded in .22 caliber shot shells) through No. 10 (which many fancied for snipe) to No. 1. Through the course of the years, though, shotgun loads (combination of sizes and kinds of shot and amounts and kinds of powder in various gauges) have been trimmed down from literally thousands to less than one hundred and fifty, and the trimming has eliminated not only the old soft shot but many odd sizes. No. 9, the smallest size currently manufactured for regular gauges, is used in skeet and sometimes on small birds. From then on the list goes No. 8, No. 7½, No. 7, No. 6, No. 5, No. 4, No. 2, and BB. BB shot is .18 inch in diameter. The table on p. 243 presents pertinent data on the various sizes of shot.

In case you don't have the table at hand, here's an easy formula for finding the actual size of shot: Subtract the size number from 17, and you'll get the pellet diameter as measured in hundredths of an inch.

As for the various charges, ½ ounce is used in the 2½-inch .410 shell. Skeet loads for the 28 gauge and the 3-inch .410 take ¾ ounce. The low-brass 20-gauge shell uses ⅞ ounce. A ⅞-ounce load is used in the 28-gauge magnum, the high-brass 20 gauge, and the low-brass 16 gauge. A charge of 1⅛ ounces is used in high-brass 16-gauge shells, in the 2¾-inch 20-gauge magnum, and in the 12-gauge trap, skeet, and field loads. High-brass 12-gauge shells use 1¼ ounces of shot, as do 20-gauge 3-inch magnum shells and 16-gauge 2¾-inch magnum shells. Magnum 2¾-inch 12-gauge loads

COMPARATIVE SHOT SIZES

SIZE	NO.00 BUCK	NO.0 BUCK	NO.1 BUCK	NO.3 BUCK	NO.4 BUCK	BB	2	4	5	6	7½	8	9
DIAMETER IN INCHES	.33	.32	.30	.25	.24	.18	.15	.13	.12	.11	.095	.09	.08

Approximate number of pellets per load

OUNCES OF SHOT TO THE SHELL	NO.00 BUCK	NO.0 BUCK	NO.1 BUCK	NO.3 BUCK	NO.4 BUCK	BB	2	4	5	6	7½	8	9
1⅞	15					93	168	252	318				
1⅝						81	146	219	276	366			
1½	12						135	203	256	337			
1⅜		12	16			69	124	186		309			
1¼					27	63	113	169	213	281	438	513	731
1³⁄₁₆								160					
1⅛	9		12				101	152	191	253	394	461	658
1				20			90	135	170	225	350	410	585
⅞								118	149	197		359	512
¾								101	128	169	263		439
½								68	85	113	175		293

Shot sizes and pellets per load.

use 1½ ounces of shot, and 3-inch 12-gauge magnum loads contain 1⅝ and 1⅞ ounces of shot. The 10-gauge 3½-inch magnum uses a full 2 ounces.

The actual number of pellets may vary a bit, depending on the make of shot, but the table given will do reasonably well for the shooter to use in figuring pattern percentages. Suppose a sharp man with a pencil shoots his favorite gas pipe at 40 yards, then draws a 30-inch circle to enclose the largest possible number of holes, and counts 215. He has used a load containing 1¼ ounces of No. 7½, which contains presumably about 430 pellets. By spending a few minutes of hard labor, he will be able to deduce that he has got a 50 percent or improved-cylinder pattern.

If he had counted 323 holes, he would eventually determine that he had obtained a good full-choke pattern of about 75 percent.

Everyone should pattern his shotgun with different combinations of shot size and powder charge, by the way, since for no good reason known to man, particular guns like particular shot sizes. The duck shooter may find that his gun will give denser patterns with No. 5 shot than with No. 6, or vice versa. It may shoot No. 4 well and then again it may not.

One season back before the days of the pie crimp my wife shot an open-bored 16 gauge, with high velocity shells containing 1⅛ ounces of No. 7½, on quail. Too late she found that at 30 yards the patterns thrown by the right barrel had holes right in the middle you could throw Mickey Rooney through. The better she held, the more certain she was to miss or merely to feather her bird. A shift to the trap load with No. 8 shot cured it.

Almost any ammunition company catalog will contain a table of shot-size recommendations like that on p. 245, which I swiped *in toto* from the *Western Ammunition Handbook*.

Many years of experience by many smart people have gone into the compilation of such lists, and most gunners will find no fault with them. There are, however, two principal schools of dissenters —the small-shot advocates and the large-shot advocates.

One correspondent of mine, a Westerner with a lot of hunting behind him, leaps right down my throat every time I write about shot sizes. He uses no shot larger than No. 7½, *even on geese.* On

FOR UPLAND GAME

	Shot Sizes
Snipe, woodcock, rails, quail in early season, and small shore birds	8 or 9
Doves, quail in late season, large shore birds, and small winged pests	7, 7½, or 8
Pheasants, prairie chickens, grouse, rabbits, squirrels	4, 5, 6, or 7

FOR WILDFOWL

Ducks over decoys	5 or 6
All other duck shooting	4
Geese	BB, 2, or 4

FOR TRAPSHOOTING

16-yd. singles and first barrel of doubles	7½ or 8
Second barrel of doubles and handicap targets	7½ or 8

FOR SKEET

For any skeet shooting	9

these big birds, he says, the gunner should hold far enough ahead to center the head and neck, then the numerous little pellets will get in their dirty work and result in a clean kill. He also claims that larger pellets ball up in the feathers and do not penetrate so deeply.

Members of the small-shot school say that the way to kill cleanly is to hit the birds in the vital areas—the brain, the spine, the neck— and that the more pellets thrown at them, the better the chances are for vital hits. The advocates of large shot say that small pellets quickly lose their velocity and energy, and lack sufficient shocking power to down a bird unless they happen to hit a vital area. In most cases, they insist, the pellets give poor penetration, cause gangrene, and slow death.

Let's take a look at a few figures on remaining energy:

Energy in Foot-Pounds of Each Pellet

Range in Yards	No. 2	No. 4	No. 6	No. 7½

12-gauge maximum load (3¾ drams of powder, 1¼ ounces of shot, muzzle velocity 1,444 foot-seconds):

Range in Yards	No. 2	No. 4	No. 6	No. 7½
10	16	10	5.9	3.6
20	12	7.5	4.3	2.65
30	10	6.1	3.5	2.05
40	8.6	5.1	2.9	1.7
50	7.3	4.4	2.4	1.38
60	6.5	3.7	2	1.1

16-gauge maximum load:

Range in Yards	No. 2	No. 4	No. 6	No. 7½
60		3.5	1.85	1

20-gauge maximum load:

Range in Yards	No. 2	No. 4	No. 6	No. 7½
60		3.6	1.92	1.06

As you see, though the smaller gauges turn up less velocity at the muzzle than the 12 gauge, at 60 yards the retained energy, size for size, is not much less. For another thing, the previous table shows that there the roughly four times as many No. 7½ pellets in a load as there are No. 2 pellets; yet it takes no seventh son of a son of a seventh son to dope out from the figures for the 12 gauge above that at 60 yards a No. 2 pellet, instead of hitting four times as hard as a No. 7½, hit nearly *six* times as hard—a gain, because of the larger, heavier shot, of almost 50 percent.

At 60 yards the velocity and energy of the little No. 7½ pellets have fallen off so much that, in spite of good pattern density, it is doubtful that even a neck shot would kill. Almost every hunter, reaching way out for a goose at 60 or 70 yards, has literally heard the small pellets rattle off its feathers and seen it go sailing majestically on.

Big birds like geese and turkeys can be killed very dead with small shot, but only at ranges where the pattern is dense enough to assure hits in the head or neck and where enough energy and velocity remain to give good penetration.

Roughly, then, with small shot the effective range on big birds is just about what it is on quail, because the head and upper neck of a goose or turkey don't offer a much bigger target than the body of a quail. If with No. 7½ or No. 8 shot a certain gun will take quail at 45 yards, it will also take geese at that distance. Actually, the man using a close-shooting gun and small shot, *and* shooting at the heads of decoyed geese at a range where such a combination is effective, will probably get more clean kills than if he were using larger shot and holding for the body.

Contrariwise, a Magnum 10 using 2 ounces of large shot, or a Magnum 12 using 3-inch shells with 1⅞ ounces of large shot, will often kill geese at 70 and sometimes 80 yards, far beyond the effective range of small shot in any amount and in any gauge.

As a practical illustration of this velocity and energy loss, at about 125 yards No. 7½ or No. 8 shot will rattle off the skin, as most every gunner knows who has shot in a hard-hunted dove flyway. No. 6 pellets will sting a little. No. 5s will hurt. No. 4s might break the skin.

In a way, changing shot sizes is like shifting something from one pocket to another. If you go to a smaller shot size, you increase pattern density and better your chances of a vital hit, but you cut down on energy delivered per pellet and, at the longer ranges, on total energy delivered. If you go to a larger shot size, you gain on energy delivered per pellet and probably on total energy delivered, but you lose on pattern density and cut down on your chances of hitting a vital area. As I mentiond at the start, we used to carry No. 2 pellets around for long shots, but a hit with those thinned-out patterns was in the nature of an act of God.

Let's draw a few conclusions about choice of shot size:

The larger the bird the larger the shot that can be used with the assurance that the necessary four or five body hits can be obtained. A goose or a wild turkey will receive the minimum four pellets from a pattern that may leave a quail or a dove entirely unscratched.

The tighter the pattern the larger the shot that can be used. A gun throwing a good full-choke pattern with No. 4 pellets can still put in as many hits (with more delivered energy per pellet) than a gun throwing a cylinder pattern with the smaller and more numerous No. 5s.

The larger the gauge the larger the shot that can be used successfully. A Magnum 10 gauge can use No. 2, but it would be silly to attempt to use them in a 20 gauge, the maximum load of which is only half that of a Magnum 10.

Other things being equal, however, the smaller the gauge, the smaller the bird, the lighter the shot charge, or the more open the boring the smaller the shot.

Under any circumstances, there seems to be no point in using shot larger than the following: in .410 or 28 gauge, No. 7½; in 20 gauge, No. 6; in 16 guage, No. 5; in 12 gauge, No. 4; and in Magnum 12 or 10 gauge, No. 2.

Effective killing range of various shot sizes: No. 9, 35 yards; No. 8, 40 yards; No. 7½, 45 yards; No. 6, 50 yards; No. 4, 60 yards; No. 2, 60 yards (in a 12-gauge Magnum, or from 65 to possibly 75 yards in a 10-gauge Magnum). From experience in the field, and from shooting at mail-order catalogs and then counting the number of pages penetrated, I'd say that's about the story—assuming, of course, that the shot is a recommended size for the birds taken.

If we had to get along with only three sizes of shot, we wouldn't be too badly off with No. 7½ for skeet, traps, and all upland shooting, even at grouse and pheasants; No. 6 for ducks, maybe grouse and pheasants too, and geese or turkeys up to 40 yards; No. 4 for pass-shooting at ducks and geese in special long-range guns. If you had to get along with only two shot sizes, you could cut out No. 4; and if only *one* shot size was permitted, I think I'd take No. 6, although No. 7½ might not be such a bad choice either.

If you're in any doubt as to which of two shot sizes to pick, choose the smaller—it patterns more densely and gives a better chance of a vital hit. I am sure it is easier to fold a duck at 35 yards with No. 6 than it is with No. 4.

The man who doesn't pattern his gun with various sizes of shot and various makes of ammunition is something like the character who blithely goes out into the deer forest come autumn without having sighted in his rifle, or who changes brands and bullet weights with no attempt to learn how performance is affected.

Besides shooting and evaluating the conventional patterns, you'll find it very revealing to draw a life-size profile of the bird you're going to hunt, then shoot at it at various ranges and *count the hits*. When a particular shot size fails to make a minimum of four hits at a certain range, you'll know you can't reach out that far with it and not cripple a lot of birds that will never reach the frying pan—yours or anybody else's!

These simple tests will tell you much about *your* gun. Maybe it has a greater affinity, say, for No. 8 shot than for No. 7½. Perhaps it performs indifferently with high-velocity loads but beautifully with standard loads. Maybe it will pattern No. 5 better than No. 4—or vice versa.

In doing your patterning, remember that the shotgun is a short-range weapon and that most ranges at which game is killed are grossly overestimated. After you draw that duck profile, take a good look at it at 50 yards, and if it doesn't seem pretty far away, I'll eat it. Now lift it 75 feet in the air and it will look twice that far away.

At 40 to 45 yards No. 6 shot will knock a duck for a loop. Move him somewhat closer and No. 7½ has all the penetration you need.

I remember the day when, on a Southwest duck marsh, one citizen was folding the birds up in a way that was something to amaze. He was using a Winchester Model 21 skeet gun and No. 8 shot. Another chap, reputed to be about as hot a duck shot as haunted the marshes along the Pee Dee River, did his shooting with a Sauer double gun, bored improved cylinder in both barrels, and he used No. 7½ shot. The secret of his success was that he never shot at a bird more than 35 yards away.

CHAPTER 22

The Elements

of Shotgun Shooting

ALMOST all Americans who shoot shotguns are completely self-taught, and that is the reason that the percentage of really good performers is small. The average young American is convinced that the ability to shoot a firearm of any sort is something that comes naturally—like having a sense of humor, being able to charm women, make a smart business deal, or whip in fair fight two Englishmen, four Germans, eight Japs, and sixteen Russians. I have yet to meet a man who would deny that he was a good natural shot, just as I have yet to meet a man who would deny that he was practically irresistible to women.

Many users of the shotgun never learn to be any good with one, but nevertheless cherish all their lives the notion that they are "natural" shots. One of the reasons that they can deceive themselves is that they generally confine their shooting entirely to the hunting season and there is no one to keep score on them. They do not count the shells they expend. They forget their misses, remember their hits.

One time I shot pen-raised pheasants with four men on a shooting preserve in the Middle West. Two were citizens who called themselves "practical" shots. Another was the sales manager of a big loading company. One of the "practical" shots not only couldn't shoot a shotgun—he couldn't even handle one. The other was a fair catch-as-catch-can shot but incredibly slow. He had been shooting a shotgun off and on for many years, but he was not nearly as effective a shot as the sales manager who had been shooting about a year but who had good instruction and had started right.

We were all using 12-gauge repeating shotguns bored improved cylinder, guns that had a killing range of about 30 to 35 yards. One chap couldn't even mount his gun, and when he fired he blew holes in the air. Another man took long and deliberate aim, but when he fired, his birds were generally beyond effective range and flew off shedding feathers. This chap would have done all right with a gun bored full choke but he was simply too slow to use an improved cylinder boring. On the other hand, the sales manager shot accurately and in good time and folded those big cackling cocks very neatly.

One of the hunters struck me as being a man of scant experience and very poor muscular co-ordination, but the rifle shooter simply did not understand the principles of shotgun shooting. He was a self-taught shot who apparently never fired at anything that didn't wear feathers. The sales manager, on the other hand, had never fired a shotgun in his life until he had gone to work for the loading company. He realized that since he was going to have to sell guns and ammunition he should know something about them and to learn about them he would have to use them. If he had to shoot, he wanted to shoot well.

He took instructions from company employees who were good shots. He practiced at skeet and traps. Since he knew nothing about shooting when he started, he began learning with an open mind and did not have bad habits to break. Within a year he was a far better shotgunner than most men who have shot twenty years or more. He who starts learning to shoot with no bad habits to break is fortunate indeed. In the army and the marine corps during the last war, it often happened that the best shot in the company was not a Kentuckian who was convinced he could shoot out the eye of a squirrel offhand at 100 yards, the Arizonan who had been plinking away at jackrabbits with a .22 since he was eight, or a Texan who felt he was a natural shot because he had a great-grand-father who had fought the Mexicans at the battle of San Jacinto, but some city kid who had never fired a rifle or seen a head of big game when he went into the service.

There is nothing natural about shooting a shotgun properly, just as there is nothing natural about a good golf swing or an effective forehand drive in tennis. Give the beginner a shotgun and tell him to hit a flying object with it and he'll do everything all wrong, just as his first swing with a golf club or a tennis racket will be all wrong. Still, becoming a good enough shotgun shot is, as accomplishments go in sports, comparatively easy. I consider it far more simple, for example, to learn to break 20 out of 25 at either traps or skeet than to learn to break 100 in golf. It is also I believe, much easier to learn to average 22 out of 25 at skeet than it is to break 90 in golf. Learning to drive, to hit fairway woods, to handle long and short irons, to chip, to putt, to blast out of a sand trap in golf are chores that make shooting a shotgun seem like child's play. The reason that there are more fairly good golfers than there are fairly good shotgun shots is that golfers have no illusions that they are born golfers the way many believe they are born shotgun shots. Almost all of those who become good golfers take lessons from professionals, watch professionals and good amateurs play, buy and read books on golf. Furthermore, they *practice*.

The average shotgunner, though, takes no lessons, reads no books on shotgun shooting, never fires a shot except in anger. No wonder he is a lousy shot. He can kid himself because, unlike the golfer, he never keeps score. If he gets his daily limit of three pheasants or five ducks, he is happy and thinks he has shot well. He may have fired twenty-four shots at the pheasants and forty shots at ducks, but, by golly, he got a limit, didn't he? What more can a man do?

This is not to say that there is no such thing as "natural" ability in shooting. Some shooters are blessed with quick-focusing eyes, fast reflexes, and good muscle memory. Some are not. There are a few people so poorly endowed by nature that they can never become good shotgun shots—and there are a few who with practice can become superlative shotgun shots. No amount of practice will ever make the average man a trap or skeet champion, just as the average writer could sit at a typewriter until he wore the seat out of his pants without ever becoming a John O'Hara or an Ernest Hemingway.

But the average man can with intelligent practice become a pretty good hand with a shotgun. In fact, he can become a far better shot than the man who has more natural gifts but who does not practice because he deludes himself into thinking he is a natural-born shot.

I consider myself a man of only average blessings in the way of muscular co-ordination. I was once a pretty fair tennis and baseball player. I shoot golf in the high 80s, occasionally slip up into the 90s, and on one red-letter day and with the aid of a lot of luck, actually scored in the high 70s. I am only about a 92-percent skeet shooter, not because I don't know how to break every target but because I am afflicted with a wandering mind and do not concentrate sufficiently. I break occasional straights and once I went 50 straight. I am a pretty fair field shot, and on many occasions I have killed twenty straight pheasants over dogs (very easy targets) without missing. However, I owe the fact that I am a fairly decent shot not to inherited natural ability but to the fact that I have given a good deal of thought to shooting and have been willing to practice.

I am a man who loves fine guns and over the years I have collected quite a number of them. In the course of a year, dozens of gun nuts come up to look at them and to fondle them. Almost always the visitor in my gun room picks up one of my fine double-barrel shotguns and throws it up as if to shoot it. As I watch, I can pick out the good shotgun shots from the poor and fair shotgun shots.

The good shotgun shot puts his gun to his face.

The fair to poor shot puts his face to his gun.

The untaught, unpracticed gunner jerks the butt up to his shoulder. Then he puts his head down so he can see barrel and target. If he is excited he often catches the butt of the gun in his clothes as he jerks the butt up. Once he has his gun to his shoulder, he puts his head down in an attempt to aim. In the field he often yanks the trigger before his head is down on the comb and consequently shoots over the bird.

The good shot does these things simultaneously:

He steps into position so that a line drawn between his toes would point to the left of the target at an angle of about 45 degrees. He leans slightly forward with slightly flexed knees to be in balance and so the recoil will not push him back on his heels. His right shoulder comes up a bit to be in the right place when the butt of the gun settles against it. His head goes forward and slightly to the right INTO THE POSITION WHERE IT WILL BE WHEN HIS GUN SETTLES INTO POSITION. As he does these things, he pushes his gun out in the direction of the bird and then brings it in so the butt is on the right place on his shoulder and the comb is against his cheek.

If his target is straightaway or slightly angling, his hips do not move. He fires when he sees the muzzle in proper relation to his target. If his shot is at a sharp angle, he is rotating his hips as he mounts his gun. The poor shot yanks his gun around with his arms; the good shot moves his gun by rotating his hips.

On a straightaway or slightly angling shot the skillful gunner has really aimed or pointed with his head, his feet, and his shoulder before the butt of the gun settles to his shoulder. The instant the butt touches his shoulder he is on. His eyes have been fixed on the target and he is not conscious of his barrels at all until suddenly they appear aligned on the target and in his field of view.

Mounting the gun speedily and correctly is half of shooting, and it was a sad day when the rules of skeet were changed to allow contestants to have the guns at their shoulder before they called for the target. When this rule change was made, half the value of skeet shooting was lost.

The shotgunner's stance should be easy and unstrained. The butt of the gun should rest just inside the pad of muscle formed by the arm and the shoulder. As we have seen, the right shoulder should be raised slightly to meet the butt, and the head inclined slightly to the right to be in position so the eye will look along the barrel. The right arm should incline naturally downward at an angle of about 45 degrees. The left hand should be well out along the fore-end or slide handle for greater leverage in guiding the piece.

The beginning shotgunner should practice mounting his gun—something he can do in his own house. He should practice fixing his eyes on some object, such as a picture, then putting his head *down* in the position it will be when he wills his shot off. Then he should step into the shot, bring the gun out and up, then back. As in any other sport, the secret of good shooting is the formation of correct habits. Not only does the good shot do things right—it is almost impossible for him to do them wrong.

The good shot looks as if he does things easily and naturally. He mounts his gun swiftly, yet it does not seem hurried because he does not jerk. His stance is easy, relaxed. He does not crouch as if he were about to jump across a mud puddle, or stand erect like a soldier at inspection.

One of the worst habits the beginning shotgunner can get into is that of closing one eye. Good shots shoot with both eyes open. Two eyes see more than one and binocular vision enables the shooter to judge range. Many good riflemen squint the left eye. Good shotgunners ALWAYS shoot with both eyes open.

It is very helpful for the beginner at shotgun shooting to take instruction at a shooting school, if there is such a thing handy. If not, the beginner should go out to a gun club and watch the best shots doing their stuff at trap and skeet. Then he should try to imitate them.

At any gun club, he will, unfortunately, notice some fairly good shots who operate from freakish stances. Some will stand ramrod stiff, some will crouch, but he should realize that these men are not good shots because of their stances but in spite of them. If he keeps his eyes open he will notice that the best shots make shooting look easy. They look relaxed and comfortable. The mediocre shots (like mediocre golf players) make their sport look like hard work. IN ANY SPORT THE BEST FORM IS THE EASIEST AND MOST EFFICIENT WAY TO DO THINGS. A Sam Snead or an Arnold Palmer steps up to a tee, swings easily and smoothly, and belts one 325 yards right down the middle of the fairway. Joe Dub sweats and groans, looks as if he were laboring hard enough to lift a house from its foundations, slices the ball 150 yards into the rough. An Alex Kerr swings swiftly, smoothly, easily, and the skeet target disappears in a cloud of blue smoke.

Subconsciously the beginner with a shotgun regards his weapon as being a variety of rifle. He wants to aim it by lining up the front sight in the middle of the receiver, and he regards the receiver as a rear sight. Then when he gets receiver (or middle rear sight in case his gun has one) lined up with the front sight and the target, he fires. He does all this because he forgets that he is not using a rifle with its single bullet. Instead he is using a shotgun and instead of hitting with a single projectile he is attempting to hit with a cloud of little projectiles (shot) that spread from 10 to 40 inches, depending upon the amount of choke and the distance. Precise aim as with a rifle is unnecessary and undesirable with a shotgun. It is unnecessary because the cloud of shot takes care of minor errors in pointing and undesirable because aiming takes the eye away from the target and slows the shooter down.

The front sight of the shotgun is the muzzle. Generally, it is made more conspicuous by the attachment of a gold, red, ivory, or fluorescent bead, or by wrapping it in white tape. Nevertheless, the end of the barrel is the front sight.

The rear sight is the eye of the shooter. If the eye is too high, he points the barrel upward in relation to the target and shoots high. If the eye is too low, the gun shoots low.

Good shotgun shots do not look straight down the barrel to the target as the marksman aims with his rifle. Instead, they see the whole barrel greatly foreshortened with the target above it.

Right now we might as well get a couple of definitions off our chests. The rifle is said to be aimed, the shotgum pointed. What is the difference? The rifleman lines up front sight, rear sight, and target. He *aims*. The shotgunner lines up only the front sight (the muzzle) in relation to his target. He *points*.

Members of one school of shotgun shooters say they never see the barrel at all, see only the target, have no notion whether they lead or not. For my part I am convinced they are talking through their hats. They just *think* they don't see their muzzles. The human eye has great depth of focus and if the barrel is aligned on the target it is impossible NOT to see it. The illusion of not seeing the barrel comes to unreflective shotgunners because their attention is on the target (as it should be) and because long practice has made much of the shooting habitual and unconscious. Many shooters are not aware of what they do. They just shoot. In the same way the man who has been tying his own shoe laces for 40 years would be hard put to tell you how he goes about it. He just does it and lets it go at that.

Shooting is like swinging a golf club in that the movements should be habitual and largely subconscious. However, at the start the movements of both sports are conscious. In addition, some people are men of muscle primarily and some are men of mind. Many superb shots who are not too bright really do not know what they do.

The shotgun is almost always fired at a moving target. In fact, shooting ground game before it flies and ducks and geese on the water (often referred to as "pot shooting" or "ground sluicing") is considered unsportsmanlike. Obviously, a flying target moves some distance before the shot reaches it and for the shot to strike it the gun must be pointed in front of the target. The distance ahead of the moving target that the gun is pointed is variously called "lead" or "forward allowance"—the British term. There are three methods by which flying targets can be struck by the shot charge.

The first is snap shooting or "spot" shooting. With this method the stationary gun is pointed at a spot ahead of the target so that shot charge and target will arrive at the same place at the same time.

The second method is called the fast swing or swinging through. With this, the gunner starts his swing behind the target, overtakes it, and fires either as the muzzle passes the target or when it gets a bit ahead. With this method only a fraction of the forward allowance necessary in snap shooting or spot shooting is needed. There are good reasons for this. Most gunners think they shoot the instant the relationship of muzzle and target look right. They do not. In fact, there is a considerable and measurable interval between the instant the gunner makes up his mind to shoot and the time the shot

STANCE, SWING AND LEAD

1. Gun position and stance as bird enters shootable range.

2. (a) Track bird along line of target.
   (b) Catch and pass bird.

3. Fire after determined lead.

4. Continue the swing of the gun —the follow through.

This is the way most Americans kill a crossing bird. They pick it up, track it, pass it, pull the trigger when the muzzle appears to be the right distance ahead. They keep the muzzle swinging AFTER they pull the trigger. Such shots are missed by slowing down the swing when the lead looks right or by stopping the swing.

gets to the target. The eyes must identify the target. The brain must give the command to the finger to pull the trigger. The message must pass through the nerves to the finger. Then the finger must obey. When the trigger is released the firing pin must fall, the primer in the shot shell must explode and ignite the powder. Then the powder must burn to generate gas and push the shot out of the barrel. Then the shot charge must wing its way to the target. If (and it is a *big* if) the shot charge intercepts the target, the result is a broken clay or a dead bird.

While all this is happening, the target is moving but so is the gun barrel. Obviously, the faster the barrel is moving, the more it moves during the time lag between impulse to fire and the arrival of the shot at their destination. In the early days of wing shooting when flintlock shotguns were used, the ignition time was very slow as anyone who has ever used a muzzle-loading flintlock knows. In addition, some people react much faster than others. The skilled react faster than the unskilled, the young faster than the old, the sharp-eyed faster than the optically handicapped. Some people swing a shotgun faster than others.

It is also obvious that the man who swings fast but who has considerable lag time will need less conscious lead than the man who swings more slowly but who has faster reaction time. This is one reason that no one can tell another just how far to lead a particular bird or clay target. When ranges are short, the fast swinger often does not consciously lead at all. The muzzle travels far enough ahead of the target during the lag time so that the shot charge hits.

This combination of gun swing and lag time results in much less practical lead than theoretical lead. A bird flying at the rate of 40 miles an hour and 20 yards away will travel about 3½ feet during the interval it takes the shot charge to intercept it. If the bird is 40 yards away and traveling at the same rate, the theoretical lead is about 8½ feet. But with a swinging shotgun no one has to point consciously that far ahead. At 20 yards and with a swinging gun, I would try to get about 1 to 1½ feet ahead of a quail passing with his steam up and at right angles. Many gunners would swear they did not lead at all—but instead shot the instant the fast-swinging gun muzzle passed the bird.

Most experienced gunners would say that they lead a passing duck or dove less than 8½ feet at 40 yards. Some (the fast swingers with slow reaction time) would say, perhaps, that they were about two feet ahead. Others, the slower swingers with the faster reaction time would guess that they lead 6 feet. My own notion is that for my own speed of swing and reaction time I have to get around 4 feet ahead in order to hit. However, again all this is relative, as what may look like 3 feet to one gunner may look like 6 to another. A few shotgunners would say that they never lead a bird at all, even one traveling at 40 miles an hour and 40 yards away. They are, I believe, kidding themselves.

The thing to be remembered is that in any case, and no matter at what angle, that barrel must be pointed (no matter what the method used)—8½ feet in front of the bird or the bird will not be hit. The gunner may think he leads 2 feet, 4 feet, 6 feet, or doesn't lead at all but he wouldn't hit the bird unless he shot the right distance ahead of it.

The third method of hitting a winging target is called "pointing out" or the "sustained lead." With this method the gunner points his muzzle ahead of the bird or target for what he considers the proper lead. Then he keeps the muzzle swinging ahead of the bird and traveling apparently as fast as the bird. Then he shoots with the gun still swinging. This method is somewhat slower than the fast swing. For many, it is more positive and more accurate.

Probably all good shots use all three methods, depending on the angle and the time available. The snap shot is used when time is of the essence. The hunter of woodcock and ruffed grouse throws his gun to his shoulder, puts the muzzle of the gun at the spot where he hopes the bird will be, and cuts loose. If he tried to kill a grouse diving out of a spruce or a woodcock disappearing into the fall foliage with the pointing out method, he'd never get one.

Snap shooting or spot shooting is indicated on a straightaway or quartering quail or pheasant. On a straightaway bird, the thing to do is to come up fast and shoot the instant the muzzle is on. If it is flying to the right, let us say, at a gentle angle the gunner should hold a bit to the right and shoot. In skeet, the best way to break the outgoing (and dropping) No. 1 high-house bird is to shoot at a spot 1½ feet or so below it.

The fast swing is best in many situations. The secret of breaking the incoming targets at the center No. 8 station at skeet is to swing like hell and shoot as the muzzle passes the bird. It is also the secret of breaking clay targets in trapshooting. The trapshot is always a fast swinger, but the greater the angle the farther he must swing *past* the target in order to break it. The fast swing is best on all upland game birds flying at a sharp angle.

Pointing out is probably the best and most exact method to use on birds shot at a high angle against the sky—pass-shooting at waterfowl and the flight-shooting on doves and bandtail pigeons. For driven Scotch grouse, the best way to make a double (or a "right and left" as the British say) is to spot shoot the first bird at about 40 yards (aim at a point a bit ahead of him unless he is coming directly toward the gun, in which case the thing to do is to shoot right at him), then to take the second bird with a fast swing, following up on the line of flight with a rapidly swinging gun, getting a little ahead and then cutting loose.

Some excellent skeet shots use the fast swing on the crossing targets at stations 3, 4, and 5, but many equally good shots point them out. At station 7, the outgoing bird is a spot shot but the incomer is best taken with a fast swing.

The good hand with a shotgun should be able to use all methods of getting that shot charge on the bird.

There are many reasons that zipping clay targets and flying birds are missed. Sometimes the reason is physical and sometimes it is psychological. I have a friend who simply cannot kill a bird over a pointing dog. When he sees the dog freeze up, his face gets the expression of a man being led to the gallows. Sometimes he cannot bring himself to boot the bird out, and when the bird comes, he simply points his gun in the general direction and shoots—probably with closed eyes. But with a flushing dog, where he does not have to go through that agony of anticipation, he is a pretty good shot. No one can shoot a shotgun well unless he has a definite picture of the relationship of target and gun muzzle when that gun goes off. The pattern of a skeet gun may cover a 30-inch circle at 20 yards, but at that the target is surrounded by a vast amount of atmosphere.

The two commonest shooting faults are shooting over and shooting behind. Shooting over comes from the gunner's not getting his cheek down on the comb. The flush catches him by surprise, and unless he has formed the habit of putting his head down automatically and putting his gun to his face, he jerks his gun up, fails to get his head down, sees too much barrel—and the shot charge is high. Shooting behind comes from slowing or stopping the swing. This is the sin of the over-meticulous gunner, the rifle-minded man, the chap who wants to get things exactly right, the shooter who is unsure of his instincts, the aimer rather than the pointer. He gets ahead of the bird, thinks his lead is exactly right; then to make sure it remains right, he slows down or stops. In the interval between the time when he tells himself to shoot and the shot charge takes off, the bird or target keeps going and he misses behind. This business of being an aimer, of being over-careful is the hardest of all shotgun sins to break.

For that reason, the mediocre shot is the aimer and the dawdler, the pokey shot. The best shots are fast, and those who want to be good shots should form the habit of shooting fast. As a great shot said many years ago, "It is better to miss a bird in good time than to hit one in poor."

Keep the head down, put the gun to the face, swing fast, and shoot the instant the relationship of muzzle and target look right. Don't try to aim. Shoot! If you get that head down, swing fast, and shoot fast, you've just about got it made!

CHAPTER 23

To Lead or Not to Lead

CERTAIN writers have for the past few years been getting a good deal of mileage out of the British or Divine Guidance school of wing shooting. Since the lads who write about it are pretty vague themselves, not a few of my puzzled correspondents have written in to ask me just what all the shouting is about.

They read that it is distinctly bad form, old boy, ever to lead a bird or a target, and that if you were ever caught doing it, a committee would wait on you and ask you (politely, of course) to turn in your old school tie. American shooters who have been taught that one of the cardinal sins of wing shooting is to get the head up, the cheek away from the comb, and the eye above the barrel, are suddenly informed that they are doing it all wrong. The thing to do, these writers say, is to keep the head up and never see the barrels. If you take a peek at the barrels, you are (a) cheating and (b) not a proper wing shot.

But of all the sins, this business of shooting in front of a bird so that in due time he'll run into the shot is, in the eyes of the Divine Guidance school, just about the worst. Not quite the worst! The unforgivable sin is to swing out farther ahead of a bird at 40 yards than you do at 20 yards. If you are guilty of that breach of etiquette you have taken a "calculated lead," and in Divine Guidance circles that is the social equivalent of drinking coffee out of a saucer or eating peas with your knife.

One man wrote a piece in which he related how he tried trap-shooting and averaged breaking about four or five birds out of twenty-five. This was because his friends had told him he had to lead his targets. Then he said to hell with it and shot right at every target. From then on his skill was spoken of in reverent whispers in all the bazaars and caravansaries throughout the realm. This chap says he never leads a bird, be it 15 or 70 yards away. No matter how far away our feathered friends are or how fast they are going, he shoots right at them and down they come.

When I was in college, I was assured I had normal intelligence, and for some years I managed to get by as a university professor. Nevertheless, I simply cannot make heads or tails out of most of the stuff turned out by the Divine Guidance school of shotgun shooting. One devotee wrote a whole book on the subject. It is too much for me, and when I open it I am as lost as a Hottentot trying to grapple with Kant's *Critique of Pure Reason.*

I read a chapter, try to figure out what the guy is trying to say, give up. Then I go back, take it paragraph by paragraph. Then I break it down sentence by sentence. The stuff still baffles me, and the only result is a slight ringing in my ears.

The fountainhead of these views is, I am convinced, the gun-makers of London. I like the British people and British products, but I have to admit that until you have been conned by an Englishman you haven't lived. Anyone who doubts this should watch a London gunmaker measuring a client for a first-quality gun. By the time the act is over, the buyer is in a trancelike state, his eyes glassy, his temperature and respiration down, and his heartbeat barely discernible. When, after a good many moons, our boy finally gets his gun, he may not be able to hit anything with it, but he's so brainwashed that he is convinced the gun fits him. If it's anyone's fault, it's his own and he does not fit the gun.

I have a quaint, old-fashioned notion that there is only one person in the world who can tell whether a gun fits—and that's the shooter himself, but only after he has shot enough to be able to judge. Like a pair of shoes, a gun either fits and is comfortable or it doesn't. If a pair of shoes hurt, they don't fit even if they were made by hand by a bootmaker to the king.

The Divine Guidance school holds that if a man's gun fits, he keeps his eyes on the bird, follows it with his left hand, shoots right at it, and never gives it any conscious lead, he will hit.

It is fairly easy to shoot much of this stuff full of holes. In the first place, the human eye is like a camera lens of extreme wide angle, and if the gun is fired from the shoulder (even with the head up and well above the barrel), the normal human eye sees not only the bird or target but the barrel as well. He can't help it, and the guy who says he never sees the barrel is kidding himself. These writers also say that no one can focus on the muzzle and the target at the same time. Actually, the human eye has great depth of focus, and if anyone has fairly good vision, he can focus well both on the end of the gun barrel and the bird or clay target. I quite agree that the scattergunner's main interest should be the target, but he should also be conscious of the end of his barrel.

The Divine Guidance school is full of astonishing inconsistencies. If the shooter does not see his barrel, how does he know he is shooting at the bird? If the shooter never sees his barrel, why does one of these writers talk about front sights for shotguns?

One writer makes much of the fact that the tennis player keeps his eye on the ball and not on his racket, the golf player keeps his eye on the ball and not on the club, the axman on the spot he wants to hit and not on the ax. All this I'll grant, but the fact is that during the back swing with any of these lethal implements the man using them simply cannot see them. On the other hand, it is impossible for the gunner *not* to see his gun barrel.

Writers of this same school advise the beginner to shoot with his head up and his eye well above the barrel—a curious piece of advice because not getting the head down is one of the major reasons for missing (by shooting over) with a shotgun.

Another tenet of the school is that no one can be a good performer with both a rifle and a shotgun, and that shooting a shotgun louses up one's rifle shooting and vice versa. It is true that many riflemen are not interested in shotguns and don't shoot them well and that many fine shotgunners can't hit a bull in the back end with a rifle. Nevertheless, I know dozens of people who are reasonably proficient with each. I count myself among them.

If anyone isn't convinced that he has to shoot ahead of a moving target in order to hit it, he should try shooting running jackrabbits with a rifle. It is rare for a shotgunner to be able to see where his shot goes, or even the wads, but in the dusty Southwest a spurt of dust usually shows where a bullet has landed.

One of the earliest discoveries the rifleman makes is that if he tries to hit a moving rabbit by shooting right at it, he'll hit well behind—even with a fast-stepping bullet like that of the .220 Swift and with his rifle moving. At a range of only 100 yards or so, and shooting at a jack loping along at no more than 20 miles an hour, the bullet will still be behind, generally not by inches but by feet. When a jack is really picking them up and laying them down and is out at 200 yards or so, it is surprising how far ahead one has to swing.

I have shot many hundreds of running jackrabbits with a rifle, and, of course, I have missed thousands. For every one missed by shooting in front, I have missed dozens by shooting behind. Yet some people will say that they never lead a moving target with either a rifle or a shotgun—just as some will say they never see the shotgun barrel or the sights on a rifle.

Many superb performers are unreflective and inarticulate men. Many are magnificiently equipped with sharp, quick-focusing eyes and fine co-ordination but are shy on brains. They are as incapable of telling anyone how they shoot as a kangaroo is of telling how he hops or a quail is of describing the mechanics of his whistle. The fact that one of these muscular geniuses can break 100 straight skeet targets while standing on one leg and shooting from the hip and swear that he never leads a target doesn't mean a thing.

There are various ways to intercept the flight of a moving object, be it bird or clay target, with a charge of shot. One can shoot with a stationary gun at the point where the target is going to be when the shot gets there as in snap shooting. Or one can swing the muzzle apparently faster than the target is moving and fire when the muzzle seems to be the proper distance in front of the target. This is generally called the fast swing. If the swing is fast, the range short, and the angle gentle, but little lead is needed. One can also swing the muzzle so that it moves apparently as fast as the target moves, maintaining the same distance between target and muzzle and getting off the shot with the muzzle moving. This is called sustained lead or pointing out.

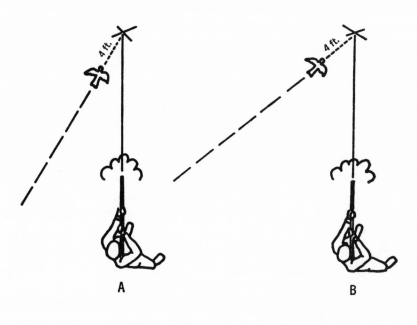

Lead at A looks greater than B. C looks still greater, but in any case the bird travels four feet while the shot is getting there.

As is known even to the most ignorant tribesman in remote Basutoland, there is a considerable interval between the instant when the shooter's brain tells him to touch old Betsy off and the instant that the shot emerges from the muzzle and begins to wing its way to the target. Various things happen. The impulse has to travel from the shooter's eye and brain to his fingertip. The muscles have to contract to pull the trigger. Then the firing pin has to fall. The primer has to shoot out its jet of flame. Then the powder must begin to burn, throw off gas, and push the charge out of the barrel. Then the shot must travel from muzzle to target.

While all this is happening, the target is moving. Lag time between two different shooters varies a great deal. Some have slow reaction times, some fast. Much experimenting has been done on this. Shooters have been told to press a button as soon as a light flashed, and then the speed of their reactions has been measured. According to a series of tests made some years ago, it takes the shooter .1 second to recognize a target once it is thrown, and then .25 second to pull the trigger. The interval from the time the trigger is released until the firing pin falls is .008, and it takes .003 for the primer to set the powder afire and for the powder gas to push the shot out of the barrel. After the shot takes off, it requires .065 second for the shot to reach a skeet target at about 20 yards. The hunter thinks things happen instantaneously after he decides to shoot, but actually almost half a second elapses between his instant of decision and the time the shot arrives at the target.

If a bird is traveling at the rate of 30 miles an hour—a modest enough speed for a quail, a dove idling along at three-quarter throttle, or a pheasant that's had time to accelerate—the theoretical lead should be about 2½ feet at 20 yards, 4 feet at 30 yards, and 6 feet at 40 yards. A bird traveling faster should have more lead— twice as much for a speeding duck or dove or for a pheasant, band-tailed pigeon, or blue grouse coming down a long hill. Even the humble clay target used in trap or skeet takes off at an initial velocity of about 60 miles per hour.

At best, wing shooting is enough to give a systematic person with a head for figures the vapors. There are too many variables. The skeet shooter fires at birds traveling known paths at known angles, and the targets are supposed to start off at a uniform speed. But in game shooting, angles vary, distances vary, and flight speed varies.

The skeet shot knows the speed and angle of the target, and it is released when he calls for it. He can therefore say that he shoots just in front of and below the No. 2 high-house bird with his gun moving faster than the bird. He can also say that he swings past the No. 4 high-house bird and shoots when the muzzle looks as if it were pointing about 4 feet in front of the target. He knows the path the target will travel and the speed. He is also used to his own speed of swing and his own reaction time. The lead is right for him.

But in the field or in the blind, the birds are coming at varying speeds and at varying angles and are taken at various distances. One day, our poor gunner may be on top of the world. His eyesight is keen, his reactions fast. But the next day he may be wary, hung over, and dopey. His reaction time is slowed up and his mind is wandering. With these complications, it is no wonder he doesn't shoot well.

The field shot has of necessity to develop a sort of a built-in fire-control system. He sees a duck coming. He hopes that the angle of flight will bring it by within range. At a certain point he decides that the bird is going to pass at about 45 yards. His head goes down into the position it will be in when he shoots. As his gun comes up, he begins to swing with his whole body. Traveling faster than the duck, the muzzle catches up with the bird, passes it, and when the muzzle appears to be the right distance ahead, our gunner pulls the trigger. If his guesses have been right, and if he has kept that muzzle moving, the bird falls.

How does our gunner know how much to lead? By hitting and missing. His subconscious mind stores the memories of thousands of shots. He knows that in other cases when a mallard drake looked about so big, so far away, and was traveling at a similar angle, he dumped it with a lead that appeared to him to be about 3 feet.

I have had people tell me they never lead a bird or target. But those who tell me that are either poor shots or good shots who are not particularly reflective people. I have never had a good shot who was also intelligent tell me that he didn't get ahead of his targets.

There may be some argument as to who is the finest skeet shot that ever lived, but if any list were compiled the name of Alex Kerr, the crack California performer, would be right there. I have known Alex many years and I have shot skeet with him. I love to see the guy shoot. He is fast, smooth, and deadly. Does Alex get in front of his targets and does he see his barrel? He tells me he does.

Bill Weaver, the scope manufacturer, is the best quail shot I have ever seen and the only upland gunner I have ever shot with who was so much better than I was that he made me feel like a clumsy oaf. He not only leads, but he can tell you just about how far ahead his muzzle looked when the gun went off.

Harold Russell of the Federal Cartridge Corp. is another scattergun great. He tells me he has to get ahead of them to hit them.

Theoretically, it is possible to hit a crossing target with no lead, but to do so the shooter would have to be a very fast swinger with a fantastically slow reaction time. Very good shots probably need somewhat less leads than ordinary shots because good shots generally swing faster. However, if the target is traveling at much of an angle, it simply must be led. There is nothing else for it.

Sometimes the lead, or forward allowance as the British say, is slight, but it has to be there. Let's take the targets at the No. 8 station in skeet. The birds come by the shooter at an angle and pass above and to one side. On those shots I pick up the bird as quickly as I can, swing rapidly, and shoot the instant the muzzle is ahead. But the range is a few yards and the gun is swinging fast.

Let's take another skeet shot—the No. 6 low-house bird. It comes from the trap to the shooter's right, angling slightly away and at about the level of his waist. It rises rapidly and its initial velocity is about 60 miles per hour. The angle is not sharp, and I break that bird the same way—by tracking past and shooting the instant I am ahead. Any slowing or stopping of the swing is bound to be fatal.

Let's take still another—the No. 1 high-house bird. It comes out of the house well above the shooter and drops rapidly away. To break that bird, the muzzle should be pointed at a spot from 18 inches to 2 feet below it when the gun goes off. Shoot right at it and you'll miss it every time.

I receive many letters asking me how far one should lead a passing duck at 45 yards or an overhead pheasant at 25 yards. I can only answer that they must be led. How far is up to the individual gunner—and it depends on his reaction time, his speed of swing, and how far his notion of 40 yards actually is. Even at skeet with the targets traveling at known speeds and at known angles, one man will tell you he leads a certain target 5 feet and another equally good shot will tell you he leads the same target 2 feet. They both hit it and they're both right.

Even if someone tells me that he shoots right at the birds and hits them, I am all for him—even if he adds that he never sees his barrel. If I wanted to get into a futile argument, I'd tell him that he just thinks he shoots right at them and he just thinks he doesn't see his barrel. I know he has to shoot ahead of them or he wouldn't hit them.

I have tried to make certain points in the preceding pages. Let's review them. It is elementary that if a target is moving the shot charge must be directed to a spot ahead in order to intercept it. However, I have tried to make the point that this matter of lead is by no means an exact science, as the amount of necessary lead differs with the speed of the target, the angle of the target, the speed of the swing, and the reaction time of the individual shooter. I have also tried to point out that what one man calls a 3-foot lead may look like a 5-foot lead to another. Two equally good skeet shooters who appear to have about the same speed of swing often give entirely different estimates of how far they are ahead of the target when their guns go off. One man may say he leads the No. 4 high-house target by 2 feet, another by 3 feet, and yet another by 8 feet. Since they all break it, their leads are obviously right for them.

Nevertheless, some estimates of necessary lead given by good shots may be helpful to those who are learning to shoot or who are trying to become better shots.

A booklet by gun and shot-shell manufacturers to promote shotgun shooting recommends, for skeet shooting, the amounts of lead listed in the table on p. 272.

These are not very different from the leads I *think* I take. I do not swing down with the No. 1 high-house bird. Instead, I spot shoot it, aiming (pointing) at what looks to me like 1½ to 2 feet below the target. Spot shooting as I do, I believe I'd shoot over the target if I held only ½ foot below (ahead of) it. The leads on the No. 1 and No. 2 low-house targets look about like what I take, but to break the difficult No. 2 high house I have to be about 1½ feet in front of it and about the same distance below it. I would say that for the high and low-house targets at No. 3 and 4 I am nearer 4 feet ahead than either 3 or 3½ feet. On the No. 6 low-house target, as I have previously written, I swing fast and shoot the instant I am ahead of it, but I have been known to miss it.

STATION	HIGH HOUSE	LOW HOUSE
1	½ ft. ahead	1 ft. ahead
2	1½ ft. ahead	1½ ft. ahead
3	3 ft. ahead	3½ ft. ahead
4	3 ft. ahead	3 ft. ahead
5	3½ ft. ahead	3 ft. ahead
6	1½ ft. ahead	1½ ft. ahead
7	1 ft. ahead	Point blank Left side
8	Cover	Cover

Nevertheless, these suggested leads should be helpful to anyone who is not already a pretty good skeet shot. They should work reasonably well for anyone who is a fairly fast swinger with an average reaction time. With these leads a very fast swinger with a slow reaction time might be ahead, and certainly anyone who checked or stopped his swing would be behind. In most wing shooting and also in clay-target shooting, misses are usually behind, seldom in front. My son Bradford is very good on quail and grouse, since he is a very fast skeet shot. But he tends to miss pheasants getting off the ground by getting too far ahead of them. I am not nearly so fast and the only bird I have ever missed by shooting ahead of is the sage grouse. This big lumbering bird gets under way so slowly that he makes the pheasant look like a rocket.

Necessary lead varies with the speed of the swing, and the speed of the swing varies with the speed of the bird as well as with the habits of the individual shooter. The shooter naturally swings faster to overtake a fast-flying bird than to overtake a slow one. He will swing faster to overtake a bird that is about to disappear. The faster the swing, the less the necessary lead. I remember one time when I was hunting pheasants in Idaho. I was hunting in the brush when I heard a pheasant get up. I saw a fine cock flash past an opening, swung rapidly, and shot just as it was going behind another bush. As I pulled the trigger I was conscious that the muzzle was a bit behind and I knew I would miss. An instant later I heard the bird hit the ground. I was swinging very fast to catch up and my reaction time was slow enough so that when the gun actually went off, the muzzle was ahead of the bird.

I have seen many tables that show the speed with which various birds fly and the theoretical lead necessary to hit them at various distances. In his excellent book, *Modern Shotguns and Loads* published in 1929, the late Capt. Charles Askins, long-time arms and ammunition editor of *Outdoor Life,* gave a list of the speed of various game birds with the theoretical and the practical leads at 40 yards. The theoretical lead is how far the gun should be pointed in front of the bird when it is fired if shot charge is to intercept the target and the "practical" lead is how far the gunner thinks he is ahead when the gun goes off. Of course, the "practical" lead is relative, as it depends on the speed of the swing and the reaction time of the shooter.

LEADS NECESSARY FOR VARIOUS GAME BIRDS

Bird	Speed in Feet Per Second	Average	Theoretical Lead at 40 Yds.	Practical Lead
Quail	60 to 80	70	8.7 ft.	4 or 5 ft.
Ruffed grouse	65 to 80	72.5	9	5
Dove	70 to 90	80	9.8	5
Mallard	50 to 90	70	8.7	4 or 5
Canvasback	90 to 100	95	11.66	6 or 7
Canada goose	80 to 90	85	10.4	5 to 6

Such tables do not mean much, but they do serve to show the beginner that he must get out in front of the bird and that he must keep his gun barrel moving. Too many variables enter into lead. A dove may be loafing along at 30 to 35 miles an hour or flying full throttle with the wind behind him at 60. He may be flying at right angles but probably he is not. What one gunner thinks is 40 yards may look like 30 to another and 50 to a third.

One time many years ago I was on a deer hunt in the Mexican state of Sonora at the point where the Cucurpi River comes out of the mountains. The doves fed during the day up on the mountain tops, 2,000 to 3,000 feet above camp. Then along in the afternoon they would fly down to roost in the big cottonwoods along the creek. They were coming down so fast they sounded like jet planes. I got enough for a dove stew and I am sure I led some of them 15 or 20 feet at 40 to 45 yards.

The upland hunter does a great deal of spot shooting. On a shot that looks straightaway or at a slight angle, the easiest way to take the bird is to shoot at the place he is going to be by holding a bit above or to one side. It would not be once in a blue moon that the upland gunner would shoot at a right-angling bobwhite quail at 40 yards. However, 40-yard crossing shots are fairly common on wild-flushing Hungarian partridges and chukar partridges. Now and then one gets such a shot at a pheasant.

In Arizona I used to do my hunting of Gambel's quail without a dog, and under such circumstances I have got a lot of wild flushes by nervous birds on bare ground. I have killed quail at around 40 to 45 yards and I generally lead them what looked to me about 3 or 4 feet. I'd lead a crossing pheasant about the same amount, unless he was coming downhill and had time to get his speed up and then I'd lead him twice as much. If a pheasant or a quail gets up in front of me within 20 yards and takes off at much of an angle, I try to get out around 6 inches to one foot in front of it, swinging fast. A pheasant getting up at a 30-degree angle at 30 yards, I'd lead 1½ to 2 feet.

Until I was well along in my forties I had never shot a pheasant, a sage grouse, a Hungarian partridge, or a chukar partridge. The first few days I shot pheasants I underled them, as they are big, conspicuous birds and it was difficult for me to believe they flew as fast as they did. By the time I had shot pheasants for a week, I found them very easy to hit. Both Hungarian and chukar partridges look as if they fly fast. For that reason I swung fast, got well ahead, and shot fast. I had no trouble hitting them from the start.

There may be those who can shoot right at everything they want to hit, be it pheasant, quail, or clay target, and knock it down, but I am not one of them. If I want to hit, I must get ahead!

CHAPTER 24

It's the Angles

A MAN I know didn't do very well on pheasants one year, something which distressed him no end. Although he used to average about four birds out of five, he got down about two out of five. All during the hunting season he was short with his wife, cross with the kids, and at night he lay awake brooding.

After a great deal of melancholy introspection, he thought he'd figured out his miseries. Until this past season he hunted with a brother who had a pointing dog. His brother always walked in on the points, and the shots our friend got were almost always at sharp angles. He knew he had to lead and he did lead. He seldom missed. But then he got a fine and hard-working pointing dog himself. He walked in on the points, and most of the shots he got were straightaway or slightly quartering. Much of the time he missed.

This is a puzzling circumstance. Until one goes into the subject, it would appear that the more gentle the angle of the bird's flight the easier the shot should be. Actually, it's just the opposite, and I believe most good shots miss more straightaway and quartering shots than any other kind, including shots at right angles.

One afternoon early in one Idaho season I was walking back toward my car in the company of the eleven-year-old son of a friend who was hunting in another direction. My dog had been acting a bit birdy, but the field was as bare as a billiard table and as unlikely a spot for pheasants as New York's Times Square. Sud-

LEAD AND ANGLE.

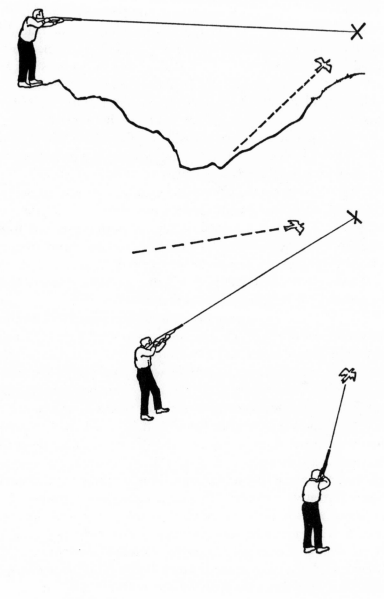

denly a big cock took off about 10 feet in front of me but never got over 3 feet off the ground. It was the easiest looking shot imaginable. I put the muzzle on his tail—and missed him with both barrels.

On another occasion I was hunting along a brushy sidehill while my Brittany worked the tall grass, brush, and weeds below me. The dog went on point about 20 feet downhill from me, but as I started toward it a rooster came flailing out. My two shots were wasted on the atmosphere. I had held right on his rear end.

The upland gunner, I am convicted, misses more straightaway shots than any other kind, and the reason is that what he generally thinks are straightaways are actually angling shots which require lead. The bird is either climbing, angling, or doing both at once. Unless the angle of climb is very sharp, a straight-stocked, "high-shooting," bird gun generally has enough built-in lead to take care of some of the upward angle, as does the pattern of the gun bored improved cylinder or modified. But even at that, the sharp-rising straightaway is powerfully easy to miss. Combine this sharp rise with an angle to one side and the gunner is dead if he doesn't make instant allowance. The trouble with the easy straightaway shot is that generally it isn't easy and it isn't a straightaway.

I can still remember a very nice miss on a pheasant that looked as big as a bald eagle one late afternoon in a Washington field. My friend Lee Sproul and I had a few birds apiece and were working back to the car when my dog Mike went on a solid point in very thick stubble. As we walked in, the bird went out almost straight up. We both shot under him. He then straightened out into a downward slant and we both shot below and behind him. I might add that we both felt exceedingly foolish. We missed because we had shot right at the rooster.

A true straightaway with the bird flying at the same elevation of the gun is relatively common in quail shooting if the gunner counts two and gives the birds a chance to flatten out before he cracks down. It is less common with pheasants because the big birds usually continue to rise as long as they're in range. But now and then the perfect shot presents itself. Once I was hunting pheasants in Idaho when my Brittany took off up a fence row, circled, and slammed into a point. When I kicked the wire of the fence, two big cocks took out, rose to about 5 feet, then leveled off. One was a bit ahead of the other. I put the muzzles of the 20 gauge on the tail of the leading bird, shot, and then swung on the other. They fell about 6 feet apart, both centered.

I like to think about that double. It makes me feel like quite a boy. But here's one I'd like to forget. My pal Bill Pinch, who lives across the street, was hunting with me one time in an enormous rolling stubble field. There were plenty of roosters in it, but the stubble was thin, the season was old, and the pheasants were as wild as snakes. We each had a bird or so, but, although we had seen a good many cocks, most of them had risen wild and we were feeling tense and thwarted. So we headed back to the car with my dog working in front of us along a steep, brushy sidehill. Then he banged into a solid point. I tossed a clod at the spot where the Brittany's nose was pointed, and a big cock came boiling out about 25 feet below us and flew straight away and close to the ground. We each shot twice, and all four shots missed. This was bad enough, but we hadn't seen the worst.

Feeling like slobs, depressed and weary, we trudged toward the car. Again Mike cracked into a point. Again the same thing happened. One would have thought we were shooting blanks. The worse part of it was that we both had missed shots like that before, and the reason we did so was perfectly obvious. Caught by surprise, we had used our muscles and our eyes but not our brains.

So let's see why we wasted those four shots and ruined our day.

We were above the birds. They were rising in relation to the ground. To our excited eyes they appeared to be flying straight away from us, but actually the angle of the birds' flight as compared with the angle of the shot charge was pretty sharp. We shot at the birds and the shot pattern was behind. The only way we could have hit those birds was to shoot in front of them by blotting them out with the barrels. If the angle is very slight, the spread of the pattern will often take care of the lead and result in a kill, but if it is a bit sharper, the result is a miss.

In the game of skeet there are two shots that appear to be

straightaways. The No. 1 high-house target sails directly away from the shooter—or so it appears. But the catch is that the target leaves the house above the shooter's head and is falling. Beginners always shoot *at* the bird, and they always miss it. There is only one way to hit it, and that's to shoot low with the muzzle of the gun a good 12 to 18 inches—or what looks like that much—below it.

The other straightaway shot is the No. 7 low-house bird. It starts out at about the level of the shooter's waist and rises rapidly. The angle is there but it isn't very sharp, and the target can generally be broken with a dead-on hold because the spread of the skeet pattern is considerable if the shooter lets the bird get out to the top of its flight. But actually, to center that target, the aim should be a bit high. The unreflective man will swear that the target is going directly away. Anyone using a tightly choked gun, or who shoots so fast that his pattern has not had time to open up, can miss that bird very neatly, as easy as it looks.

A toughie is the bird in high-level flight and going away, a shot which often presents itself when the hunter is trying to make a double or a triple on a flock of doves or ducks. Shoot right at the bird and the result will be a miss. As in the No. 1 high-house target in skeet, this shot calls for a low hold. Equally tough is the incomer right at the gun. If you see the bird you'll miss it every time, and the only way to hit it is to swing fast, blot out the bird as it comes in, and shoot while the muzzle is still moving rapidly. Even when the gunner knows how the shot should be made, he can miss it nicely because the tendency is to want to see what he's shooting at. See the bird and you'll miss it. Incomers should always be taken well out where the pattern has a chance to open up. If taken close, they are easy to miss with the small pattern.

Shooting uphill at birds that are apparently going straight away from the gun can also be rough. The hillside gives the gunner a sort of a false horizon, and the birds that appear to be flying flat are actually rising rapidly. The only way to get them is to swing up fast, blot them out, and shoot with a moving gun. I speak from bitter experience. I hunt quail in hilly country, and every now and then when my forgettery is working nicely, I can run up a streak of remarkable misses. And so can anyone else.

Some years ago another friend and I were hunting quail on a

series of steep hillsides where all the shots were sharply up or sharply down. The grass was high and thick, and the birds were lying well. My dog was having a field day, and I believe he must have made forty solid points. But for whatever the reason, I wasn't doing very well. Those birds sat so tight I had to kick them out from under my dog's nose. I was shooting too fast, wasn't figuring the angles, and for the most part shot right at the birds.

All of the birds were either sharply rising or sharply falling. Shooting at between 15 and 20 yards, as I often did, I didn't give the pattern of the modified 20 gauge a chance to open up, and generally I shot with the muzzles right on the birds' tails. When I'd used up about twenty shells I don't believe I had over five birds, and my dog was beginning to look at me with disgust. Then I sat down, meditated a while, and took stock of the situation. I knew why I was missing, and resolved to slow down so I'd have time to figure the angle and let my pattern open up a bit. From then on my shooting improved, and presently I picked up my limit of ten. I went back to the car to rest and eat a bit of lunch.

Before long my friend showed up, I'd heard him banging away as often as I had. He sat down wearily.

"How did you do?" he asked.

"Not so good," I said.

"You get a limit?" he wanted to know.

"Finally. How'd you do?" I said.

"I didn't get very many."

"How many?"

"Well, to tell you the truth I got only three." Then his voice rose. "And damn it," he said, "I'll bet I shot a box and a half of shells." When he calmed down and decided to wait the birds out a bit, he ran out his limit in a hurry.

A pheasant is a very smart creature, a bird that quickly separates the men dogs from the boy dogs. He's a tough bird to get a shot at but a very easy bird to hit. Once he gets wound up he can make knots, but he is large, heavy, and underpowered, and he gets off the ground slowly. If there is any excuse for missing a pheasant that gets up within 30 yards I have never been able to figure it out.

And what are the shots I miss? You know. Those easy straightaways. I miss them because they look easy. Without thinking, I shoot at them and miss. Give me a sharply angling shot—a rooster sailing by at 45 degrees and I almost never miss. The ones I foul up are those I should have got with a fly swatter—those easy straightaways.

With the crossing shot, I know I have to lead. I swing ahead, see plenty of air between the bird and the muzzle, keep the gun swinging, and hit.

Why do I go into those declines on the easy shots?

Generally, I believe, because the bird startles me, or for some reason I am overanxious. Or maybe I'm tired. Then my brain ceases to function. I don't take that necessary split second to figure the angle, and I miss.

Straightaway?

Once my wife and I were hunting some hills without much success. The dog was ranging wide and moving fast, and presently the little woman grew weary of the whole business. She announced she was tired of running after that darned dog and said she'd hunt slowly back to the car and take it easy. Half an hour later my Brittany went on point in some high grass on the hillside just beyond the stubble. I started to walk in, but those pheasants knew the facts of life. When I was about 35 yards away, they both took off downhill. I was presented with a beautiful chance for a double, but I knew I'd have to shoot fast. I did shoot fast. The result was that I shot right at birds angling down and missed both of them. As luck would have it, they headed right toward my wife, who was sitting on a rock about 150 yards away resting her weary legs. She heard me shoot and saw the two cocks coming. Wisely, she stayed still until they crossed about 30 yards away. Then she rose and killed them both.

"I knew I didn't have to chase that silly dog to get birds," she told me.

So the next time those easy straightaways begin to throw you, do a little mental geometry and find out why the angle of the shot charge and the angle of the bird's flight aren't getting together. Don't shoot too fast. Wait for the pattern to open up a bit, and then hold high or low, right or left, as the case may be, and do your stuff.

The reason the easy straightaway shot is so tough is that generally it isn't a straightaway. It just looks as if it is.

CHAPTER 25

Hitting Birds Afield

FIELD shooting is far more difficult than either trap or skeet shooting. There are hundreds of shooters in the United States who can quite often break fifty or a hundred straight clay targets at either trap or skeet, but no man has ever lived who could kill fifty straight quail, fifty straight doves, or fifty straight ducks.

Clay targets are by no means easy, but the man who shoots them knows where they are coming from and when. The trapshooter who fires at 16 yards or handicap does not know the angle the target will take but at least he knows it isn't going to set up behind him. The man shooting doubles or skeet knows not only when the targets will appear and where they will come from but the paths they will follow.

Not so with the bird hunter! When he hunts upland game, he does not know exactly when the bird will appear, where it will come from, or what angle it will take. Even when hunting with a pointing dog, the gunner often gets fooled. A covey of quail may fly straightaway or at an easy angle, but they may fly at right angles or even come boiling right at the hunter. The cock pheasant may sneak away from the dog and come out from a spot where it was not expected. Instead of flying straightaway or at a gentle angle, a single quail may hug the ground and fly a circle around the gunner.

Even in flight shooting for ducks and doves, the birds fly at different speeds, at various angles, and various distances. Live targets can dodge and swerve and change pace.

Many are the marvelous tales one hears of wing shooting. Some of the old market hunters are supposed to have been able to kill fifty straight ducks without a miss. I hate to be cynical but I put these tales in the same category as those of the buffalo hunters who thought nothing of killing buffalo at 800 yards with their old black-powder buffalo rifles. Many gunners today talk a fine bird hunt, but when they are in the field they don't do quite as well as they do at cocktail time. Years ago when I was living in Arizona I told an acquaintance that never in my life had I killed ten straight Gambel's quail. He told me that he was astonished at my ineptness —that many times he had not only commonly killed ten straight, but as many as fifteen straight. I resolved to take this guy hunting some day and get a load of that wonderful shooting. I did. Apparently that wasn't his day. He didn't get a bird until he had fired six shots, and he had only five birds for his first twenty-five shells. When I chided him a bit he told me he couldn't understand it, that he had never done such lousy shooting in his life.

It is very easy for most of us to forget just how many shells we use to bag our birds and in retrospect our performance seems much better than it actually is. We cherish the memories of the times we were hot, forget the times we didn't do so well.

Upland game over a pointing dog should not be as difficult as it is. Generally, quail, pheasants, Huns, chukar partridges are shot going away from the gun and are easy targets. There seems to be no excuse for missing them, but we do. Let's look at the reasons. The first, I believe, is psychological. A covey of twenty-five quail flushes. The hunter is startled. He lets off both barrels. Not a feather! How come? The startled hunter often fails to get his head down on the stock. He jerks his gun up, then shoots before he gets his head down. He has tried to put his face to his stock instead of getting his head down as the gun comes up and putting the stock to the cheek. The result is that he sees too much barrel and shoots over.

The startled hunter can also miss because he shoots at the covey instead of picking out one particular bird and killing it. This is a beginner's trick but something that even an experienced hunter can do when he is jumpy enough. It is also easy for the startled hunter to misjudge the angle. As I have pointed out in the chapter called "It's the Angles," it is seldom that the upland hunter gets an absolutely true straightaway with the bird flying directly away from the hunter in even flight. A high proportion of upland birds are taken by spot shooting—throwing the gun up and shooting at the spot where the bird is going to be. On these gentle angles there is no need to swing. Instead, the thing to do is to hold to one side of the slightly angling bird. The spooky hunter forgets to do this, just as he also is apt to forget to get his head down and sees too much barrel.

The flush, particularly if unexpected, makes the flustered upland hunter feel rushed. The birds seem to be traveling at rocket speed. He feels that if he doesn't shoot instantly his chance will be gone forever. He jerks his gun up, bangs away with no clear picture of relationship between muzzle and bird—and misses.

When I find myself nervous and missing quail, I *make* myself take a little more time. I have tried the experiment of deliberately holding on a bird but not shooting. It is surprising how much time one actually has. Then I make myself step into my shot with my left foot forward, get my head down, put up the gun, see the relationship of muzzle and bird, and fire. It may help to count to get the proper rhythm: 1. Step into the shot and get the head down; 2. Mount the gun; 3. Get on the bird and fire.

Killing two birds out of a covey rise is just about as easy as taking one. Perhaps it is actually easier, as the man who has made up his mind to take a double has less of a tendency to dwell on his aim than if he is content with one—just as it is easier to break the doubles in skeet than it is to break the singles. The thing to do is to kill that first bird, wipe it from the mind, then take another. Concentration is one of the secrets of successful shooting. No one can hit that first bird if he is worrying about killing the second, and he can't kill the second if he is wondering whether he will be able to pick up the first. A good, cool shot should make a fairly high percentage of doubles on covey rises, and a superlative shot using a repeater should make some triples.

Bobwhite quail lie tight. They are almost always killed inside of 30 yards, often inside of 20 yards. The man who uses a full-choke gun on bobwhites is handicapping himself, and unless he is a slow and pokey shot he is doing himself a disservice even if his gun is bored modified. Ideal medicine for bobwhites is a light double-barrel 20 gauge with 26-inch barrels bored improved cylinder and modified or improved cylinder in both barrels. The double-barrel skeet guns bored Skeet No. 1 and No. 2 (about the same as cylinder and modified) are also good. The best shot size is No. 8.

The California valley quail, if given a chance in proper cover, will lie almost as tight as the bobwhite and he is shot at just as short range. In areas of light cover, these little rascals will flush a bit wilder. In addition, the valley quail is, I think, a tougher bird, harder to kill and with more of a tendency to run and hide when wounded. If the hunter can forego the occasional 35 and 40-yard shot, he'll do nicely on valley quail with a bobwhite gun, but if he cannot, he needs more gun than an improved cylinder 20 bore. Instead, he should use a modified 20 with 1 ounce of shot or an improved cylinder 16 or 12 with 1⅛ or even 1¼ of No. 7½.

The Gambel's quail and scaled quail of the Southwest can lie very tight when he is found in heavy grass or weed cover, but these arid country birds are generally shot in badly grazed-over cattle country. In such chewed-off land they run like rabbits and flush wild. I have shot more Gambel's quail than any other variety, and I believe I did my best shooting with an L. C. Smith double bored modified and full with 1 ounce of No. 7½ shot. I once tried a Winchester Model 21 bored Skeet No. 1 and No. 2 on them, but I lost too many wounded birds. When I got an extra set of barrels bored modified and full for the 16, the trouble stopped. The scaled quail or "cottontop" is as bad a runner as the Gambel's and the same medicine applies to him.

But all quail shooting is fast shooting, and a long, heavy, full-choked gun is the worst possible medicine. In my youth I used to try to hit them with full-choked pumps with 30-inch barrels. I had scant success. A light 20-gauge double changed me overnight from being a poor quail shot to at least an average shot. With the sluggish, heavy, long-barrel guns I was too often below and behind.

What is good quail shooting? I'd say that anyone who averages a bird in hand to two shells expended is doing very well. I am not sure that I average that, although I don't miss it far. Sometimes I do a good deal better, sometimes worse. The late Bill Weaver, the scope manufacturer, was the best quail shot I ever hunted with. He would average at least three birds in the hand to four shells. This is on valley quail. Carroll Lemon of Tucson, Arizona, is another very fine quail shot, and I have seen Jim Rikhoff, the former Winchester public relations man, do some classy shooting on Georgia bobwhites.

Shooting pen-raised bobwhites over a couple of fine pointing dogs at the Nilo Farms near Alton, Illinois, the late Larry Koller, editor of *Guns & Hunting*, Warren Page, then shooting editor of *Field & Stream*, and I once killed eighteen birds with nineteen shots. I was shooting over my head that day. As for the others, I cannot say. My wife, Eleanor, is a good quail shot, and on a Georgia plantation one day she killed nine wild birds over dogs with twelve shots. That's better than I did. She was using a 20-gauge Winchester Model 21 bored improved cylinder and modified. Her shooting astounded our host.

I never shot a pheasant until I was forty-six, but since that time I have killed a lot of the big gaudy cocks. The first few days I didn't find them easy to hit, as I couldn't get it through my head how slowly a pheasant moves when he is first getting up and how fast he can move when he has time to get wound up, particularly if he is coming downhill. But after the first few days I found pheasants very easy to hit, probably the easiest of all game birds, particularly if they are shot over a pointing dog.

Why are pheasants missed if they are so easy? Primarily, I believe, because they are big and beautiful and even when they are in front of the nose of a pointing dog, they have a tendency to scare the hell out of a gunner. Then our hunter doesn't get his head down, gets tangled in his feet, and commits all the other sins of upland gunnery. I know the birds I miss are almost always the ones that catch me by surprise. Then I shoot too fast, before my pattern has a chance to open up, shoot right at the bird instead of taking a fraction of a second to size up the angle.

The pheasant is generally a sharply rising target. Sometimes he will fly almost straight up. Straightaway birds are usually missed by shooting under, and on such birds I have the best luck by swinging up fast under them and touching off the shot when the muzzles are on the cock's head. It is generally wise to shoot a pheasant while he is still going up, as there is then a chance to put a shot or two into the head. Most shots at pheasants are straightaways or at gentle angles and on the angles one should shoot a bit above and to one side of the bird. If as often happens the bird flushes well ahead and takes off at an angle, the gunner should take his time, swing with the bird, and be sure to give him some lead. At 25 or 30 yards I lead a rooster getting under way what looks to be about 1½ to 2 feet. At 40 yards I try to get about 3 feet ahead and at 45 maybe 4 or 5 feet. For me the easiest of all shots on pheasants is the one at a right angling bird at between 25 and 35 yards. These I almost never miss. The toughest are birds at gentle angles and birds that flush below me on a hill. These I often miss because I shoot right at them.

I have often heard it said that one should shoot at the pheasant's body and not at his long tail. I do not think I have ever had that fault but possibly others have. My own faults are getting flustered and shooting too fast and misjudging gentle angles.

Driven pheasants that have had time to get their steam up are something else again. In England pheasants are driven so as to fly over rows of trees to a line of gunners. I have shot such birds only once. Mostly, the shots are overhead incomers. They are taken by starting under the bird, swinging fast, and shooting when the bird is blotted out by the muzzles. Any tendency to check the swing when the bird disappears is fatal.

In Idaho, where I live, birds are often flushed from wheat fields on top of hills and they fly down into the creek bottoms to cover. A bird that has traveled several hundred yards mostly downhill is going so fast that he whizzes. I saw one of the finest shots I have ever known stand in his tracks and shoot behind five such birds in succession.

Often the pheasant hunter is tempted to take long shots at wild-flushing pheasants—at 50, 60, 65 yards. It is best not to. If the bird is not missed, he flies off with two or three shot in him to die eventually of peritonitis.

A pheasant is a tough bird, and he is particularly hard to kill when he has leveled out and all one has to shoot at is his rear end. Then unless a wing is broken, he'll probably fly on even though fatally wounded. On many occasions I have seen pheasants shot like that fly from 100 to 400 yards until they fell dead, and I have had my dog find birds stone dead after they had flown out of sight. Because there is more area to shoot at and less meat to penetrate, a pheasant is far easier to kill stone dead from the side.

Men who have shot far more pheasants than I have recommended full-choke guns for pheasants. I do not like them as I find them great wounders with anything except a perfect hold. With their dense centers and thin fringes, full-choke patterns are poor medicine at less than 40 yards. For all-around use on pheasants a 55 or 60 percent 16 or 20 or a 45 to 50 percent 12 is about right. The man who shoots over a pointing dog and who has enough fortitude to keep from taking the long, uncertain shots will kill more birds stone dead with an open-bored gun than he will with a full choke. In the fall of 1963 a friend of mine with a new automatic bored full choke knocked down eight pheasants the first day of the Idaho season and recovered one. He told me his shells were not strong enough. I told him he was using more choke than he could handle and was hitting the birds with the edges of this pattern. I suggested a more open boring. He found a skeet barrel for his automatic at a local dealer's place, and from then on he averaged a bit better than one bird for two shells.

I have shot pheasants with everything from a modified 28 gauge and an improved cylinder 20 to a 12 gauge bored 55 and 65 percent. This is a Winchester Model 21 double with 26-inch barrels. It is a deadly pheasant gun but a bit heavy, and I have done my best pheasant shooting with it. On two occasions I have killed between twenty and twenty-five straight birds with it. Of late years I have been using another Model 21 bored modified and full with a 1-ounce load in the modified barrel and a 3-inch magnum load with 1¼ ounces of shot in the full-choke barrel. When I am feeling particularly lazy, I go out with a little 5¼-pound European 28-

gauge double bored modified and full. I use the 1-ounce magnum loads and with the full-choke barrel, I once killed stone dead a pheasant crossing at forty long paces.

One of the best pheasant shots I know shoots a Model 21 bored Skeet No. 1 and No. 2 and uses No. 4 shot. Some recommend No. 7½ but I have lost too many well-hit straightaway birds with it because of insufficient penetration. I think No. 6 is the best compromise for pattern density and penetrating power.

For whatever the reason, I have always found Hungarian and chukar partridges easy to hit. I have also found them easy to kill. When hit, they generally stay put instead of running off and hiding like a pheasant or a Gambel's quail. On numerous occasions I have killed five straight partridges. Since both have a tendency to flush wild, the gun used on them should be bored about modified and carry at least 1⅛ ounces of shot. For me No. 7½ or No. 6 seem to work equally well. On these, one bird picked up to 2 to 2½ shells is probably good shooting.

A grouse of any sort caught in the open is easy to hit, but flashing through brush and pitching out of trees, he is a difficult target. A typical shot at a blue grouse in the Northwest is at a bird pitching out of a conifer tree on the other side and glimpsed only through the branches or diving out into a canyon. In each case, the gunner must swing rapidly down, pass the bird, and shoot. To me this is the toughest shooting I have ever tried, possibly because I am a bit on the pokey side. If I get one bird in five shots, I am doing well. I have hunted with some gunners, though, who can average 50 percent. I'd say one bird for every 3 to 3½ shells was good shooting. A fast, light, open-bored gun and No. 6 shot is the business.

The fast, maneuverable mourning dove is the No. 1 upland game bird in North America, and one of the most missed. This is partly because he flies fast, because he is often shot at out of range, and because he can swerve and dodge. A score of years ago I was shooting one day on a flyway near Tucson, Arizona. I asked five ordinary shots to keep careful record for me of the number of shells they fired and the number of birds they picked up. I also asked five good shots who did a lot of skeet and trapshooting as well as bird hunting. The average shots averaged one bird to eight shells, if I remember correctly, the good shots one bird to 3 to 3½ shells. All volunteered that they had never done such miserable shooting in their lives. Later I asked one of the best shotgun handlers in the United States how he averaged on doves shooting on a flight and taking everything he considered was within range. He told me that he picked up about one bird for every three shells expended. I'd call that very good shooting.

I have been shooting doves off and on since I was ten years old. It is a wonderful but frustrating sport, and there is generally a lot of air around each dove. Birds coming into a water hole with their flaps down are easy to hit and a reasonably good shot should miss few of them. Birds walked up in a wheat field where they are feeding are likewise easy to hit. It is flight shooting that is tough.

Most gunners use too much choke on doves and shoot at too many birds out of range. Anyone who wants to make himself look good should shoot an improved cylinder barrel and limit his shots to 35 yards. A dove is easy to bring down and when he lands he stays put. The gunner should also stay out of sight until he is ready to shoot.

But shooting on a flight with a full-choke gun and taking everything that comes within 45 or 50 yards, anyone who can average one bird to 3 to 3½ shells is doing remarkably well. I am a spotty shooter under these conditions. I may miss five or six straight birds or I may kill that many straight. I notice that if a dove sneaks up on me and I have to swing and shoot fast, I generally get it, but if I have all the time in the world, see the bird coming a quarter of a mile away, I have a tendency to ride it out and miss it. This is the reason most gunners miss doves, I am convinced. Almost anyone can improve his dove shooting by keeping his gun down until the bird is almost on him, then throwing up his gun, swinging fast, and shooting.

Shooting driven birds is a European institution, but it is practiced in the United States to some extent on game preserves. The famous Scotch grouse is driven to a line of "guns" by a line of beaters. The birds come in flocks flying fast and generally fairly low. I found the birds fairly easy to shoot and any skeet shooter should have no difficulty since the shots he'll get are incomers about like the No. 1 and No. 2 low-house birds. He should take his first bird out at 40 yards or so, then swing up rapidly and take another at short range. An ideal gun is a 12-gauge double bored improved cylinder or modified or Skeet No. 1 and No. 2. The choked barrel should be fired first. I averaged about 50 percent on Scotch grouse, maybe a bit better. I was using the British game loads with 1 1/16 ounces of British No. 6 shot. My gun was bored modified and improved-modified, a bit tight for such shooting. With practice and a more open gun, I think I could do better.

SIZE DUCKS APPEAR AT VARIOUS DISTANCES

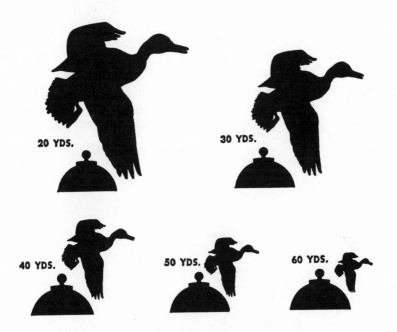

20 YDS.   30 YDS.

40 YDS.   50 YDS.   60 YDS.

Every gunner has a sort of built-in radar by which he judges the range. Here is about the way the mallard looks over a single-barrel gun at various ranges.

—courtesy Browning Arms Co.

Ducks coming into decoys are generally easy to hit if the gunner lets them get close, and up to 30 yards a skeet-bored 12 gauge used with 1½ ounces of No. 6 shot is incredibly deadly. So armed and on decoyed birds, a reasonably good shot should average 50 percent. Pass-shooting is something else. I think ducks are a good deal easier to hit on a pass than doves, but the gunner should never shoot at a bird until he can see his markings plainly and he should fight the natural tendency to ride his birds out. I have seen duck and goose hunters shoot at birds that were out of range for anything less than an anti-aircraft gun.

The extreme range of even a magnum 12 gauge using 1⅞ ounces of shot is only about 65 yards. Ducks will be killed farther than that when hit by a single shot in the head or neck or in the body by a lucky cluster. But such luck should not be counted upon. Furthermore, the lead necessary to knock off a speeding duck at 65 yards is beyond the skill of 99 gunners out of 100. Those who confine their pass-shooting to 40 to 45 yards, will get more ducks, wound fewer ducks, waste fewer shells, and register far better averages than those who blast away at long and doubtful ranges. I have always found ducks easier to hit than doves, and I think a reasonably good shot ought to pick up one duck for every 2 to 2½ shells if he doesn't try the long ones. Crack shots will do better, poor ones far worse.

CHAPTER 26

Big Game
with a Shotgun

USED with the proper ammunition, there isn't any doubt but that the shotgun is one of the world's deadliest weapons at short range on soft-skinned game. Used at too great a distance or with the wrong ammunition, there isn't any doubt but that it is one of the world's worst wounders.

In the game fields of Africa a standard piece of equipment for a safari is a double-barrel shotgun. Generally, it is carried in the hunting car to be used in an emergency, particularly if the white hunter's client is after leopards. So deadly is the shotgun at close range that it is almost impossible for a dangerous soft-skinned animal to get past one to drive home his charge if the gun is in the hands of a cool man who doesn't panic and who reserves his shot for the proper time.

Some years ago an American tycoon plugged a leopard too far back and the cat took refuge in a big pile of rocks sick and mad with pain. A few hours later the white hunter finished it off with a load of British SSG buckshot, which is about the same as our No. oo buck. When the leopard collapsed, it was all of four feet from the muzzle of the shotgun. Many a white hunter and many a colonist in Africa has been saved from being chewed up by the old reliable smoothbore and the proper amount of medicine in the form of buckshot.

A friend of mine, a famous big-game hunter in the Middle East, once went into a pile of rocks after another wounded leopard—but with a rifle. He got the leopard but the experience was a pretty hairy one. From that time on he has always had one of his shikaris (guides) carry at all times a Browning automatic shotgun equipped with sling and swivels and loaded to the hilt with buckshot.

Whenever another famous big-game hunter, this time a Britisher, took on a lion (particularly when that lion was in the company of some unpredictable mamma lions), he *sat down* with a repeating rifle in his hands and a shotgun loaded with SSG buck across his knees. If he bowled over his lion with his rifle, all was well; but if he got a charge, he waited until the lion was within a few yards and then let him have both barrels from the shotgun full in the head and chest. He wrote that on short-grass plains and so armed he wasn't afraid of any lion that ever walked.

This lethal weapon, the shotgun, is being used more and more widely on deer in the United States. The reason is that those two adaptable and prolific creatures, the human being and the whitetail deer, go on increasing cheek by jowl. In many areas the use of any weapon but a shotgun would be pretty dangerous business. Oddly enough, the notion is prevalent that the shotgun shooting a rifled slug has about the danger zone of a BB gun. Actually the shotgun slug fired at an angle of about 25 degrees has a range of well over a half mile. In heavy woods I'd rather have my hunting compadres armed with .220 Swifts or with .243s than with slugs, as the big, blunt slugs will penetrate far more brush. However, the shotgun shooting buckshot has far less range than a rifle as the round and ballistically inefficient pellets quickly disperse their energy and there is less chance for them to plaster some comely milkmaid in the back 40 or some suburban matron in Windemere Manor, the new housing development.

It grieves me to admit this, but as a gun editor I ought to get around more. I have never killed a deer with either a load of buckshot or with a slug. I have shot two deer with bird shot—one with

No. 7½ and one with No. 6, if I remember correctly—and at a distance measured in feet not yards. If anyone thinks bird shot won't kill a buck, he should take a crack at one at a few yards while the charge is still hanging together.

After the bird-shot pattern opens up, the small shot are worthless. Many years ago in southern Arizona I was hunting quail when my wife and I blundered into a coyote convention. It had been a very dry year and the coyotes had gathered around a well they had dug about six feet deep down to water in a dry arroyo. We must have seen a dozen at ranges from 40 to 70 yards and the bird shot did nothing but speed them on their way.

Buckshot, as the name would indicate, are designed for use on deer. In size they run from .24 inch for No. 4 to .33 inch for No. oo. No. 3 measures .25; No. 1, .30; and No. o, .32. The larger sizes of buckshot are loaded only in the 12 gauge, as they do not pattern well in the smaller gauges. Buckshot loads available in 12 gauge are No. oo with 9 pellets, No. o with 12, No. 1 with 16, and No. 4 with 27. In addition, a 12-gauge 2¾-inch magnum shell is loaded with 12 pellets of No. oo buck and a 3-inch 12-gauge magnum shell with 15 pellets. There are no buckshot loads available in 10 gauge.

The 12 gauge is generally used for deer hunting with buckshot, but buckshot loads are also available in the smaller gauges. The 16 gauge is generally loaded with 12 pellets of No. 1 buck and the 20 gauge with 20 pellets of No. 3. In the South where deer are hunted with shotguns and where the 16 gauge is very popular, many deer are shot with that load of 12 pellets of No. 1 buck.

What is the killing range of a 12-gauge shotgun with buckshot? It depends on the shotgun—and also on luck. I have heard of lucky kills to around 80 yards, but in all cases the damage was done by one pellet in the brain, spine, or heart. When deer are killed cleanly with buckshot, it is from multiple hits, just as a pheasant or duck is killed.

A friend who has done a good deal of deer hunting down in South Carolina has a theory about hits with buckshot. He says that 2 pellets, instead of having twice the shock power of 1 pellet, have about 4 times as much, and 3 pellets have about 12 times as much, and 4 pellets about 24 times as much. He also tells me that unless a pellet strikes the spine or brain, a deer almost never goes down with 1 hit. With 2 hits, he says, the deer sometimes goes down, with 3 he often goes down, and with 4 he *always* goes down. He considers the sure killing range of a gun is as far as 4 No. 0 pellets can consistently be put on a deer-size target.

Another friend of mine who has done a good deal of deer hunting with buckshot says he always used No. 4 buck, which carry 27 pellets to the normal load. He says he always holds for the head and neck, never for the body, and never shoots at over 40 yards. He also says that 2 or 3 pellets of No. 4 in the head and neck will always knock a deer down.

But the killing pattern of buckshot is thin. I once saw a buck wounded with buckshot and chased by hounds take refuge in a little pond. He stayed right out in the middle, about 65 yards from the bank. The hunter shot at the buck's head and neck at that distance about a dozen times and I am sure he hit it only twice.

Some correspondents have written me that they get very good buckshot patterns with full-choke guns. Much depends on the gun —the particular bore diameter, the amount of constriction at the muzzle, and the size of buckshot used. Every hunter who plans to use buckshot on deer should do considerable experimenting with different sizes of buckshot to see which size patterns best in his own gun. Generally speaking, it has been my own experience that the best patterns are shot with guns with less than full-choke boring—modified and improved cylinder. Twenty years ago Ithaca Gun Company made a gun for a hunter who wanted to use it with nothing but No. 00 buck from an open boat on swimming polar bears. Ithaca took plenty of time with the reaming of the choke, taking out a bit of metal at the muzzle, patterning it, taking out a bit more. It wound up as an improved cylinder with about 8 points of constriction, if I remember correctly the story as told me by the late Lou P. Smith. So bored the gun would pattern 100 percent—every single one of the pellets in a 30-inch circle at 40 yards. Such a gun would be very deadly indeed. Among the South Carolina deer hunters I talked to, the general consensus was that the 16-gauge guns they mostly used patterned No. 1 buck best on the average in barrels bored improved cylinder.

Deer are generally wounded with buckshot because hunters take rear-end shots and the pellets do not have the power to penetrate into the vitals. They also shoot out of range. I once saw a native hunter in India blast off with buckshot at a herd of spotted axis deer at somewhere around 70 or 80 yards. How many deer he wounded I cannot say. A companion and I needed meat and shot two of the deer with rifles. Both had buckshot in them.

In the old days before the invention of the American rifled slug, the man who wanted to use a single missile in a shotgun had no other choice but to use the round "pumpkin ball." These are miserable things. Because they have to get through the tightest choke they are made small. Those for a 12-gauge gun are really about 16 gauge—16 to the pound.

They are very inaccurate and they are also low on killing power. When I was hunting tigers in India, I saw 12-gauge balls of English manufacture put into two tigers. In both cases the penetration was unsatisfactory—only 2 or 3 inches in solid rump muscle, for example. Unless the shooter was very lucky, such a missile would only stir a tiger up. Most of the man-eaters in India have been wounded and incapacitated by balls and buckshot so that they cannot kill game and hence take to killing naked and defenseless men.

Until recent years the British gunmakers turned out smoothbore guns rifled at the muzzles. Various makers called them by different names—"Paradox," "Explora," and so on. These were supposed to be all-around weapons for brush and jungle—accurate with balls and conical bullets and useful with buck or bird shot. Barrels were regulated to shoot together with solid bullets and the guns were sighted like double rifles. There is no doubt but that at close range (up to 100 yards) those ball-and-shot guns would be deadly on soft-skinned game and many lions and tigers have been killed with them.

In Africa native hunters use smoothbore muzzle loaders on all manner of big game and wound far more than they kill. In my bullet collection I have an iron ball which I dug out of the fanny of a 44¼-inch sable bull I shot in 1953 in Tanganyika. It had been pounded into a more or less spherical shape, and apparently it had been in the sable's rump for years, as it was heavily encrusted with rust.

I have never run into any ballistic data on pumpkin balls but rifled slugs are something else again—powerful and reasonably accurate missiles with adequate killing power for deer at short range.

As developed in the United States about thirty year ago, the slugs are made of pure, soft lead. They have hollow bases, so they will "upset" (expand) to fill the bore and yet swage down when they strike the constriction of the choke. Because of their material and construction, they will not harm a gun. "Rifling" is swaged on the outside of the slugs, and the original theory was, I believe, that the rifling made the slugs spin and hence remain stable in flight and accurate. I am told, however, that the only result of the rifling is a reduction of bearing surface and hence a bit lower pressure. The slugs remain point on and stable only because they are heavier at the front end. They do not spin in flight.

The rifled slugs are made in 12, 16, 20, and .410 gauge. Weights are as follows: 12 gauge 1 ounce, 16 gauge ⅞ ounce, 20 gauge ⅝ ounce, and .410 gauge ⅕ ounce.

At the muzzle, the 12-gauge slug has the very respectable velocity of 1,600 foot-seconds and 2,480 foot-pounds of energy. Out at the deer range of 50 yards retained velocity is 1,370 foot-seconds and the energy is 1,365 foot-pounds, or about that of the .30/30 at 100 yards. However, the slug has a very poor ballistic coefficient and at 100 yards the velocity had dropped·to 960 foot-seconds and the energy to 895 foot-pounds—or to less than that of the .25/35 at the same distance.

At 100 yards the 16-gauge slug has a retained velocity of 1,010 foot-seconds and energy of 870 foot-pounds, the 20 gauge 940 and 535. The worthless little .410 slug should never be used on anything larger than rabbits. It weighs only 93 grains, has only 650 foot-pounds of energy at the muzzle, 270 at 50 yards, and 155 at

100 yards. It is not accurate enough for small game or powerful enough for deer. Why it is made at all, I'll never know.

A famous shotgun slug used to some extent in this country is the Brenneke, which is manufactured in Germany and imported by Stoeger. It is made in 12, 16, and 20 gauge. Like the American slug, the Brenneke is rifled, but also like the American slug, it is relatively stable because it is heavier at the front end—in this case, because a bore-sealing wad is attached to the rear end of the slug. The Brenneke slugs are a bit heavier than those of the American variety, penetrate somewhat deeper, have a bit better ballistic coefficient and get to 100 yards with a bit more soup. In Europe the slugs have been used successfully on the Scandinavian elk (which is related to the North American moose and about the size of the Wyoming variety of that animal). In India, where shotguns are often used on tiger, the Brenneke slug is highly thought of. Like the American slug, the Brenneke can be used in full-choke guns without harm to them.

Slugs are capable of reasonably good accuracy but the average double-barrel bird gun won't ordinarily give it. Double-barrel shotguns will generally crossfire with slugs, the right barrel to the left and the left barrel to the right. But this is not alway true. My wife once had a 20-gauge Ithaca double that would shoot slugs like a double rifle up to about 60 yards.

Shotguns are made and sighted to hit things by "pointing" (seeing the target in relation to the muzzle), whereas rifles are made to hit things by aiming (seeing the target in relation to front and rear sights—or with a scope, which serves as both front and rear sights). Shot *à la* rifle (using the receiver as a rear sight), a shotgun generally doesn't hit very close to where it looks. Furthermore, the slugs give their best accuracy in a straight cylinder barrel that does not deform them, and their poorest accuracy when they are squeezed down in a full choke.

As a consequence, many an innocent hunter who simply had bought himself a box of rifled slugs and took his full-choke pump or automatic with 30-inch barrel out for a deer hunt has had some rude surprises. It is routine for such innocent characters to miss standing deer cold at 50 yards and then to wonder how it happened. Then these lads do last what they should have done first. They go out and shoot their *escopetas* with slugs at paper. Old Betsy, they find, is grouping (if it can be called that) at from 1 to 2½ feet from where they want it to. Then they tear their hair and shout for the U. S. Marines.

The answer to all this is that since the shotgun with slugs is in effect a makeshift rifle, the thing to do is to fit it with sure-enough sights and to sight it in like a rifle. Various outfits make receiver peepsights for shotguns that can be fitted to the receivers of pumps and automatics. Weaver makes both top and side mounts so his 1X (K–1) shotgun sight can be fitted to a repeater—or for that matters so the K 2.5 can be used. Either a 1X or 2½X scope is easy to adjust and a shotgun equipped with a scope can be sighted in like a rifle.

Remington, Winchester, Mossberg, Browning, High Standard, and Ithaca make special shotguns equipped with open rear sights with barrels bored straight cylinder for slugs. Surprisingly accurate shooting can be done with these "slug specials." With a 12-gauge Ithaca that Shelley Smith, Ithaca boss, lent me, I had no trouble shooting groups that ran about 6 inches at 50 yards, 12 inches at 100 yards. This from the sitting position. This entirely practical short-range deer-hunting accuracy is closer than many hunters can hold with a rifle. Incidentally, these cylinder bore barrels are excellent for skeet and for short-range bird shooting—grouse, quail in brush, and woodcock. With one of these "slug-special" barrels and another bored modified for waterfowl, pheasants, and doves, a hunter has a close approach to an all-around weapon.

But whatever kind of sights the slug-hunter has on his scatter gun, he should probably sight in to hit the point of aim at 50 yards. Then his slugs will strike about 2 inches low at 75 yards and about 5 inches low at 100. Beyond 100 yards, the slugs drop rapidly and the killing power is also a good deal less. I doubt whether anyone is justified in taking a crack at a deer at much beyond 100 yards. But at up to 100 yards, I'd hate to have a good shot equipped with one of those slug specials, or any other open-bored shotgun with good sights. Chances are I'd get hit!

In 1963 Winchester-Western announced a rather remarkable break-through in the neglected field of buckshot loads. They call the new development the Mark 5 buckshot load. It uses a plastic collar around the charge of buckshot and the shot are further protected from deformation by being nested in powdered polyethylene. The result is fewer deformed buckshot, a tighter pattern, and greater energy delivered out at 30 to 60 yards where the bucks are, because the undeformed shot are traveling at higher velocity. From the patterning I have done with the Mark 5 buckshot loads, it would appear that the range with a given barrel is extended from 30 to 50 percent. So they can nest better the new buckshot are slightly smaller than the old. No doubt other loading companies will bring out similar loads.

SHOT-SIZE DIMENSIONS

Old Line			New Line (*Mark V*)		
No. Pellets	Name	Pellet Diameter (inches)	No. Pellets	Name	Pellet Diameter (inches)
9	oo	.330	—	—	—
12	oo	.330	12	oo–o	.323
15	oo	.330	15	oo–o	.323
12	o	.320	—	—	—
16	1	.298	16	1 Specl	.289
27	4	.235	27	3–4	.233
41	4	.235	41	3–4	.233
12	1	.298	12	1 Specl	.289
20	3	.250	20	3–4	.233

BALLISTICS FOR BRENNEKE SLUG

Gauge	Weight of bullet including wad (grains)	Length of barrel (inches)	Velocity (feet per second)					Energy (foot-pounds)				
			0	25 yds.	50 yds.	75 yds.	100 yds.	0	25 yds.	50 yds.	75 yds.	100 yds.
12	491	30	1593	1384	1213	1083	977	2756	2090	1606	1280	1049
16	427	28	1510	1303	1129	997	903	2163	1606	1208	947	774
20	364	28	1513	1300	1123	988	890	1852	1367	1020	788	637

CHAPTER 27

Learning

on Clay Targets

WHEN I was a boy in the early years of this century, flying game in Arizona and in general over most of the Uinted States was much more plentiful than it is today and there were far fewer gunners. If there were any bag limits, I did not hear of them and I had graduated from college before I ever saw a game warden. Before the First World War, I used to shoot whitewings and mourning doves with my grandfather and we considered a combined bag of about a hundred birds for an afternoon to be about right. An uncle of mine had a ranch house over which a flight of whitewings passed every afternoon. During the years from the time I was eight until I was thirteen or fourteen, I used to go outside with a single-barreled 20 gauge, a couple of boxes of shells, and a cracker box to sit on. Then I would shoot at the whitewings as they came over.

In those days people could learn to shoot by shooting at game. My grandfather was a crack shot and I don't suppose he ever shot at a clay target in all his life. Today in most places the opportunities for shooting game are so limited that it is impossible to learn to become a good shot simply by shooting at birds. In some places the pheasant season is ten days long and the limit is two birds a day. In the Sacramento Valley of California, hunters wait in line all night for an opportunity to hunt pheasants on open land. When a cock rises, a dozen guns bang away at it.

If anyone is going to become a good shot today, he will have to learn on clay targets. Remington, Western-Winchester, and Federal all sell hand traps by which with a little practice a clay target can be thrown rapidly and accurately. In addition, there are other privately made target throwers, some of which can throw two or more clay targets for practice in shooting doubles and triples. These hand traps are ideal for teaching youngsters to shoot and for keeping the older shooter in practice. All one needs is a case of clay targets and permission to shoot in some open country. The number of angles which can be presented to the gunner are limited only by the imagination of the thrower. With any of these hand traps, the thrower can make the target go sharply up like a towering pheasant or he can make it skim flat just above the ground like a foxy quail.

Perhaps the best way of all to become interested in shotgun shooting and to become proficient in the use of the shotgun is to take up one of the two clay target-shooting games, either skeet or traps. Both games are excellent practice and both games teach the gunner to handle his gun, track his target, shoot quickly, and break it. Possibly even more important is that these games bring the beginning shooter in contact with good shots who are willing to give him shooting tips and who will also furnish examples of how it should be done. One of the best ways for the beginner to learn to perform any athletic feat is to watch a skilled performer.

Trapshooting is the oldest and most popular of the clay target-shooting games, and the first American trapshooting championship was held as long ago as 1885 in New Orleans. There are four different kinds of trapshooting—16-yard singles, handicap, doubles and international trapshooting. In trapshooting, the shooters shoot in a squad or a line of five. They fire twenty-five shots and change stations every fifth shot. The targets "rise," or come out of the trap house, 16 yards from the shooter. The shooter always knows where the birds are coming from. He mounts the gun before he calls for the bird but he does not know what angle the target is going to take. The trapshooter picks the bird up as quickly as he can see it, tracks rapidly past it and shoots with the muzzle moving faster than the target. Trapshooting is all done by the "fast-swing" method. The targets are all rapidly rising, but depending on weather conditions, the angle of the rise is not always the same. In an incoming wind, the targets rise at a sharper angle. When the wind is behind them, they fly flatter. The trapshooter varies his lead by swinging farther past the targets which fly at a sharper angle than he does at targets which fly at a more gentle angle.

Some very fast trapshooters break their targets quite quickly, but the average reasonably fast trapshooter breaks his target after it has traveled 20 to 21 yards. For 16-yard singles, a modified choke is the best because it gives a little more leeway for error and yet has sufficient pattern density so that the clay targets do not get through the pattern. For handicap shooting a full choke is a must. Handicap is shooting singles but from different distances. Depending on their average scores, the shooters are handicapped by being put back from the 16-yard line. The skilled shooter may be required to fire from as far as 25 yards.

Double targets are shot from the 16-yard position and are thrown simultaneously. The traps are so regulated that the right-hand target is a straightaway from station 1 and the left-hand target is a straightaway from station 5. At the other stations, 2, 3, and 4, there are no straightaways. Shooting doubles is a pretty tough game, and to be good at it the shooter has to be fast enough to break both targets before either begins to fall. The shooter should align his gun to spot about where he is going to break his first target and then swing fast to break his second target while it is still rising. If he shoots his first target too slowly, he will have to shoot under his second—and falling targets are notoriously hard to hit.

International clay-pigeon shooting is a very difficult version of the sport, but until recently it has seldom been shot in the United States. In international traps, the field consists of a trap house in which there are fifteen traps arranged in a straight line. The stations are situated 16½ yards to the rear of the traps. There is one station for every three traps. All traps are adjusted to throw targets in a 45-degree angle right and left of the center trap of each group. The up and down angles are also varied and since both horizontal and vertical angles vary this is a tougher game than is American trapshooting. Furthermore, the international targets are faster than American targets since the traps are set to throw the bird 77 yards instead of the 52-yard maximum for the American style. In international clay-pigeon shooting, the shooters move from one station to the next after each shot. They shoot at twenty-five targets and may fire two shots at each target without penalty, just as they are allowed to fire two shots at each live pigeon.

Skeet is a much younger game than traps. The game started around Boston and was originally called "shooting around the clock." At first, only one trap was used and the shooters moved around in a circle. Then the game was standardized with the targets to be thrown from two "houses," one high and one low. The targets follow a fixed path but always, as is the case with traps, the wind will make them tower or dive. There are seven stations in a semi-circle and another station, No. 8, midway between the two houses. The path of the targets is slightly away from the opposite house. A round of skeet consists of twenty-five shots at twenty-five targets. The gunner fires at a pair of singles at each station, one from the high house and one from the low house. Then the squad of five moves to the next station. In the middle, No. 8 station, the targets come almost at the shooter and must be broken very rapidly. These No. 8 shots are the most spectacular of all those on the skeet field. They are not difficult once they are learned. The squad then moves to the high-house No. 1 station and fires at double targets thrown simultaneously. He also shoots doubles at No. 2, No. 6, and No. 7. The optional shot is another shot at the first target missed. If the gunner fires twenty-four shots without a miss he may take his optional at any station he chooses. Almost without exception, skeet shooters take as their optional shot the No. 7 low-house target, which is an easy straightaway.

Until after the war, the skeet shooter had to hold his gun away from his shoulder and down so that the butt of the gun could be seen under the right elbow. Then when he called for his target, he had to mount the gun, track the bird, and shoot. This practice in speedy mounting of a gun was exceedingly valuable, particularly to the beginning shooter, as fast gun mounting is a very important part of good and accurate shotgun shooting, particularly in the uplands. Human beings, however, are competitive creatures and most skeet shooters will do anything to break an extra bird or two on a round. The rules now are that the gun can be mounted before the bird is called for. Much of the value of skeet has been lost through this rule. Because I shoot skeet to keep in practice for upland shooting, I keep my gun down and mount it after the target appears. So do many other skeet shooters.

Skeet is, in my opinion, better practice for the hunter than trap-shooting. The skeet shooter has a greater variety of angles. They vary from targets traveling directly away from him, as at stations 1 and 7, and coming almost directly at him, as at station 8, to targets that are traveling at a right angle like the low-house bird at station 3 and the high-house bird at station 5. In skeet shooting the gunner must shoot in different styles as he would in the field. I spot-shoot the No. 1 high-house target and the No. 7 low-house target. I break both targets at station 8 with a very fast swing starting behind and shooting the instant the muzzle covers the target. Most of the targets shot at wider angles can be taken either by the fast swing or by the sustained lead.

Skeet targets are broken at from three or four yards, as in the case of the No. 8 station, to 22 yards or thereabouts in the case of targets shot from No. 3, 4, and 5. Today most skeet is shot with pump or automatic shotguns with ventilated ribs and bored what is called Skeet No. 1, which is about straight cylinder. Side-by-side doubles are seldom seen on the skeet field today but quite a few over-and-under shotguns bored Skeet No. 1 and Skeet No. 2 or about cylinder and weak modified are seen.

Skeet is not as popular as trapshooting even though in many ways it is a better game. Trapshooters shoot for money prizes. Skeet shooters shoot for glory and practice.

The game of trapshooting got its name and much of its vocabulary because it started out as a game by which live pigeons were shot. That is why the mechanism which throws the clay target is

referred to as a "trap" and that is why the targets are often referred to as "birds." I have read that in its earliest form pigeons
were simply put under old stovepipe hats. Then the hats were
jerked over by a string, the pigeon fluttered out, and the sport shot
him.

Live-pigeon shooting has been outlawed in most American states
but a few still permit it. As it is shot today, there are five little
traps, and when they are sprung they are opened up and a jet of
compressed air is supposed to send the pigeon on its way. The
gunner does not know which trap the bird is coming from. A low
fence surrounds the traps. Any bird which gets over the fence even
though it falls dead beyond the fence is considered lost. The gunner gets two shots at each bird without penalty and an experienced
live-pigeon shot always drives in a second shot as rapidly as possible even though the pigeon may be lying dead on the ground. One
can never tell what the pigeon is going to do when the jet of air
hits him. He might tower straight up. He might fly directly away.
He might fly at a sharp angle—or he might even fly right at the
shooter. He also might walk out of his trap, stand beside it, coo, and
preen his feathers. Even seasoned clay target shots get jittery when
shooting at pigeons.

In another form of the game, the birds are thrown by hand by
a thrower who generally plucks feathers from one wing to give the
bird an erratic flight. The thrower tries to hurl such difficult birds
that the gunner will miss. I have never shot these hand-thrown
pigeons although I have shot a few boosted out by jets of air. I
have seen these thrown pigeons shot in Mexico and in Spain. Believe me, they look tough. Live-pigeon shooting of both varieties is
a great gambling game and often $10,000 is laid on a single bird.
Most live-pigeon shooters that I have seen use over-and-under
shotguns and the classic live-pigeon load is 1¼ ounces of No. 7
shot and 3 drams of powder—a load, incidentally, which is a good
one for chukar and Hungarian partridges and not bad for pheasants.

Intelligent practice is the secret of becoming a good shotgun
shot, just as it is the secret of becoming a good golfer, a good tennis
player, or a good swimmer. A man may own the finest shotgun in

the world, one with gold-plated locks and a Circassian walnut stock, but if he seldom shoots it, he won't shoot well. In these days of short seasons, of limited game, and of many hunters, the only way any of us can do enough shooting to get good at it is by shooting clay targets.

One thing I have noticed is that the man who does his first shooting on clay targets is almost always a fast shot. If he isn't reasonably fast, he simply does not hit them. Many of us who learned on game and are relatively self-taught have a tendency to be pokey. He who learns to shoot on ducks or doves can dwell on his aim, can ride his bird out, can take three times as long to shoot as he needs to and yet still have the bird within range. Where I grew up, even quail were generally shot in rather open country and the slow shot with a full-choke gun could ride his birds out and often kill them at 40 to 45 yards.

But anyone who is going to break many clay targets at trap-shooting has to be fast. He must break the target while his pattern retains sufficient density for the saucer not to slip through it, and he must break it before it starts to fall and before the wind has time to get in all of its dirty licks.

The skeet shot can ride out some of his targets and still break them, but most of them must be broken quickly or they aren't broken at all. Shooting doubles at either skeet or traps requires that the first target be broken quickly if the shooter has any chance to break the second.

Shooting a shotgun well is a game of speed. A pokey shot can never shoot better than fairly well. He can kill some game and break some clay targets, but he is never a top hand with a shotgun. Crack shotgun pointers are always fast. One thing that I have noticed about top shotgun shots is that they never dwell on their aim, even when they have an opportunity to do so. The ordinary shotgun shot, when on a stand for doves or in a blind for ducks, brings his gun up, follows his bird along. Eventually he shoots. All too often he misses. The crack performer almost never raises his gun until the moment of truth has come. Then his head goes down, his right shoulder comes up. As the gun comes to his shoulder, he has already started his swing by rotating his hips. The gun swings rapidly and when it goes off the bird falls. The crack shot can kill a bird while the mediocre shot is thinking about it.

Every beginning shooter should strive to be fast. The faster the gunner shoots the less the chance of his slowing or stopping his swing. The faster he shoots the less chance he has to dwell on his aim, to check and double check, to hesitate.

I notice that when I am shooting doves and see a bird winging its twinkling way toward me a quarter of a mile away and have all the time in the world, I very often miss. Why? Because unconsciously I am aiming. I am making sure that I am leading that damned dove exactly five feet. When the lead looks just right, I slow down, shoot, and miss.

But if a dove sneaks on me and I have to swing and shoot fast, I almost invariably hit. Why? I have had no time to take a precise lead or to slow my swing. This is why the fair-to-middling skeet shooter will miss one or two of the easy crossing shots at singles on which he has all the time in the world. He misses them because he is too slow. He rides them out, slows his swing, lets them drop below his pattern, shoots above and behind them. He takes his doubles in better time because he has to—and he will average breaking a higher percentage of doubles than of singles.

Some people have better eyes than others. Some have better muscular co-ordination than others. Some are fast by nature and others are slow by nature. But everyone who wants to shoot a shotgun well should strive to shoot quickly. Above all, he should form the habit of shooting the instant the relationship of muzzle and target look right. If he does, he'll shoot while the barrel is still moving and he'll hit. But if he makes sure the relationship is exactly right, he'll probably slow down his swing and he'll miss!

The shotgunner is NOT trying to hit something with a single bullet. He is trying to hit with a cloud of shot pellets that cover from 8 to 50 inches, depending on the range at which he is shooting. The spread of the shot makes up for minor errors in pointing. The best way to learn to trust this spread of the shot and to shoot fast is on clay targets!

CHAPTER 28

Handloading
Shot Shells

WHEN I moved to Idaho in 1948 and for two or three years after that, there were piles of empty shot shells all over the grounds of the Lewiston gun club. About once a week the caretaker would rake the shells into piles and burn them.

Then in the early fifties, those piles of shells disappeared. They have not been seen since. Many of the shooters started wearing wide-mouthed sacks and every time they ejected shells they carefully put them in the sacks. On the skeet range I began to notice many more malfunctions, particularly with automatic shotguns, and every now and then the hollow boom of a "blooper" echoed around the club grounds. About the same time, the numbers of the shooters started to increase. Now, in 1964, there are probably five times as many skeet and trap shooters as there were in 1950.

The explanation of all these phonomena is that the boys have begun handloading. Now at the local club I'd guess that four out of five shells fired at the skeet and trap are hand loaded. Probably the figures wouldn't be very different at any other trap or skeet club in the country.

Throughout the 1890s and until the early years of this century, a great many shotgunners reloaded their fired shot shells. They used simple hand tools, dip measures for shot and powder. Sometimes they used brass shells, sometimes paper. I have been told that in those days gunners used to take their reloading equipment to their duck blinds and reload between flights. Then gradually the handloading of shot shells died out. One of the reasons was that the factory shot shells were cheap and very good. Another was that many of the reloaders had trouble with the new dense powders and many were afraid of them. Before the war when I used to shoot skeet in Tucson, I don't think a single member of the skeet club reloaded. Since the war, the increase in the reloading of centerfire metallics and shot shells has been an astounding phenomenon. Dozens of firms making loading tools and components have sprung up and prospered. There are now probably twenty-five times as many reloaders of centerfire metallics as there were before the war, but shot-shell reloading has increased at least a hundred fold. Before the war, the reloader of shot shells was so rare that he was looked upon as a sort of a nut. Now must gunners who do much shooting reload.

The loading of shot shells has become so universal that the big ammunition loading companies, who at first opposed the whole business, have now decided to relax and enjoy it under the sensible theory that if you can't lick them the only thing to do is to join them. At one time, at least one of the major loading companies had seriously thought about putting out shot shells that could not be decapped and reprimed, with the notion of discouraging reloading. Today they give tender and solicitous attention to the whims of the handloader because a large proportion of the loaded shot shells purchased in the United States today are bought by the people who expect to reload them. The reloadability of the shell is an important factor in its salability.

The handloader of rifle cartridges can actually produce a superior product. He can select what he wants from a wide choice of bullets. He can seat his bullets out just right for the throat of his individual rifle. He can select his powder and vary his charge until he gets top accuracy. The skillful and knowledgeable handloader of rifle cartridges can generally produce ammunition for his own particular rifle that gives somewhat better accuracy than factory ammunition.

In spite of the rather romantic tales one hears to the contrary, the reloader of shot shells does not produce a product superior to that turned out by the automatic machinery of the loading companies. In fact, if he can turn out ammunition about as good, he is doing very well indeed. The handloader of shot shells hasn't gone into it because he wants a superior product but because he wants to save money. And save money he does. Maybe his reloads produce an occasional "blooper." Maybe he gets an occasional malfunction on the skeet field. On rare occasions he may get a bit careless, put in a double charge, and blow up a gun—something a pal of mine did once with a double gun. But for the most part he produces usable ammunition and he saves money.

In an old gun catalog published along in the 1930s during the depression, I find Winchester field loads in 12 gauge and loaded with 3 drams equivalent of powder and 1⅛ ounces of shot listed at retail for 75 cents. In 1964 the same load was listed at $2.90. In the prewar catalog, the premium "high-velocity" duck loads like Super Speed were listed at $1.10 for a box of 25. Today the same load retails at $3.50.

However, the trapshooter who uses his fired cases and who does not figure in his time or the cost of his tools can reload a box of 25 shot shells with trap loads for the average component cost below:

Primers, Battery Cup	.38	
Powder, Red Dot	.30	
Wads, Overpowder	.04	
Wads, Fibre Filler	.08	
Shot, 1⅛ oz.		
chilled	.50	=$1.30
Savings per box		$1.60

But this isn't quite the whole picture. Most gun clubs sell shells to their members at wholesale cost, or from $2.25 to $2.50 a box. Furthermore, the distribution of shot shell components to handloaders these days is, like much of the sporting goods business, a cut-throat proposition. If the handloader is willing to buy his components in fairly large lots or chip in with a companion or two to do the buying, he can probably buy components wholesale, since most larger dealers manage to get them at jobbers' discount anyway. Then the individual handloader can save a little more money, and his box of 25 reloads may come as cheaply as $1.15.

It is this business of being able to shoot shells that have cost him from $1.15 to perhaps $1.50 that has got the skeet and trap shooter back to shooting. They are mostly the ones who are justified in handloading shot shells. Let us suppose that the handloader pays $50 for his tool, and just to make the arithmetic come out easy, let us suppose he saves $1 a box. Then he'd have to load 50 boxes of shells in order to pay for his tool. The chap who shoots four or five rounds of trap or skeet on Sunday would be justified in laying out the $50 for the tool, but the field shooter who went out four or five times after pheasants and a couple of times after ducks wouldn't shoot 50 boxes of shells (1,250 individual shells) in five years and maybe not in ten years. Some people are gimmick happy, just as some are gun happy and automobile happy. The gimmick-happy man who likes to have the basement crowded with curious machines will get his loading tool anyway. I doubt whether the field shooter has any business owning one.

The steps for reloading a fired shot shell are essentially like the steps for reloading a fired centerfire-rifle cartridge case.

Step 1. The shell must be decapped and recapped. That means the fired primer must be pushed out of the primer pocket in the head of the case and a new primer must be seated.

Step 2. The shell itself must be prepared for firing by inserting it into a die to bring it back to something like its original dimensions and it must then be removed from the die. Paper shot shells are not springy like brass. After they are fired, they are "dead" and never come back to their original dimensions like full-length resized brass centerfire rifle cases.

Step 3. The shell case is now prepared for loading. The spent primer is out, a new one in. It has been resized. It is now charged with powder. It can be weighed, dipped, or thrown by a measure that is part of the tool.

Step 4. The wad column must now be inserted. This may be a plastic wad column such as the Winchester Win-Wad, the Remington Power Piston, or the Alcan Max Flite. Or it may consist of an overpowder wad and a couple of greased felt filler wads, or of a plastic "H"-type wad, and a filler wad of fiber or felt. Then the wads must be seated on the powder with the amount of pressure given in the directions. The wad column should be of such length that it leaves about one half inch at the mouth of the case for the star crimp. Wads are made of various materials and come in various thicknesses so that the loader can make up wad columns of proper length. Obviously the use of a denser powder makes a longer wad column necessary. More shot in the case means a shorter wad column. Loading tools have adjustments for various amounts of wad pressure, but plastic wad columns will hold little if any pressure.

Step 5. This is charging with a measured amount of shot.

Step 6. This is the crimping. Most shells today use the star or pie crimp but some use a rolled crimp with a top wad. The shell has now been reloaded.

My advice to anyone starting to reload for the shotgun is to spend a few evenings with a friend who reloads, as it is much easier for most of us to pick up the fine points of any mechanical process by watching and doing than by reading. A useful book for the shotgun handloader to have is the *NRA Illustrated Shotgun Handbook*. It contains two chapters of detailed instructions on reloading shot shells and gives tested loads for various purposes and for various gauges.

The Alcan Company, Seminary Road, Alton, Illinois, is a very large wholesaler and importer of shotgun reloading supplies. The firm publishes an excellent and comprehensive handbook on reloading shot shells. Alcan imports powder from Sweden and Italy and other components from various European countries. Some of the components, I believe, are made by Alcan. The Alcan manual recommends various powder-wad-shot combinations for the different gauges. Its section on how the loader can tell what is wrong with his ammunition is excellent.

The Chemical Products Sales Division, Explosives Department, E. I. du Pont de Nemours & Company, Wilmington 98, Delaware, has compiled a list of recommended loads with Du Pont powders in all the gauges and will send it free on request. Hercules powder Company, Wilmington, Delaware, also sends a free folder on loads with its famous powders to those who request it. B. E. Hodgdon, Shawnee Mission, Kansas, puts out a reloader's catalog which he sells for $1.50. Much of it is taken up with other material but he does publish some shot-shell loading data with his own powders, which I understand are government surplus and are renamed standard powders. *Speer's Reloading Manual,* available for $2.95 from Speer, Inc., Lewiston, Idaho, or from dealers in reloading supplies and equipment, is mostly on reloading of rifle and pistol cartridges, but gives instructions in reloading shot shells and also lists recommended loads. The *Lyman Reloader's Handbook* published by the Lyman Gun Sight Corp. of Middlefield, Connecticut, for $2, contains good loading data for the various gauges with different powders, cases, and other components and also extensive instructional material.

Specific loading data should include case, primer, powder, wad column, wad pressure, shot charge, and type of crimp.

A very specific set of recommendations for loads for various purposes is found in the *NRA Illustrated Shotgun Handbook.* Here is an example: Shell: Federal Hi-Power; Primer: Federal 209; Powder: 23 grains of Hercules Red Dot; Wads: one .200-inch overpowder wad, two ¼-inch, one ³⁄₁₆-inch filler wads; Wad pressure: 78 pounds; Shot charge: 1⅛ ounces; Crimp: folded. The above load is suitable for trapshooting and upland hunting.

In the area where I live, the most-used trap load consists of 19 to 20 grains of Red Dot, with a one-piece plastic shot column like the Win-Wad or the Power Piston, and 1⅛ ounces of shot, No. 7½ or No. 8 for trap and No. 8 or No. 9 for skeet.

Like factory-loaded shot shells, those that are handloaded fall into the categories of target (trap and skeet), field (upland hunting), and wildfowl (heavy and magnum loads with progressive-burning powders).

Anyone who plans to do his own loading, either to save money or simply as a hobby, should ground himself in theory. The handloading manuals I have mentioned above are useful; so is a general book on shotguns and shotgun shooting such as this one. The man well grounded in theory is not going to increase his charge of some fast-burning powder to get a magnum load and hence blow himself up. Neither will he make the mistake of using a light charge of progressive-burning powder in a trap load.

As we have seen, the steps necessary to turn a fired and empty shot shell into a live and loaded cartridge ready for clay target or game are few and simple. Tools to perform these functions can be cheap or expensive. Satisfactory loaded shells can be turned out by one tool which sells for about $10. Beautifully machined, power-driven tools sell from $400 to $600. With the $10 outfit, I think that anyone would be doing well to reload one box of 25 shells in an hour. With the power-driven tools it is not difficult to load 50 or 60 boxes of shells in an hour. Actually, about the only legitimate use for the fast power tools is loading for a gun club or loading on a custom basis.

Perfectly satisfactory tools for the individual sell for from $35 to $100. Again the difference is speed. The $35 machine will turn out about 100 loads or four boxes an hour, but the $100 machine will furnish about 250 shells or 10 boxes an hour. Anyone using such a machine would have to do a lot of shooting before reloading became burdensome. With the fast machines the shells travel from station to station. At every movement of the handle, the operator inserts a new case to be decapped, recapped, sized, charged with powder, wads, shot, and then crimped. As he puts in the new case, he takes out a finished, reloaded shell.

The more highly developed (and also the more expensive) shot-shell loading machines have built-in powder and shot magazines and measures. These measure powder and shot automatically. Some even insert the wads automatically, and all the operator has to do is to put in the empty shells, keep the magazines filled, and operate the handle. The speediest and most highly developed machines will load up to 60 boxes of shells an hour.

The reloader of shot shells should expect to save substantial money and have fun, if he does not go gimmick happy and get a tool so expensive that he could not load enough shells to pay for it if he lived to be 175. If he simply loves gimmicks and wants to charge his $400 reloading machine off to fun and games, that is all right with me too. It is a much less harmful, less expensive, and less self-destructive hobby than skiing, skin diving, drag racing, or pub crawling.

The handloader should listen with a skeptical smile to other practitioners of the art who tell him of their super loads that pattern 85 percent and kill geese at 90 yards. If he tries to work up loads that equal these wonders, he is going to be pretty disappointed. To those who want dense patterns, an average of 70 percent is good and 75 is excellent. Actually, patterns with a very high count are very often a sign of sub-standard velocities, low pressure, and poor killing power.

Also, the handloader should regard with healthy skepticism some of the claims of the component manufacturers. One says the use of a certain type of plastic overpowder wad will increase pattern density 10 percent. Another claims that his variety of copper-coated shot will increase pattern density from 10 to 15 percent. The handloader has also read that the use of the star crimp and doing away with the overshot wad has thickened up his average pattern at least 5 percent. Then he is informed that if he uses a certain type of variable choke device on his gun, he'll also get 10 to 12 percent better patterns. When he adds all this up, he will discover that unless someone was pulling his leg he should be getting patterns of well over 100 percent.

The reloader should be leery of trying to save too much money. Some varieties of cheap foreign shot-shell cases are of such poor quality that they burn through on the second or sometimes on the first loading. Reclaimed shot dug out of the ground at some trap club is apt to be filled with sand and grit. It will ruin the barrel. Some cheap wads do not give a good gas seal and produce inferior loads.

The handloader should approach his loads with extreme caution by sticking to time-tried standard loads. He should never try to interpolate loads from one gauge to another, to guess the identity of a powder.

He should learn to investigate any out-of-the-ordinary performance. Does his barrel lead badly? Do his loads seem to give extra recoil? Are his pattern percentages markedly lower or higher than the ones his barrel gives with factory loads? Do some of his loads give the hollow boom and the muzzle flash of a "blooper"? If any of these conditions exist, our handloader should find out what is wrong. The big loading companies develop their loads with the assistance of pressure guns and chronographs and by shooting hundreds of patterns and evaluating them. The handloader has to use his head and proceed with caution.

Before the man interested in reloading his own shot shells jumps into it, he should talk to several acquaintances and get their reactions to the tools they use, to the loads they have liked, and to shot shell reloading in general. The potential reloader will find that he can get good advice on the choice of tools, the selection of components, and on proper loads from sporting-goods dealers who specialize in the sale of loading equipment and supplies.

I shall list some time-tried loads worked up by one of the helpful dealers I know. He is Paul Nolt, who runs Lolo Sporting Goods in Lewiston, Idaho, and who probably sells more loading tools and shot-shell components than any other dealer in the Northwest. Paul got into the sporting-goods business about the time gunners began to get interested in handloading. He tries out all tools, all powders, all components. He is the president of the Lewiston Gun Club, a crack shot, a dedicated bird hunter, and a practical ballistician of no mean attainments.

Here are his pet loads for 12 to 20:

12-GAUGE TRAP SHELLS (HIGH INSIDE BASE WINCHESTER AND REMINGTON):

Target Load

> 20 grains 450LS Winchester Ball powder, air-wedge overpowder wad, ⅜ to ½ inch filled wad, 1⅛ ounces shot, 60 pounds wad pressure.

Field Load (low inside base tube)

> 30 grains 500HS Winchester Ball powder, Win-Wad, 1¼ ounces shot, 60 pounds pressure.

2¾-inch Short Magnum Load (low inside base shell)

> 39 grains AL-7, .70 overpowder wad, 2¼-inch filler wads, 1½ ounces shot, 70 pounds pressure.

16 GAUGE:

Target Load (*high inside base tube*)

19 grains 450LS, .200 overpowder wad, ½-inch filler wad, 1 ounce shot, 70 pounds pressure.

Field Load (*low inside base tube*)

28 grains Herco, .70 overpowder wad, 2¼-inch filler wads, 1⅛ ounces shot, 100 pounds pressure.

Magnum Load (*low inside base tube*)

30 grains 540MS, .135 overpowder wad, ⅜-inch filler wad, 1¼ ounces shot, 60 pounds pressure.

20 GAUGE:

Target Load (*high inside base shell or tube*)

16 grains Red Dot, .70 overpowder wad, ½-inch filler wad, ⅞ ounce shot, 50 pounds wad pressure.

Field Load (*low inside base tube*)

20 grains 500HS, .135 overpowder wad, 2¼-inch filler wads, 1 ounce shot, 70 pounds pressure.

or

25 grains 540MS (same wad column as above)

Magnum 2¾-inch Load (*low inside base tube*)

33 grains AL-8, 1.70 overpowder wad, 2¼-inch filler wads, 1⅛ ounces shot, 70 pounds pressure.

Wad columns will vary slightly with various brands of shells.

CHAPTER 29

Shotgun Miscellany

Care and Cleaning

Books on shotguns almost always wind up in some words of wisdom on the care and cleaning of shotguns, so here goes. Shotguns are easier to care for than they were a generation or two ago. The use of non-corrosive primers in shot shells has made regular cleaning of the bores much less necessary than it used to be. Nowadays primer residue does not attract moisture and neither does that of modern smokeless powders. However, the residue left in the barrels after firing contains nothing to repel moisture and prevent rust either, and an uncleaned barrel will eventually rust if the moisture content of the air is high enough.

Since cleaning and oiling the barrel is a simple matter, I almost always clean the bore when I get back from hunting. I put the felt ball that comes with most cleaning rods on the end of the rod. I then take a clean flannel patch of the size used with .30 calliber rifles, saturate it with some good powder solvent like Hoppe's No. 9, and push it through the bore. This pushes out the carbon and other residue from the combustion of the powder and may also push out a few flakes of lead. I throw that patch away, put on a clean one saturated with some good preservative gun oil. I push that through and the bore will be rust free even in a damp climate for a good many weeks. If I plan to use the gun within a week or so, I omit the second patch.

In these days of hard shot and shot coated with copper and nickel and the use of plastic collars around the shot charge and of plastic shot columns, there is little trouble with leading. Barrels lead because they are rough or because soft shot is used. If shells without a plastic collar are used, many new shotguns will lead for a time just forward of the forcing cone. The lead can be seen as a rough and silvery-looking deposit. It is not difficult to remove with any of a variety of brass and bronze brushes used in connection with a powder solvent. Steel brushes should not be used as they may scratch the bore. Then when the barrel is wiped out with a solvent-saturated patch, flakes and flecks of lead will be found on the patch. In time the passage of the shot will smooth up the bore and leading will be a thing of the past. Some fine shotguns that are handfinished and at least partly handmade do not lead at all, for the bores are polished mirror-smooth with a mild abrasive before the guns are delivered. However, it should not be forgotten that the choke of a shotgun barrel can be too smooth, and that often the patterning of a barrel is improved by roughing up the choke.

When the gunner comes in from the field or the gun club, he should make it a practice to wipe off the outside metal parts of his gun with an oily rag. Then it will not rust. If the gun is to be stored for some time, it should be protected inside and out with a heavier oil that will not evaporate or run off.

Those who know no better squirt oil (usually some gummy oil that they use for the lawn mower and squeaky door hinges) into every hole and crevice they can find in their guns. This rots the wood of the stock and in general does no good. A few drops occasionally on the working parts in the action of a repeating shotgun is all that is needed. A gas-operated automatic should have the gas port cleared of carbon and the carbon cleared out of the gas cylinder now and then. The owner of a shotgun with hand-detachable locks like those seen in high-class European doubles should remove them perhaps once a year, wipe them off, and oil them very lightly with a light, high-quality oil.

If a gunner gets his weapon thoroughly wet, as sometimes happens when hunting waterfowl, he should wipe it off with a dry cloth when he gets home. Then he should wipe all exterior metal parts with an oily rag. The warm air in a centrally heated house will soon dry off any moisture he hasn't wiped away.

Some men take pride in the appearance of their guns and some do not. It happens that I do. I have rifles that have been used on tough mountain hunts in various parts of the world and have been carried hundreds of miles in saddle scabbards and yet show little signs of wear and none of abuse. A shotgun is apt to take a worse beating than a big-game rifle. It is used more often, and if it is a wildfowl gun, it is exposed to wet weather. The hunter may use it to press down barb wire fences, and he may carry it uncased from place to place in a car.

In time the much-used gun will show some blue wear and there will be some nicks and dents in the stock. But with anything like reasonable care, the shotgun should look good for many years. I have a Winchester Model 21 in 12 gauge with two sets of barrels. I have shot a lot of skeet with it using open barrels. I have hunted upland game with it in Idaho, Washington, and Oregon. I have shot grouse with it in Scotland and francolin and guinea fowl with it in Tanganyika. It shows that it has been used, but it is still a handsome and sleek-looking gun. My wife's Model 21 in 16 gauge is twenty-five years old but it is still a handsome gun.

Gun Cases

One of the secrets of keeping a shotgun looking good is having the proper gun cases. For shipping by plane or for carrying from place to place as hand luggage or in an automobile, I like best the traditional British trunk case made of leather over oak or plywood and with heavy brass corners. These cases are made to fit the individual gun. They are lined in good-quality red or green felt billiard cloth and have compartments for a square oil can, a cleaning rod, patches, and snap caps. These should be ordered with a canvas cover that buckles on, for what airline baggage handlers can't do to anything made of leather isn't worth doing.

I have only one top-quality British trunk case. I had it made in

London and got it through the now defunct W. J. Jeffery & Company, which was then on Pall Mall. I furnished them with the outline of the taken-down Model 21, one barrel with fore-end, the other without, and the handsomely done case fits the gun to perfection. At the time, I paid about $65 for the case with canvas cover. Today, I understand that such a case costs over $150. I can well believe it since a canvas case with brass corners and lined with billiard cloth which I got for my .450/400 Jeffery double rifle from Holland & Holland in 1962 cost me $85.

Trunk-type cases made in Belgium of leather and with corners reinforced with leather can be obtained from Abercrombie & Fitch in New York, Chicago, or San Francisco. Browning Arms Company also imports such a case from Belgium. Excellent trunk-type cases on the British pattern are also made in Austria and Germany and may be ordered from Waffen-Franconia of Würzburg. The German name for such a case is *Gewehrkoffer*. The quality is good and the prices are lower than the ones for British cases. Similar cases with brass or nickel-plated corners and lined with felt are made in Spain and are quite cheap, but the felt is not of high quality and the leather is generally of goat or domestic hog hide. Though they are good looking, the cases are not so nicely made or as durable as the best British cases. I bought a couple of them in Madrid for about $20 apiece and shipped a gun in one by air freight to Nairobi and back some years ago. It looks as if a half-dozen horses had stepped on it. It should have had an outer canvas cover.

The trunk-type cases I have seen have all been made in Europe. A solid type of case that is traditionally American is the leg-of-mutton case made of heavy leather to hold a double with one or two sets of barrels or a pump or automatic. Such cases are, to my notion anyway, not as handsome as the trunk-type cases, but they do a good job of protecting the gun when carried long distances in an automobile or as airline baggage.

I can remember when just about anybody with any pretensions to amounting to anything had a good leg-of-mutton gun case for his Parker, his Fox, or his L. C. Smith. He put the gun in the case when he rode out to shoot quail or doves in his buggy behind his fancy trotting mare, or when he boarded his sleeper on the train of cars bound for the Dakotas for some prairie chicken and duck shooting. Then when he got to the scene of action he put his gun together. When he was through he cleaned out the barrels, wiped the metal parts with an oily rag, and back into the leg-of-mutton case it went.

Today, although the traditional leg-of-mutton case is still made, I do not think many are sold. Most gunners seldom take their pumps and automatics down. Instead, they clean them from the muzzle. When they transport them, they usually do so by automobile, and they put them in long leather, leatherette, canvas, or plastic cases lined with sheepskin, flannel, or artificial fleece. These protect the guns from scratches but they do not protect them from hard knocks as do the leg-of-mutton and the trunk-type cases. However, all gun owners should have cases of this type as they protect the guns on casual automobile hunts. Leaning two unprotected guns up against the back seat is a fine way to dent them, nick then, and scratch them up.

Refinishing Stock and Metal

The run-of-the-mine pump or automatic shotgun made in the United States has a stock made of plain and generally soft and porous American black walnut. The latest models generally have checkering that is pressed in. Older models are usually machine checkered with hand-cut borders. Even most postwar Model 21 Winchesters have checkering that can only be described as fairly good.

To see genuinely first-rate checkering, one has to go to high-grade American, Belgian, and German guns, mostly made before the war. Some very handsome checkering was done on high-grade Parkers, Winchester Model 21s, L. C. Smiths, and Foxes. It is still possible to get very good checkering on Browning shotguns and other guns made in Belgium. Some fine checkering has been done on British guns in the past but the checkering on a $2,500 Purdey today leaves a good deal to be desired. The checkering on the better-grade Merkel, which is made in East Germany, is usually

very good, as is the checkering on the high-grade Belgian Fran-
cottes and Italian Berettas.

Probably the finest checkering in the world today is being done
by a handful of talented American craftsmen—Mews, Biesen,
Fisher, and Brownell—to name some of them. Anyone who loves
fine weapons and fine workmanship will add to his pleasure of
ownership and to the value of his gun by having one of these artists
rechecker an otherwise excellent foreign gun or a beloved old
gun.

The finish on most factory shotguns is some sort of shellac or
varnish which is generally sprayed on. Some of the newest plastic
varnishes are quite durable, but they make the stock glitter like the
mouth of hell. To me they look cheap. Some of the worst factory
finishes flake and chip off at the slightest bump. I took a factory
rifle on a shoot in Mozambique and Angola in the summer of 1962
and when I got back great hunks of the varnish had fallen off—this
in spite of the fact that I treat firearms with great tenderness.

The classic finish for a fine gunstock is straight linseed oil. This
works well enough on very fine-grained European walnut. On
open-grained wood, however, so much oil seeps in that the wood
turns dark and the grain is hidden.

To refinish an old stock or put a finish on a new one, I like to go
about it as follows: If the stock is an old one, I brush on varnish
remover, then scrape the loosened varnish off with a dull knife.
When the varnish is off, I wipe and scrub the whole stock thoroughly with alcohol. Dents in the stock can be raised by putting a
wet cloth on the stock and then holding a hot iron on the cloth to
let the steam work into the fibers of the wood. Another method of
removing dents is to put alcohol on the stock at the point of the
dent and then setting it afire. Old checkering has generally accu-
mulated oil, blood, dead skin, dirt, and all manner of crud. It can be
cleaned out by soaking in varnish remover, then scrubbing along
the line of the checkering with an old toothbrush or with the sort
of a brush five-and-ten-cent stores sell for cleaning suede shoes.
Then the checkering should be scrubbed out with alcohol to the
bottom of the lines.

With the old finish off and the checkering cleaned out, the stock should be thoroughly sanded with wet-or-dry sandpaper used wet and on a large art-gum eraser. At first, the wet stock should be dried quickly and the "whiskers" cut off with fresh sandpaper. The finish sanding should be done with very fine sandpaper, No. 600 grit wet-or-dry if you can get it. This paper is so fine that it polishes.

The next step is to brush on a coat of good spar varnish and let the stock set until the varnish is bone dry. Then this coat of varnish should be sanded off right down to the bare wood with No. 400 grit wet-or-dry sandpaper used wet. Again one should finish up with No. 600. The stock should now be as smooth as the damask cheek of a sixteen-year-old maiden and all the pores of the wood should be filled. This can be seen by holding the stock so that the varnish in the pores reflects the light.

As the next step, I rub a coat of George Brothers Lin-Speed or boiled linseed with about one-fourth spar varnish added. Then I take a clean, dry rag and rub off all the oil I possibly can. I let the stock set for two or three days to get thoroughly dry. Then I do the same thing again. The coats put on that way are microscopically thin, get tough and dry, have a deep, rich sheen but no glitter. A few drops of boiled linseed oil rubbed on by hand, rubbed off with a dry, clean rag, and then polished by hand will renew the finish of the stock, do away with minor scratches, and add to the luster.

In time the finish wears off the metal of a much-used shotgun and the owner will want a re-blue job done. The hot-salt bluing process which came into wide use during the war and which is almost universally used today on rifles and repeating shotguns is poison on doubles. It dissolves the solder by which the barrels and ribs are joined. Before the word got around, many an innocent smith was badly shaken when he dunked the barrels of a double gun into his pet hot-salt solution and had them come out in several pieces. This solution also dissolves aluminum.

The hot-salt process is widely used not because it is the best but because it is quick, cheap, relatively foolproof, and fairly satisfactory. Shotgun barrels must be blued by the cold-rusting process or the hot-niter process, neither of which harm the solder. Both processes take more time and more skill than the hot-salt process, and both are better looking. Most local gunsmiths can reblue a repeating shotgun, but the owner of a double must send his gun to some firm such as Griffin & Howe in New York or Pachmayr Gun Works in Los Angeles.

Gadgets

Most German and Austrian shotguns are fitted with sling swivels and are used with light ⅝ and ¾-inch slings. American, British, Belgian, and Italian guns are not so fitted. I have never had a shotgun with swivels, and I think permanent swivels detract from the looks of a gun. But a friend of mine who does a lot of chukar-partridge hunting with the resultant climbing and walking has a 20-gauge Winchester Model 21 double with quick detachable swivels, one on the bottom of the buttstock, the other attached to the lower rib of the barrel. He claims that for that type of hunting he would not be without his sling.

Many European shotguns are made with separate firing pins. Often these break when the gun is snapped on an empty chamber. Actually, there is no particular reason to snap a gun when it is put away, for the springs can stay under tension for years without harm, but most gun owners worry if their guns are put away cocked. For these worriers a pair of snap caps is in order. These are dummy metal cartridges with fiber backed up by coil springs in the place of primers. The firing pins can fall on these without harm. British gunmakers furnish snap caps with their custom guns as a matter of course, and most British cases have compartments for them. Snap caps can be ordered from Abercrombie & Fitch or direct from Holland & Holland or any other British gunmaker. Snap caps are not needed on guns with integral firing pins like the Winchester Model 21.

When most of us go gunning, we go by automobile. We take our extra ammunition in the original boxes and we put it on the floor of the automobile. The boxes often break and the shells roll around, get dirty, are stepped on, and collect feathers and trash. The British and Continentals take extra shells with them in leather and canvas bags that look something like camera-gadget bags.

These can be obtained at the ritzier sporting-goods stores like Abercrombie & Fitch and can also be ordered from Norm Thompson, the Portland, Oregon, sporting-goods store that does a large mail-order business. The Lawrence Company of Portland makes a heavy leather case that holds four boxes of 12-gauge shells. Abercrombie & Fitch imports from Britian a little leather box on an oak frame and with brass corners. It is a handsome piece of equipment and holds four boxes of shells. A gadget like any of these is worth acquiring.

On Shooting Clothes

I have been shooting a shotgun at feathered game for about fifty years and during that time I have seen many changes take place. I have seen the numbers of hunters increase until there are now thousands where there were once dozens. I have seen free and unrestricted hunting vanish over a large part of the United States. I have seen the double gun largely replaced by the pump and the automatic, but I believe I see now a revival of interest in the double as a prestige item.

I have seen shooting preserves come into being around a great many of the large cities, and I am aware that the future of gunning in the United States lies in paid hunting of some sort. At the present time there is no incentive for the farmer to manage his land for the benefit of upland game, and there will not be until his palm is crossed with a bit of silver. The day when anyone who would pay a few dollars for a hunting license could have unlimited shooting is rapidly coming to an end—even in the more thinly populated states of the West.

Another gunning tendency that I think I detect anyway is for the better-heeled shooters to look less like indigents when they go out hunting. In Europe shooting is for the most part the privilege of the well-to-do. When an Englishman goes gunning for grouse or pheasants, he wears a tweed jacket and plus fours or sometimes, if he is a Scot, he wears kilts. On his head he wears a tweed hat or cap. A clean shirt and a necktie complete his costume. The American gunner may drive out in a $7,000 automobile, but he is apt to wear a pair of dirty pants ripped and torn from barbed wire fences and an ancient and baggy canvas coat that stinks of blood and guts and is plastered with feathers.

But in the past few years I have seen an increasing number of neat and personable looking upland gunners even in the unsophisticated states of Idaho, Washington, and Oregon where I do most of my shooting. These chaps manage to wear clean shooting jackets, often over clean red-flannel shirts. They apparently change their pants now and then. They often wear brown or green Tyrolean hats. Often they have their wives with them and they invariably wear smart hats, neat pants and jackets, and manage to look charming even as they knock cock pheasants for a loop.

We Americans are descended largely from European peasants who if they had hunted at all in Europe did so by poaching and were primarily after the meat. Then when they moved to the New World and set out to conquer a continent, they and their descendants remained meat hunters. I live by choice in a small Idaho city just across the Snake River from Washington. I moved here as a refugee from urban sprawl, freeways, noise, parking problems. The pioneer tradition is strong among most of my neighbors. They are meat hunters who refuse to shoot quail because a quail costs in ammunition more than it is worth in meat. Although a few nail elk and deer heads to the garage or barn, most simply leave the heads in the woods. They cannot understand why I should want to hunt in Asia, Africa, or the Yukon when I cannot bring the meat back with me.

But even way out here in the boondocks, we refugees from progress are starting to spruce up a bit. Down South, where bobwhite quail are hunted in style on horseback or in rubber-tired hunting wagons pulled by matched mules, the gunners dress well indeed. More and more the gunners around the cities are looking neat and sporty. I think it is a good idea!

Index

Abercrombie & Fitch, 38, 62, 156, 326, 330-1
Acme Steel, 88
Adjustomatic Choke, 117
Aguirre & Aranzabal, 38, 40-1, 49-50
aiming, 256, 301, 311, 312
Alcan Company, 216, 317
Alcan Max Flite, 317
all-around guns, 26, 162-6, 236; see also shotguns
American choke, 95, 96
American-made double-barrel shotguns, 53-68
American Rifleman, 178
American trapshooting championship, first, 306
angles, 276-83
Anson & Deeley hammerless box-lock action, 8, 28, 30, 46, 56
Aristocrat, 49
Arizaga, 33, 48-9, 51, 185, 188, 189
Arizaga, Esubio, 50
army muskets, 3, 41
Arthur, Chester A., 135
Asian wild sheep, 16-17
Askins, Captain Charles, 93, 234, 273
Aubrey, 11
Austrian-made guns, 88, 144-5, 151, 165, 183, 205
automatic ejectors, 5, 9, 18, 24, 31-2, 51, 58-61, 66-8
automatic safeties, 34, 64
automatic shotguns, 13-14, 21-3, 76-83; gas-operated, 22, 80-3, 170, 173, 236, 239; see also shotguns
AYA, 38, 49-50, 51, 52

Baker, 57
Baker, Sir Samuel, 177
Baker, W. H., 57

Baker Gun Company, 31, 53
ballistics, 222-40; for Brenneke slug (chart), 304; see also shot shells
Bannerman, 69-70
barrels, 84-92; fluid steel, 7, 11-13, 59, 60, 70, 71, 87; twist, 7-8, 11, 85-6, 129; Damascus, 8, 11-14, 59, 66, 70-2, 85-6; laminated, 12, 13, 85; stationary, 29; L. C. Smith, 59; Winchester 21: 63, 88; Remington, 66; Browning, 68; Winchester 1887: 70; decarbonized steel, 84; early, 84-5; skelp, 85; Parker, 86; replacement, 87; European-made, 87-8; Winchester 59: 89; cockeyed, 89-90; chambers in, 90-1; lengths of, 91-2; see also choke boring
beavertail forends, 9, 45-6, 50, 57, 61, 64, 143, 148, 198
Bee .218: 207
Beesley, Frederick, 43
Belgian-made guns, 13-14, 22, 24-5, 38, 47, 68, 101, 145-6, 151, 165, 183, 198
Beretta, 37, 38, 41, 47-8, 67, 168, 188, 189, 327-8
Bernardelli, 48
Biesen, Al, 42, 51, 151, 328
big-game combination guns, 204-5
big game rifles, 123
big-game shotguns, 295-303
bird shot, 204, 242, 299
birds, see game birds
Black Beauty, 11
black powder, 4, 71, 85, 91, 177, 181, 184, 206, 214-16, 223-4
black-powder burns, 8
Blitz action, 30-1, 46
block action, 19
bolt-action shotguns, 19, 143, 185
bolting, 29-30

Boss, 17, 37, 38, 41, 43, 46, 67, 144, 155, 196

box-lock action, 8, 28, 30, 37, 47, 56, 58, 62, 67; Anson & Deeley, 8, 28, 30, 47, 56

Breda, 77, 118

breech-loading shotguns, 5, 17, 28–9, 145, 176, 178, 211, 222–3

Brenneke slug, 301; ballistics chart for, 304

British-made guns, 17, 30–1, 33, 35, 37–9, 41–7, 68, 143–8, 151, 196, 198, 203–4, 209, 299

British trunk cases, 325–6

Brown, Myles, 207

Brownell, Lenard, 42, 151, 328

Browning, John M., 12–14, 20, 22, 24, 67, 70, 76

Browning, Matthew, 76

Browning, Val, 78

Browning Arms Company, 13–14, 24–5, 47, 68, 76, 181, 302

Browning automatics, 13–14, 22, 26, 76–8, 239, 296

Browning Double Automatic, 23, 78, 79, 239

Browning over-and-unders, 37, 78, 172, 185

Browning Pigeon, 68

Browning-Remington, 76–7

Browning Superposed, 24–5, 36, 37, 67–8, 165, 172–3, 198, 209

buckshot, 17, 156, 159, 196, 204, 230–1, 295–9, 303

buffalo, 34, 204

Burgess, 12

Burrard, Major Gerald, 109

buttplates, 147

C-Lect Choke, 74, 118

Canuck trap shells, 213

caplocks, 4

cartridges, rifle, handloading of, 314

cases, 4, 325–7; leg-of-mutton, 60, 200, 326–7

cast-off, 148, 159, 160

cast-on, 148, 160

Central Arms Company, 54–5

Challenge Ejector, 11

chambers, 90–1

checkpieces, 145

Chicago, 11

chilled shot (hard), 179, 214, 241

choke boring, 5, 88–9, 93–114, 223; full, 86, 89, 91, 94, 95, 99–104, 107,

109, 112; swaged, 89, 96; modified, 94, 95, 100–2, 104, 106, 109–13; specifications charts for, 94, 98, 100, 102, 109, 113–14; standard, 95; American, 95, 96; English, 95, 96; improved-cylinder, 95, 97, 99, 100, 102, 104, 110, 111; conical, 95–7, 99; conical-parallel, 95–8; taper, 95, 99; jug, 96; skeet, 96–7, 99, 100, 106–7, 109–11; recess, 96, 97; improved-modified, 97, 99–102, 106; quarter, 99, 101, 111; selection of, 106–14

choke devices, variable, 12, 26–7, 74, 92, 97, 103, 105, 115–22, 129, 132, 189, 198, 207, 227, 237, 239

Chromax Steel, 88

chronograph, use of, 224

Churchill, 43, 45, 50

clay-pigeon shooting, international, 307–8

clay targets, 5, 26, 134–6, 162, 180, 261, 305–12

clothes, shooting, 331–2

cockeyed barrels, 89–90

cockeyed stock, 148

collet-type choke devices, 97, 116–19, 121, 132

Colt, 5, 12, 55

Colt Ace pistol, 79

Colt cap-and-ball revolver, 12

Colton Firearms Company, 11

comb, 9, 26, 52, 70, 72, 137, 142, 145–7, 154–61; Monte Carlo, 9, 137, 146, 148, 158–9, 161

combination guns, 202–7

conical choke, 95–7, 99

conical-parallel choke, 95–8

constriction, see choke boring

Continental Arms Company, 38, 220

Continental guns, 9, 29, 30, 35–8, 90, 146–8, 183, 203, 205, 209

Coxe, Wallace H., 212

Crescent Firearms Company, 54

crimping, 93, 105, 217, 223, 244, 317, 319

crossbolt, Greener, 29, 37

crossbolt safeties, 75

crows, loads for (chart), 169

Cutts Compensator, 115, 116, 121, 128–9, 139–40, 173

Cyclone Choke, 117, 118

Damascus barrels, 8, 11–14, 59, 66, 70–2, 85–6

Darne, 29

decoys, 112, 130, 168, 230
deer: loads for, 17, 156, 159, 169, 196, 204, 230–1, 295–9, 303; guns for, 26, 74, 174, 196, 204, 302
Deer Slayer, 26, 174
Diana, 51
Dickson, John & Son, 41, 43, 46
Dickson round action, 31, 46
Divine Guidance School, 263–5
doll's head, 29
double-barrel shotguns, 23–4; types of, 28–39; European-made, 40–52; American-made, 53–68; *See also* shotguns
doves: loads for (chart), 169; shot sizes for, 245; leads for (chart), 273; guns for, 291–2
drop, 9, 26, 52, 70, 72, 142, 146–7, 154–61
drop shot (soft), 214, 241
ducks: loads for (chart), 169; shot sizes for, 245–9; leads for (chart), 273; guns for, 294
Du Pont powders, 212, 214–16, 224, 236–8, 317–18; recoil in foot-pounds of (chart), 238

Eastern Arms Company, 11
Elgin Arms Company, 54–5
Empire Arms Company, 11
Emsco Choke, 121
English choke, 95, 96
English grip, 145
English shotguns, *see* British-made shotguns
Englishing, 89
European-made double-barrel shotguns, 40–52
Explora, 203, 299

Fabri, 48
Fabrique Nationale, 22, 41, 47, 67, 76
falling block action, 19
fast swing, 138, 257–61, 266, 307
Featherlight, 11
Federal Cartridge Company, 105, 185, 229, 270, 306
Federal Firearms Act, 176
Federal Hi-Power, 224, 230, 318
Federal shot shells, 213, 217, 218, 221, 224, 230
field shooting, 284–94
Field & Stream, 288
fit, shotgun, 154–61
flintlocks, 3–4, 16–17

fluid-steel barrels, 7, 11–13, 59, 60, 70, 71, 87
Folsom Arms Company, 54
Forsyth, Alexander, 4
forward allowance, *see* lead
Fox, 8, 24, 31, 33, 53–4, 67, 150–1, 172
Fox, A. H., Company, 53–4, 67, 149
Fox-Kautsky single trigger, 67
Fox Model B, 33–4
Franchi, 33, 38, 41, 49, 51, 77
Francotte, 38, 47, 327–8
French-made guns, 29, 47, 52, 74, 88, 165
Fryberg & Company, 11
full choke, 86, 89, 91, 94, 95, 99–104
fulminate, first use of, 4

game birds: loads for (chart), 169; shot sizes for, 245–9; leads for (chart), 273; methods of shooting, 284–94
Garand, 10, 80
Garbi, 50–1
gas-operated automatics, 22, 80–3, 170, 173, 236, 239
gauges, 176–85; bore diameters of, 177, 181
Geco, 19
geese: guns for, 168–71; loads for (chart), 169; shot sizes for, 245–9; leads for (chart), 273
General Recreation, 57
George Brothers Lin-Speed, 329
German-made guns, 37–8, 81, 87, 88, 101, 144–5, 151, 165, 183, 205–6
Gewehr, 41, 81
Gewehrkoffer, 326
Gibraltar, 11
Greener, W. W., 29, 84
Greener crossbolt, 29, 37
Greener safeties, 34, 207
Griefelt, 49
Griffin & Howe, 51, 77, 161, 330
grips, 143–6
grouse: loads for (chart), 169; shot sizes for, 245–9; leads for (chart), 273; guns for, 291–3
Gun and Its Development, The (W. W. Greener), 29
gun cases, 4, 325–7; leg-of-mutton, 60, 200, 326–7
gun fit, 154–61
Guns & Hunting, 288

half pistol grip, 145–6
hammerless shotguns, 5, 8, 14, 21, 28, 30, 47, 56, 72–5
hand traps, 306
handicap shooting, 34, 112, 179–80, 307
handloading, 180, 184, 313–22
Harrington & Richardson, 10, 19, 75
Harrison & Hussey, 43
Hartford Gun Choke Company, 117, 118
Hartley, Marcellus, 22
Hawker, Colonel Peter, 4
Herco, 229
Hercules Powder Company, 216, 229, 318
Herter, George Leonard, 121
Herter Company, 117
Herter Vari-Choke, 121
Hibbard, Spencer & Bartlett, 10
high-house target, 270–2, 309
High Standard, 14, 21, 74–5, 81, 118, 302
High Standard automatic, 22, 239
High Standard J. C. Higgins, 81
Hodgdon, B. E., 216–17, 318
Hoenig, George, 51
Holland & Holland, 17, 37, 38, 41–4, 46–7, 326, 330
Hollenbeck Gun Company, 54, 206
Holliday, Doc, 175
Hopkins & Allen, 10, 55
Hornet .22: 207, 229
Hunter Arms Company, 5, 24, 31, 54, 59, 61
Husquvarna, 40, 52
Hydro-Coil, 237, 239

Imperial Chemical Industries, 43–4
improved-cylinder choke, 95, 97, 99, 100, 102, 104, 110, 111
improved-modified choke, 97, 99–102, 106
Instructions to Young Sportsmen (Colonel Peter Hawker), 4
international clay-pigeon shooting, 307–8
Italian-made guns, 33, 37, 38, 41, 47–8, 77, 145, 151, 166, 198
Ithaca, 8, 14, 29, 31, 33, 57–9, 166, 174
Ithaca 37, 73–4
Ithaca Field Grade, 58
Ithaca Gun Company, 5, 14, 21, 23, 33–4, 53, 57–8, 73, 149, 298, 302
Ithaca NID, 58

Ithaca SKB, 48
Iver Johnson, 31, 54, 60
Iver Johnson Champion, 18

Japanese-made guns, 25, 52, 65, 165
Jarvis Choke, 117, 120–1
J. C. Higgins (High Standard), 81
Jeffery, W. J., 43, 325–6
Jeffery Nitro Express, 87
Johnson, Peter H., 56
Johnson, Thomas C., 14, 76, 79
jug choke, 96

Kemble, Fred, 93, 95
Kennedy, Monte, 151
Kerr, Alex, 191, 256, 269–70
Kersten fastener, 37
Kessler, 19, 70
killing range, 112, 130, 133, 233–5, 248; of various shot sizes, 248; of buckshot, 297–8
Koller, Larry, 288
Krieghoff, Heinrich, 66
Krupp, 87
Krupp Flusshahl, 87

La Beau Corelay, 47
laminated barrels, 12, 13, 85
Lancaster, Charles, 43
Lancaster and Daw, 5
La Salle, 20
Lawrence Company, 331
L. C. Smith, 5, 8, 24, 29, 31, 33, 41, 54, 57, 59–61, 86, 172
L. C. Smith Crown Grade, 61
L. C. Smith De Luxe, 61
L. C. Smith Field Grade, 60–1, 199
L. C. Smith Ideal Grade, 61
L. C. Smith Monogram, 60, 61
L. C. Smith Pigeon, 60
L. C. Smith Premier, 61
L. C. Smith Specialty Grade, 61
lead, 257–60, 263–75; sustained, 138, 260; theoretical, 259–60, 273; calculated, 263; for skeet shooting, 270–2; for game birds (chart), 273; practical, 273
Le Boulengé chronograph, 224
Lefaucheux pinfire cartridge, 5
Lefever, 33–4, 86
Lefever, Frank & Sons, 87
Lefever Arms Company, 58
Lefever Company (Uncle Dan), 5, 53, 58

Lefever Nitro Special, 58
leg-of-mutton case, 60, 200, 326–7
Lemon, Carroll, 288
leopards, 203–4, 295–6
lever-action shot guns, 18–19, 70
lions, 296, 299
live-pigeon shooting, 4, 5, 310
Livermore, George, 57
loads: buckshot, 17, 156, 159, 196, 204, 230–1, 295–9, 303; number of pellets in (charts), 132, 243; for various game (chart), 169; for pheasants, 186–92; for quail, 193–201; types of, 230–2; *see also* shot shells; specific game
Lolo Sporting Goods, 321
Long Range Wonder, 11, 15, 18
long-recoil system, 13–14, 21–3, 76–9, 170, 173
Long Tom, 11, 92
low-house target, 270–2, 309
Lyman Gun Sight Company, 115, 318
Lyman Reader's Handbook, 318

M-1 Garand, 10, 80
Manton, Joseph, 4, 55
Marlin, 14, 19, 21, 24, 54, 166, 207
Marlin 42-A, 74
Marlin 43-A, 74
Marlin .410 gauge, 70
Marlin 53-A, 74
Marlin 90: 33, 54
Marlin 1898: 72
Marshall, Wells Company, 10
Mathieson, Olin, 189, 198
Mauser, 43–4, 206
Mauser 98: 19
Mauser 1891 7.65 mm., 55
McIntire, Dwight, 57
Medicus, Philip J., 206
Meriden, 11
Meriden Arms Company, 10, 55
Merkel, 37–8, 67, 101, 327–8
Mews, Leonard, 42, 328
military muskets, 3, 41
Miller single trigger, 33
Miller Trigger Company, 33, 51
Modern Shotgun, The (Major Gerald Burrard), 109
Modern Shotguns (W. W. Greener), 84
Modern Shotguns and Loads (Captain Charles Askins), 273
modified choke, 94, 95, 100–2, 104, 106, 109–13

Monte Carlo comb, 9, 137, 146, 148, 158–9, 161
Montgomery Ward, 10
Mossberg, 14, 19, 21, 302
Mossberg C-Lect Choke, 74, 118
muskets, 3, 41
muzzle bandage, 139
muzzle loaders, 3–4, 16–17, 176, 222–3
Mysteries of Shotgun Patterns, The (Oberfell and Thompson), 98

Nilo Farms, 80, 189, 288
Noble Manufacturing Company, 75, 185
Nolt, Paul, 321
NRA Illustrated Shotgun Handbook, 317, 318

Oberfell, George G., 98, 104
O'Connor, Bradford, 42, 62, 189, 272
O'Connor, Eleanor, 33, 42, 43, 58, 62, 189, 194, 202, 244, 288, 297
Olin, John, 182, 224
Olin, Spencer, 182
Outdoor Life, 93, 115, 206, 210, 273
Outdoor Recreation, 70
over-and-under guns, 24–5, 27, 36–9, 52, 78, 172, 185; combination, 206–7
Ovis poli, 16–17

Pachmayr Gun Works, 116, 161, 330
Page, Warren, 288
Palmer, Arnold, 255
Pape, W. R., 95, 97
Paradox, 203–5, 299
Parker, 5, 8, 23, 24, 31, 33, 41, 53, 55–7, 86, 150–1, 172, 185
Parker AAHE, 56, 57
Parker AHE, 56, 57
Parker A-1 Special, 56, 151
Parker BHE, 56, 57
Parker CHE, 56, 57
Parker DH, 14
Parker DHE, 56
Parker, The: America's Finest Shotgun (Peter H. Johnson), 56
Parker Gun Company, 8, 55–7, 149
Parker Trojan, 10, 56, 57
Parker VH, 14, 56, 57
partridge: loads for (chart), 169; guns for, 291
patterning, 123–33
Pedersen patents, 14
peepsights, receiver, 302

pellets, 240–9; number of in loads (charts), 132, 243; energy in foot-pounds of (chart), 246; velocity of, 246–7; *see also* shot
Perazzi, 48
Peters, 220
pheasants: suggested loads for (chart), 169; guns and loads for, 186–92, 288–91; shot sizes for, 245–49
pie crimp, 93, 105, 217, 244, 317
pigeon shooting, live, 4, 5, 310
Pinch, Bill, 279
pistol grips, 143–6
pitch, 159–61
plastic-collared shot shells, 93, 104, 105, 217–18, 220, 223, 324
plastic shot shells, 220–1, 223
plastic stocks, 150
pointing, 256–7, 301
pointing out, 138, 260, 261
Poly Choke, 103, 105, 116–18, 121, 122, 198
pot shooting, 257
powder: early improvements in man-ufacture of, 4; black, 4, 8, 71, 85, 91, 177, 181, 184, 206, 214–16, 223–4; smokeless, 8, 72, 181, 184, 215–16, 222, 223; fast-burning, 105, 216, 318–19; progressive-burning, 181, 184, 217, 223, 224, 227, 229, 230, 318; Du Pont, 212, 214–16, 224, 236–8, 317–18; dram equivalents of, 214–15, 227, 230, 236–7; bulk, 215–16; dense, 215–16, 223, 229; double-base, 216; single-base, 216; foreign-made, 216–17; slow-burning, 216, 217, 229; Hercules, 216, 229, 318; recoil in foot-pounds of (chart), 238
POWer PAC, 116, 118
Power Piston, 105, 218, 317
prairie chicken: loads for (chart), 169; shot sizes for, 245
primers, 162, 180, 208, 210, 213–14
pump guns, 12–14, 20–1, 69–76
pumpkin balls, 17, 156, 177, 203, 204, 299, 300
Purdey, 17, 41–4, 45–6, 47, 144, 196, 198

quail shooting: 285–8; suggested loads for (chart), 169; guns and loads for, 193–201; shot sizes for, 245–9; leads for (chart), 273
quarter choke, 99, 101, 111

rabbits: loads for (chart), 169; shot sizes for (chart), 245
rail: loads for (chart), 169; shot sizes for, 245
Ranger, 11
receiver peepsights, 302
recess choke, 96, 97
recoil, 9, 37, 71–2, 142, 147, 157–60, 170, 179, 235–9; long-recoil system, 13–14, 21–3, 76–9, 170, 173; short-recoil system, 13–14, 22, 79, 173, 239; in foot-pounds of smokeless powder (chart), 238
recoil pads, 147, 161, 195, 237
Red Dot, 318
Remington, 5, 22, 23, 31, 53, 55–6, 76, 149–50, 217, 218, 220, 302, 306
Remington 10: 14, 20–1, 72–4
Remington 11: 13–14, 22, 76–7, 81
Remington, 11–48: 13, 22, 77, 78, 81, 82, 83, 151, 185, 198, 236, 239
Remington 17: 20, 21, 58, 73, 74
Remington 29: 21, 73
Remington 31: 21, 73
Remington 32: 25, 36, 37, 66, 165, 172–3
Remington 58: 81–2, 83
Remington 550: 79
Remington 742: 80
Remington 870: 73, 75, 151, 157, 236
Remington 878: 82, 83, 171
Remington 1100: 23, 82–3, 151, 174, 185, 236, 239
Remington 3200: 66
Remington Express, 220, 230
Remington Nitro Express, 125, 181, 213, 224
Remington-Rider rolling block ac-tion, 19
Remington Shur Shot, 220, 224
Remington Whitmore, 65
repeating shotguns, 11–12, 14, 19–21; *see also* shotguns
Richards, Ken, 120, 132
rifle cartridges, handloading of, 314
rifle grips, 145
rifled slugs, 156, 159, 174, 203, 204, 230–1, 299–302; Brenneke, 301; bal-listics chart for Brenneke, 304
Rigby, John, 43–4
Rikhoff, Jim, 288
riot guns, 27, 72, 118–19, 175
rolling block action, 19
Roper, 12
Roper choke, 12, 115

Index

rotary bolt, 29
Royal Gun Company, 54, 206
Russell, Harold, 270

S.A.A.I. standards, 231
safeties, 34–5; automatic, 34, 64; tang, 34, 74, 75, 207; Greener, 34, 207; crossbolt, 75
Sam Holt, 14–15
Savage Arms Corporation, 14, 53–4, 67, 92, 151, 207
Savage automatics, 13–14, 22, 74, 77, 239
Savage 99, 207
Savage over-and-under, 25
Savage-Stevens, 21, 24, 118
sawed-off shotgun, 27
scopes, 134–41; on big-game shotguns, 302
Sears, Roebuck, 10, 11, 14, 28, 55, 74, 81, 92
selective automatic ejector, 5, 24, 31–2, 51
self-loaders, see automatic shotguns
self-opening shotguns, 35
Selous, Frederick Courteney, 177
Shapleigh Hardware Company, 10
Shaw, Joshua, 4
shells, see shot shells
shooting, elements of, 250–62; fast swing, 138, 257–61, 266, 307; pointing out, 138, 260, 261; stance, 254–5, 258; mounting, 254, 255; pointing, 256–7, 301; snap shooting, 257, 260; spot shooting, 257, 260, 274; see also lead
shooting clothes, 331–2
shooting loose, 30
Shooting Master, 20, 132
shooting range, 227–30
short-recoil system, 13–14, 22, 79, 173, 239
shot, 240–9; buckshot, 17, 156, 159, 196, 204, 230–1, 295–9, 303; chilled (hard), 179, 214, 241; bird, 204, 242, 299; drop (soft), 214, 241; formula for finding size of, 242; manufacture of, 242; comparative sizes of (chart), 243; sizes for various game, 245–9; choice of size, 247–8; killing range of, 248; see also pellets
shot-shell cases, 211, 220
shot shells, 208–21; invention of, 5, 28; low-brass, 85, 213, 242; Western Super-X, 88, 125, 181, 213, 220, 224, 229, 230; plastic-collared, 93, 104, 105, 217–18, 220, 223, 324; scatter, 110; brush, 110, 214; velocities of, 122, 210, 214–15, 217, 223–7; Remington Nitro Express, 125, 181, 213, 224; primers in, 162, 180, 208, 210, 213–14; handloading of, 180, 184, 313–22; brass, 180, 208–10; high-velocity, 181, 184, 213, 224, 227, 230, 315; Winchester-Western, 184, 185, 217–20; paper, 208, 210, 211; wadding in, 208, 210–13, 217–18, 220; lengths of, 209; foreign, 209–11, 214, 320; pressures of, 210, 216, 223–4; storing of, 211; Federal, 213, 217, 218, 221, 224, 230; high-brass, 213, 220, 242; plastic, 220–1, 223; ballistics of, 222–40; see also loads, powder, shot
shotgun fit, 154–61
shotgun grips, 143–6
shotgun loads, see loads
shotguns: brief history of, 3–15; flintlock, 3–4, 16–17; muzzle loaders, 3–4, 16–17, 176, 222–3; caplock, 4; hammerless, 5, 8, 14, 21, 28, 30, 47, 56, 72–5; breech-loading, 5, 17, 28–9, 145, 176, 178, 211, 222–3; brand names of, 10–11, 54–5; repeating, 11–12, 14, 19–21; single-barrel, 11–12, 17–18; pump, 12–14, 20–1, 69–76; automatic, 13–14, 21–3, 76–83; turn-of-century prices of, 17, 66; classification of, 16–27; current prices of, 17; lever-action, 18–19, 70; bolt-action, 19, 143, 185; gas-operated automatics, 22, 80–3, 170, 173, 236, 239; double-barrel, 23–4, 28–68; over-and-under, 24–5, 27, 36–9, 78, 172, 185; upland, 25–6, 90–2, 167–8, 186–92; for deer, 26, 74, 174, 196, 204, 302; all-around, 26, 162–6, 236; wildfowl, 26, 170–1; trap, 26, 171–2; skeet, 26–7, 172–4; riot, 27, 72, 118–19, 175; self-opening, 35; European-made double-barrel, 40–52; American-made double-barrel, 53–68; depression prices of, 56, 58, 60–1, 64, 68, 165; slug, 174; gauges of, 176–85; combination, 202–7; big-game, 295–303; care and cleaning of, 323–5
Shur Shot, 220, 224
sidelock action, 8, 30, 37, 46, 47, 59
Siemens, 87

) 339 (

sights, 134–41; on big-game shotguns, 302
Silver Hawk, 38
Simmons Choke, 116, 189
Simmons Hardware Company, 10
Simmons Specialties, 116
single-barrel shotguns, 11–12, 17–18
skeet choke, 96–7, 99, 100, 106–7, 109–11
skeet gun, 26–7, 172–4
skeet shooting, 36, 56, 64–6, 72–9, 91, 119, 128, 305–12; loads for (chart), 169; shot sizes for, 245; leads for, 270–2
skelp barrel, 85
sling swivels, 145, 330
slug gun, 174
Slug Special, 26, 302
slugs, rifled, 156, 159, 174, 203, 204, 230–1, 299–302; Brenneke, 301; ballistics chart for Brenneke, 304
Slugster, 26, 74
Smith, L. C., *see* L. C. Smith
Smith, L. H., 57
Smith, Lou P., 298
Smith, Shelley, 302
smokeless powder, 8, 72, 181, 184, 215–16, 222, 223; recoil in footpounds of (chart), 238
Smokeless Shotgun Powders, 212
snap caps, 330
snap shooting, 257, 260
Snead, Sam, 255
Southgate ejector, 32
Spanish-made guns, 38, 48–52, 145–6, 165, 182, 185, 188, 198
Spanish Mauser, 206
Speer, Inc., 318
Speer's Reloading Manual, 318
Spencer, 12, 69–70
Spencer, Christopher C., 69
Sporting Arms and Ammunition Manufacturers Institute, 183, 231
spot shooting, 257, 260, 274
Springfield, 10
Sproul, Lee, 204, 278
squirrel: loads for (chart), 169; shot sizes for, 245
stance, 254–5, 258
standard choke, 95
star crimp, 217, 223, 317
Sterlingworth, 67
Stevens, 19, 54, 67
Stevens Arms Corporation, 10, 150

Stevens .410/.22: 206
Stevens 520: 20
stock fit, 154–61
stocks, 142–53; pre-World War I, 9–10, 147; single-barrel, 18; Parker, 56, 150–1; Ithaca, 58–9; L. C. Smith, 60–1; Winchester 21: 62, 64–5, 151; Fox, 67, 150–1; Browning, 68; dimensions of, 142–3, 156–7, 160–1; one-piece, 143; grips on, 143–6; British, 143–8; checkering designs on, 144, 150–2, 327–8; engraved, 145; crooked, 147, 158, 161; cockeyed, 148; woods used for, 148–50; plastic, 150; Parker, 150–1; finishing of, 152–3; trap-gun, 172; skeet-gun, 173; refinishing of, 327–30
Stoeger, 38, 64, 301
Super Ranger, 11
sustained lead, 138, 260
swaged choke, 89, 96
swan shot, 3
swedging, 98
Swedish-made guns, 40, 52
swinging through, 257–61, 266, 307
swivels, sling, 145, 330
Syracuse, 8
Syracuse Arms Company, 5, 149
Syracuse Gun Company, 58

tang safeties, 34, 74, 75, 207
taper choke, 95, 99
targets: clay, 5, 26, 134–6, 162, 180, 261, 305–12; high-house, 270–2, 309; low-house, 270–2, 309
Thompson, Charles E., 98, 104
Thompson, Norm, 331
Three-Barrel Gun Company, 54, 206
tigers, 203–4, 299, 301
top bolting, 29–30
top-break system, 29
trap gun, 26, 171–2
trapshooting, 5, 23, 64–6, 72–5, 91, 112, 146, 157, 305–12; loads for (chart), 169; shot sizes for, 245
trigger-plate lock system, 30–1, 47
triggers, 32–5; on Spanish guns, 50–1; Parker, 56; Ithaca, 58–9; L. C. Smith, 60; Winchester 21: 61–4; Remington 32: 66; Fox, 67; Browning Superposed, 68
trunk cases, 325–6
turkey: loads for (chart), 169; shot sizes for, 246–7
twist barrels, 7–8, 11, 85–6, 129

Ugartechea, 50–1
Union Arms Company, 14–15, 31, 55, 58, 70, 72
upland-game shooting, 284–94; guns for, 25–6, 90–2, 167–8, 186–92; loads for (chart), 169; shot sizes for, 245–9; leads for (chart), 273

Valmet, 52
Van Natta, J. E., 57
variable choke devices, 12, 26–7, 74, 92, 97, 103, 105, 115–22, 129, 132, 189, 198, 207, 227, 237, 239
velocity: of shot shells, 122, 210, 214–15, 217, 223–7; of pellets, 246–7; of rifled slugs, 300–1
Ventilated Poly Choke, 116
ventilated ribs, 139, 170, 171
Vickers, 88

Waffen-Franconia, 326
Watrous, George R., 64
Watson Brothers, 43
Watts, William, 4
Weatherby rifles, 7
Weaver, W. R., 120, 139, 270, 288
Weaver, W. R., Company, 116, 120, 138, 302
Weaver Choke, 116, 120, 207
weaver scopes, 138–9
Western Ammunition Handbook, 244
Western Arms Long Range gun, 58
Western Cartridge Company, 58, 182, 209, 224, 229, 233–4
Western Mark V, 218
Western Super-X, 88, 125, 181, 213, 220, 224, 229, 230
Western X-Pert, 220
Westley Richards, 41, 43, 46, 55, 87
Wheeling Gun Company, 54, 206
White, E. Field, 103, 115, 117
Whitney, Eli, 41
Whitworth, Sir Joseph, 59, 60, 66, 88
wild sheep, Asian, 16–17
wildfowl: guns for, 26, 170–1; loads for (chart), 169; shot sizes for, 245–9; leads for (chart), 273
Wilkes-Barre Gun Company, 58
Williams, "Carbine," 22, 79

Williams Gun Sight Company, 101, 102
Winchester, 21, 22, 29–30, 42, 76, 149, 302
Winchester 12: 14, 21, 22, 73, 75, 77, 157, 185, 194
Winchester 21: 17, 24, 29–31, 33, 41–2, 45, 61–5, 88, 96, 106, 151, 165, 168, 185, 188, 189, 196, 198, 199
Winchester 24: 65
Winchester 40: 14, 77
Winchester 42: 73, 77, 185
Winchester 50: 79–80
Winchester 59: 22, 80, 89, 98, 131, 166, 189, 239
Winchester 89: 19
Winchester 94: 15
Winchester 95: 15
Winchester 97: 53
Winchester 100: 80
Winchester 101: 25, 39, 65, 165
Winchester 1200: 21, 73
Winchester 1400: 22, 80, 83, 239
Winchester 1887: 12–13, 18–19, 70, 86, 180
Winchester 1893: 13, 20, 70–1, 86
Winchester 1897: 13, 15, 20, 53, 71–2, 86, 193, 197
Winchester 1901: 13, 18, 70, 180
Winchester 1911: 14, 77–9
Winchester Ammunition Handbook, 100
Winchester Grand American, 65
Winchester Mark 5, 105, 303
Winchester museum, 13, 63, 71
Winchester Pigeon, 65
Winchester Ranger, 220, 224
Winchester Rifles & Shotguns, (George R. Watrous), 64
Winchester Super Speed, 220, 227, 315
Winchester Super-X, 83
Winchester-Western, 184, 185, 217–20, 303, 306
Win-Lite Choke, 80
Win-Wad, 218, 317, 318
woodcock: loads for (chart), 169; shot sizes for, 245
Woodward, 37, 38, 43, 45–6, 47

Zeiss scopes, 138

A Note on the Type

The text of this book was set on the Linotype in Janson, a recutting made direct from type cast from matrices long thought to have been made by the Dutchman Anton Janson, who was a practicing type founder in Leipzig during the years 1668–87. However, it has been conclusively demonstrated that these types are actually the work of Nicholas Kis (1650–1702), a Hungarian, who most probably learned his trade from the master Dutch type founder Dirk Voskens. The type is an excellent example of the influential and sturdy Dutch types that prevailed in England up to the time William Caslon developed his own incomparable designs from these Dutch faces.

Composed, printed, and bound by
The Haddon Craftsmen, Scranton, Pa.
Typography by Albert Burkhardt